Addressing Violence Against Women on College Campuses

EDITED BY
CATHERINE KAUKINEN, MICHELLE HUGHES MILLER,
AND RÁCHAEL A. POWERS

Addressing Violence Against Women on College Campuses

TEMPLE UNIVERSITY PRESS
Philadelphia • *Rome* • *Tokyo*

TEMPLE UNIVERSITY PRESS
Philadelphia, Pennsylvania 19122
www.temple.edu/tempress

Library of Congress Cataloging-in-Publication Data

Names: Kaukinen, Catherine E., editor. | Miller, Michelle Hughes, editor. | Powers,
   Ráchael A., editor.
Title: Addressing violence against women on college campuses / edited by Catherine
   Kaukinen, Michelle Hughes Miller, and Ráchael A. Powers.
Description: Philadelphia, Pennsylvania : Temple University Press, [2017] | Includes
   bibliographical references and index.
Identifiers: LCCN 2017017379 (print) | LCCN 2016055654 (ebook) |
   ISBN 9781439913758 (cloth : alk. paper) | ISBN 9781439913765 (pbk. : alk.paper) |
   ISBN 9781439913772 (E-Book)
Subjects: LCSH: Campus violence—United States. | Campus violence—United States—
   Prevention. | Women college students—Crimes against—United States. | Rape
   in universities and colleges—United States.
Classification: LCC LB2345 .A35 2017 (ebook) | LCC LB2345 (print) | DDC 371.7/82—dc23
LC record available at https://lccn.loc.gov/2017017379

∞ The paper used in this publication meets the requirements of the American National
Standard for Information Sciences—Permanence of Paper for Printed Library Materials,
ANSI Z39.48-1992

Printed in the United States of America

9 8 7 6 5 4 3 2 1

To the next generation of college women,
in the hope they do not face the harms experienced
by those who came before them

Contents

Exhibits and Figures

Exhibits

Figures

Preface

January 2017 Reflections on the 2016 Election and the Unknown Future That Awaits Our College Campuses

When we finished this edited volume in fall 2016, we were hopeful about future efforts to better understand and address violence against women on college campuses. The progress during the past several years has been palpable, especially given the confluence of student and survivor activism, policy enactments, expanding assessment and etiology research, and significant efforts by institutions of higher education to improve their responses to victims and innovative prevention efforts. In our concluding chapter, we wrote about the progress that has collectively been made, and what we see as areas where more work still needs to be done. We ended this book asking ourselves: Do we know enough? And are we doing enough?

And then came November 9, 2016, when we learned that a sizable minority of U.S. voters elected Donald J. Trump as president. The weeks before the election were rife with discourse and images that devalued and denigrated women, including the often-seen "Trump That Bitch" (Johnson 2016). But most disturbing was the remarkably misogynistic language from the president-elect himself (Timm 2016), including his brag about his celebrity-acquired ability to sexually assault women ("I don't even wait . . . you can do anything, grab 'em by the pussy") coupled with a victim-blaming negation of several women who claimed that he had sexually assaulted them during his lengthy career, instead calling himself a "victim" of their lies.

It is fair to say that this misogynistic, violent, and victim-blaming discourse is antithetical to the work of those activists, scholars, and practitioners cited in this volume, and it is especially contrary to our goals for this book. In fact, in our conclusion, we bemoan the continuing presence of such attitudes within our culture that we argue perpetuate, even encourage, the high levels of violence against women we currently see. Indeed, when he laughed at his supporters' use of these misogynistic slurs (Bellstrom 2016), we worried about a generation of young people feeling empowered to be similarly crass and disrespectful. And when he said women could falsely claim sexual assault about anyone, we worried about whether reporting rates on college campuses would go down because victims will have another reason to fear they will not be believed.

We especially worried about the message our student athletes heard when President-elect Trump characterized some of his statements as "locker room banter" (Timm 2016). Prevention efforts have focused on creating a culture of bystander intervention within athletics for years, instead of a culture where misogynistic language or behavior reigns. Here, we are somewhat optimistic, as college and professional male athletes from across the country, our allies in this fight to end violence against women, have strongly rejected President-elect Trump's claim. One of the most profound responses to this "locker room talk" narrative was from Marvin Williams of the Charlotte Hornets, who noted, "I don't know what locker rooms he hangs out in or what they talk about, but I have never heard that in any locker room and I hope I never do" (Bonnell 2016).

But our worries, and the worries of others in the anti-violence movement, are about more than discourse. Policies may change under the new administration that reflect the president-elect's language and an accompanying Republican platform that already proposes to shift the process of addressing sexual violence away from educational institutions and into courts of law (New 2016). Such a change would potentially bring with it enhanced due process rights for those accused and the higher burden of proof found in criminal cases, significantly transforming our understandings of the importance of educational institutions in the prevention of violence. The already insufficient budget for the Office for Civil Rights within the Department of Education may be cut even further, which would restrict the staff's ability to enforce current Title IX expectations, making them a nonviable resource to address institutional inadequacies for student survivors. It is even possible that the current interpretation of Title IX may be rolled back entirely (New 2016), removing the burden and promise of institutional Title IX responses to campus violence. And, if Title IX is redefined, what could be the future of the Violence Against Women Act (VAWA), the Clery Act, and the Campus SaVE Act—repeal, strip funding, or fail to enforce? If any of these changes occur, the corresponding effect on institutions of higher education and, more important, on their students, may be substantial. In 2014, more than 16,000 VAWA offenses were reported on our college campuses (Department of Education n.d.). What happens to the individuals who make similar reports in 2017 and beyond? Will the compilation of such data, let alone the processes that work to bring redress to the victim while ensuring that the rights of those accused are protected, even be seen as valuable? How will we ensure both due process and educational support when both universities and criminal justice agencies investigate and adjudicate?

As of yet, however, we do not know what the outcomes of this election will be on efforts to address violence against college women. We hope that we will continue to see research being funded, prevention programs being expanded, offices and staff being supported through training and resources, and survivors being heard and believed. We hope that this momentum continues beyond any one presidential administration. But after November 9, 2016, our optimism has faltered. While at the beginning of the writing of this book we were full of hope at the thought of continued change, we now have concern and worry.

Nevertheless, we ask the reader to recognize our initial framework of optimism and its source: the phenomenal ongoing work of activists, advocates, and academics. We are grateful for and confident in these efforts to eradicate violence against women. The recent emergence of campus-based violence into the public discourse coupled with institutional and student-led efforts to change the social climate on college campuses and the tireless work of academics and practitioners is empowering. Across professions, perspectives, and platforms people have, and will continue to, come together to address a whole host of issues—including the virulent discourse mentioned previously—that face our nation and threaten those living at the margins. So although we are worried, we also believe in the power of many to eliminate violence against women. In that spirit, as Maya Angelou encourages us, we are: "hoping for the best, prepared for the worst, and unsurprised by anything in between."

REFERENCES

Bellstrom, K. 2016. Trump supporters are selling "Trump That Bitch" t-shirts featuring Hillary Clinton. *Fortune*, April 25. Available at http://fortune.com/2016/04/25/trump -clinton-misogynistic-merch/.

Bonnell, R. 2016. What kind of locker room does Donald Trump hang out in? asks Charlotte Hornet Marvin Williams. *Charlotte Observer*, October 10. Available at http:// www.charlotteobserver.com/sports/nba/charlotte-hornets/article107365047.html.

Department of Education. n.d. *Campus safety and security.* Available at http://ope.ed.gov /campussafety/#/.

Johnson, J. 2016. Donald Trump calls her "Crooked Hillary," but his fans just say "b----." *Washington Post*, June 16. Available at https://www.washingtonpost.com/politics /donald-trump-calls-her-crooked-hillary-but-his-fans-just-say-b----/2016/06/15 /b33e166c-330c-11e6-8ff7-7b6c1998b7a0_story.html?utm_term=.3e3f2df52816.

New, J. 2016. Campus sexual assault in a Trump Era: President-elect Trump has offered few details on how his administration might deal with campus sexual assault, but his surrogates and other Republicans say they would scale back enforcement of Title IX. *Inside Higher Education*, November 10. Available at https://www.insidehighered.com /news/2016/11/10/trump-and-gop-likely-try-scale-back-title-ix-enforcement-sexual -assault.

Timm, J. C. 2016. Trump on hot mic: "When you're a star . . . you can do anything" to women. NBC News, October 7. Available at http://www.nbcnews.com/politics/2016 -election/trump-hot-mic-when-you-re-star-you-can-do-n662116.

Acknowledgments

This book is the culmination of years of experience of academics, practitioners, and activists, whose work can, on the whole, be found in the references throughout this volume. We thank all of the researchers, activists, and practitioners who work tirelessly to assist our student victims and improve responses to violence against women on college campuses. We strongly believe that their collective efforts will change the future experiences of college students, and we are humbled to be working alongside them. We are grateful to the authors of the chapters in this volume for sharing their expertise with us and our readers and for thoughtful, well-researched, and articulate contributions. We also thank those who assisted our work in various ways, whether by providing us with connections or materials, helping with the technical aspects of the volume, or offering emotional and professional support: Diane Price Herndl, Kim Golombisky, and Jennifer Ellerman-Queen from the Department of Women's and Gender Studies at the University of South Florida; Zoe Ridolfi-Starr from Know Your IX; and Ethan Wade, whose tireless efforts engaging students in preventing violence against women is inspiring. We are also grateful to Temple University Press, particularly Aaron Javsicas and Marinanicole "Nikki" Dohrman Miller, for the opportunity to publish this work and for their patience and assistance throughout the process.

On a personal level, Michelle wants her partner, Rob Benford, to know that she is fully aware of everything he did to make her life easier as she worked to complete her share of this project. She is very grateful for his decades of loving support and encouragement. Katie is grateful for the continued and unwavering support of her husband, Ted, who stands behind all of her professional endeavors and research projects and never failed to ask how the book was coming along. Ráchael would like to thank family and friends who supported her with their interest, encouragement, and feedback.

Finally, we thank the students, often women, who have survived violence while attending college, for sharing their experiences and strength, which have helped us understand the patterns and contexts of violence, and for their persistence in seeking justice, which has guided our collective efforts to hold perpetrators accountable and to prevent future violence. We honor their courage as we share their voices in this volume.

Addressing Violence Against Women on College Campuses

1

Violence Against College Women

Unfortunately, It Is Not a New Problem

CATHERINE KAUKINEN,
RÁCHAEL A. POWERS, AND
MICHELLE HUGHES MILLER

The context for this book is the recent "discovery" of violence against women on college campuses. While researchers have long noted that violence against women on college campuses remained underreported and largely unaddressed by campus and local law enforcement, as well as by campus administrators, the April 4, 2011, "Dear Colleague Letter" from the U.S. Department of Education and its Office for Civil Rights (OCR) was a game changer. The 2011 Dear Colleague Letter has served as an articulation of campus responsibilities to address sexual violence under Title IX. In Chapter 7, Michelle Hughes Miller provides a detailed outline and analysis. The obligations under the Dear Colleague Letter have altered the way college campuses must address, investigate, and adjudicate disclosures and complaints of sexual violence (along with intimate partner violence and stalking). The letter also put in place a number of requirements for campuses to act to prevent violence against women and ensure that the campus community understands its role in the process of reporting. In doing so, it reinforced a system of accountability for campuses to comply with these requirements or face sanctions from the OCR. This theme of accountability runs throughout the chapters of this book. The shift to making universities responsible and accountable in cases of sexual violence places a heavy burden on universities to ensure the protection of victims and the safety of their campuses. Many campuses do not have the administrative capabilities and are not financially prepared for such an unfunded mandate. At the same time, in

ensuring compliance with the newest interpretations and policy requirements of Title IX, some campuses may have lost sight of the very goal of the
Dear Colleague Letter: the protection of our student victims. As schools
shifted to formal legal compliance they may have lost sight of their need to
protect and serve their student victims and to prevent future victimizations.
We believe that if institutions protect their student victims and ensure they
are not further victimized by the process, they will more than likely also be
in compliance with Title IX. See Figure 1.1 for a timeline of federal legislation
that has affected the response of institutions of higher education to sexual
violence and violence against women.

The guidance provided by the 2011 Dear Colleague Letter has been followed by additional interpretations of Title IX that also have implications for
how campuses comply with the Clery Act, legislation requiring campuses to
both keep and publicly disclose information about crime, including sexual
assaults, intimate partner violence, and stalking, on and near their respec-
tive campuses. The passage of the Campus SaVE Act (along with the broader
Violence Against Women Act), the White House Task Force to Protect Students from Sexual Assault, the "It's on Us" campaign, the adoption by many
campuses of the "No More" campaign, and the 2014 Campus Accountability
and Safety Act (which remains pending in the U.S. Senate as of this writing)
bring still more obligations. Together these new legislative requirements and
task force directives describe how college campuses need to engage in prevention efforts to reduce the incidence of violence, respond to their student
victims in terms of interim measures, investigations, adjudications, and
sanctions, and make clear to faculty, staff, and students (bystanders, victims,
and accused individuals) their responsibilities, obligations, and rights with
respect to dating violence, domestic violence, sexual assault, and stalking.
With these directives comes potential sanctions if institutions fail to adhere
to these new legislative mandates. It is clear that many institutions of higher
education are not prepared to address these mandates or have the resources
to do so. Ultimately the question is this: Given the growing number of unfunded mandates placed on colleges and universities, how can campuses and
their administrators handle their investigative responsibilities while also
ensuring the safety of the campuses and the victims of these crimes?

While the problem of violence against women on college campuses is not
new, the shift to making campus personnel responsible to redress the victimizations experienced by their students is a relatively new perspective and one
slow to be adopted by administrators. At the same time, many campuses
have for decades had allies and advocates committed to prevention efforts
and victim assistance, recognizing the impact of violence against women.
Academic research, feminist advocacy, and victim service provision have addressed campus-based violence against women since the late 1960s and
1970s. For example, research by E. J. Kanin (1967) on a sample of college men

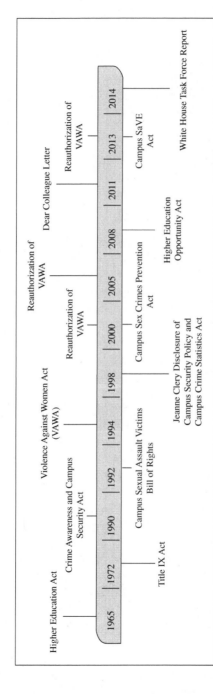

Figure 1.1 Timeline of Federal Legislation Impacting Institutions of Higher Education Response to Sexual Violence (and Violence Against Women)

showed that the incidence of exploitive sexual behavior was high among both aggressive and nonaggressive college men. As many as 80 percent of aggressive college men and 27 percent of nonaggressive college men indicated that they had used at least one exploitive tactic to gain access to sexual intercourse (e.g., attempting to get a young woman intoxicated or threatening to terminate a relationship). His research also demonstrated that sexually aggressive men were able to justify their behavior in terms of their perceptions of women as "teasers," "golddiggers," or "loose women"—perceptions that both stigmatize women and legitimate targeting them for any type of sexual approach.

The research on dating violence had its advent in 1981 (Makepeace, 1981). In the 1980s research had begun to estimate the extent and correlates of sexual violence against college women (Berkowitz 1992; Muehlenhard and Cook 1988; Muehlenhard and Linton 1987). Alan Berkowitz's (1992) summary of the literature from the 1980s notes efforts to identify *perpetrator* characteristics, situations associated with *sexual assault*, and *men's misperception* of *women's sexual intent*. Research in the 1980s focused attention on the relationships between justifications for sexual aggression, sex-role stereotyping, adversarial sexual beliefs, acceptance of interpersonal violence, and belief in rape myths (Burt 1980; Muehlenhard, Friedman, and Thomas 1985). Throughout the 1980s and 1990s campus-based interventions focused on the strategies that women could implement to reduce their risk, including practicing self-defense and changing routine activities, along with other victim-centered approaches. Today, campus efforts continue these emphases, but they also focus on offender accountability and a host of bystander programs, student activism initiatives, and widespread mandatory reporter training, all of which are designed to impact the cultural and community contexts within which violence against college women takes place.

The research today also includes large-scale climate surveys, as well as evaluations of prevention and intervention efforts (McMahon and Banyard 2011), which have recently been identified as a new means for addressing the problem of sexual violence on campuses. Along with federal legislative initiatives, the Association of American Universities (AAU) has encouraged its member schools to commit to new campus climate surveys in order to measure the extent and impact of sexual violence across campuses using comparable measures. These types of data are largely already available from previous data collections, including data collected by the authors, albeit from individual campuses which limits the generalizability to all campuses. The limitations of previous data collections have also been that they were collected as one-time, cross-sectional research projects and not part of an on-going effort to explore the climate of campuses. At the same time, there are significant questions about the purpose and publication of this new climate survey, and the effect such a survey would have on existing campus data collections. Louise Fitzgerald, a professor emerita of psychology at the University of Illinois at Urbana-Champaign, had this to say about the planned AAU climate survey: "To ignore the combined experience of the country's most prominent and experienced researchers and attempt to reinvent the wheel is intellectual arrogance of the worst sort. Worse, it risks compromising the validity and thus policy usefulness of the project" (quoted in Bonine 2014). While many scholars, researchers, and advocates have led the charge to address violence against women on college campuses, it may be that ownership of this social and public health problem is shifting to the federal government and campus administrators without the input of those who initiated the charge. The question is whether federal legislation and campus administrations will address the long-term problem, providing remedies for the victims of crime and ensuring safety to all students on our college and university campuses, or merely engage in a series of prescribed measures to ensure that they follow the letter of the law and are in compliance with Title IX requirements, rather than its spirit.

The editors and authors of this volume highlight research on the extent, nature, and dynamic of both interpersonal and sexual violence against women and examine the contexts in which violence against women occurs on college campuses. Opening chapters cover such topics as the pervasiveness of drinking and rape culture, victim blaming, and problematic masculine identities and behaviors that have led to campus crimes against women persisting, with little variation, for the past twenty to thirty years. The book then shifts to an extensive discussion of the ways in which college and university campuses and the federal government have attempted to prevent victimization, attend to victims of crime, and hold offenders accountable, as well as the implications of these attempts for higher education actors, including campus administrators, victim advocates, and student activists. The book also highlights the work done to provide accurate estimates of the problem of violence against women along with challenges to the collection of accurate climate survey data from college campuses. The chapters explore the importance of campus efforts that focus on educating young men and women on the nature of sexual and dating violence; attempting to make men accountable and to empower bystanders to act; conducting outreach and awareness that meets students where they are; and changing cultural norms by both including men as allies in preventing violence against women and making violence prevention an integral part of the student experience.

This book lays out a number of goals that may facilitate an ongoing discussion of violence against college women and point to how to best prevent, investigate, and intervene to assist victims; reduce the impact of these crimes; and hold perpetrators accountable to ensure safety on our college and university campuses. Outlining the extent of violence against women on college campuses and analyzing the data used for these estimates, the book also explores the various explanations for our problem of violence against women on college campuses and the strategies and prevention efforts that will best address the problem. The current legislative landscape and federal mandates, including where they came from and how they are changing campuses' responses to violence against women, are also addressed. This discussion identifies resistance to, or, more accurately, a backlash against, the identification of problems and the search for and enactment of solutions. This backlash includes a denial of the often cited "1 in 4 women" statistic (proportion of women who are victims of sexual violence), and a push to shift responsibility for adjudication and victim services to criminal justice agencies off campus.

The contributing authors and the editors of this book bring diverse perspectives to the issues of violence against college women and the prevention of violence on college campuses. Researchers, administrators, victim advocates, and Title IX experts can all help address this important social problem and suggest how colleges and universities should best approach solving it.

In Part I we provide a historical and contemporary overview of the extent, nature, and dynamics of violence against women on college campuses. Starting with what we know about these issues, the chapter authors go on to consider how we got to where we are in terms of policies, practices, and campus-based interventions. They also examine the risk factors for violence against women, as well as protective measures, and highlight research into the causes of the pervasiveness of rape culture, victim blaming, and unhealthy masculinities. Paying special attention to the role of alcohol in sexual conduct on college campuses, Part I further considers the relationship between drinking and violence in campus cultures, its effects on women, and ways that reporting victimization can be effective.

When looking at the extent and nature of sexual violence, intimate partner violence (IPV), and stalking of college women, it is important to recognize that developing instruments to measure these phenomena is a challenge, especially across academic disciplines. The first estimates of campus sexual violence came from data gathered between 1993 and 1994 from a large, nationally representative sample of students enrolled in four-year colleges. Since that time, estimates of the percentage of women who were the victims of a completed rape and/or completed sexual assault (e.g., forced kissing or unwanted groping of sexual body parts) have ranged from 3 to 20 percent. It is also crucial to note that for almost every measure of sexual violence considered, college women were victimized at higher rates off campus than they were on campus—a finding that has implications for how campuses address the problem of sexual violence against college women and how to make perpetrators who commit their offenses off campus accountable. Moreover, as Callie Marie Rennison, Catherine Kaukinen, and Caitlyn Meade note in Chapter 2, research of on-campus sexual violence against college women is limited, and what is known must be pieced together from multiple sources. In this chapter, they also examine estimates of college women's experience of sexual violence, which suggest that roughly one in five senior college women were victims of a completed rape and/or completed sexual assault, while also pointing to a number of challenges to studying sexual violence, including failure to report and underreporting of victimizations, nonresponse in data gathering, limitations of samples used, variable attention to contextual factors, and mixed interpretations of results.

In Chapter 3, Ráchael A. Powers and Catherine Kaukinen turn to IPV and estimates of dating violence that range from 10 percent to 50 percent, including both physical and psychological abuse of women. Studies consistently find that emotional and psychological abuse are more frequent than physical abuse, and several studies find that the majority of male and female college students have experienced psychological abuse within a dating relationship. Strikingly—and this has implications for prevention and intervention—both women and men are more likely to be victims and perpetrators of violence within a mutually violent relationship. As the authors further note, while much of what is known regarding dating violence comes from quantitative surveys that may be valid and reliable, it is difficult to ascertain how young adults, particularly young women, understand their relationships and the use of violence in them. Likewise, they suggest that identifying the primary motivations for violence and determining whether motivations for, severity of, and reactions to dating violence differ in casual and serious relationships are both important.

In Chapter 4, which focuses on stalking, Matt R. Nobles and Kate Fox point to the paucity of research in the area. What we know, in general, are some basic characteristics of victims, including demographics, and some facts, such as how many acknowledge their own victimization, how many report it to the police, and under what circumstances they may be more likely to do so. Nobles's and Fox's extensive work on stalking among college students has led them to conclude that stalking victimization and perpetration often share important similarities and that self-reported history of intimate partner violence and sexual assault are strongly associated with stalking outcomes. Yet they also point out that much of the research on stalking at present can speak only to such issues as acknowledgment of victim status, decisions to report to police, and self-protective behaviors. Victim-coping strategies, including counseling and advocacy, have typically been a focus. In their work, however, Nobles and Fox find that stalkers score significantly higher on the insecure-anxious scale of attachment and lower on the insecure-avoidant scale. They also note that other psychological variables, ranging from major to minor psychiatrically diagnosed problems and including depression and a history of anger-related diagnosis or treatment, are positively and significantly associated with stalking perpetration.

Observing that no study has systematically evaluated a prevention or intervention that targets stalking offenders, Nobles and Fox point to the challenges posed by disparate definitions of stalking and different approaches to measuring it, which have important implications for the validity, reliability, and generalizability of knowledge about stalking victimization and perpetration among college students.

Part I of the book also includes an exploration of the broader context in which violence against women occurs. Thus, in Chapter 5, Walter S. DeKeseredy considers reasons for violence against women by drawing on male peer support theory and feminist routine activities theory. Broadly, male peer support theory suggests that individual and cultural factors give rise to conditions wherein men (and women) are socialized to accept male dominance. This translates into an environment that is conducive to violence against women, especially when factors such as alcohol consumption are involved. Feminist routine activities theory also acknowledges the larger role of culture in shaping risk of violence by reintroducing the motivated offender into the theory and considering how alcohol use contributes to creating suitable targets. Taken together, these theories aim to explain how campuses that are generally non-criminogenic become high-risk environments for women.

In Chapter 6 Antonia Abbey focuses more closely on the role of alcohol in violence against women, a factor that has recently received considerable attention from academics and the media. On the basis of her own extensive work in this area, she provides a conceptual model for understanding its role in acquaintance sexual assaults. This model explains the mechanisms by which alcohol consumption increases the risk of a victimization occurring. Alcohol has both psychological and pharmacological effects, which, combined with preexisting beliefs and attitudes about women and relationships, interact with personality characteristics of perpetrators. Abbey thus explains not only why alcohol is a factor in so many sexual assaults of college women, but also how alcohol impacts how we respond to such crimes, including mitigating responsibility of the offender and blaming the victim.

Part II of this book moves on to focus on recent legislative changes associated with Title IX, the Clery Act, and the SaVE Act. It begins with Michelle Hughes Miller's examination of the evolution of Title IX and of the legal, political, and social conditions that gave rise to the 2011 Dear Colleague Letter (DCL). While the letter is generally thought to be a turning point in how violence against college women is addressed, Hughes Miller argues that the DCL represents a shift in emphasis, but not understanding, as the OCR had recognized, albeit subtly, institutions' obligations to address sexual violence under Title IX since at least 1997. However, what the 2011 DLC did articulate was how institutions are to respond to violence against college women.

Chapter 8 considers the Campus SaVE Act, contextualizing the act within the histories of the reauthorized Violence Against Women Act (VAWA) and the Clery Act, which expand a campus's responsibilities to address intimate partner violence and stalking. Identifying the major elements of this legislation as they relate to prevention of and response to violence against women on college campuses, Michelle Hughes Miller and Sarah L. Cook discuss the explicit transparency and compliance requirements. They also consider the ongoing debates about the scope and mandate of the SaVE Act: Who is included in the SaVE Act? What elements of the act are requirements and what elements are just suggestions? Most important, how do universities demonstrate compliance?

In Chapter 9, Catherine Kaukinen reviews the political context for current efforts to address campus violence against women, including recommendations stemming from the 2014 White House Task Force to Protect Students from Sexual Assault, which also focuses on improving the safety of American college and university campuses and helping them meet their obligations in compliance with federal regulations in this area. The chapter also explores the White House Task Force's "It's on Us" program, which encourages college and university campuses to initiate violence prevention campaigns that engage students in campus-based events and programming as allies in addressing violence against women, and to use student leaders who take "The Pledge" to serve as role models.

In Chapter 10, Carmen Suarez returns to the topic of Title IX to discuss its organizational prevention and response dimensions. On the basis of her own experiences as vice president for global diversity and inclusion at Portland State University and interviews with other Title IX coordinators, Suarez discusses balancing the needs/rights of complainants and respondents and the struggle to apply a victim-centered approach to investigations and adjudication. She also explains the role of the Title IX coordinator in this process and demonstrates how coordinators have met both institutional support and interference. Although compliance is often the metric used to evaluate the effectiveness of responses to Title IX cases, Suarez emphasizes that the ultimate goal is cultural change and that compliance is the means, not the end.

In Chapter 11, Helen Eigenberg and Joanne Belknap present an in-depth discussion of mandatory reporting, a controversial aspect of Title IX. Proponents of mandatory reporting argue that it puts the needs of students above the university's reputation and that it will ultimately make campuses safer as more perpetrators are removed and victims receive needed services that they would not have received without disclosure. Opponents, on the other hand, argue that mandatory reporting takes agency away from the victim, that it may additionally traumatize victims, and that it may discourage victim reporting to nonconfidential personnel, such as professors. From this point of view, mandatory reporting may actually have the opposite effect than intended. In addition, Eigenberg and Belknap note that regulations do not give much guidance to Title IX coordinators, who must balance the student's desire for confidentiality with the safety of the university with little guidance from the regulations. Moving on to evaluate recent legislative efforts to mandate reporting beyond campus walls to local law enforcement and prosecutors' offices, Eigenberg and Belknap conclude the chapter with recommendations for increasing transparency and improving confidence in the system.

The degree to which college campuses are equipped to provide victim services and advocacy for victims and the crucial role such services play in preventing and responding to violence against women are the focus of Chapter 12. While federal policy clearly indicates that institutions should address the needs of victims, currently there is tremendous variability in the availability and breadth of victim advocacy across different institutions, as Ráchael A. Powers, Alesha Cameron, and Christine Mouton point out. Smaller community colleges and universities may lack the resources and/or the caseload to support a dedicated office on the campus, and rural universities may not have local victim services available at all. In addition, there are also institutional and cultural barriers to providing services on a campus, including the question of confidentiality for reports made to such offices. This chapter highlights the approaches to campus-based victim advocacy that have been most validated by research.

Part III shifts attention to how to prevent violence against college women and reviews strategies such as campus climate surveys, campus outreach efforts, and student-led social movement organizations, which seek to create awareness and provide students with information regarding their rights under Title IX. Educational programming that emphasizes women's actions and bystander programs and national campaigns that engage men as allies in violence prevention are also considered.

Campus surveys are the focus of Christine Lindquist and Christopher P. Krebs in Chapter 13. As other authors in this volume observe, obtaining accurate estimates of victimization can be difficult, but climate surveys can provide much-needed information to a university regarding the extent of victimization of its students, which can then be used to inform prevention and intervention efforts. Furthermore, standardized climate surveys, which can be used to compare institutions, can help highlight best practices for violence reduction. Reviewing efforts made by individual institutions and in collaboration with federal agencies to create and implement climate surveys, Lindquist and Krebs also draw from their own work to offer several recommendations for maintaining methodological rigor in view of the difficulty of capturing experiences and attitudes of a large population of students. The chapter concludes with a discussion of the future of climate surveys, including legislation that may mandate their implementation in schools.

Once there is some understanding of students' experiences, beliefs, and attitudes, prevention of violence ultimately relies on the education that incorporates this information. In Chapter 14 Sarah McMahon focuses on the role of bystander education, a mandatory part of the SaVE Act. She provides an overview and history of bystander programs, detailing how they arose in response to critiques of traditional sexual violence prevention programs, which focus on individual behaviors and attitudes and could result in victim blaming. In contrast, bystander programs treat sexual violence as a community health issue and involve everyone in sexual violence prevention efforts and thereby also change social norms that are supportive of violence against women. Reviewing several popular programs, McMahon notes studies showing that these programs can affect attitudes and, to a lesser extent, behaviors and these changes may persist over time. McMahon concludes with several recommendations for bystander programs and encourages continued evaluations to assess their effectiveness as sexual violence prevention strategies.

In Chapter 15, Ráchael A. Powers and Jennifer Leili explore men's antiviolence programs and men's engagement in efforts to combat violence against women. Given that men are the main perpetrators of violence, they play an important role in the acceptance of gender-based violence. Thus, involving men in efforts to prevent violence against women is vital. Reviewing some of the best practices for these programs, Powers and Leili look at several prominent examples of men's college-based anti-violence programs and consider evidence for their effectiveness in changing norms and behaviors. Non-institutional efforts to engage men in anti-violence efforts, such as SlutWalks and Take Back the Night events are also covered here, as are critiques of them, such as the claim that men receive accolades "just for showing up" or that they downplay the seriousness of victimization. The authors conclude with a discussion on the future of these programs, including the role of social media and the need to be culturally relevant.

In Chapter 16, Ava Blustein considers the rise of local and national student campaigns and political protests against campus violence against women, which have increased in recent years, as organizations such as Know Your IX attest. Blustein, who works with Know Your IX, looks at important efforts on the part of student-activists, many of whom are victims themselves, and examines both the goals of these social movement organizations and the extent to which they have been successful in changing campus culture and climate. In particular, she describes how Title IX has provided students with a means to protest, while also holding universities accountable for their responses to sexual assault on college campuses. Further considering how social media offers a way for students to expand the reach of their activism, broaden support, and increase awareness of their issues and the efficacy of their efforts, she concludes by calling attention to the growing diversity of the movement, as it recognizes the interconnections between sexual violence and other forms of oppression on college campuses.

In Part IV, our authors offer guidance for and critical discussion about ways to prevent and intervene in violence against women. Drawing on her expertise as a Title IX coordinator, Meredith M. Smith reviews the origins of the 2011 DCL and argues that concerns about compliance may hinder the ultimate goal of this legislation to prevent gender-based violence and support victims. While sexual harassment and violence have always been part of Title IX, frustrations of victims and the community over mishandled incidents of sexual violence brought about refinements in how schools should respond to such cases. As a result, Title IX investigations increased exponentially, as did administrators' concern with ensuring compliance with regulations, which soon overshadowed the intent of the legislation. Smith urges us to move beyond concerns about compliance and embrace the spirit of the legislation, the call to create meaningful cultural change that will reduce violence against college women.

In response to the federal mandates that have led to changes in the ways that law enforcement and campus policies address campus violence against women, claims about the inappropriateness of universities responding to a "criminal" problem have increased, as have significant concerns about the rights of the accused. In fact, the most prevalent critique is that Title IX and other federal initiatives fail to take adequate steps to prevent false allegations and wrongful convictions of young men. In Chapter 18, Helen Eigenberg, Stephanie Bonnes, and Joanne Belknap review the significant national and legal challenges associated with federally mandated requirements to address campus rape. They point out that these changes have reinvigorated a backlash, which uses many of the tactics of 1980s and 1990s critics, including attempts to minimize the extent of the problem, redefine rape in ways that are consistent with rape mythology, challenge procedural and legal responses to rape on campuses, and "blame" feminists for the ways that overzealous officials are responding to this issue.

While there exist attempts to minimize the extent and impact of violence against women on college campuses, there has also been an opposing cultural shift that includes the engagement of bystanders and allies. Bystander intervention has gained prominence in recent years, to the point that it is now mandated within VAWA legislation, because it recognizes and works to transform the culture of campuses within which violence against women occurs. While we applaud these efforts, the monumental task of changing campus culture must acknowledge all of the elements that individually and synergistically create the milieu in which college students live and learn. Thus, in our concluding chapter we consider the challenges and opportunities for universities and colleges seeking to address violence against women. The challenges are many, from victim-blaming beliefs that affect reporting, to victim services that are understaffed and face questions about their advocacy and confidentiality, to expectations that campus administrators can somehow find justice for survivors and perpetrators within their policies and programming. Fortunately, survivor-activists, the detailed guidance of Title IX offered by the OCR, and the explicit mandates of the Campus SaVE Act have created pressure on campus administrators and service providers to do more, and to do it better. But, in fact, universities already have the means to respond to campus violence against women by virtue of the campus missions of teaching, research, and service. Programs that attempt to transform campus culture can build upon existing teaching platforms and educational strategies. Assessing these programs and getting detailed information about the experiences of students in climate studies are what scholars and researchers already do, and do well. The direct care provided in reporting offices, counseling centers, and victim services is aligned with the existing service mission for university students and communities.

At the same time, universities must still select and implement policies, programs, and services. But the questions are which programs, which services, and for whom? Addressing these challenges in the Conclusion, we look at several questions: How do colleges and universities design their systems of prevention and response to fulfill the needs of all of their constituents? How do they continue to grow and improve their services? And, ultimately, how do they ensure that they are, in fact, creating the safe, inclusive communities of higher education that we all envision?

REFERENCES

Berkowitz, A. 1992. College men as perpetrators of acquaintance rape and sexual assault: A review of recent research. *Journal of American College Health* 40 (4): 175–181.

Bonine, J. E. 2014. Surveys, secrecy, and sexual assault. *Chronicle of Higher Education*, November 26. Available at http://chronicle.com/blogs/conversation/2014/11/26/surveys-secrecy-and-sexual-assault/.

Burt, M. R. 1980. Cultural myths and supports for rape. *Journal of Personality and Social Psychology* 38 (2): 217–230.

Kanin, E. J. 1967. An examination of sexual aggression as a response to sexual frustration. *Journal of Marriage and the Family* 29 (3): 428–433.

McMahon, S., and V. L. Banyard. 2011. When can I help? A conceptual framework for the prevention of sexual violence through bystander intervention. *Trauma, Violence, and Abuse* 13 (1): 3–14.

Muehlenhard, C. L., and S. W. Cook. 1988. Men's self-reports of unwanted sexual activity. *Journal of Sex Research* 24 (1): 58–72.

Muehlenhard, C. L., D. E. Friedman, and C. M. Thomas. 1985. Is date rape justifiable? The effects of dating activity, who initiated, who paid, and men's attitudes toward women. *Psychology of Women Quarterly* 9 (3): 297–310.

Muehlenhard, C. L., and M. A. Linton. 1987. Date rape and sexual aggression in dating situations: Incidence and risk factors. *Journal of Counseling Psychology* 34 (2): 186–196.

I

The Extent, Nature, and Causes of Violence Against Women on College Campuses

2

Sexual Violence Against College Women

An Overview

CALLIE MARIE RENNISON,
CATHERINE KAUKINEN,
AND CAITLYN MEADE

Introduction

Although sexual violence against college women has been a topic of much academic interest for decades, it has become the subject of intense interest in the popular media only in recent years. This heightened concern reflects increased publicity about federal mandates to address sexual violence against college women and on college campuses, including the 2011 Dear Colleague Letter (DCL) and the reauthorized Violence Against Women Act (VAWA). Recently, the notion that one in five college women are sexually assaulted has become "common knowledge," leading to the belief that college campuses are foci of sexual violence where especially female students are at great risk. Research indicates that college students, especially women, express high levels of fear that they will be victimized (Fisher and Sloan 2003; Jennings, Gover, and Pudrzynska 2007). It is clear that sexual violence continues to be a major problem on college campuses (and beyond). Yet the underdeveloped extant research demonstrates that campus sexual violence—that which specifically occurs on campus—happens less frequently than sexual assaults of college women occurring off campus. This has important implications for college women and for college administrators who are accountable for responding to their student victims. The notion that college campuses are dangerous likely comes from using evidence of sexual violence against college women (that could occur anywhere) as proof that college and university campuses experience extreme rates of sexual violence.

The purpose of this chapter is twofold. First, it provides an examination of the extent and nature of sexual violence against college women that occurs both on and off campus. This includes the identification of the risk factors for sexual violence and also its physical and psychological consequences. Second, it explores the differences between on- and off-campus sexual violence and their relevance as campuses move forward in their prevention and response efforts. The chapter closes with a review of what is known, and ways in which this area of inquiry can be expanded for both policy and prevention.

Koss's Foundational Sexual Aggression/Sexual Violence Studies

A natural starting point in a discussion about sexual violence against college women begins with the research of Mary Koss and associates. Koss's initial research was not to understand sexual violence against college students per se, but more broadly to improve the measurement and methodology used to study sexual violence, especially in regard to detecting sexual violence that may not have been disclosed (Koss 1985; Koss and Oros 1982). To this end, Koss and Oros (1982) developed a self-report instrument that measured the violent act of "rape on a continuum of normal male behavior within the culture. The continuum of sexual aggression would range from intercourse achieved through verbal coercion and threatened force to intercourse achieved against consent through use of physical force (rape)" (455). The twelve-question instrument—the (initial) Sexual Experiences Survey—was administered to 1,846 male and 2,016 female students enrolled at Kent State University. Utilizing a sample of college students was clever, efficient, and convenient because it provided a large number of respondents in the age range most associated with higher risk of sexual aggression/victimization. Although the results were not generalizable, given they were based on a single university, Koss and Oros's (1982) findings—at a time when the use of official records, victimization studies, and other means that underestimated sexual violence were the standard—confirmed that a self-report survey approach is a feasible alternative approach in sexual violence research.

Extending this line of inquiry, Koss, Gidycz, and Wisniewski (1987) estimated sexual aggression and sexual violence against college students using a nearly representative sample of university students attending thirty-two institutions. This National College Women Survey gathered data from 3,187 women and 2,972 men using an extensive survey instrument that included about 330 questions (twelve of which were from the Sexual Experiences Survey). An important methodological element of this work is the use of behaviorally specific questions (see, e.g., Russell 1982). This approach improved chances of gathering data from acknowledged and unacknowledged rape victims. Results indicated that since age fourteen, 28 percent of college women reported an attempted rape (12 percent) or a completed rape (15 percent). Koss, Gidycz, and Wisniewski (1987) also estimated that in the prior year, 10 percent of college women had been raped and 7 percent were victims of attempted rape (which corresponds to a rate of 166 per 1,000 college women). These findings and others in the field formed the basis of the frequently cited conclusion that "rape is much more prevalent than previously believed" (Koss, Gidycz, and Wisniewski 1987, 170). Nevertheless, this work did not delve into the location (on or off campus) of sexual violence, an issue we discuss in detail later in this chapter.

Contemporary Research on Sexual Assault Against College Women

Young men and women are exposed to a variety of new experiences when they begin their postsecondary education. Newfound freedoms and friendships can alter their lifestyles and choices. With college often comes partying, alcohol and drug use, decreased supervision, and interactions with strangers—factors correlated with increased risk of victimization. Crime on college campuses has received extensive attention in recent decades, bringing to light the high prevalence of victimization that college students' experience. Sexual violence is one of the most studied types of victimization that students, especially women, face during their college years. Harassment, unwanted sexual contact, and coerced sexual conduct are among the types of sexual victimization that are reported (Fisher, Cullen, and Turner 2000) and categorized under the umbrella term "sexual violence."

The rather broad definition of sexual violence lends varying figures to the prevalence of victimization. This has also led to a variety of methodological techniques using different types of data, beginning with Koss's work, discussed previously. Depending on the reference period used in an administered self-report survey, between 3 percent (Fisher, Daigle, and Cullen 2010a) and 28 percent (Hickman and Muehlenhard 1997) of college women reported an attempted or completed rape (Rennison and Addington 2014). In comparison, Clery statistics, those data on crimes reported to universities that are publicly distributed annually in their security reports, indicate rather low numbers of sexual assaults officially reported on campus. However, noncompliance of universities and low official reporting by victims produce these underestimates of sexual violence (Gardella et al. 2015). Similarly, official police records indicate much lower rates of sexual violence than self-report studies do. Researchers attribute the difference between self-reported and officially reported victimization to a variety of reasons, such as knowing the perpetrator, minimization of the experience, and fear of retribution (Fisher, Cullen, and Turner 2000). Much of this research has focused on women. While the continued study of violent victimization of both men and women is warranted, women are much more likely to be victims of sexual violence. Research by Gardella and colleagues (2015) found that female students reported sexual victimization four times more than males.

The most widely cited contemporary statistic regarding sexual violence is the "1 in 5" statistic (see also Chapter 18 for a discussion of this statistic and its critics). This statistic comes from various reports, including the Campus Sexual Assault (CSA) Study, the goal of which was "[t]o examine the prevalence, nature, and reporting of various types of sexual assault experienced by university students in an effort to inform the development of targeted intervention strategies" (Krebs et al. 2007, vii). This research is based on a random sample of eighteen- to twenty-five-year-old college students attending two large public universities. The survey was fielded via the Internet in late 2006 and gathered data from 5,466 women and 1,375 men. Among many findings was that "[n]ineteen percent of the women reported experiencing completed or attempted sexual assault since entering college" (Krebs et al. 2007, xiii). Stated differently, 19 percent of senior college women were victims of completed rape and/or completed sexual assault (e.g., forced kissing or unwanted groping of sexual body parts) since they had enrolled in college.

While the "1 in 5" statistic clearly denotes an unacceptable level of sexual violence, the research by Krebs et al. (2007) and others has sometimes been distorted to inaccurately reflect the extent, nature, and dynamic of sexual violence against college women. First, findings in Krebs et al. (2007) are not representative of all colleges, nor of all college students. Later studies, such as the Campus Climate Survey Validation Study (CCSVS) by Lindquist and Krebs (discussed further in Chapter 13), while also not representative of the nation, add to our understanding. Krebs and colleagues (2016) note that neither the sample for the CCSVS of nine schools nor the data collected from the students attending them are intended to be nationally representative of all college students or institutions of higher education (IHE). The authors indicate that the goal of the research was on methodological testing, and "the results can be compared to those of other campus climate surveys and from other federal surveys, however, in an effort to improve understanding of the impact that methodological decisions have on the magnitude and validity of victimization estimates" (15).

Second, the "1 in 5" statistic has sometimes been misused to describe the extent of college women's experience of completed rape, yet the authors clearly identified that the 19 percent referred to both completed rape and other forms of completed sexual assault such as forced kissing (Krebs and Lindquist 2014; Krebs et al. 2007). Similarly in line with the "1 in 5" statistic, the CCSVS found an average prevalence rate of 21 percent for completed sexual assault experienced by undergraduate females since entering college (including completed rape; in the CCSVS, "sexual assault is the term used to describe any unwanted and nonconsensual sexual contact that involved either sexual battery or rape. It does not include sexual harassment or co-erced sexual contact, which were measured separately," 16). Clarification of what the "1 in 5" statistic refers to, then, is particularly important. Third, the "1 in 5" statistic refers to undergraduate seniors only, not to college females generally. This is therefore a "lifetime" college risk (similar to the CCSVS study) and does not represent the experiences of first-year students (or other students such as graduate students and those on medical school campuses, which frequently were found to be higher). A fourth issue is that many be-lieve the statistic means that one in five women was raped *on campus*. In most studies, the percent victimized refers to completed sexual violence that occurred to female college students, on and off campus. Unfortunately, mis-understandings about the "1 in 5" statistic by the federal government and those trying to eradicate violence have been picked up by those who wish to challenge viewing sexual violence of college women as an important social problem. Cantor and colleagues (2015) noted that one universal statistic to represent women's risk of sexual violence, such as the "1 in 5" statistic, is not particularly valuable. It likely over- or underestimates the actual risk on any given campus. Moreover, it also fails to address how differential risk and protective factors shape risk. The authors conclude that the "1 in 5" statistic is misleading at best.

Recently, Cantor and colleagues (2015) investigated student attitudes and experiences, as well as the incidence, prevalence, and characteristics of sexual assault and misconduct at twenty-seven IHE. The survey—the AAU Campus Climate Survey on Sexual Assault and Sexual Misconduct—was fielded to the IHE via the Internet in the spring semester of 2015. The final sample size included 89,115 female students. Average survey response was low (19 percent—response rates differed greatly across campuses) and non-random, leading to a caution that estimates may be biased upward. One very important finding is a great deal of variation in sexual assault and sexual misconduct rates across IHE, which means that using any one estimate to represent all IHE is unwarranted and misleading at best. Four findings are particularly noteworthy: First, 36 percent of female undergraduate students and 32 percent of female graduate/professional students "believe it is very likely or extremely likely that campus officials would take action to address factors that may have led to the sexual assault or sexual misconduct on cam-pus" (Cantor et al. 2015, xxii). Second, 27 percent of undergraduate females and 19 percent of graduate/professional female students believe that sexual assault or sexual misconduct is a problem at their IHE (Cantor et al. 2015, 164). Third, 10 percent of undergraduate females and 5 percent of graduate/professional female students believe that they are very or extremely likely to experience a sexual assault or sexual misconduct at their IHE (44, 164), and an identical percentage of respondents believe that they are very or extremely likely to experience a sexual assault or sexual misconduct at an off-campus, university-sponsored event (164). These findings suggest that the "1 in 5" message regarding the prevalence of sexual violence against college women is being heard, and that a small percentage of women students may have translated that awareness into increased perceived risk of personal victimization.

Certain demographics are also predictive of sexual assault victimization. Age is one of these predictors, with younger women between the ages of eighteen and twenty-four being at heightened risk for sexual violence and, more important, the clustering of this age group on college and university campuses. Research has demonstrated that women aged eighteen to twenty-four had higher rates of rape and sexual assault than females in all other age groups (Sinozich and Langton 2014). Similarly, Breiding (2014) finds that among women victims of sexual violence, approximately 79 percent experienced their first sexual victimization before the age of twenty-five; further, 40 percent experienced their first sexual victimization before the age of eighteen. While college students represent a diverse range of ages, as of 2013, approximately 40 percent of college students were between eighteen and twenty-four years of age; this is up from 36 percent in 2000 (National Center for Education Statistics 2016). Further, this age group represents what we think of as traditional college students. Within the college student population, seniors were more likely to report sexual victimization than other class years (Gardella et al. 2015). Unfortunately, there has been less research conducted on racial differences in college sexual assault victimization, though existing research has found that African American women reported higher rates of forced sexual intercourse than White women (Gross et al. 2006), but White students were more likely to report incapacitated sexual assault than African American students (Krebs et al. 2011). In addition, a study by Krebs and colleagues (2011) found that the context in which sexual assault occurs at historically Black colleges or universities is the same as non-historically Black schools. With regard to sexual orientation, research examining whether heterosexual students are victimized more often than sexual minority students has produced mixed results. Edwards and colleagues (2015) found that sexual minority students were more likely than their heterosexual counterparts to be victims of sexual assault, while Jones and Raghavan (2012) found that there were no significant differences in victimization between the two groups.

Many studies have examined correlates of sexual violence perpetration such as alcohol use (Abbey 2002), though more attention is being paid to correlates of victimization. Alcohol use has been highlighted as one of the biggest contributors to sexual assault victimization and perpetration, with around 50 percent of rape survivors and 74 percent of rape perpetrators reporting that they consumed alcohol before the sexual violence occurred. Given these figures, it is not surprising that studies have found those students who drink less are not as likely to report being a victim of sexual violence (Gardella et al. 2015; Krebs et al. 2011). Beyond alcohol use, other research has examined the relationship between casual and hookup sex and the risk of sexual assault (Adams-Curtis and Forbes 2004; Flack et al. 2007). The hookup culture often involves high rates of alcohol use and spontaneous, casual sexual activity (Barriger and Vélez-Blasini 2013). Engaging in this culture has been found to be related to sexual victimization among women and perpetration by men (Sutton and Simons 2015). This is discussed in detail by Antonia Abbey in Chapter 6.

The topic of consent has been brought to the forefront of the college sexual victimization conversation, in particular, how consent for sexual activity is interpreted and communicated among college students. The term sexual assault conjures images of a stranger ambushing a surprised victim, but studies have found that between 83 percent and 90 percent of sexual assaults of college students are perpetrated by a dating partner, a friend, or an acquaintance (Abbey 2002; Fisher, Cullen, and Turner 2000). Sexual scripts indicate that women are supposed to resist sex to maintain their reputation and men are expected to try to convince women to give in to sex (Gagnon and Simon 2009). Such scripts imply that men are supposed to interpret women's communication of consent. Research has indicated that men and women typically are successful at assessing and interpreting consent cues, but sometimes men overinterpret women's interest in sex as being in favor of consent (Abbey 1987) or men (choose to) interpret women saying no as "token resistance." Nonverbal cues may be heavily relied on by young men for a variety of reasons, such as cultural promotion of sexual scripts, embarrassment in asking for verbal consent, or an expectation that consent is always implied unless directly stated otherwise (Jozkowski et al. 2014). This points to the need for continued educational efforts within college campus sexual assault prevention programs to adopt a definition of consent that is affirmative, and to clearly state that the absence of verbal nonconsent ("no") is not sufficient for consent.

The physical and psychological impacts of sexual assault can be far-reaching and include posttraumatic stress disorder (PTSD), substance abuse, depression, and suicidal ideation (Chang et al. 2015). Forcible rape is likely to result in physical injury due to more resistance by the victim (Abbey et al. 2004; Kilpatrick et al. 2007). Furthermore, victims of forcible rape exhibit physical symptoms of stress during the attack, such as shortness of breath and rapid heart rate (Clum, Nishith, and Calhoun 2002). Incapacitated rape, or rape that occurs while the victim is intoxicated, may not be as physically traumatic as forcible rape, though the two may result in similar emotional trauma (Brown, Testa, and Messman-Moore 2009). Clum, Nishith, and Calhoun (2002) found no difference in the perceived severity of the event for victims of either type of rape, nor did they find a difference in emotional stress symptoms, such as confusion or guilt, during the assault. Further-more, victims of either type of rape did not differ in their perceptions of responsibility (Abbey et al. 2004) or in emotional affect (Schwartz and Leggett 1999). Given the high rate of alcohol use during campus sexual vio-lence, it is important to understand that the negative consequences are just as salient for incapacitated victims as for sober victims.

Empirical work on campus sexual assault has highlighted additional is-sues such as barriers to help-seeking, disclosure, and reporting (e.g., Sable et al. 2006), along with university and college reporting policies and proce-dures (e.g., Krivoshey et al. 2013). These studies have found that there are many reasons victims fail to report assault, such as shame, guilt, perceived lack of evidence, self-blame, and fear of not being believed (Sable et al. 2006). Research has also concluded that victim alcohol use during a sexual assault decreases reporting of sexual victimization. Krebs and colleagues (2007) found that only 2 percent of drug- or alcohol-incapacitated victims reported their victimization to the police, compared to 13 percent of physically forced victims.

Historically, few universities and colleges responded to sexual assault disclosures and reports in ways that protected the victims of sexual violence, nor did they, in many cases, comply with Title IX and Clery Act legislation (Fisher, Cullen, and Turner 2002). Recent political initiatives were designed to fully address all instances of sexual violence on college campuses and the failure of colleges and universities to adequately investigate these cases. The Sexual Assault Violence Elimination Act (SaVE), an amendment to the re-authorized Violence Against Women Act, passed in 2014. This act requires schools to provide information and statistics on sexual violence, information on bystander intervention programs, and to guarantee certain protections and rights for crime victims. In time, research should indicate whether these changes in policy increase reporting of and response to sexual victimization. Federal legislation, after and including the 2011 Dear Colleague Letter, is discussed in detail later in this volume in Chapter 7.

On-Campus Sexual Violence Is Not Synonymous to Sexual Violence Against College Women

It is important to note that on-campus sexual violence is not equivalent to sexual violence against college students more broadly. On-campus sexual violence refers to sexual violence that occurs on a college campus, while sexual violence against a college student is committed in any location, on or away from a college campus. This is not a new distinction, but one that ap-pears overlooked in contemporary literature, despite its implications for how colleges and universities document these cases for Clery and how these assaults are investigated. Distinguishing between on-campus sexual violence and sexual violence against college students more generally has been recognized by some researchers, who note the importance of context. Wooldredge, Cullen, and Latessa (1995) emphasized the "importance of examining victimization in different environmental settings" (119). These sentiments are equally applicable in references to sexual violence.

Making the distinction between on-campus and off-campus sexual violence against college women does not suggest that one location for sexual violence is more or less important or serious than the other. Both are serious, occur far too frequently, and demand consideration. Yet there are several reasons why making the distinction is important. First, and most simply, using precise definitions and measurement can reveal if a location in which sexual violence against college women occurs has distinct correlates, and if predictors vary in significant ways. Second, failure to clearly distinguish between locations of sexual violence inhibits our ability to design or enhance programs to reduce or eradicate sexual violence across all of its contexts. Policies designed to eradicate, approaches used to educate, and strategies to police on-campus sexual violence may need to differ from those related to sexual violence against college women occurring off campus. For example, research may indicate that on-campus victimizations against college women are less likely than off-campus victimizations of women to result in a physical injury and involve an intimate partner (Rennison 2015a). Third, the current conflation of the two is being frequently misunderstood to indicate that *college and university campuses* are the epicenters of sexual violence against college women. As a result, some parents have opted to keep their daughters at home and away from college due to safety concerns (see, e.g., Fisher and Nasar 1992). C.M. Rennison also noted communications with parents who have opted to keep their daughters at home and away from college due to safety concerns on college campuses (Rennison 2015b). This confusion may mislead current college students into believing that campuses themselves are unsafe, causing them to opt instead for residence in off-campus homes, apartments, or other locations where the actual risk of sexual violence may be far greater. Fourth, conflating the locations of sexual violence may lead to poor allocation of resources that are dedicated to responding to these attacks. If these scarce resources are earmarked incorrectly based on a misunderstanding of where the sexual violence is occurring, some victims may not be receiving needed assistance. For example, targeting interventions and educational programming within on-campus housing is appropriate and at the cornerstone of most campuses' educational activities. Yet campuses have less often collaborated with private off-campus apartment complexes to offer education and messaging. Finally, using precise language has important campus policy ramifications. Policies designed to make college and university campuses safer are being shaped based on findings about sexual violence against college students that are occurring both on and off campus. However, the perception that campuses are unsafe is being used to promote such policies as allowing concealed carry of weapons on college campuses and rejecting unisex campus bathrooms.

Correlates of Crime and Sexual Violence on Campus

To understand the correlates of campus violence, researchers had historically focused largely on on-campus characteristics (e.g., campus security expenditures and activities, administrative staffing, student population characteristics, cost of enrollment, campus wealth, on-campus housing) and off-campus characteristics (e.g., unemployment rate, location, city populations, city crime rates, and other exogenous forces "that may induce outsiders to perpetrate criminal acts on campus property" [McPheters 1978, 48]). Most of this research did not directly discuss sexual violence. Nevertheless, consistent findings emerged from this body of work. Most important, crimes committed on campus are generally property crimes; violent crime is relatively rare (Barton, Jensen, and Kaufman 2010; Henson and Stone 1999), and students are considerably safer on campus as compared to off campus (e.g., Rennison 2015a; Volkwein, Szelest, and Lizotte 1995). In addition, a higher number of students living on campus in dormitories or other residences (especially male students) is correlated with higher crime rates on campus (Bromley 1995; Fernandez and Lizotte 1995), as is higher levels of crime deterrents on campus such as police enforcement and/or police expenditures (McPheters 1978; Morriss 1993). Greater accessibility to and from campus (e.g., public transportation) and visibility of the campus (e.g., more acreage, greater number of buildings) is related to higher campus crime rates (Fox and Hellman 1985; Moriarty and Pelfrey 1996). Financial characteristics of campuses are also associated with campus crime rates: higher tuition costs, total tuition costs per student per term, and the greater wealth of the campus are associated with higher campus crime rates (Fernandez and Lizotte 1995; Volkwein, Szelest, and Lizotte 1995). Finally, a higher quality of education is related to higher campus crime rates (Morriss 1993; Sloan 1992, 1994).

Estimates of Sexual Violence Against College Women on Campus

Unfortunately, the investigation of crimes occurring on campus lacks sufficient development in the field (Nobles et al. 2012), as evidenced by the lack of scholarship on this topic since the 1990s. This is especially the case for sexual violence on campus. For instance, Moriarty and Pelfrey (1996) investigated the role of campus and community characteristics for several types of crime. Using data from 354 campuses, findings showed that the number of students living in campus housing, the number of buildings on campus, the number of acres of campus (i.e., visibility), and the population of the surrounding community were positively related to campus rape. The strongest relationship was measured to be between the size of the student population and campus rape. Henson and Stone (1999) also attempted to focus on specific types of crime including sexual violence, but their sample size was "too small to detect the more serious crimes such as rape" (301). Today, a leader of this inquiry into campus sexual violence against college women is Bonnie Fisher and her colleagues.

The first estimates of on-campus sexual violence came from data gathered between 1993 and 1994 from a large, nationally representative sample of students enrolled in four-year colleges (Fisher et al. 1998). The data gathered in 1993 via telephone came from a two-stage instrument based on the methodology and instruments used by the National Crime Victimization Survey (NCVS) and included information on a wide range of victimizations experienced. While the purpose of the research was not to gather location information on sexual violence, it did collect data about whether the incident occurred on or off campus. Findings failed to support the notion that universities are rife with predatory offenses, although results showed that students are not free from victimization on campus. In terms of sexual violence, statistically equal rates of rape against students were measured on and off campus (4.0 sexual victimizations per thousand on campus; 4.3 sexual victimizations per thousand off campus). Findings also showed that on-campus sexual assault rates were 1.4 times higher than off-campus rates (12.7 sexual victimizations and 8.9 per thousand, respectively). While this research does not offer gender-specific estimates, it provides an initial, important glimpse into on-campus sexual violence.

Fisher, Cullen, and Turner (1999, 2000) next focused specifically on sexual violence occurring on campus against college women. In 1996, they fielded a nationally representative telephone survey of randomly selected college students enrolled in either a two- or four-year program (n=4,466). This survey—the National College Women Sexual Victimization (NCWSV) Survey—used behaviorally specific questions in keeping with the best methodological practices (e.g., Kilpatrick, Edmunds, and Seymour 1992; Koss and Oros 1982), and utilized a two-stage instrument approach developed and used by the NCVS (i.e., a screener instrument to uncover victimizations and an incident instrument to gather incident details). Estimates suggested that 3 percent of college women experienced attempted or completed rape in the current school year, which corresponds to a rate of twenty-eight attempted or completed rapes per thousand college women (Fisher, Cullen, and Turner 2000). The NCWSV gathered information about the location of sexual violence and found that for almost every measure of sexual violence considered, college women were victimized at higher rates off campus as compared to on campus. The categories of sexual violence considered were completed rape, attempted rape, completed sexual coercion, attempted sexual coercion, completed sexual contact with force or threat of force, completed sexual contact without force, attempted sexual contact with force or threat of force, attempted sexual contact without force, threat of rape, threat of contact with force or threat of force, threat of penetration without force, and threat of contact with force. Two-thirds (66 percent) of rapes occurred off campus and 34 percent on campus. In addition, 55 percent of attempted rapes were perpetrated off campus while 45 percent occurred on campus.

The CSA study, previously mentioned, also contributes to our understanding of differences between acts of sexual violence against college women on and off campus. It estimates that 37 percent (n=49) of forced sexual assault victims and 39 percent (n=196) of incapacitated sexual assault victims were victimized on campus (Krebs et al. 2007, 5–16). As such, "the majority of sexual assault victims of both types reported that the incident had happened off campus" (5–19).

Aside from methodological contributions, NCVS data have been silent on the issue of location. One exception is Sinozich and Langton (2014), who used 1995 to 2013 data from the NCVS to compare estimates of females aged eighteen to twenty-four in college with those who are not. One estimate in this report noted that 4 percent of sexually violent victimizations against college women occurs on campus. This is markedly lower than extant findings and should be viewed with caution because it is based on ten or fewer sample cases. In addition, although the NCVS sexual violence questions are undergoing revision to improve measurement, this estimate is not based on behaviorally specific questions. Given that, this estimate certainly misses a proportion of unacknowledged rape victims (see Fisher et al. 2003; Koss 1985).

Conclusion

At first glance, it appears there is a large and growing body of literature devoted to sexual violence against college women, paralleling the growing media discussion of this important issue. This is true, but only to a point. What exists is a fairly large and somewhat disparate literature on sexual violence against college women broadly, and little research on demographic differences of experiences or risk and protective factors. In addition, contemporary data is sorely lacking on the relevant question of location, with no piece of research devoted specifically to an examination of on-campus sexual violence against college women. Instead, what is known about this topic, and the topic of demographic differences for victims of sexual violence, must be pieced together from multiple sources. This chapter, therefore, ends with a call for more targeted, but still generalizable research on the experiences and risk and protective factors for the diversity of college students who experience sexual violence on and off college campuses.

Nevertheless, we do know a bit about sexual violence against college women:

1. There is tremendous variation in the estimates of college women's experiences of sexual violence, both across studies (dependent on definitions, data, and methodology) and across institutions. However, when a broad definition is used for traditional universities and a restricted age group (not community colleges or those campuses with noncommuter populations and face-to-face instruction), roughly one in five senior college women has been the victim of a completed rape and/or completed sexual assault (e.g., forced kissing or unwanted groping of sexual body parts) since enrolling in college.

2. College women were victimized at higher rates off campus compared to on campus for nine of the ten categories of sexual violence considered in the NCWSV, with approximately two-thirds (66 percent) of rapes occurring off campus, and 34 percent occurring on campus. Slightly more than half (55 percent) of attempted rapes occurred off campus and 45 percent occurred on campus (Fisher, Cullen, and Turner 2000). Only the threat of sexual contact without force occurred at higher rates off campus than on campus. This has significant policy and program implications for universities that have yet to be fully discussed.

3. The AAU Campus Climate Survey indicates that a significant minority of female students believe sexual assault or sexual misconduct is a problem at their IHE (Cantor et al. 2015, 164). This finding is a stark reminder of the power of social media and our various prevention campaigns to inform students of the issue of sexual violence against college women. The AAU study's further finding that a small proportion of women perceive they are at very high risk for sexual assault is a sad commentary on young women's perceptions of their safety as college students—perceptions that enhanced research can address.

Future research will have to contend with the methodological difficulties inherent in sexual violence research generally, and on- and off-campus sexual violence specifically. Attention must be given to clear and reasonable definitions used, as it captures the diversity of our college student population. Aside from the usual definitional issues related to sexual violence (i.e., researchers use terms such as rape, sexual assault, sexual battery, sexual violence, and sexual misconduct to mean different things across studies), research must also address definitions such as "on campus" and "college student." Defining a student's experience using a simple dichotomy (on campus and off campus) fails to capture important nuances that location might hold. Some off-campus locations are strongly associated with the university (e.g., nonsponsored sorority and fraternity houses located off campus), while others are not. In addition, greater attention to defining "college students" is needed. Identifying exactly what is meant by a "college student" is particularly relevant now, as an increasing array of postsecondary educational options are available, and adults of many ages (i.e., not just those eighteen to twenty-four years of age) are pursuing college degrees on campus, online, and in other hybrid formats.

With clearer definitions and related measurement, a greater understanding of the context and patterns of sexual violence perpetrated against college women is possible. This is important not just in our work to prevent future assaults but also in our assessment of how existing survivors understand and seek support for their victimizations, so we can continue to improve current interventions and responses. Nonetheless, other challenges related to studying sexual violence will remain, including unacknowledged victims (together with those who were incapacitated), failure to report and under-reporting of victimizations, poor access to victim services, nonresponse in data gathering, differential response based on victimization experiences, limitations of samples used, attention to contextual factors, and interpretation of the results. It is a challenging field of inquiry, but extant gaps in our understanding and filling them represent important opportunities for future inquiry.

ACKNOWLEDGMENTS

A debt of gratitude is owed to the researchers who have focused their research on sexual violence generally, and sexual violence against college students specifically, regardless of whether it occurred on or off campus. There are many dedicated researchers in addition to those cited in this chapter who are richly deserving of appreciation. It is our hope that with continued inquiry into sexual violence, society, the criminal justice system, and policy makers will eventually treat sexual violence with the seriousness and severity it richly deserves.

REFERENCES

Abbey, A. 1987. Misperceptions of friendly behavior as sexual interest: A survey of naturally occurring incidents. *Psychology of Women Quarterly* 11 (2): 173–194.
———. 2002. Alcohol-related sexual assault: A common problem among college students. *Journal of Studies on Alcohol*, Supplement No. 14, 118–128.
Abbey, A., T. Zawacki, P. O. Buck, A. M. Clinton, and P. McAuslan. 2004. Sexual assault and alcohol consumption: What do we know about their relationship and what types of research are still needed? *Aggression and Violent Behavior* 9 (3): 271–303.

Adams-Curtis, L. E., and G. B. Forbes. 2004. College women's experiences of sexual coercion: A review of cultural, perpetrator, victim, and situational variables. *Trauma, Violence, and Abuse*, 5 (2): 91–122.

Barriger, M., and C. J. Vélez-Blasini. 2013. Descriptive and injunctive social norm overestimation in hooking up and their role as predictors of hook-up activity in a college student sample. *Journal of Sex Research* 50 (1): 84–94.

Barton, M.S., B. L. Jensen, and J. M. Kaufman. 2010. Social disorganization theory among college campuses. *Journal of Criminal Justice* 38 (3): 245–254.

Breiding, M. J. 2014. Prevalence and characteristics of sexual violence, stalking, and intimate partner violence victimization—National Intimate Partner and Sexual Violence Survey, United States, 2011. *Morbidity and Mortality Weekly Report: Surveillance Summaries* 63 (8): 1–18.

Bromley, M. 1995. Factors associated with college crimes: Implications for campus police. *Journal of Police and Criminal Psychology* 10 (3): 13–19.

Brown, A. L., M. Testa, and T. L. Messman-Moore. 2009. Psychological consequences of sexual victimization resulting from force, incapacitation, or verbal coercion. *Violence Against Women* 15 (8): 898–919.

Cantor, D., B. S. Fisher, S. Chibnall, R. Townsend, H. Lee, C. Bruce, and G. Thomas. 2015. *Report on the AAU Campus Climate Survey on sexual assault and sexual misconduct.* Rockville, MD: Westat.

Chang, E. C., T. Yu, Z. Jilani, E. E. Fowler, A. Y. Elizabeth, J. Lin, and J. K. Hirsch. 2015. Hope under assault: Understanding the impact of sexual assault on the relation between hope and suicidal risk in college students. *Journal of Social and Clinical Psychology* 34 (3): 221.

Clum, G. A., P. Nishith, and K. S. Calhoun. 2002. A preliminary investigation of alcohol use during trauma and peritraumatic reactions in female sexual assault victims. *Journal of Traumatic Stress* 15 (4): 321–328.

Edwards, K. M., K. M. Sylaska, J. E. Barry, M. M. Moynihan, V. L. Banyard, E. S. Cohn, W. A. Walsh, and S. K. Ward. 2015. Physical dating violence, sexual violence, and unwanted pursuit victimization: A comparison of incidence rates among sexual-minority and heterosexual college students. *Journal of Interpersonal Violence* 30 (4): 580–600.

Fernandez A., and A. J. Lizotte. 1995. An analysis of the relationship between campus crime and community crime: Reciprocal effects? In *Campus crime: Legal, social and policy perspectives,* 2nd ed., ed. B. S. Fisher and J. J. Sloan III, 79–102. Springfield, IL: Charles C. Thomas.

Fisher, B.S., F. T. Cullen, and M. G. Turner. 1999. *Extent and nature of the sexual victimization of college women: A national-level analysis.* U.S. Department of Justice, National Institute of Justice (NCJ 179977).

———. 2000. *The sexual victimization of college women.* U.S. Department of Justice, National Institute of Justice and Bureau of Justice Statistics (NCJ 182369). Retrieved from the National Criminal Justice Reference Service, https://www.ncjrs.gov/pdffiles1/nij/182369.pdf.

———. 2002. Being pursued: A national-level study of stalking among college women. *Criminology and Public Policy* 1 (2): 257.

Fisher, B. S., L. E. Daigle, and F. T. Cullen. 2010a. What distinguishes single from recurrent sexual victims? The role of lifestyle-routine activities and first-incident characteristics. *Justice Quarterly* 27 (1): 102–129.

———. (2010b). *Unsafe in the ivory tower: The sexual victimization of college women.* Thousand Oaks, CA: Sage.

Fisher, B. S., L. E. Daigle, F. T. Cullen, and M. G. Turner. 2003. Acknowledging sexual victimization as rape: Results from a national-level study. *Justice Quarterly* 20 (3): 535–574.

Fisher, B. S., and J. L. Nasar. 1992. Fear of crime in relation to three exterior site features: Prospect, refuge, and escape. *Environment and Behavior* 24 (1): 35–65.

Fisher, B. S., and J. J. Sloan III. 2003. Unraveling the fear of victimization among college women: Is the "shadow of sexual assault hypothesis supported?" *Justice Quarterly* 20 (3): 633–659.

Fisher, B. S., J. J. Sloan III, F. T. Cullen, and C. Lu. 1998. Crime in the ivory tower: The level and sources of student victimization. *Criminology* 36 (3): 671–710.

Flack, W. F., K. A. Daubman, M. L. Caron, J. A. Asadorian, N. R. D'Aureli, S. N. Gigliotti, A. T. Hall, S. Kiser, and E. R. Stine. 2007. Risk factors and consequences of unwanted sex among university students hooking up, alcohol, and stress response. *Journal of Interpersonal Violence* 22 (2): 139–157.

Fox, J. A., and D. A. Hellman. 1985. Location and other correlates of campus crime. *Journal of Criminal Justice* 13 (5): 429–444.

Gagnon, H., and W. Simon. 2009. *Sexual conduct: The social sources of human sexuality.* New Brunswick, NJ: Aldine Transaction.

Gardella, J. H., C. A. Nichols-Hadeed, J. M. Mastrocinque, J. T. Stone, C. A. Coates, C. J. Sly, and C. Cerulli. 2015. Beyond Clery Act statistics: A closer look at college victimization based on self-report data. *Journal of Interpersonal Violence* 30 (4): 640–658.

Gross, A. M., A. Winslett, M. Roberts, and C. L. Gohm. 2006. An examination of sexual violence against college women. *Violence Against Women* 12 (3): 288–300.

Henson, V. A., and W. E. Stone. 1999. Campus crime—an analysis of reported crimes on college and university campuses. *Journal of Criminal Justice* 27 (4): 295–307.

Hickman, S. E., and C. L. Muehlenhard. 1997. College women's fears and precautionary behaviors relating to acquaintance rape and stranger rape. *Psychology of Women Quarterly* 21 (4): 527–547.

Jennings, W. G., A. R. Gover, and D. Pudrzynska. 2007. Are institutions of higher learning safe? A descriptive study of campus safety issues and self-reported campus victimization among male and female college students. *Journal of Criminal Justice Education* 18 (2): 191–208.

Jones, C. A., and C. Raghavan. 2012. Sexual orientation, social support networks, and dating violence in an ethnically diverse group of college students. *Journal of Gay and Lesbian Social Services* 24 (1): 1–22.

Jozkowski, K. N., Z. D. Peterson, S. A. Sanders, B. Dennis, and M. Reece. 2014. Gender differences in heterosexual college students' conceptualizations and indicators of sexual consent: Implications for contemporary sexual assault prevention education. *Journal of Sex Research* 51 (8): 904–916.

Kilpatrick, D. G., C. N. Edmunds, and A. Seymour. 1992. *Rape in America: A report to the nation.* Arlington, VA: National Victim Center.

Kilpatrick, D. G., H. S. Resnick, K. J. Ruggiero, M. A. Conoscenti, and J. McCauley. 2007. *Drug-facilitated, incapacitated, and forcible rape: A national study.* Washington, DC: U.S. Department of Justice (Doc No: 219181).

Koss, M. P. 1985. The hidden rape victim: Personality, attitudinal, and situational characteristics. *Psychology of Women Quarterly* 9 (2): 193–212.

Koss, M. P., C. A. Gidycz, and N. Wisniewski. 1987. The scope of rape: Incidence and prevalence of sexual aggression and victimization in a national sample of higher education students. *Journal of Consulting and Clinical Psychology* 55 (2): 162–170.

Koss, M. P., and C. J. Oros. 1982. Sexual Experiences Survey: A research instrument investigating sexual aggression and victimization. *Journal of Consulting and Clinical Psychology* 89 (3): 455–457.

Krebs, C. P., K. Barrick, C H. Lindquist, C. M. Crosby, C. Boyd, and Y. Bogan. 2011. The sexual assault of undergraduate women at Historically Black Colleges and Universities (HBCUs). *Journal of Interpersonal Violence* 26 (18): 3640–3666.

Krebs, C. P., and C. H. Lindquist. 2014. Setting the record straight on "1 in 5." *Time,* December 15. Available at http://time.com/3633903/campus-rape-1-in-5-sexual-assault-setting-record-straight/.

Krebs, C. P., C. Lindquist, M. Berzofsky, B. Shook-Sa, K. Peterson, M. Planty, L. Langton, and J. Stroop. 2016. *Campus Climate Survey Validation Study final technical report.* Department of Justice (R&DP-2015: 04, NCJ 249545).

Krebs, C. P., C. H. Lindquist, T. D. Warner, B. S. Fisher, and S. L. Martin. 2007. *The campus sexual assault (CSA) study.* Washington, DC: U.S. Government Printing Office.

Krivoshey, M. S., R. Adkins, R. Hayes, J. M. Nemeth, and E. G. Klein. 2013. Sexual assault reporting procedures at Ohio colleges. *Journal of American College Health* 61 (3): 142–147.

McPheters, L. R. 1978. Econometric analysis of factors influencing crime on the campus. *Journal of Criminal Justice* 6: 47–52.

Moriarty, L. J., and W. V. Pelfrey. 1996. Exploring explanations for campus crime: Examining internal and external factors. *Journal of Contemporary Criminal Justice* 12 (1): 108–120.

Morriss, S. B. 1993. *The influences of campus characteristics on college crime rates.* Paper presented at the Thirty-Third Annual Forum of the Association for Institutions Research held at the Chicago Marriott downtown, Chicago, IL, May 16–19.

National Center for Education Statistics. 2016. *The condition of education 2016: Fast facts.* U.S. Department of Education (NCES 2016-144). Available at http://nces.ed.gov/fastfacts/display.asp?id=372.

Nobles, M. R., K. A. Fox, D. N. Khey, and A. J. Lizotte. 2012. Community and campus crime: A geospatial examination of the Clery Act. *Crime & Delinquency* 59 (8): 1131–1156.

Rennison, C. M. 2015a. *Violence against females on college campuses—1995–2013.* Paper presented at the Seventy-First Meeting of the American Society of Criminology held at the Hilton, Washington, DC, November 18–21.

———. 2015b. Personal communication with an unnamed parent, January 8.

Rennison, C. M., and L. A. Addington. 2014. Violence against college women: A Review to identify limitations in defining the problem and inform future research. *Trauma, Violence, and Abuse* 15 (3): 159–169.

Russell, D. 1982. The prevalence and incidence of forcible rape and attempted rape of females. *Victimology* 7 (1–4): 81–93.

Sable, M. R., F. Danis, D. L. Mauzy, and S. K. Gallagher. 2006. Barriers to reporting sexual assault for women and men: Perspectives of college students. *Journal of American College Health* 55 (3): 157–162.

Schwartz, M. D., and M. S. Leggett. 1999. Bad dates or emotional trauma? The aftermath of campus sexual assault. *Violence Against Women* 5 (3): 251–271.

Sinozich, S., and L. Langton. 2014. *Rape and sexual assault victimization among college-age females, 1995–2013.* Washington, DC: U.S. Government Printing Office.

Sloan III, J. J. 1992. Campus crime and campus communities: An analysis of crimes known to campus police and security. *Journal of Security Administration* 15 (2): 31–47.

———. 1994. The correlates of campus crime: An analysis of reported crimes on college and university campuses. *Journal of Criminal Justice* 22 (1): 51–61.

Sutton, T. E., and L. G. Simons. 2015. Sexual assault among college students: Family of origin hostility, attachment, and the hook-up culture as risk factors. *Journal of Child and Family Studies* 24 (10): 2827–2840.

Volkwein, J. F., B. P. Szelest, and A. J. Lizotte. 1995. The relationship of campus crime to campus and student characteristics. *Research in Higher Education* 36 (6): 647–670.

Wooldredge, J., F. T. Cullen, and E. Latessa. 1995. Predicting the likelihood of faculty victimization: Individual demographics and routine activities. In *Campus Crime: Legal, social, and policy perspectives*, 2nd ed., ed. B. S. Fisher and J. J. Sloan III, 133–122. Springfield, IL: Charles C. Thomas.

3

Intimate Partner Violence on College Campuses

RÁCHAEL A. POWERS AND
CATHERINE KAUKINEN

Introduction

Intimate partner violence (IPV) is a substantial public health problem, and increasing attention is being focused on the prevalence and consequences of dating violence among younger populations. This is true especially among college students, who experience violence within their intimate relationships as both victims and perpetrators. While researchers studying violence against women have long looked at the causes and consequences of IPV among college samples, this has only recently become a mandate for prevention and intervention efforts on college campuses. The 2014 Violence Against Women Reauthorization Act (VAWA) imposed new obligations on colleges and universities under its Sexual Assault Violence Elimination Act (SaVE) provision. Under VAWA, colleges and universities are now required to report domestic violence, dating violence, and stalking in addition to the crime categories previously mandated by the Clery Act. Furthermore, VAWA requires that all new students and new employees must be offered primary prevention and awareness programs that promote awareness of domestic violence, dating violence, sexual assault, and stalking. Attention is crucial since some research suggests that younger women may be at an increased risk of IPV, not only in relationships where they are the primary victims of violence and abuse but also where the violence is in the context of a mutually violent relationship. Understanding both contexts is important for preventing violence against women and its impact and addressing prevention more broadly on college campuses. Bachman and Saltzman (1995) found that women between nineteen and twenty-nine years old reported higher prevalence of IPV. Estimates of dating violence among college women range from 10 percent to 50 percent (Barrick, Krebs, and Lindquist 2013; Kaukinen, Gover, and Hartman 2012). Although IPV can encompass physical and psychological abuse and feature ongoing or former relationships, studies differ in their definitions of IPV, which accounts for some of the variability in prevalence estimates. Studies consistently find that emotional and psychological abuse is more frequent than physical abuse, and several studies find that the majority of college students have experienced psychological abuse (Cercone, Beach, and Arias 2005; Harned 2001).

College men and women are particularly vulnerable to IPV, both as victims and perpetrators, in part because many of them become involved in their first serious romantic relationship during those years. Previous research has concluded that the nature of romantic relationships influences IPV. Using a college student sample and an experimental design, Bethke and DeJoy (1993) found that students were more accepting of violence in the relationship when the relationship was depicted as serious (versus casual). The onset of serious relationships, coupled with autonomy from parental authority and other health risk behaviors contribute to the prevalence and frequency of IPV among college students.

This chapter explores the extent, nature, and dynamic of dating violence among college students. First, the extent of IPV among various subgroups (gender, race, and sexual orientation) is reviewed. Second, risk factors are discussed with a focus on lifestyle factors that may particularly impact college students (e.g., sexual risk taking and alcohol/drug consumption). Although the majority of research on IPV focuses on risk factors, protective factors are also reviewed, especially those salient to students such as engagement in academic activities. Third, the physical and psychological consequences of IPV are discussed, as well as the implications for these adverse conditions on academic performance. Finally, this chapter concludes with a series of recommendations for future research and policies/practice.

Differential Risk by Gender, Race, and Sexual Orientation

A major focus of research on IPV in general and among college students has been on assessing gender symmetry. Earlier studies on dating violence reported that for college students, women were more likely to be victims and men were more likely to be aggressors (Makepeace 1981). However, more recent work has shown similar rates of perpetration (Follette and Alexander 1992) or higher rates of perpetration among female college students (Cercone, Beach, and Arias 2005; Kaukinen, Gover, and Hartman 2012). Measures of dating violence victimization and perpetration among college samples are most frequently assessed using survey designs that utilize a modified version of the Revised Conflict Tactics Scale, or CTS2 (Straus et al. 1996). These instruments first ask questions on victimization experiences by an intimate partner and then also ask if the respondent had perpetrated the same behavior on his or her partner. Dating violence perpetration and victimization are often measured as dichotomous variables that indicate whether the respondent engaged in (or experienced) at least one conflict resolution tactic in the last twelve months (or some other observation period). Other researchers point to similarities in physical violence but also differences in the types of violence experienced, with women more likely to suffer sexual violence and men more likely to be subjected to psychological aggression (Harned 2001). Taken as a whole, these studies suggest that college dating violence often occurs within the context of a mutually violent relationship.

However, although these studies imply gender symmetry, the dynamics and outcomes of this violence are still gendered. Cercone, Beach, and Arias (2005) found that men were more likely to endorse instrumental views of violence where violence was used to control the partner. Although self-defense is an often-cited reason to explain women's use of violence in relationships, the motivations for female-perpetrated dating violence may be more complicated. For example, Leisring (2013) found that the three most commonly reported motives for college women engaging in physical aggression were anger, retaliation, and stress. Less than 5 percent of the women reported self-defense as a motivation. In addition, women who previously had been victimized were more likely to report feelings of fear, which suggests that IPV may differentially impact men and women (Cercone, Beach, and Arias 2005). Although the overall prevalence of perpetration may be comparable, men's violence against women is more likely to lead to injuries (Harned 2001).

Research has also explored the risk of IPV victimization by race and ethnicity. Tjaden and Thoennes (2000) found that non-White women were more likely to experience physical violence than their White counterparts. In particular, studies indicate that African American women have a higher or equal risk to Hispanic women and both are greater than the risk for White women (Caetano et al. 2000; Vest et al. 2002). However, other studies found no differences with regard to race (Bachman and Saltzman 1995). There is some evidence to suggest variability in rates of IPV by racial composition of the campus. Barrick, Krebs, and Lindquist (2013) found that the rate of IPV victimization among undergraduate women at historically black colleges and universities (HBCUs) is strikingly high. Estimates ranged from 18 percent for physical abuse to 34 percent for emotional abuse. In addition, approximately 30 percent of women reported experiences of coercion or stalking. Although formal comparisons cannot be made due to methodological differences, the authors note that these estimates are much higher than those provided in a comparable study of two predominately White institutions (Barrick, Krebs, and Lindquist 2013; Krebs et al. 2009).

Research on LGBTIQ (lesbian, gay, bisexual, transgender, intersex, and questioning) college students is rare; however, studies have begun to explore prevalence and consequences of IPV in the LGBTIQ community. Some studies on adolescents indicate that LGBT youth may experience higher rates of dating violence victimization than heterosexual couples. Transgender and female youth appear to be at a particularly high risk (Dank et al. 2014). These findings are also echoed in surveys of adults. Tjaden and Thoennes (2000) found that women in same-sex relationships were more likely to experience physical abuse, sexual violence, and stalking compared to their heterosexual counterparts. This pattern may also be present in colleges and universities (Porter and McQuiller Williams 2013). Using a community sample of twelve- to twenty-two-year-olds, Freedner and associates (2002) found that the risk of victimization was comparable overall between LGBTIQ and heterosexual adolescents and young adults, but bisexual men and women reported higher rates of abuse. Threats to reveal sexual orientation to family, friends, or others (i.e., "outing") may be particularly salient for bisexual adolescents. In a more thorough examination of the dynamics of IPV among LGBT students, Edwards and Sylaska (2013) used a minority stress framework to examine how sexual minority stigma, internalized self-homonegativity, and sexual identity concealment shaped the risk for perpetration among college students and found that internalized homonegativity and sexual identity concealment were related to physical abuse perpetration and homonegativity was also related to sexual violence perpetration. Their results point to the need for colleges to institutionalize social support networks for LGBTIQ students.

Child Abuse and Childhood Exposure to Domestic Violence

Experiencing child abuse and maltreatment is consistently related to later dating violence perpetration and victimization for women (Gover, Kaukinen, and Fox 2008; Leisring 2013). The relationship between early childhood physical, sexual, and emotional abuse and later involvement with IPV is commonly referred to as the cycle of violence theory. Research often draws from a social learning perspective where children learn methods of conflict resolution from their experiences with their caregivers. Research has demonstrated that the magnitude of these effects can be quite large. For example, using the National Longitudinal Study of Adolescent Health data, Gómez (2011) found that experiencing child abuse increased the odds of later perpetration of IPV by 90 percent. Similarly, in a study of adolescents, Hamby, Finkelhor, and Turner (2012) concluded that the odds of teen dating violence victimization at least doubled with experiences of physical abuse, psychological abuse, and custodial interference. Using longitudinal data that spanned students' college careers, Smith, White, and Holland (2003) found that women who were most likely to be physically or sexually victimized were those with a history of both childhood abuse and adolescent violence.

In addition, Black, Sussman, and Unger (2010) argue that because the family is a key socializing factor in the lives of children, witnessing parental IPV also has a significant role to play in dating violence perpetration and experiences. These effects are quite large, increasing the odds of adolescent IPV by 120 percent in one study (Hamby et al. 2012). Similar to experiencing child abuse, those who witness parental violence may model this behavior in their own intimate relationships because they have learned that it is a viable option for conflict resolution.

The effects of experiencing or witnessing violence as a child may be mediated or moderated by demographic characteristics such as gender (Laporte et al. 2009) or other factors such as low self-control (Sellers 1999). For example, Gover and colleagues (2008) found that for young women, experiences of child abuse increase the risk for both dating violence victimization and offending, and in particular mutual violence. In addition, recent research suggests that child abuse may be only one of many negative conditions that increase the likelihood of IPV perpetration or victimization (Jennings et al. 2014).

Behavioral and Mental Health Risk Factors

Within the literature on college dating violence, researchers have also explored how a variety of behaviors and risk factors impact the risk for both dating violence victimization and the risk of mutually violent relationships.

Sexual Decision Making

Recent sexual activity with respect to the number of sexual partners increases women's risk for involvement in a violent dating relationship (Cleveland, Herrera, and Stuewig 2003). Some studies argue that the number of partners increases women's risk for IPV victimization and perpetration (Cleveland, Herrera, and Stuewig 2003; Gover 2004). However, others have pointed out that the number of partners is not the sole risk factor; rather, day-to-day sexual decision making, relationship control, and contraceptive autonomy and control are also associated with sexual activity and IPV. Purdie, Abbey, and Jacques-Tiura (2010) conclude that violent and abusive relationships are associated with decreased contraceptive use, and physically and sexually abusive men are less likely to engage in monogamy. Therefore, sexual activity as a risk factor may be more closely tied to women's autonomy and the power dynamics of the relationship. Indeed, research has found that higher levels of sexual relationship power provide a protective factor against IPV among college women (Buelna, Ulloa, and Ulibarri 2009). In addition, Buelna, Ulloa, and Ulibarri also found that young women who had lower sexual relationship power were more likely to have been treated for a sexually transmitted infection. Their findings point to the need for the inclusion of women's empowerment and contraceptive autonomy within college dating violence prevention and education, along with the need to work with campus health centers to identify and provide support for IPV victims.

Another way to conceptualize sexual risk taking relates to the nature of sexual intimacy and its associated risk. Casual relationships, marked with the absence of monogamy and explicit emotional commitment, have implications for the risk of violence because the nature of these relationships is ambiguous and, as a result, may be more likely to feature sexual infidelity and jealousy (Bogle 2008; Garcia and Reiber 2008). For example, Manning, Giordano, and Longmore (2006) found that approximately one-third of those engaged in these nondating sexual relationships desire or expect eventual emotional commitment and monogamy. These expectations, combined with the ambiguity in these relationships, may make violence more likely. This may be particularly the case in relationships in which IPV is mutual in nature and not motivated by power and control.

Alcohol and Drug Use

College students may also be particularly susceptible to IPV because of risky lifestyle choices that often have their onset during the college years. In particular, sexual risk taking and alcohol use have both been identified as salient risk factors for IPV perpetration and victimization. The use and abuse of alcohol and drugs are sometimes viewed as part of a larger group of behavioral and health-risk behaviors that are associated with multiple forms of violence, including dating violence (Lormand et al. 2013; Temple et al. 2013). For example, drawing on longitudinal data from adolescents, Temple and colleagues (2013) examined whether alcohol use and exposure to parental violence predicted physical dating violence perpetration among young men and women. They found that alcohol use was significantly associated with subsequent dating violence perpetration and there was a continuity of both substance use and dating violence over time. The authors' findings point to the importance of implementing and continuing substance abuse prevention programs with younger adolescents, and continuing these programs in colleges and universities. At the same time, the continuity of dating violence demonstrates the difficulties that college-based education will have in reversing a pattern of unhealthy behaviors, including dating violence and substance abuse.

Gidycz, Warkentin, and Orchowski (2007) note that using drugs and alcohol may increase the likelihood of dating violence because potential male perpetrators may perceive the use of such substances as reducing a victim's ability to resist unwanted physical or sexual advances and/or as preventing them from being able to interpret warning cues of a potential assault. This correlate of the risk for IPV has implications that have the potential for victim blaming. This points to the need for strong prevention messages that highlight the need to not blame the victims of IPV for their experiences, but rather address the nature and extent of both drinking and IPV on college campuses.

Alcohol also allows perpetrators to excuse their behavior, therefore mitigating their own responsibility for the violence (Koss and Cleveland 1997). Similarly, Abbey (2002) notes that women who drink alcohol are seen as promiscuous and suitable targets, and the negative stigmas regarding sexually active women are used by sexually violent men to mitigate their culpability. In sum, alcohol and substance use may operate as situational inducements for perpetrators who are intent on engaging in IPV.

Although alcohol is thought to operate partially on mitigating responsibility, some research has suggested that it has unique pathways to intimate partner victimization for women. Howard and Wang's (2003) empirical work broadened the profile of at-risk females and examined dating violence, emotional health, sexual behavior, and substance use within a cluster of risk factors. Their findings indicate that these risk factors together increase the likelihood of experiencing adolescent dating violence victimization. Also, they suggest that for some young women, health-risk behaviors and relationship decision making may be reflective of decisions made in the context of sadness and hopelessness. Therefore, mental health may also be an important factor to consider.

Mental Health as a Risk Factor

Some scholars suggest that symptomatic mental health may be a precursor to dating violence victimization and offenses. Negative mental health, as measured by anger, self-esteem, anxiety, and depression has been associated with experiences of IPV. For example, Follingstad and colleagues (1999) found that perpetrators of dating violence were more likely to express anger and be more irrational and impulsive in their behaviors and beliefs. The need for control in a relationship not only predicted the likelihood of violence but also the frequency. Likewise, Follingstad and colleagues (2002) examined the psychological roots of dating violence, specifically the relationship between anxious relationship attachment, angry temperament, controlling behaviors, and dating violence severity. They found that anxious attachment and angry temperament influence the desire for control within the relationship. Therefore, negative mental health may directly and indirectly impact perpetration of IPV among young men and women.

Mental Health Consequences of Dating Violence

Negative mental health serves not only as a risk factor but also as a common consequence of dating violence. Victims, particularly young women, are at higher risk for a variety of mental health outcomes, including but not limited to depression, posttraumatic stress disorder, and anxiety (Kaura and Lohman 2007). Negative health symptoms may further exacerbate students' risk for violent relationships and negative academic performance (including lower grade point average [GPA] and course failure), and also may result or interact with substance use as a coping behavior. For example, Swahn and colleagues (2013) found that multiple forms of violence, including dating violence experienced by young men and women, were highly associated with negative impacts on mental health and substance use risk behaviors, including sadness, early alcohol use, binge drinking, drug use, and suicide attempts. Women who are victims of violence may use and abuse alcohol and drugs as a form of self-medication in an attempt to cope with the trauma of violence and alleviate the symptoms associated with victimization (Saunders et al. 1999). Lormand and colleagues (2013) conclude that drug and alcohol use may not only be a coping mechanism for those in a violent relationship, but that substance abuse may also increase the likelihood that a more potentially dangerous, violent outcome may occur. Therefore, drinking may place victims at an increased risk for further and more severe violence. Self-medication may actually impede the acquisition of healthy coping skills and interfere with personal relationships along with social and academic functioning. These findings point to the importance of viewing substance abuse as part of a wider set of health-risk behaviors and focusing prevention and intervention on healthy attitudes, relationships, and behaviors as a whole.

IPV victimization may directly impact academic performance or indirectly impact achievement through negative mental health symptoms and the use of alcohol or drugs as a coping mechanism. DeKeseredy and Schwartz (1998) found that female student victims may disengage from academia, drop or miss classes, perform poorly, and sometimes withdraw completely from college. Beyond mental health and alcohol/substance use presenting a barrier to academic achievement, perpetrators may also engage in behaviors that prevent victims from fully engaging in college (DeKeseredy and Schwartz 1998). It is not uncommon for victims to be stalked after dissolving a relationship, and those behaviors may create an environment where victims feel unsafe and ultimately withdraw from school. For example, Logan,

Leukefeld, and Walker (2000) found that approximately a quarter of their sample was stalked after a breakup and that stalking was associated with both physical and psychological victimization (see Chapter 4 for more information on stalking).

Protective Factors

Comparatively, there is less research on protective factors, which insulate college women from IPV, than there is on risk factors. However, research has identified several protective factors for the likelihood of perpetrating or experiencing dating violence. In addition, several researchers have identified protective factors that mediate the psychological impact of dating violence victimization.

Several studies have established a link between engagement in sports and academia and the likelihood of dating violence. With a sample of college students, Mason and Smithey (2012) found that hours spent engaged in academic activities may decrease opportunities for dating violence. These activities place both victims and perpetrators in a context in which IPV is less likely. Beyond directly impacting the risk of dating violence, several studies have illustrated that engagement in academics and athletics may serve to mediate the impact of dating violence on victims. While other research has shown the mental health impacts of IPV (outlined earlier), victims engaged in academic and athletic activities are able to use these as coping strategies.

Using data on young adults from the Rochester Youth Development Study, Smith and colleagues (2013) examined the role of educational experiences in moderating the impact of child abuse on dating violence. Their findings indicate that the impact of child abuse and maltreatment is mediated by academic performance, specifically GPA. They conclude that school GPA serves to protect abused children from later engagement in dating violence perpetration. Taylor and associates (2012) looked at the role of protective factors and, in particular, participation in athletics and self-esteem. Drawing on data from a sample of African American girls, they found that not only did involvement in athletics decrease the risk of dating violence victimization but also that this relationship largely operates through self-esteem. Participation in athletics is positively related to girls' self-esteem, particularly feelings of competence, and this in turn serves as a protective factor against dating violence victimization.

Research also suggests that social support may serve to buffer the relationship between victimization and psychological outcomes (McNally and Newman 1999). For example, Richards and Branch (2012) found that female students with higher levels of support were significantly less likely to perpetrate and experience dating violence. Other research has also pointed to the impact of social support as a protective factor for women in particular. In a study of adolescents, Cleveland, Herrera, and Stuewig (2003) found that maternal attachment is associated with reduced risk for young women to be victims of dating violence.

Summary of Research and Future Directions

Young women in heterosexual relationships are at risk for involvement in dating violence as both perpetrators and victims. This finding of the mutuality of IPV not only has important implications for women's experience of violence, the impact they experience, and their utilization of services on college campuses, but also for the development of effective campus-based dating violence interventions and prevention messaging. Further, preliminary research indicates that LGBT students may be at a heightened risk for all types of dating violence compared to heterosexual students. There are several risk factors associated with increasing the likelihood of perpetration or victimization among college women. Experiencing child abuse or witnessing domestic violence impacts later experiences of dating violence, and these relationships vary by gender. Other health and behavioral factors exacerbate risk, such as substance use and sexual activity. Dating violence has implications beyond physical injuries, as victimization causes psychological distress, substance use disorders, and academic disengagement. However, academic engagement, self-esteem, and familial attachment may serve as buffers to both the likelihood of perpetrating or experiencing violence and the negative outcomes associated with victimization.

While there is now a large body of research that explores the risk of dating violence, the dynamics of these encounters, and the consequences of victimization, much of this research is cross-sectional. However, as this chapter demonstrates, with the exception of experiencing child abuse or witnessing domestic violence, many of these risk and protective factors occur in young adulthood. Therefore, future research should strive to disentangle the progression of dating violence within and across relationships. Furthermore, research should explore how these risk and protective factors are related to each other and to the frequency and severity of dating violence.

Along those same lines, much is known regarding risk factors for dating and IPV, while much less is known regarding protective factors in general. This line of inquiry is important, as previous research has demonstrated that factors related to engagement in prosocial institutions can decrease the negative effects of experiencing dating violence. These mediators to the psychological and academic consequences of dating violence can be incorporated into policy and practice.

Much of what is known regarding dating violence has relied on quantitative surveys. Although the measures may be valid and reliable, it is difficult to ascertain the meanings that young adults, particularly young women, ascribe to their relationships and the use of violence in those relationships. Given that one of the primary motivations for the use of violence among college women is jealousy and control in light of the college climate of "hooking up," future research should use qualitative narratives to examine how young adults define the use of violence in monogamous and non-monogamous relationships and whether motivations, severity, and reactions to dating violence differ between casual and serious relationships.

Implications for Policy and Practice

In a recent review of dating violence among college students, Kaukinen (2014) outlined a number of implications for universities and colleges to prevent violence, identify victims and perpetrators, and intervene to limit negative consequences of abuse.

In particular, these recommendations point to the need to educate faculty, staff, and administrators as to the nature, extent, and dynamics of women's experiences of dating violence on campus. First, it is important for schools to recognize that many of these relationships are mutually combative and that there is an overlap between victims and perpetrators. This has implications for preventing violence against women on college campuses and ensuring that victims utilize services. Therefore, staff and faculty should be cognizant of identifying the nature of the dating violence before intervening. Given that dating violence often co-occurs with other problematic health and behavioral issues such as substance use, academic disengagement, and mental health problems, college staff should be trained to screen for possible domestic violence when treating issues and adjust interventions accordingly. The co-occurrence of these behaviors and problems also means that universities need to establish working relationships among the student service centers that handle counseling, athletics, and academics. See Exhibit 3.1 for a discussion of implications for practice, policy, and research.

An ecological framework should be utilized to inform primary prevention programs. Such a framework is the understanding that community- and sociocultural-level factors contribute to violence against women. Therefore, intervention efforts should be aimed at changing social norms that contribute to the use of violence. For example, bystander programs are popular violence prevention programs on college campuses that take this approach to addressing dating violence. As more thoroughly discussed in Chapter 14, the other advantage of bystander programs is that they involve men in efforts to end violence against women. This is pertinent, as masculine scripts and gender roles often provide justification for young men to use violence, yet they feel alienated from violence prevention programs that label them as perpetrators (for more discussion on engaging men in violence prevention, see Chapter 15).

Exhibit 3.1 Implications for Practice, Policy, and Research

- There is an absence of longitudinal studies on college dating violence, which has prevented a thorough understanding of the extent, dynamic, and nature of dating violence and its associated risk and protective factors.
- Among college students, it is important for both researchers and those working with students to recognize that much of the experience of dating violence includes students' experiences as both victims and offenders. This finding has implications for developing violence prevention education and interventions.
- College campuses need to collaborate with researchers to be sure that they develop interventions that draw on the most recent scientific research and evidence in building on the protective factors for dating violence.
- Many faculty, staff, and administrators are likely to hold a set of ideas and assumptions on the nature and extent of dating violence. This may be particularly true around gender. This points to the need for researchers to educate and challenge these assumptions, and work with campuses in the development of educational messages and intervention materials.
- Faculty, academic advisers, and other college staff need to be educated on the prevalence and nature of college dating violence victimization and offending. This education should also include how to respond to reports of violence and how to provide students with pathways to resources and recovery.
- Universities and colleges need to identify the problems their students face with respect to dating violence and associated health-risk behaviors. This suggests the need for resources to collect regularly scheduled climate surveys that measure student involvement in risky health behaviors and dating violence.
- College staff that interact with students on a regular basis need to be equipped to screen for victimization and recognize that the experience and impact of dating violence is likely to manifest in a variety of student outcomes—including substance abuse, mental health, and sexual risk taking—and negatively impact academic success and engagement.
- Universities need to create collaborative working groups on campus that may be brought together to evaluate research and develop education and awareness programming that cuts across a continuum of health-risk behaviors. These collaborations might include counseling centers, health centers, student conduct offices, housing, athletics, women's centers, and student success centers.
- University and college health and mental health providers need to properly identify the treatment needs of victims with diverse co-occurring problems.

Kaukinen, C. 2014. Dating violence among college students: The risk and protective factors. *Trauma, Violence, and Abuse* 15 (4): 283–296.

The ecological model of violence also illustrates that these factors are embedded and related to other attitudes and behaviors that support or increase the likelihood of dating and sexual violence. As reviewed earlier, there is a relationship between risky health and behavioral factors and dating violence among college students. Educational programming should highlight the nature of healthy relationships and behaviors as it applies to intimate partners and alcohol/drug use, mental health, and academic achievement. While federal regulations and university initiatives have ensured that campuses provide a variety of health promotion workshops geared at addressing mental and physical health, general well-being, and academic engagement, they should also be explicitly tied to programming aimed at preventing dating violence.

REFERENCES

Abbey, A. 2002. Alcohol-related sexual assault: A common problem among college students. *Journal of Studies on Alcohol and Drugs* 14: 118–128.

Bachman, R., and L. E. Saltzman. 1995. *Violence against women: Estimates from the redesigned National Crime Victimization Survey*. Washington, DC: Department of Justice.

Barrick, K., C. P. Krebs, and C. H. Lindquist. 2013. Intimate partner violence victimization among undergraduate women at historically black colleges and universities (HBCUs). *Violence Against Women* 19 (8): 1014–1033.

Bethke, T. M., and D. M. DeJoy. 1993. An experimental study of factors influencing the acceptability of dating violence. *Journal of Interpersonal Violence* 8 (1): 36–51.

Black, D. S., S. Sussman, and J. B. Unger. 2010. A further look at the intergenerational transmission of violence: Witnessing interparental violence in emerging adulthood. *Journal of Interpersonal Violence* 25 (6): 1022–1042.

Bogle, K. A. 2008. *Hooking up: Sex, dating, and relationships on campus*. New York: New York University Press.

Buelna, C., E. C. Ulloa, and M. D. Ulibarri. 2009. Sexual relationship power as a mediator between dating violence and sexually transmitted infections among college women. *Journal of Interpersonal Violence* 24 (8): 1338–1357.

Caetano, R., C. B. Cunradi, J. Schafer, and C. L. Clark. 2000. Intimate partner violence and drinking patterns among white, black, and Hispanic couples in the U.S. *Journal of Substance Abuse* 11 (2): 123–138.

Cercone, J. J., S. R. Beach, and I. Arias. 2005. Gender symmetry in dating intimate partner violence: Does similar behavior imply similar constructs? *Violence and Victims* 20 (2): 207–218.

Cleveland, H. H., V. M. Herrera, and J. Stuewig. 2003. Abusive males and abused females in adolescent relationships: Risk factor similarity and dissimilarity and the role of relationship seriousness. *Journal of Family Violence* 18 (6): 325–339.

Dank, M., P. Lachman, J. M. Zweig, and J. Yahner. (2014). Dating violence experiences of lesbian, gay, bisexual, and transgender youth. *Journal of Youth and Adolescence* 43 (5): 846–857.

DeKeseredy, W. S., and M. D. Schwartz. 1998. *Woman abuse on campus: Results from the Canadian national survey*. Thousand Oaks, CA: Sage.

Edwards, K. M., and K. M. Sylaska. 2013. The perpetration of intimate partner violence among LGBTQ college youth: The role of minority stress. *Journal of Youth and Adolescence* 42 (11): 1721–1731.

Follette, V. M., and P. C. Alexander. 1992. Dating violence: Current and historical correlates. *Behavioral Assessment* 14 (1): 39–52.

Follingstad, D. R., R. G. Bradley, C. M. Helff, and J. E. Laughlin. 2002. A model for predicting dating violence: Anxious attachment, angry temperament, and need for relationship control. *Violence and Victims* 17 (1): 35–47.

Follingstad, D. R., R. G. Bradley, J. E. Laughlin, and L. Burke. 1999. Risk factors and correlates of dating violence: The relevance of examining frequency and severity levels in a college sample. *Violence and Victims* 14 (4): 365–380.

Freedner, N., L. H. Freed, Y. W. Yang, and S. B. Austin. 2002. Dating violence among gay, lesbian, and bisexual adolescents: Results from a community survey. *Journal of Adolescent Health* 31 (6): 469–474.

Garcia, J. R., and C. Reiber. 2008. Hook-up behavior: A biopsychosocial perspective. *Journal of Social, Evolutionary, and Cultural Psychology* 2 (4): 192–208.

Gidycz, C. A., J. B. Warkentin, and L. M. Orchowski. 2007. Predictors of perpetration of verbal, physical, and sexual violence: A prospective analysis of college men. *Psychology of Men and Masculinity* 8 (2): 79–94.

Gómez, A. M. 2011. Testing the cycle of violence hypothesis: Child abuse and adolescent dating violence as predictors of intimate partner violence in young adulthood. *Youth and Society* 43 (1): 171–192.

Gover, A. R. 2004. Risky lifestyles and dating violence: A theoretical test of violent victimization. *Journal of Criminal Justice* 32 (2): 171–180.

Gover, A. R., C. Kaukinen, and K. A. Fox. 2008. The relationship between violence in the family of origin and dating violence among college students. *Journal of Interpersonal Violence* 23 (12): 1667–1693.

Hamby, S., D. Finkelhor, and H. Turner. 2012. Teen dating violence: Co-occurrence with other victimizations in the National Survey of Children's Exposure to Violence (NatSCEV). *Psychology of Violence* 2 (2): 111–124.

Harned, M. S. 2001. Abused women or abused men? An examination of the context and outcomes of dating violence. *Violence and Victims* 16 (3): 269–285.

Howard, D. E., and Q. M. Wang. 2003. Risk procedures of adolescent girls who were victims of dating violence. *Adolescence* 38 (149): 1–14.

Jennings, W. G., M. Park, T. N. Richards, E. Tomsich, A. R. Gover, and R. A. Powers. 2014. Exploring the relationship between child physical abuse and adult dating violence using a causal inference approach in an emerging adult population in South Korea. *Child Abuse and Neglect* 38 (12): 1902–1913.

Kaukinen, C. 2014. Dating violence among college students: The risk and protective factors. *Trauma, Violence, and Abuse* 15 (4): 283–296.

Kaukinen, C., A. R. Gover, and J. L. Hartman. 2012. College women's experiences of dating violence in casual and exclusive relationships. *American Journal of Criminal Justice* 37 (2): 146–162.

Kaura, S. A., and B. J. Lohman. 2007. Dating violence victimization, relationship satisfaction, mental health problems, and acceptability of violence: A comparison of men and women. *Journal of Family Violence* 22 (6): 367–381.

Koss, M. P., and H. H. Cleveland. 1997. Stepping on toes: Social roots of date rape lead to intractability and politicization. In *Researching sexual violence against women: Meth-*

odological and personal perspectives, ed. M. D. Schwartz, 4–21. Thousand Oaks, CA: Sage.

Krebs, C. P., C. H. Lindquist, T. D. Warner, B. S. Fisher, and S. L. Martin. 2009. The differential risk factors of physically forced and alcohol- or other drug-enabled sexual assault among university women. *Violence and Victims* 24 (3): 302–321.

Laporte, L., D. Jiang, D. J. Pepler, and C. Chamberland. 2009. The relationship between adolescents' experience of family violence and dating violence. *Youth and Society* 43 (1): 3–27.

Leisring, P. A. 2013. Physical and emotional abuse in romantic relationships: Motivation for perpetration among college women. *Journal of Interpersonal Violence* 28 (7): 1437–1454.

Logan, T., C. Leukefeld, and B. Walker. 2000. Stalking as a variant of intimate violence: Implications from a young adult sample. *Violence and Victims* 15 (1): 91–111.

Lormand, D. K., C. M. Markham, M. F. Peskin, T. L. Byrd, R. C. Addy, E. Baumler, and S. R. Tortolero. 2013. Dating violence among urban, minority, middle school youth and associated sexual risk behaviors and substance use. *Journal of School Health* 83 (6): 415–421.

Makepeace, J. M. 1981. Courtship violence among college students. *Family Relations* 30 (1): 97–102.

Manning, W. D., P. C. Giordano, and M. A. Longmore. 2006. Hooking up: The relationship contexts of "nonrelationship" sex. *Journal of Adolescent Research* 21 (5): 459–483.

Mason, B., and M. Smithey. 2012. The effects of academic and interpersonal stress on dating violence among college students: A test of classical strain theory. *Journal of Interpersonal Violence* 27 (5): 974–986.

McNally, S. T., and S. Newman. 1999. Objective and subjective conceptualizations of social support. *Journal of Psychosomatic Research* 46: 309–314.

Porter, J. L., and L. McQuiller Williams. 2013. Dual marginality: The impact of auditory status and sexual orientation on abuse in a college sample of women and men. *Journal of Aggression, Maltreatment, and Trauma* 22 (6): 577–589.

Purdie, M. P., A. Abbey, and A. J. Jacques-Tiura. 2010. Perpetrators of intimate partner sexual violence: Are there unique characteristics associated with making partners have sex without a condom? *Violence Against Women* 16 (10): 1086–1097.

Richards, T. N., and K. A. Branch. 2012. The relationship between social support and adolescent dating violence: A comparison across genders. *Journal of Interpersonal Violence* 27 (8): 1540–1561.

Saunders, B. E., D. G. Kilpatrick, R. F. Hanson, H. S. Resnick, and M. E. Walker. 1999. Prevalence, case characteristics, and long-term psychological correlates of child rape among women: A national survey. *Child Maltreatment* 4 (3): 187–200.

Sellers, C. S. 1999. Self-control and intimate violence: An examination of the scope and specification of the general theory of crime. *Criminology* 37 (2): 375–404.

Smith, C. A., A. Park, T. O. Ireland, L. Elwyn, and T. P. Thornberry. 2013. Long-term outcomes of young adults exposed to maltreatment: The role of educational experiences in promoting resilience to crime and violence in early adulthood. *Journal of Interpersonal Violence* 28 (1): 121–156.

Smith, P. H., J. W. White, and L. J. Holland, L. J. 2003. A longitudinal perspective on dating violence among adolescent and college-age women. *American Journal of Public Health* 93 (7): 1104–1109.

Straus, M. A., S. L. Hamby, S. Boney-McCoy, and D. B. Sugarman. 1996. The revised Conflict Tactics Scales (CTS2): Development and preliminary psychometric data. *Journal of Family Issues* 17 (3): 283–316.

Swahn, M. H., R. M. Bossarte, J. B. Palmier, H. Yao, and M. H. Van Dulmen. 2013. Risk factors for multiple forms of violent experiences: Analyses of the 2009 Youth Risk Behavior Survey. *Vulnerable Children and Youth Studies* 8 (3): 225–236.

Taylor, M. J., R. A. Wamser, D. Z. Welch, and J. T. Nanney. 2012. Multidimensional self-esteem as a mediator of the relationship between sports participation and victimization: A study of African American girls. *Violence and Victims* 27 (3): 434–452.

Temple, J. R., R. C. Shorey, P. Fite, G. L. Stuart, and V. D. Le. 2013. Substance use as a longitudinal predictor of the perpetration of teen dating violence. *Journal of Youth and Adolescence* 42 (4): 596–606.

Tjaden, P., and N. Thoennes. 2000. *Full report on the prevalence, incidence, and consequences of violence against women: Findings from the National Violence Against Women Survey* (NCJ 183781). Washington, DC: Office of Justice Programs.

Vest, J. R., T. K. Catlin, J. J. Chen, and R. C. Brownson. 2002. Multistate analysis of factors associated with intimate partner violence. *American Journal of Preventative Medicine* 22 (3): 156–164.

4

Stalking on College Campuses

Matt R. Nobles
and Kate Fox

Introduction

In 2008, a man stalked the famous ESPN reporter Erin Andrews by covertly identifying her hotel room, obtaining a room adjacent to hers, tampering with her peephole to film the celebrity, and posting the nude videos of her online. In April 2016, after serving two and a half years in prison, the stalker and the hotel settled with Andrews to award her $55 million (Byers 2016). In a series of public appearances, Andrews has explained the detrimental and long-term effects of being a stalking victim, including stigma, embarrassment, humiliation, and paranoia. Although the specifics of this case are certainly unique, the same traumatizing and terrorizing effects of stalking impact many other young women who are not celebrities—many of whom are college women.

This chapter provides an overview of the state of the literature on stalking among college students and details specific gaps in the literature that require future investigation. We identify definitional aspects of stalking, discuss the prevalence rates and trends observed by prior literature, synthesize the observed characteristics of victims and offenders, and present responses of the justice system. A substantial portion of this chapter is devoted to the need for future research because—despite the advancements within this body of knowledge—much remains unknown.

What Is Stalking?

Stalking is a crime that cannot be defined in terms of its objective circumstances. Instead, stalking is generally delineated based on two criteria: (1) there must be a repeated course of unwanted conduct that (2) creates an emotional reaction in the victim or "a reasonable person" as identified by the law (e.g., feeling threatened and/or frightened). While stalking definitions vary widely across laws and within the research and practitioner communities, these two components are prominently featured across disciplines and practices (Fox, Nobles, and Fisher 2011). Stalking, therefore, possesses an unusual attribute not generally shared by more common forms of crime: almost any type of behavior could fit the definitional criteria and, in some cases, the same behaviors could be viewed as alternatively benign and menacing. For example, ordinarily *legal* behaviors such as leaving flowers or gifts for someone to find may actually be *illegal* behaviors (stalking) if other conditions are met (e.g., unwanted, frightening and/or threatening, and occurring repeatedly). Under the umbrella of stalking is another relatively new phenomenon termed cyberstalking. Cyberstalking involves the use of electronic means to facilitate stalking, such as via text messaging and social media, among a seemingly endless array of other electronic possibilities. Importantly, the adoption of social media and other technology-enabled means of communication among younger adults is both more common and less understood in terms of expectations and normative behavior. Thus, identifying the contours of stalking, its correlates, and its consequences is a challenge, especially across academic disciplines.

There is still considerable inconsistency in stalking measurement among researchers, despite calls for standardization and closer adherence to "typical" statutory definitions. Fox, Nobles, and Fisher (2011) discuss measurement issues in stalking research, including the use of behavioral checklists and the proliferation of diverse legal standards for stalking and cyberstalking. In particular, they note that stalking surveys that operationalize the phenomenon into single-item, self-report measures ("Have you ever been stalked?") can be especially problematic because many victims are poorly informed about the legal criteria that apply to their experiences. For example, Jordan, Wilcox, and Pritchard (2007) reported that only 42.1 percent of college students who met objective behavioral screening criteria for stalking victimization correctly acknowledged their victim status; later estimates have been even more pessimistic (McNamara and Marsil 2012). It is also likely that the younger generation (i.e., college- and high school–age individuals) sometimes uses the term "stalking" inappropriately to casually refer more generally to noncriminal romantic pursuit (i.e., behavior that is not frightening, harassing, or threatening). While we are currently unaware of any empirical data to support this suspicion, we invite future research to investigate the ways in which popular culture and language impacts perceptions of, knowledge about, and experiences with stalking.

Regardless of the differences in stalking measurements, research clearly points to the serious—and sometimes long-term—consequences that stalking victims often experience. In terms of emotional effects, some stalking victims exhibit feelings of paranoia, fear, anxiety, nightmares, suicidal thoughts, and posttraumatic stress symptoms (Hall 1998; Pathé and Mullen 1997; Spitzberg and Cupach 2003). A number of physical consequences of stalking have also been identified, including appetite disturbance, headaches, asthma attacks, persistent nausea, and chronic sleep disturbance (Pathé and Mullen 1997).

What We Know about Stalking on Campus

Prevalence Estimates and Trends

The modern era of stalking research followed from the implementation of the first antistalking criminal statutes in 1990. The earliest peer-reviewed research in this era, however, was unsuitable for stalking prevalence estimates in the aggregate because it originated from clinical/forensic samples (Meloy 1996) and was primarily oriented toward the diagnostic criteria required for use by court-ordered evaluators (Meloy 1997). Since the mid-1990s, however, criminology and criminal justice scholars have expanded methodological and conceptual approaches and adapted behavioral checklists administered in survey-based data collection efforts, many of which have been used with college student samples. Tjaden and Thoennes (1998) pioneered a stalking behavioral measurement approach in the National Violence Against Women Survey (NVAWS), which was the first national study to incorporate measures of stalking. Based on the NVAWS national sample, approximately 74 percent of stalking victims were between eighteen and thirty-nine years old, suggesting substantial overlap with traditional college student populations. In addition to providing the first prevalence estimates for stalking, the NVAWS was noteworthy for shaping several subsequent generations of survey-based data collection on stalking phenomena.

The issues with definitions, measurement, and identification of long-term trends are interrelated, but trends are beginning to be accessible to stalking researchers now that we have ten to fifteen years of survey-based research from which to draw. Prevalence estimates are difficult to describe because of underreporting and definitional differences. National trends in the United States contrast with common estimates derived from college student samples. For instance, Tjaden and Thoennes (2000) reported lifetime stalking victimization prevalence of 8 percent for women and 2 percent for men, although these estimates were contingent on victims experiencing "high" fear. When the fear threshold was relaxed to "somewhat" or "a little" frightened, the estimates showed 12 percent and 4 percent lifetime victimization for women and men, respectively. Subsequently, Basile, Swahn, Chen, and Saltzman (2006) estimated national lifetime prevalence of stalking victimization at 7 percent for women and 2 percent for men. The most recent nationally representative evidence on stalking prevalence appears to trend closer to common college student–based estimates, with lifetime stalking victimization of approximately 15.2 percent for women and 5.7 percent for men (Breiding 2014).

Estimates of stalking victimization range from 13 percent to 30 percent for college women (Fisher, Cullen, and Turner 2002; Fremouw, Westrup, and Pennypacker 1997) and from 11 percent to 19 percent for college men (Bjerregaard 2000; Fremouw, Westrup, and Pennypacker 1997; Haugaard and Seri 2003). Victimization prevalence estimates in samples of men and women combined also vary, but measurement using behavior checklists suggests a proportion of 27 percent overall, with between 1 percent and 6 percent of students self-reporting stalking perpetration (Fremouw, Westrup, and Pennypacker 1997; Nobles, Fox, Piquero, and Piquero 2009). Variation in these collective estimates are likely a function of several factors, including differences in state laws and methods of operationalizing stalking on student surveys. Nevertheless, per U.S. Department of Education (2014) statistics, assuming approximately 20.4 million students were enrolled in degree-granting institutions and projections of 24 percent victimization and 3 percent perpetration, stalking *on American college and university campuses alone* would affect nearly 5 million victims and implicate some 612,000 offenders. The magnitude of these projections is generally congruent with recent studies of victimization prevalence for sexual assault on college women, which is estimated at 23 percent (Cantor et al. 2015).

Characterizing College Student Stalking Victims and Offenders

Characteristics of stalking victims and offenders available in the literature are unquestionably sample- or population-dependent. For example, the early work on stalking likely overstated the prevalence of offender psychiatric disorders because of the focused attention on clinical/forensic samples. In general, however, stalking research in criminology has often made use of college student samples, and most of the peer-reviewed work has focused on circumstances and outcomes related to victimization rather than on perpetration. The picture of demographics and behavioral traits regarding offenders is murkier, and much of the offender-centric work comes out of the forensic psychology literature, which focuses on clinical markers and classification typologies.

As a result of typical sampling and data collection methodologies, victims are often described as being disproportionately female and younger adults, while stalking offenders are stereotypically described as male and younger or middle-aged. Some estimates have placed the mean age of onset for both stalking victims and perpetrators around age twenty (Nobles et al. 2009). Typical estimates for the duration of stalking episodes for college students range between twelve and twenty-six weeks (Bjerregaard 2000; Fisher, Cullen, and Turner 2002), a finding that seems consistent for both victims and perpetrators (Nobles et al. 2009). Notably, however, contemporary research challenges many of these common assumptions. Several studies have presented evidence that the stereotype of the female victim and male stalker is unfounded, although important differences in perceived fear and self-reported physical and psychological harm disproportionately affect female victims (Sheridan, North, and Scott 2014). In addition, analysis of stalking perpetration and victimization by age shows that stalking behaviors are largely consistent in terms of their nature and the potential for violent outcomes, indicating an important exception to the common focus on college-age victims and offenders (Sheridan, North, and Scott 2014). For example, stalking is sometimes a precursor to homicide and attempted homicide among female victims (McFarlane et al. 1999).

Very little research has explicitly addressed stalking within the subcategories of race and ethnicity, perhaps due to underrepresentation in the available samples, but the existing evidence shows that stalking tends to be intraracial in the general population (Baum et al. 2009). Some limited evidence suggests potential differences in the manifestation of stalking—similar to other categories of intimate partner violence—in lesbian, gay, bisexual, and transgender (LGBT) relationships (Sheridan, Scott, and Campbell 2016), perhaps due to factors such as the implicit threat of "outing" closeted minorities and other dynamics that are uncommon in heterosexual populations. Overall, the consensus in the criminology literature seems to suggest that the experience of attending college, as well as the timing of transition into young adulthood, makes university campuses an ideal setting for stalking to occur and for researchers to study stalking phenomena.

The stalking literature also features empirical evidence associating stalking victimization and perpetration outcomes with criminological theory constructs—and most of this research has been done among college samples. For example, college women victims of stalking have been found to have less self-control than college women who were not stalking victims (Fox, Gover, and Kaukinen 2009). Social learning theory has been extended to explain stalking victimization and offending among college students, yielding support to the idea that stalking behaviors can be learned or reinforced through social interactions with others (Fox, Nobles, and Akers 2011). Additionally, college student stalkers were significantly more likely to have insecure, anxious adult attachment styles as compared to nonstalkers (Patton, Nobles, and Fox 2010). In a test of control balance theory, college student men who stalked had significantly higher control surpluses (i.e., believed they had more control over others than others had over them), while college women in the sample who stalked or were stalked had significantly higher control deficits (i.e., believed others had more control over them than they had over others) (Nobles and Fox 2013). Finally, lifestyle/routine activity theories have been tested and supported in the context of stalking, demonstrating that people who engage in certain types of social behavior are significantly more likely to become stalking victims (Reyns et al. 2016). Specifically, lifestyle/routine activities that have been linked to stalking victimization among college students are substance use, public activities, and off-campus residence (Mustaine and Tewksbury 1999).

Additionally, researchers have begun to address theoretical competition and integrative approaches to describe stalking (Fox, Nobles, and Fisher 2016). Because stalking phenomena seem to be especially prevalent in college-age populations and, at least to some extent, overrepresented in campus environments, discussion about the theoretical correlates of stalking is appropriately concentrated on this setting. Studies of this type also directly inform discussion about stalking on college campuses because many of them have incorporated smaller samples with college student-based survey data.

Justice System Response

With respect to criminal justice system responses, researchers are beginning to understand some aspects involving victim help-seeking behavior as well as law enforcement investigation. Prior work with college samples suggests a relatively dim view of system response, which is perceived to be influenced by bias and neglect (Cass and Rosay 2012). These perceptions are also exaggerated by the relative infrequency with which stalking victims recognize and acknowledge their own victim status (Jordan, Wilcox, and Pritchard 2007). Several studies have outlined circumstances under which victims may be more likely to seek help from others outside of the criminal justice system (Buhi, Clayton, and Surrency 2009; Reyns and Englebrecht 2010), and what types of self-protective behaviors they adopt as a result of their experience (Nobles et al. 2014). These factors are intrinsically, if indirectly, linked to the overall picture of the justice system response to stalking.

Regarding stalking in the formal criminal justice system, current knowledge is limited and based largely on data representing the general population. For example, a recently published study (Brady and Nobles 2015) identified the progression of law enforcement response to stalking and stalking-related calls for service and determined that almost no cases that involve an initial call or incident report actually result in an arrest for stalk-ing. This suggests that police may be unable or unwilling to identify cases in which a pattern of conduct rises to the level of criminal stalking when re-sponding to incidents. For instance, they may be reluctant to make arrests under the stalking charge, perhaps in consultation with prosecutors who understand that stalking carries a much higher evidentiary burden than many of the individual violations representing a "course of conduct." A sep-arate but related study (Nobles unpublished manuscript) describes recidivism risk factors for stalkers released from Florida prisons, concluding that for-merly incarcerated stalking offenders exhibit fewer traditional risk factors when compared to a similar, nonstalker offender sample. For example, while several risk factors (i.e., prior time served, race, marital status, and employ-ment status) were significantly associated with rearrest within three years of release from prison, for a comparison group of similar offenders, none of these factors were significantly associated with rearrest for stalking offend-ers. This evidence highlights the ongoing difficulty in using the criminal justice system as a formal mechanism for deterrence in stalking cases, and it also provides insight into the challenges in stalking prevention and response on college campuses.

Gaps in What We Know about Stalking: Directions for Future Research

Based on past findings (Fisher, Cullen, and Turner 2002) as well as current prevalence estimates (Breiding 2014), stalking is a crime that affects millions of Americans on and off college campuses, and it is often enormously disrup-tive and traumatic for victims. Coupled with the relative underdevelopment of knowledge on its formal and informal responses and consequences, stalk-ing research needs to move into the criminology "mainstream," and the study of stalking phenomena and antistalking policy should be prioritized. Researchers need to communicate more effectively that these are not phe-nomena affecting only celebrities and that stalkers are not merely socially isolated, maladjusted, or pitiable. As previously discussed, more research— especially beyond clinical case studies—should be devoted to systematically studying the characteristics among college and noncollege stalkers.

More and better data is always beneficial to stalking researchers who wish to answer challenging empirical questions, as well as those wishing to identify heretofore unrecognized patterns leading to inductive theories. Na-tionally representative and/or longitudinal data on stalking victims and of-fenders would be a treasure trove of information. Certain questions may require a mixed-mode or qualitative approach; for example, many questions surround the apparent reluctance among prosecutors to file stalking charges, as noted earlier. Virtually all of the public domain data on stalking (National Crime Victimization Survey [NCVS], Supplemental Victim Survey [SVS]) is

badly out of date and does not reflect essential elements such as the contemporary ubiquity of social media. One tool that would greatly aid in establishing trends and bolstering objective empirical measures of stalking would
be to revisit the representation of stalking in the NCVS. A targeted SVS
specifically addressing stalking was attached to the 2006 NCVS, but there
were several limitations to the resulting data, including the orientation of
screening questions and the comparatively small supplemental sample size,
not to mention the language and content of the questions. In general, however, the NCVS is a valuable data source that could be leveraged by stalking
researchers and practitioners, particularly the regularity with which data are
collected (i.e., annually), the typical number of respondents (i.e., approximately 90,000 households per year), the national representativeness of NCVS
samples, and the potential for comparison with victims of other crimes (e.g.,
sexual assault, robbery, and physical assault). Stalking researchers would
therefore benefit from an update to the SVS and potentially from lobbying
to include additional stalking questions as part of the "main" NCVS.

Although stalking research has already relied to a great extent on college
student samples, there is still much to learn. Existing studies have noted that
awareness of stalking victimization is low, even among victims themselves
(Jordan, Wilcox, and Pritchard 2007), but additional research could help to
judge whether on-campus awareness efforts have substantially altered the
discrepancy between objective and subjective definitions. For instance, side-
by-side comparison of the steps involved in victims' decisions to report and
steps involved in formal investigations of stalking cases could help to identify commonalities and pitfalls that result in failed prosecutions or other
undesirable outcomes. Further study could also help to establish the sensitivity of individual and circumstantial thresholds for stalking awareness by
examining the degree to which personal characteristics, relationship dynamics, or social situations in which stalking occurs contribute to specific
outcomes. College students may be even more likely to over- or underesti-
mate their risk of stalking victimization because some behaviors may be
perceptually exaggerated in common college student social situations (e.g.,
"This creepy guy was stalking my friends and me at the bar last night," or "I
don't want to call the police; it was just a bad breakup and she's trying to win
me back").

Interventions and Programming

Anecdotally, practitioners in the law enforcement and victim services fields
seem to be ahead of academics and much of the public in that they are more
aware of the contemporary stalking problem. Thus, it is paradoxical that we
know very little overall about stalking intervention efforts. Much of the re-

search on stalking at present can only speak to issues such as acknowledgment of victim status and the decision to report to police (Jordan, Wilcox, and Pritchard 2007) as well as self-protective behaviors (e.g., carrying a weapon, avoiding places/people, or changing contact information), and even among those topics, there is not a clear consensus on which strategies are "effective." Other than examples related to victim coping strategies (Kamphuis and Emmelkamp 2001), antistalking programming seems to be either poorly documented or lacking entirely.

Few peer-reviewed studies have attempted a systematic review of antistalking programming on college and university campuses. Findings to date indicate that most institutions make general stalking information available to students (Truman and Mustaine 2009), although it is unclear whether or how this information translates into enhanced self-awareness, reporting, or disciplinary outcomes. Also, although there are some tools available in the public domain to facilitate risk assessment and expert testimony in stalking cases (Rugala, McNamara, and Wattendorf 2004), these resources are generally limited to rubrics for professionals whose primary responsibility is to support court proceedings (see Proctor 2003 for a victim-focused exception). We are not aware of any peer-reviewed research that has systematically evaluated any prevention or correctional intervention (e.g., diversion programs, standard parole vs. intermediate sanctions, or examination of specific elements of intensive supervision) targeting stalking offenders. The psychology literature has suggestions regarding clinical case management and treatment strategies such as dialectical behavior therapy (Rosenfeld et al. 2007) to address physiological arousal and extreme forms of behavior reactions to ordinary stimuli in a cognitive-behavioral therapy context, but these are likely to be of little utility to law enforcement, court, and corrections practitioners. One strategy moving forward is to identify existing stalking interventions at the state and local levels, and to conduct formal program evaluations with cooperating agencies. Another strategy might involve proposals for a new type of intervention based on successful models that target related crimes such as dating or intimate partner violence.

Justice System Response

Regarding the campus environment specifically, both researchers and policy makers could benefit from further investigation into informal and semiformal system responses to stalking cases. Given the cynicism that college students express toward the anticipated police response to stalking victims (Cass and Rosay 2012), other avenues may be more promising. For example, many college and university student handbooks and codes of conduct specifically identify stalking as a prohibited and punishable offense, but it is unclear how frequently these mechanisms are used to facilitate reporting, investigation, and discipline. In addition, more-focused attention toward Title IX as the basis for reporting and prosecuting sexual assault in recent years suggests potential impacts on the identification of stalking patterns and/or referral to appropriate authorities, but the scope and magnitude of this effect is unknown. Finally, given that victim help seeking for stalking involves reliance on informal social support networks (i.e., peers, family, or classmates) in approximately 90 percent of cases (Buhi, Clayton, and Surrency 2009), future research could help to outline the interaction between victims and support network members, as well as the presumed influence of networks on victim awareness of the stalking label, subsequent decisions to seek formal intervention from administrators or police, and the potential to mitigate victim consequences such as depression and posttraumatic stress disorder (Kamphuis and Emmelkamp 2001; Blaauw et al. 2002).

Beyond the campus context, researchers point to evidence that hard-fought legislative victories to criminalize this behavior are being rendered effectively obsolete because so few cases ever result in arrest, prosecution, or conviction (Brady and Nobles 2015). Researchers need to address this area more comprehensively, including with mixed methods and qualitative work, and they need to suggest course corrections as appropriate. This will require long-term partnerships with cooperating agencies in order to collect data and collaboratively discuss programming solutions. The sensitivity of this form of interpersonal crime and the challenges for victims and agencies to cooperate with the stalking research enterprise remain important challenges.

Frontiers of Stalking Research

Apart from the criminal justice system response, there is still a great deal that researchers and practitioners need to know about the origins of stalking. Some clues from psychological and criminological theory have been empirically evaluated, but the field would benefit from in-depth examination of offender modalities such as onset, frequency, specialization, and desistence in order to inform actuarial risk assessment and related objectives. Critically, this work must move beyond small clinical/forensic samples to consider other environmental and social process variables. For example, with the exception of clinical evaluation of psychiatric disorders and other Diagnostic and Statistical Manual of Mental Disorders (DSM)–style conditions, it is unclear whether and how certain risk and protective factors (employment, relationships, social support, and the like) can be instrumental in preventing stalking offenders from recidivating. For instance, the stability offered by regular employment and exposure to prosocial others like family members could be especially important in preventing stalking offenders from recidivating by disrupting their course of conduct or sensitizing them to the emotional consequences of their behavior. Pioneering work in biosocial criminology may also help to identify biological predispositions to stalking, including the association with behavioral genetic markers such as monoamine oxidase A (MAOA), serotonin, and other commonly flagged mechanisms implicated in aggression and pursuit behavior (Meloy and Fisher 2005).

Finally, cyberstalking needs careful conceptual and empirical study. If definitional problems still plague "classic" stalking research, then cyberstalking should be considered a true frontier. Some work has attempted to disaggregate both conceptual and practical contrasts between cyberstalking and traditional forms by discussing cyberstalking as a subset of all stalking, and by comparing features of victimization experiences including the presence of fear, financial impacts, and the number and type of self-protective behaviors (Nobles et al. 2014), but virtually none have yet attempted an evaluation of university responses to cyberstalking. Systematic review of statutes, which are evolving yearly, would be a reasonable beginning for outlining the legalistic evolution. However, many open questions revolve around the similarities and differences in victimization and offending behaviors when contrasting cyberstalking and stalking cases (Reyns, Henson, and Fisher 2012), and this gap seems especially pertinent to current and future generations of college students ubiquitously exposed to smartphones, social media, and other developments. Beyond a handful of very recent studies, we know virtually nothing about overall prevalence, offender characteristics, or victim and system responses to cyberstalking.

Conclusion

The body of knowledge on stalking has grown tremendously within the past nearly three decades. A general consensus about the definition has been established across legislation and disciplines (i.e., unwanted, frightening/threatening, repeated behavior that causes the victim or a reasonable person to feel afraid). National and smaller-scale studies have clearly identified that younger, college-age women are at significantly higher risk of stalking victimization than men and as compared to the general public. And several promising theoretical explanations for stalking victimization and perpetration have recently been empirically tested (e.g., self-control, social learning, control balance, and routine activity). Yet many important questions remain unexplored. It is our hope that scholars continue to devote much-needed attention to the gaps in the stalking literature, especially as they relate to the lives and safety of college students.

REFERENCES

Basile, K. C., M. H. Swahn, J. Chen, and L. E. Saltzman. 2006. Stalking in the United States: Recent national prevalence estimates. *American Journal of Preventive Medicine* 31 (2): 172–175.

Baum, K., S. Catalano, M. Rand, and K. Rose. 2009. *Stalking victimization in the United States*. Washington, DC: Office of Justice Programs, Bureau of Justice Statistics, Department of Justice.

Bjerregaard, B. 2000. An empirical study of stalking victimization. *Violence and Victims* 15 (4): 389–406.

Blaauw, E., F. W. Winkel, E. Arensman, L. Sheridan, and A. Freeve. 2002. The toll of stalking: The relationship between features of stalking and psychopathology of victims. *Journal of Interpersonal Violence* 17 (1) 50–63.

Brady, P. Q., and M. R. Nobles. 2015. The dark figure of stalking: Examining law enforcement response. *Journal of Interpersonal Violence,* doi: 0886260515596979.

Breiding, M. J. 2014. Prevalence and characteristics of sexual violence, stalking, and intimate partner violence victimization—National Intimate Partner and Sexual Violence Survey, United States, 2011. *Morbidity and Mortality Weekly Report Surveillance Summaries* 63 (8): 1–18.

Buhi, E. R., H. Clayton, and H. H. Surrency. (2009). Stalking victimization among college women and subsequent help-seeking behaviors. *Journal of American College Health* 57 (4): 419–426.

Byers, D. 2016. Erin Andrews settles stalker lawsuit with hotel. *CNN Money*, April 25. Available at http://money.cnn.com/2016/04/25/media/erin-andrews-hotel-settlement/.

Cantor, D., W. Fisher, S. Chibnaill, R. Townsend, H. Lee, C. Bruce, and G. Thomas. 2015. Report on the AAU campus climate survey on sexual assault and sexual misconduct. Available at http://sexualassaulttaskforce.harvard.edu/files/taskforce/files/final_report_harvard_9.21.15.

Cass, A. I., and A. B. Rosay. 2012. College student perceptions of criminal justice system responses to stalking. *Sex Roles* 66 (5–6): 392–404.

Fisher, B. S., F. T. Cullen, and M. G. Turner. 2002. Being pursued: Stalking victimization in a national study of college women. *Criminology and Public Policy* 1 (2): 257–308.

Fox, K. A., A. R. Gover, and C. Kaukinen. 2009. The effects of low self-control and childhood maltreatment on stalking victimization among men and women. *American Journal of Criminal Justice* 34: 181–197.

Fox, K. A., M. R. Nobles, and R. L. Akers. 2011. Is stalking a learned phenomenon? An empirical test of social learning theory. *Journal of Criminal Justice* 39 (1): 39–47.

Fox, K. A., M. R. Nobles, and B. S. Fisher. 2011. Method behind the madness: An examination of stalking measurements. *Aggression and Violent Behavior* 16 (1): 74–84.

———. 2016. A multi-theoretical framework to assess gendered stalking victimization: The utility of self-control, social learning, and control balance theories. *Justice Quarterly* 33 (2): 319–347.

Fremouw, W. J., D. Westrup, and J. Pennypacker. 1997. Stalking on campus: The prevalence and strategies for coping with stalking. *Journal of Forensic Science* 42 (4): 666–669.

Hall, D. M. 1998. The victims of stalking. In *The psychology of stalking: Clinical and forensic perspectives,* ed. J. R. Meloy, 113–137. San Diego, CA: Academic Press.

Haugaard, J. J., and L. G. Seri. 2003. Stalking and other forms of intrusive contact after the dissolution of adolescent dating or romantic relationships. *Violence and Victims* 18 (3): 279–297.

Jordan, C. E., P. Wilcox, and A. J. Pritchard. 2007. Stalking acknowledgement and reporting among college women experiencing intrusive behaviors: Implications for the emergence of a "classic stalking case." *Journal of Criminal Justice* 35 (5): 556–569.

Kamphuis, J. H., and P. M. Emmelkamp. 2001. Traumatic distress among support-seeking female victims of stalking. *American Journal of Psychiatry* 158 (5): 795–798.

McFarlane, J. M., J. C. Campbell, S. Wilt, C. J. Sachs, Y. Ulrich, and X. Xu. 1999. Stalking and intimate partner femicide. *Homicide Studies* 3 (4): 300–316.

McNamara, C. L., and D. F. Marsil. 2012. The prevalence of stalking among college students: The disparity between researcher-and self-identified victimization. *Journal of American College Health* 60 (2): 168–174.

Meloy, J. R. 1996. Stalking (obsessional following): A review of some preliminary studies. *Aggression and Violent Behavior* 1 (2): 147–162.

———. 1997. The clinical risk management of stalking: "Someone is watching over me." *American Journal of Psychotherapy* 51 (2): 174.

Meloy, J. R., and H. Fisher. 2005. Some thoughts on the neurobiology of stalking. *Journal of Forensic Sciences* 50 (6): 1472–1480.

Mustaine, E. E., and R. Tewksbury. 1999. A routine activity theory explanation for women's stalking victimizations. *Violence Against Women* 5 (1): 43–62.

Nobles, M. R. (unpublished manuscript). Stalking recidivism: Estimates and correlates from a large correctional sample.

Nobles, M. R., and K. A. Fox. 2013. Assessing stalking behaviors in a control balance theory framework. *Criminal Justice and Behavior* 40 (7): 737–762.

Nobles, M. R., K. A. Fox, N. Piquero, and A. R. Piquero. 2009. Career dimensions of stalking victimization and perpetration. *Justice Quarterly* 26 (3): 476–503.

Nobles, M. R., B. W. Reyns, K. A. Fox, and B. S. Fisher. 2014. Protection against pursuit: A conceptual and empirical comparison of cyberstalking and stalking victimization among a national sample. *Justice Quarterly* 31 (6): 986–1014.

Pathè, M., and P. E. Mullen. 1997. The impact of stalkers on their victims. *British Journal of Psychiatry* 170 (1): 12–17.

Patton, C. L., M. R. Nobles, and K. A. Fox. 2010. Look who's stalking: Obsessive pursuit and attachment theory. *Journal of Criminal Justice* 38 (3): 282–290.

Proctor, M. 2003. *How to stop a stalker*. Charleston, SC: Prometheus Books.

Reyns, B. W., and C. M. Englebrecht. 2010. The stalking victim's decision to contact the police: A test of Gottfredson and Gottfredson's theory of criminal justice decision making. *Journal of Criminal Justice* 38 (5): 998–1005.

Reyns, B. W., B. Henson, and B. S. Fisher. 2012. Stalking in the twilight zone: Extent of cyberstalking victimization and offending among college students. *Deviant Behavior* 33 (1): 1–25.

Reyns, B. W., B. Henson, B. S. Fisher, K. A. Fox, and M. R. Nobles. 2016. A gendered lifestyle-routine activity approach to explaining stalking victimization in Canada. *Journal of Interpersonal Violence* 31 (9): 1719–1743.

Rosenfeld, B., M. Galietta, A. Ivanoff, A. Garcia-Mansilla, R. Martinez, J. Fava, V. Fineran, and D. Green. 2007. Dialectical behavior therapy for the treatment of stalking offenders. *International Journal of Forensic Mental Health* 6 (2): 95–103.

Rugala, E., J. McNamara, and G. Wattendorf. 2004. Expert testimony and risk assessment in stalking cases: The FBI's NCAVC as a resource. *FBI Law Enforcement Bulletin*, November, 8–17.

Sheridan, L. P., A. C. North, and A. J. Scott. 2014. Experiences of stalking in same-sex and opposite-sex contexts. *Violence and Victims* 29 (6): 1014–1028.

Sheridan, L. P., A. J. Scott, and A. M. Campbell. 2016. Perceptions and experiences of intrusive behavior and stalking: Comparing LGBTIQ and heterosexual groups. *Journal of Interpersonal Violence,* doi: 0886260516651313.

Spitzberg, B. H., and W. R. Cupach. 2003. What mad pursuit? Obsessive relational intrusion and stalking related phenomena. *Aggression and Violent Behavior* 8 (4): 345–375.

Tjaden, P. G., and N. Thoennes. 1998. *Stalking in America: Findings from the National Violence Against Women Survey.* Washington, DC: National Institute of Justice and Centers for Disease Control. Available at http://www.ncjrs.gov/pdffiles/169592.pdf.

———. 2000. *Full report on the prevalence, incidence, and consequences of violence against women: Findings from the National Violence Against Women Survey* (NCJ 183781). Washington, DC: Office of Justice Programs.

Truman, J. L., and E. E. Mustaine. 2009. Strategies for college student stalking victims: Examining the information and recommendations available. *American Journal of Criminal Justice* 34 (1): 69–83.

U.S. Department of Education, National Center for Education Statistics. 2014. Digest of Education Statistics, (NCES 2016-006), chap. 3. Available at http://nces.ed.gov/programs/digest/d14/ch_3.asp.

5

Explaining Campus Violence Against Women

Unhealthy Masculinity and Male Peer Support

Walter S. DeKeseredy

M any people define American colleges as "ivory towers" divorced from the harsh realities of the "everyday world," while countless others view these institutions of higher learning as "places where the pursuit of truth and the exercise of reason prevail, and where it is assumed our daughters will be safe from the 'lion in the streets'" (Pierson 1991, 10). What is seldom addressed by the general public, however, is that North American college campuses have long been breeding grounds for high levels of crime (Fisher and Sloan 2013; Schwartz and DeKeseredy 1997). For example, more than 170 years ago, Harvard University complained that students frequently committed "crimes worthy of the penitentiary" (Shenkman 1989, 135). Since then, college students have steadily engaged in a host of crimes, with male violence against heterosexual women being one of the most common (Daigle et al. 2015).

Survey research on campus violence against women dates back to Kirkpatrick and Kanin's (1957) self-report sexual assault study, but it was not until the results of Koss, Gidycz, and Wisniewski's (1987) pathbreaking national representative sample survey were published that this harm started to garner national attention. Many surveys on a wide range of violent behaviors experienced by female undergraduates have since been conducted, including another national U.S. project and a Canadian countrywide study (DeKeseredy and Schwartz 1998; Fisher, Daigle, and Cullen 2010). Like their predecessors, the bulk of more recent studies estimate that at least one out of four undergraduate women is victimized by some type of sexual assault and that approximately the same number is targeted by physical assault during their college careers (DeKeseredy and Schwartz 2013). Moreover, the vast majority of perpetrators are not strangers. Rather, they are either male acquaintances, classmates, friends, "hookup" partners, boyfriends, or former boyfriends (Krebs et al. 2007; McOrmond-Plummer, Easteal, and Levy-Peck 2014).

Generations have gone by since Kirkpatrick and Kanin (1957) and Koss, Gidycz, and Wisniewski (1987) conducted their studies. It says much about our society, our interests, and our sensibilities that this disturbing research was ignored for so many years. There is now definitely much more awareness of, and concern about, campus violence against women, due in large part to the ongoing efforts of feminist coalitions' lobbying and education initiatives, the establishment in 2014 of the White House Task Force to Protect Students from Sexual Assault, the widespread viewing of Kirby Dick's (2015) documentary *The Hunting Ground*, and the creation of the Sexual Violence Elimination Act (SaVE). Starting in 2014, SaVE has required incidents of "domestic violence, dating violence, sexual assault, and stalking" to be revealed in yearly campus crime statistics reports and includes procedures that survivors should follow if they have been harmed by these crimes (Daigle et al. 2015). What is more, SaVE dictates that campuses must have ongoing primary prevention education programs such as bystander intervention and policies on disciplinary procedures.

In addition to SaVE, under the Violence Against Women Act (VAWA), congress authorized the U.S. Department of Justice's Office of Violence Against Women to implement the Grants to Reduce Sexual Assault, Domestic Violence, Dating Violence, and Stalking on Campus Program (Daigle et al. 2015). Also referred to as Campus Program grants, funds are awarded to colleges that develop a comprehensive, coordinated response to these harms. Thus, collectively, the initiatives briefly discussed here have raised "the specter of the dark side of the ivory tower" (Sloan and Fisher 2011, 3).

Violence against women on college campuses is now extensively discussed and debated, with many commentators asserting that U.S. colleges are experiencing an *epidemic* of woman abuse. Actually, the concept of epidemic is out of place here. To health officials, an epidemic is a disease that devastates a population before eventually subsiding. Yet violence against women, as demonstrated by decades of sound research, is deeply entrenched in the North American college population. Thus, if woman abuse on college campuses is a disease, then it is in its endemic phase, possibly to be compared with methamphetamine use among rural residents of West Virginia (Garriott 2011).

Violence against women, regardless of where it occurs, cannot be eliminated solely through the gathering of quantitative data on its extent, distribution, correlates, and consequences. To advance a better understanding of the violent plight of college women, and to both prevent and control this problem, more than just accurate statistics are required. We need to explain *why* college men engage in different types of woman abuse, including behaviors that involve the use of new electronic technologies, such as image-based sexual abuse and cyberstalking.[1] Thus, the main objective of this chapter is to offer two widely read and cited explanations for the presence, prevalence, and persistence of campus male heterosexual violence against women: male peer support theory and feminist routine activities theory.

Male Peer Support Theory

Most college men never physically, sexually, or electronically abuse female undergraduate and graduate students. Still, *all* men live in a society that can accurately be termed a *rape-supportive culture*, where values and beliefs that support and encourage the victimization of women are widely available (Cross 1993; DeKeseredy and Schwartz 2013). This does not mean every man will adopt such attitudes and values, but they are so prevalent in popular culture that they are readily and easily accessible to all men. These attitudes and values are not only available but also seem to be culturally approved for those men who choose to adopt them (DeKeseredy and Schwartz 2016). A rape-supportive culture also refers to "the set of cultural expectations, practices and standards that seek to erase the realities of sexual violence through a certain kind of story—one that says if a woman is assaulted, it is because of what she was wearing, drinking, doing, or saying—not because of the person who assaulted her" (Healey 2016, 1). The relationship between a rape-supportive culture and male-to-female violence on campus is fairly complex, but *male peer support* reflects, amplifies, and buttresses patriarchal attitudes and values, making it an integral part of today's modern and expanded rape-supportive culture that contributes to various types of woman abuse (De-Keseredy and Schwartz 2016).

There are conflicting definitions of patriarchy and it is a heavily contested concept (DeKeseredy 2011; Hunnicutt 2009). However, for the purpose of this chapter, following Renzetti (2013), it is defined here as "a gender structure in which men dominate women, and what is considered masculine is more highly valued than what is considered feminine" (8).

I originally developed the concept of male peer support to recognize the attachments to male peers and the resources provided by these men that encourage and legitimate woman abuse (DeKeseredy 1988a). Men (and women) are exposed to a wide variety of messages that support and oppose various behaviors, something that is the core of much criminological theorizing (Lilly, Cullen, and Ball 2015). In the context of a world that is still heavily patriarchal, with regular and extensive social and media messages offering excuses and justifications for the exploitation and victimization of

women, many men (and women) are concerned and confused by their relations with the opposite sex. *Male peer support theory* suggests that when
some men seek the advice of their peers, they are given both encouragement
and advice on how to abuse women who "talk back" or do not provide sex
on demand. Nearly thirty years of large- and small-scale research shows that
having friends who offer such advice is one of the most powerful determi-
nants of when a college male engages in physical or sexual assault of female
intimate partners or acquaintances (DeKeseredy and Schwartz 2015).

Although this chapter focuses on college students, our review of an international body of qualitative and quantitative research (DeKeseredy and
Schwartz 2013) supports what Bowker (1983) said close to thirty years ago
about all-male subcultures of violence:

> This is not a subculture that is confined to a single class, religion,
> occupational grouping, or race. It is spread throughout all parts of
> society. Men are socialized by other subcultural members to accept
> common definitions of the situation, norms, values, and beliefs about
> male-dominance and the necessity of keeping their wives in line.
> These violence-supporting social relations may occur at any time and
> in any place. (135–136)

To explain various types of violence against women on campus, DeKeseredy and Schwartz (1993) crafted the model depicted in Figure 5.1. It links
macro- and microlevel factors, and it is a modified version of DeKeseredy's
(1988a) original male peer support theory (see Figure 5.2), which we deemed
to be too focused on individual factors.

DeKeseredy (1988a) argued that many men experience various types of
stress in heterosexual dating relationships, whose sources range from sexual
problems to challenges to their perceived male authority. Some men try to
deal with these problems themselves, but other men turn to their male friends
for advice, guidance, and various other kinds of social support. The resources
provided by these peers may encourage and justify woman abuse under certain conditions. Furthermore, male peer support can influence some men to
victimize their dating partners regardless of stress. There is some support for
my model (see DeKeseredy 1988b), but it is missing some other related de-
terminants, including broader social factors, that can motivate a college man
to abuse a woman.

In the newer model presented in Figure 5.1, DeKeseredy and Schwartz
(1993) argue that four especially important factors need to be added: the
ideologies of familial and courtship patriarchy, alcohol consumption, membership in social groups (e.g., fraternities and combative sports teams), and
the absence of deterrence.[2] Figure 5.2 was informed by feminist thought, but
Figure 5.1 more specifically takes into account various social forces impor-

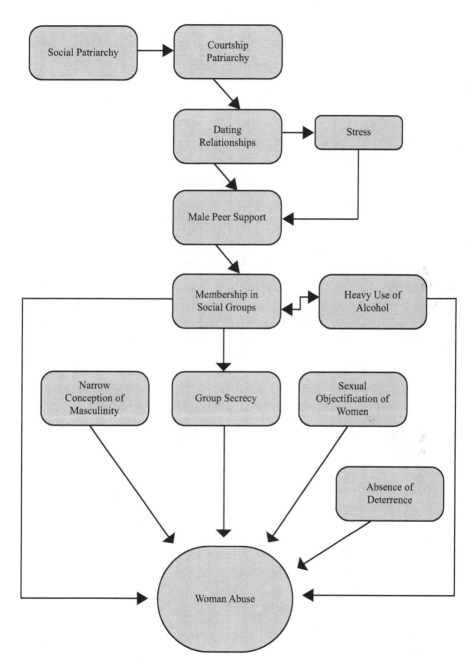

FIGURE 5.1 Modified Male Peer Support Model

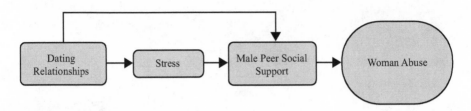

FIGURE 5.2   DeKeseredy's Original Male Peer Support Model

tant in feminist theory. In particular, the modified model recognizes how the broader social patriarchy acts as an ideology that justifies—not only to men but also to many women—why male superiority should reign in many fields and endeavors. Familial and courtship patriarchy is a subset of this thinking that describes domestic or intimate situations: who makes decisions, who drives, who pays for dinner, and who determines when to engage in sexual relations (DeKeseredy and Schwartz 2015; Dobash and Dobash 1979).

Figure 5.1 incorporates the same stressful situations in college dating as Figure 5.2, but situates them in a much broader context, particularly on the college campus, of male social groups such as fraternities, sports teams, and single-sex dorms. Such organizations too often champion the objectification and exploitation of women through songs, newsletters, and group showings of pornography (DeKeseredy and Corsianos 2016; Kimmel 2008). Others teach that "no means yes," or that sex with women who are unable to consent is acceptable. Many more simply provide a culture of sexual entitlement that raises both male expectations of "scoring" and worry and shame if a member were to allow a date to say no. More broadly, alcohol also seems related to much campus sexual assault (Weiss 2013). Perhaps, most important, there seems to be a lack of deterrence on virtually all college campuses because few men are ever punished for sexual or physical assaults on women, and when they are, the punishments are mild. Few local prosecutors will push such cases, especially against athletes (DeKeseredy and Flack 2007; DeKeseredy and Schwartz 2013). The full theory is more complex than this, but the major point is that although society gives many messages feminists often term a rape-supportive culture, those who have friends who reinforce such messages are the ones most likely to become physical and sexual predators.

Figure 5.1 is superior to Figure 5.2, but it too has shortcomings. Perhaps the most salient is that although most of the individual elements have been repeatedly tested empirically, there have only been limited tests of the entire model. Yet, in their attempt to test the entire model on a single campus sample, Franklin, Bouffard, and Pratt (2012) were able to produce empirical support. Given the complexity of some of the variables, it may not be possible to completely measure some of the core elements. The model may have more value for teaching than for predicting. Put another way, its greatest strength may lie in summarizing the complex relevant literature and proposing important ways to theorize and conceptualize male influence, rather than mathematically isolating and predicting which men are most likely to abuse women.

A Feminist Routine Activities Theory

The literature in psychology may disagree on many things, but one point of agreement is that men who are identified as sexual aggressors on college campuses are generally immature, irresponsible, and have less respect than others for society's rules.[3] What is more, men who are the least motivated to obey societal norms are the most likely to be attuned to messages from peers who approve of woman abuse (Franklin, Bouffard, and Pratt 2012). These men not only have callous sexual attitudes toward women but also see violence and danger as masculine and exciting. The combination of these traits in young men means that they can reaffirm their masculinity by being sexually aggressive toward young women on college campuses (DeKeseredy and Schwartz 2013; Schwartz and DeKeseredy 1997). These men are "doing masculinity" by acting sexually aggressive around women (Messerschmidt 1993).

There is another way to deal with the problem of locating just exactly what might be the psychological motivation of sexually aggressive men. Still one of the most popular theories today is Cohen and Felson's (1979) *routine activities theory*. This theory remains one of the most widely discussed, cited, and tested mainstream criminological approaches, although it succeeds only partially at one of its original goals, namely, deflecting attention from offenders' motivation. This lack of concern about motivation is one of the primary criticisms of the theory, but virtually all of those who now use it build motivation back in.

The key part of routine activities theory is that the amount and the location of crime are affected, if not caused, by three important factors: (1) the presence of likely offenders who are presumed to be motivated to commit the crimes; (2) the absence of effective guardians (i.e., police or security guards); and (3) the availability of suitable or vulnerable targets (Cohen and Felson 1979). While this point is rarely discussed, an important element of this theory is that there must be offenders who are likely to commit crimes if they have the opportunity to do so. All commentators refer to this factor as *motivated offenders,* but Felson (1994) reports that he did not use the word *motivation*; he even avoided discussing how the probability of victimization differed across groups, "since that would bring up the forbidden topic of motivation" (Clarke and Felson 1993, 2). Still, Cohen and Felson (1979) did not rule out the use of motivation explanations; they felt that these "might in the future be applied to the analysis of offenders and their inclinations as well" (605).

Nevertheless, research on traditional routine activities paid scant attention to what motivates offenders to approach any particular suitable target. Thus, with motivation presumed from the presence of offenders, researchers made little attempt to discover what makes offenders different from other persons at the scene (Lilly, Cullen, and Ball 2015).

In its original formulation, routine activities theory helps to explain high rates of sexual assault on college campuses (Schwartz et al. 2001). Surely the very factors discussed by Cohen and Felson (1979) are present on campuses. If motivation is to be measured by the number of offenses, certainly a large number of sexual victimizations occur, although most are not reported to the authorities (Daigle et al. 2015; Richards and Restivo 2015). "Suitable targets" abound in the number of women who voluntarily ingest large amounts of alcohol or drugs on campus, and the lack of effective deterrence or punishments on most campuses is tantamount to an absence of effective guardians (Fisher, Daigle, and Cullen 2010). Nevertheless, this theory fails to account for numerous factors. One is the presence of so many "likely offenders" in an environment that often contains very few persons with criminal records, or those who might be considered worrisome to the average citizen. "It simply assumes that such persons exist and that they commit crimes in a certain places and times at which the opportunities and potential victims are available" (Akers 2000, 35). Fisher and colleagues (1998) therefore argue that because numerous sexual crimes are committed on campus, the requirement of "proximity to crime" is maximized.

Schwartz and Pitts's (1995) *feminist routine activities theory* attempts to make explicit how a supposedly low-crime environment such as the college campus could also be considered a high-crime arena. Their perspective maintains that a disproportionately large number of sexual assaults occur on North American campuses because a large number of *criminogenic convergences* are most likely to occur in these settings. In this context, criminogenic convergence means that there are male students who are motivated to assault women sexually, that available ("suitable," in the words of the original theory) female targets are present, and that capable guardians who would be willing to intervene are absent.

In explaining why motivated offenders are present on college campuses, Schwartz and Pitts contend that feminist theory is strongest exactly where mainstream routine activities theories are weakest. Of course, problems arise in using feminist theory to fill this gap because there are different feminist theories (Renzetti 2013), which lead to different feminist explanations of this phenomenon. Schwartz and Pitts's feminist perspective, though, emphasizes the presence of male peer groups that perpetuate and legitimate the sexual exploitation of women, especially those who are intoxicated. Male members of these social networks are much more likely than nonmembers to be motivated to sexually assault women. For instance, several studies show that men who report having friends who support getting women drunk so that they cannot resist sexual advances are themselves likely to report using similar strategies (e.g., Boeringer, Shehan, and Akers 1991; Schwartz and Nogrady 1996).

Schwartz and Pitts contend that two lifestyle factors increase women's "suitability" as targets of sexual assault: (1) drinking to the point where they are vulnerable to sexually predatory men, and (2) attending parties and social events frequented by a large number of potential offenders, such as those who belong to pro-abuse subcultures (e.g., fraternities). Nonetheless, Schwartz and Pitts's theory fundamentally disagrees with the notion that women who become targets deserve their victimization because they engaged in risky behavior. The strength of a routine activities approach is that it emphasizes only one point: motivated male sexual aggressors are searching for situations where they have an advantage or the ability to take the upper hand in victimization (Schwartz et al. 2001).

Unfortunately, college campuses too often are "effective-guardian absent." Many campus administrators do not seriously punish men who abuse women physically and sexually, even when they engage in extremely brutal behavior such as gang rape (DeKeseredy and Schwartz 2013). Criminal justice personnel, too, often disregard acquaintance and/or date rapes, essentially telling men that their sexually aggressive behavior is acceptable (Maier 2014).

In sum, according to Schwartz and Pitts, it is on college campuses that one is most likely to find the copresense of motivated male offenders, vulnerable or "suitable" victims, and the absence of effective guardians. This criminogenic convergence helps explain the high rates of sexual assault in North American institutions of higher learning. But what do the data say? Statistics generated by a small-scale campus study and a Canadian national representative sample survey provide some support for Schwartz and Pitts's preliminary effort to develop a feminist routine activities theory. One of the most important findings uncovered by the aforementioned national study was the combined effect of three variables; Canadian undergraduate men who drank two or more times a week and who had friends who gave them peer support for both psychological and physical partner abuse were more than nine times as likely to report committing sexual abuse as men reporting none of these three characteristics (Schwartz et al. 2001).

Schwartz and Pitts's theory has some limitations (see DeKeseredy and MacLeod 1997), but Schwartz and Pitts should be commended for constructing a theory that is both logical and simple because it involves only three variables (Ellis and DeKeseredy 1996). Unlike earlier versions of routine activities theories (e.g., Cohen and Felson 1979), their perspective is also one of the very few attempts to examine the relationship between gender and crime.

Conclusion

At the time of this writing in May 2016, many schools, in accordance with Title IX requirements, conducted (or were in the process of conducting) campus surveys of sexual assault and other types of victimization. The results of these projects will likely confirm what we already know and have known for decades: woman abuse on campus is a major social problem. Still, there remains a conspicuous absence of sound theoretical work on this topic, which was an issue raised nearly twenty years ago by Schwartz and DeKeseredy (1997). Perhaps this can be explained in part by the fact that much of the social sciences in this current era (especially in the United States) is dominated by measurement and statistical analysis (DeKeseredy 2012; Young 2011).

Regardless of why theoretical developments have not kept pace with the burgeoning empirical literature on campus violence against women, whether we like it or not or whether we realize it or not, "theory is a fundamental part of our everyday lives" (Curran and Renzetti 1994, 2). What is more, we need good theories not only for scientific reasons but also to inform effective policies. As Kurt Lewin (1951), the founder of modern social psychology, puts it, "There is nothing so practical as good theory" (169). Indeed, before we can develop effective policies to curb woman abuse on campus, we must first determine what causes or motivates men to engage in this behavior. The theories reviewed here constitute good sociological starting points, but there is still much more work that should be done.

There is a major need as well to develop theories of same-sex violence against women and violence against transwomen on campus. The bulk of the literature on campus violence against women is heteronormative and the same can be said about the bulk of the empirical, theoretical, and policy work on any type of intimate partner violence. There is, to be sure, much violence in same-sex relationships that warrants theoretical attention. For instance, about one-third of lesbian, gay, and bisexual (LGB) people experience this harm in their lifetime, and it is estimated that intimate sexual violence is experienced by 5 percent of LGB people during the same time frame (Messinger 2014).

More recommendations for further theoretical work could easily be offered here, but in the meantime, college women who are currently being victimized by men cannot afford to sit back and hope that researchers will develop greater theoretical insight. Using theories, such as those discussed in this chapter, to identify locations and strategies for social change initiatives would be an excellent start.

NOTES

1. Image-based sexual abuse is often referred to as "revenge porn." Some academic and legal circles also call it "nonconsensual pornography" or "involuntary pornography" (Franks 2014). See McGlynn and Rackley (2016) for the rationale behind using the term image-based sexual abuse.

2. See DeKeseredy and Schwartz (2013) and Schwartz and DeKeseredy (1997) for a detailed explanation of this complex modified model.

3. This section includes modified portions of work published previously by Schwartz and DeKeseredy (1997) and Schwartz et al. (2001).

REFERENCES

Akers, R. L. 2000. *Criminological theories*, 3rd ed. Los Angeles, CA: Roxbury.

Boeringer, S. D., C. L. Shehan, and R. L. Akers. 1991. Social contexts and social learning in sexual coercion and aggression: Assessing the contribution of fraternity membership. *Family Relations* 40 (1): 58–64.

Bowker, L. H. 1983. *Beating wife-beating.* Lexington, MA: Lexington Books.

Clarke, R. V., and M. Felson. 1993. Introduction: Criminology, routine activity, and rational choice. In *Routine activity and rational choice,* ed. R. V. Clarke and M. Felson, 1–14. New Brunswick, NJ: Transaction.

Cohen, L. E., and M. Felson. 1979. Social changes and crime rate trends: A routine activities approach. *American Sociological Review* 44 (4): 588–608.

Cross, W. F. 1993. *Differentiation of sexually coercive and noncoercive college males.* Unpublished doctoral dissertation. Athens: Ohio University.

Curran, D. J., and C. M. Renzetti. 1994. *Theories of crime.* Boston: Allyn and Bacon.

Daigle, L. E., S. Mummert, B. S. Fisher, and H. L. Scherer. 2015. Sexual victimization on college campuses. In *Sexual victimization: Then and now,* ed. T. Richards and C. D. Marcum, 83–102. Thousand Oaks, CA: Sage.

DeKeseredy, W. S. 1988a. Woman abuse in dating relationships: The relevance of social support theory. *Journal of Family Violence* 3 (1): 1–13.

———. 1988b. *Woman abuse in dating relationships: The role of male peer support.* Toronto: Canadian Scholars' Press.

———. 2011. *Contemporary critical criminology.* London: Routledge.

———. 2012. The current condition of criminological theory in North America. In *New directions in criminological theory,* ed. S. Hall and S. Winlow, 66–79. London: Routledge.

DeKeseredy, W. S., and M. Corsianos. 2016. *Violence against women in pornography.* New York: Routledge.

DeKeseredy, W. S., and W. F. Flack Jr. 2007. Sexual assault in colleges and universities. In *Battleground criminal justice,* ed. G. Barak, 693–697. Westport, CT: Greenwood.

DeKeseredy, W. S., and L. MacLeod. 1997. *Woman abuse: A sociological story.* Toronto: Harcourt Brace.

DeKeseredy, W. S., and M. D. Schwartz. 1993. Male peer support and woman abuse: An expansion of DeKeseredy's model. *Sociological Spectrum* 13 (4): 394–414.

———. 1998. *Woman abuse on campus: Results from the Canadian national survey.* Thousand Oaks, CA: Sage.

———. 2013. *Male peer support and violence against women: The history and verification of a theory.* Boston: Northeastern University Press.

———. 2015. Male peer support theory. In *Sisters in crime: Bringing gender into criminology*, ed. F. T. Cullen, P. Wilcox, J. L. Lux, and C. Lero Johnson, 302–322. New York: Oxford University Press.

———. 2016. Thinking sociologically about image-based sexual abuse during and after separation/divorce: The contribution of male peer support theory. Paper presented at the annual meetings of the American Society of Criminology, New Orleans, LA, November.

Dobash, R. E., and R. P. Dobash. 1979. *Violence against wives: A case against the patriarchy*. New York: Free Press.

Ellis, D., and W. S. DeKeseredy. 1996. *The wrong stuff: An introduction to the sociological study of deviance*, 2nd ed. Toronto: Allyn and Bacon.

Felson, M. 1994. *Crime and everyday life*. Thousand Oaks, CA: Pine Forge.

Fisher, B. S., L. E. Daigle, and F. T. Cullen. 2010. *Unsafe in the ivory tower: The sexual victimization of college women*. Thousand Oaks, CA: Sage.

Fisher, B. S., and J. J. Sloan. 2013. *Campus crime: Legal, social, and policy perspectives*, 3rd ed. Springfield, IL: Charles C. Thomas.

Fisher, B. S., J. J. Sloan, F. T. Cullen, and C. Lu. 1998. Crime in the ivory tower: The level and sources of student victimization. *Criminology* 36 (3): 671–710.

Franklin, C. A., L. A. Bouffard, and T. C. Pratt. 2012. Sexual assault on the college campus: Fraternity affiliation, male peer support, and low self-control. *Criminal Justice and Behavior* 39 (11): 1457–1480.

Franks, M. A. 2014. Drafting an effective "revenge porn" law: A guide for legislators. Available at http://papers.ssrn.com/sol3/papers.cfm?abstract_id=2468823.

Garriott, W. 2011. *Policing methamphetamine: Narcopolitics in rural America*. New York: New York University Press.

Healey, E. 2016. Jian Ghomeshi trial exposes troubling double-standard. *Toronto Star*, February 15. Available at http://www.thestar.com/opinion/commentary/ 2016/02/15 /jian-ghomeshi-trial-exposes-troubling-double-standard.html.

Hunnicutt, G. 2009. Varieties of patriarchy and violence against women: Resurrecting "patriarchy" as a theoretical tool. *Violence Against Women* 15 (5): 553–573.

Kimmel, M. 2008. *Guyland: The perilous world where boys become men*. New York: Harper.

Kirkpatrick, C., and E. J. Kanin. 1957. Male sex aggression on a university campus. *American Sociological Review* 22 (1): 52–58.

Koss, M. P., C. Gidycz, and N. Wisniewski. 1987. The scope of rape: Incidence and prevalence in a national sample of higher education students. *Journal of Consulting and Clinical Psychology* 55 (2): 162–170.

Krebs, C. P., C. H. Lindquist, T. D. Warner, B. S. Fisher, and S. L. Martin. 2007. *The campus sexual assault (CSA) study*. Washington, DC: U.S. Department of Justice, National Institute of Justice.

Lewin, K. 1951. *Field theory in social science: Selected theoretical papers*, ed. D. Cartwright. New York: Harper and Row.

Lilly, J. R., F. T. Cullen, and R. A. Ball. 2015. *Criminological theory: Context and consequences*, 6th ed. Thousand Oaks, CA: Sage.

Maier, S. L. 2014. *Rape, victims, and investigations: Experiences and perceptions of law enforcement officers responding to reported rapes*. New York: Routledge.

McGlynn, C., and E. Rackley. 2016. Not "revenge porn," but abuse: Let's call it image-based sexual abuse. *Inherently Human: Critical Perspectives on Law, Gender and Sexuality*, February 15, 41. Available at https://inherentlyhuman.wordpress.com/2016/02/15/not -revenge-porn-but-abuse-lets-call-it-image-based-sexual-abuse/.

McOrmond-Plummer, L., P. Easteal, and J. Y. Levy-Peck. 2014. The necessity of appropriate service response to intimate partner sexual violence. In *Intimate partner sexual violence*, ed. L. McOrmond-Plummer, P. Easteal, and J. Y. Levy-Peck, 18–29. London: Jessica Kingsley.

Messerschmidt, J. W. 1993. *Masculinities and crime: Critique and reconceptualization*. Lanham, MD: Roman and Littlefield.

Messinger, A. M. 2014. Marking 35 years of research on same-sex intimate partner violence: Lessons and new directions. In *Handbook of LGBT communities, crime, and justice*, ed. D. Peterson and V. Panfil, 65–85. New York: Springer.

Pierson, R. R. 1991. Violence against women: Strategies for change. *Canadian Women's Studies* 11 (4): 10–12.

Renzetti, C. M. 2013. *Feminist criminology*. London: Routledge.

Richards, T. N., and L. Restivo. 2015. Sexual victimization among intimates. In *Sexual victimization: Then and now*, ed. T. N. Richards and C. D. Marcum, 69–82. Thousand Oaks, CA: Sage.

Schwartz, M. D., and W. S. DeKeseredy. 1997. *Sexual assault on the college campus: The role of male peer support*. Thousand Oaks, CA: Sage.

Schwartz, M. D., W. S. DeKeseredy, D. Tait, and S. Alvi. 2001. Male peer support and routine activities theory: Understanding sexual assault on the college campus. *Justice Quarterly* 18 (3): 701–727.

Schwartz, M. D., and C. A. Nogrady. 1996. Fraternity membership, rape myths, and sexual aggression on a college campus. *Violence Against Women* 2 (2): 148–162.

Schwartz, M. D., and V. Pitts. 1995. Exploring a feminist routine activities approach to explaining sexual assault. *Justice Quarterly* 12 (1): 10–31.

Shenkman, R. 1989. *Legends, lies, and cherished myths of American history*. New York: Harper and Row.

Sloan, J. J. III, and B. Fisher. 2011. *The dark side of the ivory tower: Campus crime as a social problem*. New York: Cambridge University Press.

Weiss, K. G. 2013. *Party school: Crime, campus, and community*. Boston: Northeastern University Press.

Young, J. 2011. *The criminological imagination*. Malden, MA: Polity Press.

6

Alcohol-Related Sexual Assault on College Campuses

A Continuing Problem

ANTONIA ABBEY

I n recent years, the White House, congressional committees, and survivors have focused attention on sexual assault and other forms of sexual misconduct that occur on college campuses. These groups have spotlighted a problem that has often been trivialized, despite reports of disturbingly high rates of sexual aggression by college men against women since the 1950s (Kirkpatrick and Kanin 1957; Koss, Gidycz, and Wisniewski 1987). The sexual violence that occurs on college campuses is part of a much larger problem. Men's violence against women is a serious health and human rights issue throughout the world that is often motivated by the desire to control women's sexuality (World Health Organization 2013). In a large U.S. nationally representative survey conducted in 2010 by the Centers for Disease Control and Prevention, 18.3 percent of women reported being raped during their lifetime and 44.6 percent experienced another form of sexual violence; more than 93 percent of the perpetrators were men (Black et al. 2011). Etiological research has focused on the most common type of sexual assault, which involves female victims and male perpetrators who use verbal threats, physical force, and/or the victim's impairment, often within a casual or steady dating relationship (Black et al. 2011; Koss 1988). Thus, this chapter focuses on men's sexual aggression against women, recognizing that men and transgendered individuals are also victims of sexual assault and that sexual violence also occurs in same-sex relationships (Black et al. 2011; Edwards et al. 2015).

Alcohol is associated with approximately half of sexual assaults, including those on college campuses, with estimates ranging from about 40 percent to 75 percent (Abbey 2002). Typically, if alcohol is consumed, the perpetrator and victim spent some time drinking together in a social setting. Recognizing alcohol as a risk factor for perpetration does not excuse perpetrators; they are responsible for their actions whether they were sober or intoxicated. Recognizing alcohol as a risk factor for victimization is not victim blame; no one is responsible for being sexually assaulted and all survivors should be treated with empathy to avoid causing further trauma.

This chapter expands on a model of alcohol's role in acquaintance sexual assault that the author has been developing for several decades (Abbey 1991, 2002, 2011). It does not include a systematic review of all the empirical studies that have found associations between alcohol and sexual assault (see Abbey et al. 2014; Ullman 2003). Instead, the goal of this chapter is to highlight the mechanisms through which alcohol consumption in a potential sexual situation increases the likelihood that sexual assault will occur. As can be seen in Figure 6.1, alcohol has both psychological and pharmacological effects on potential perpetrators and victims. Men who commit acts

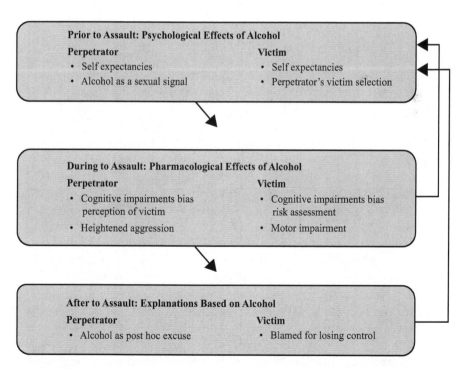

Figure 6.1 Conceptual Model on Alcohol's Roles in Acquaintance Sexual Assault

of sexual aggression typically have extreme scores on multiple risk factors, including hostility toward women, rape myths, sexual dominance, callous affect, positive attitudes about casual sex, number of sex partners, childhood victimization, and peer approval of sexual coercion (Malamuth et al. 1991; Wheeler, George, and Dahl 2002). Alcohol works in concert with perpetrators' beliefs about women and relationships, as well as with their personalities and past experiences. Empirical research demonstrates that alcohol increases the risk of sexual aggression among men who are already predisposed to act aggressively (this is described in more detail below under "Pharmacological Effects of Alcohol on Perpetrators"). Alcohol also affects a woman's ability to evaluate risky situations, thus increasing her vulnerability if targeted by a sexually aggressive man (Norris, Nurius, and Graham 1999).

Traditional heterosexual gender roles, sexual double standards, and perceived norms regarding heavy drinking and casual sex contribute to rape culture on college campuses. Thus, the next sections describe alcohol and sexual norms and behavior on college campuses, followed by theoretical and empirical evidence to support the model depicted in Figure 6.1.

The College Context: Alcohol and Sexual Norms and Behavior

Prevalence of Alcohol Consumption, Heavy Drinking, and Alcohol-Related Problems

Recent nationally representative data from the Monitoring the Future study indicate that 79 percent of college students have tried alcohol at some point in their lives, and 65 percent report that they have consumed alcohol in the past month (Johnston et al. 2015). Heavy episodic drinking is typically operationalized as consuming five or more drinks in a two-hour time period for men; the cutoff is four or more drinks for women. Across the past thirty years, full-time college students have had higher rates of heavy drinking than other same-age adults, with peaks in 1993 and 2008 of 40 percent. In 2014, 35 percent of college students reported at least one occasion of heavy episodic drinking in the past two weeks, as compared to 31 percent of same-age adults not in college. In the National Longitudinal Study of Adolescent Health, attending a four-year college was positively associated with heavy drinking among White young adults and negatively associated with heavy drinking among African American and Asian young adults (Paschall, Bersamin, and Flewelling 2005). A sizable proportion of heavy drinkers consume much more than four or five drinks per occasion; researchers estimate that 24 percent of male college students and 7 percent of female college students consumed at least ten drinks per occasion at least once in the past two weeks (White and Hingson 2014). Both individual and campus factors are associated with heavy drinking. It is highest among men, Whites, members of Greek organizations, students on campuses with low proportions of older students, students on campuses with low proportions of minority students, students on campuses surrounded by a high density of alcohol outlets, and students in states with few alcohol control policies (Wechsler and Nelson 2008; White and Hingson 2014).

Heavy drinking is associated with a myriad of serious consequences. Approximately 1,800 college students die from alcohol-related unintentional injuries each year (Hingson, Zha, and Weitzman 2009). These deaths are attributed to traffic fatalities, alcohol poisoning, drowning, falls, fires, gunshots, and hypothermia. An additional 20,000 college students are hospitalized for alcohol overdoses annually (White and Hingson 2014). Approximately 599,000 students experience nonfatal, unintentional injuries attributed to alcohol each year (Hingson, Zha, and Weitzman 2009). Additional common consequences include sexual assault, physical assault, suicide attempts, blackouts, and property damage (Hingson, Zha, and Weitzman 2009; White and Hingson 2014). Approximately one-quarter of college students report negative academic consequences due to their drinking, including missing classes or assignments and receiving low grades (White and Hingson 2014). Most of these studies do not provide breakdowns by gender or race/ethnicity, although more White college students than African American college students report that they experience negative consequences associated with drinking (Skidmore et al. 2012).

Traditional Heterosexual Dating and Sexual Scripts Are Still Commonly Endorsed

Many scholars have described traditional heterosexual gender role norms about dating and sexual behavior (Gagnon and Simon 1973; Vannier and O'Sullivan 2011). One major theme is that men are expected to initiate sex and women are expected to serve as gatekeepers, telling men when to stop. There are several assumptions underlying this theme, including that men always want sex, that women are less interested in sex than men are, and that it is the woman's obligation to limit sexual activities. Sexual scripts build on traditional distinctions between men's agency and women's communion, reinforcing the expectation that men assertively act on their sexual desires and women passively respond to their partner's needs. Although this script sounds outdated and does not apply to all young adults, these themes still consistently emerge in the sexual narratives of adolescents, college students, and young adults who are not in college (Bartoli and Clark 2006; Sakaluk et al. 2014).

A second, related theme is that sex is a game or conquest and that "all is fair in love and war." This stereotype supports the narrative that "no" means "try later" or "convince me," thereby legitimating seduction strategies that cross the line to verbal coercion and threats (DeGue and DiLillo 2004; Ryan 2011). Although many colleges have recently developed active consent policies that require students to explicitly ask their partners for consent prior to each sexual activity (LaFrance, Loe, and Brown 2012), most young people are not taught to use active consent by their parents or through school curricula, nor is active consent modeled in most media depictions of sexual encounters. Thus, it is not surprising that indirect strategies are still commonly used to ascertain partners' willingness to engage in specific sexual activities and that stereotypes like those described earlier guide perceptions of sexual interest (Powell 2008).

Sexual Double Standards

Sexual double standards are still common such that women are judged more harshly than men for engaging in sexual behavior outside of long-term, committed relationships (Crawford and Popp 2003; Sprecher, Treger, and Sakaluk 2013). Women with many sexual partners are still much more likely to be stigmatized than men with a similar number of partners. Women recognize that this double standard affects others' perceptions of them, and their desire to avoid negative sanctions can stop them from engaging in wanted casual sex (Conley, Ziegler, and Moors 2012; Townsend and Wasserman 2011).

Prevalence of Casual Sex, Hooking Up, and Alcohol Consumption

Short-term sexual relationships have a long history (Reay 2014). American scholars have documented changes in dating and sexual norms, beginning with the opportunities that automobiles provided youth to socialize without supervision in the 1920s, and continuing with widespread access to reliable birth control and the free love movement in the 1960s (Garcia et al. 2012; Stinson 2010). A recent nationally representative sample of individuals aged fourteen to fifty-four in the United States found that the median age of first sexual intercourse was 16.2 for women and 16.1 for men born in the 1980s; the median number of lifetime sexual partners was 5.3 for women and 8.8 for men (Liu et al. 2015). In contrast, the median age of first marriage has been climbing in the United States to age 25.8 for women and 28.3 for men (Copen et al. 2012). Researchers have speculated that the long gap between puberty and marriage has made casual sexual relationships more desirable and acceptable, as many young adults delay marriage and childbearing until they have completed school and established themselves in careers (Stinson 2010).

Approximately 50–80 percent of college students report that they have engaged in a hookup, defined as "brief uncommitted sexual encounters among individuals who are not romantic partners or dating each other" (Garcia et al. 2012, 161). Although the term casual sex typically refers to penetrative sex, researchers and social pundits have noted that the term hookup is deliberately vague regarding the type of sexual activity that occurred (e.g., kissing, oral sex, vaginal sex). Thus, the wide variation in estimates across studies can be attributed to differences in question phrasing (e.g., any sexual activity vs. sexual intercourse), sampling (e.g., proportion of traditional vs. nontraditional students), and time period covered by the questions (e.g., lifetime vs. past year) (Garcia et al. 2012; Owen et al. 2010). Some studies find that female college students are less likely to hook up than male college students (Grello, Welsch, and Harper 2006; Kuperberg and Padgett 2015), while others find no gender differences (Owen et al. 2010). Although some researchers have argued that casual sex and hooking up are more common among college students than other young adults, other researchers have found comparable rates (Conley et al. 2012; Lyons et al. 2013). The conflicting findings across studies may reflect different definitions of hookups being used in different populations.

Many researchers and commentators have suggested that hooking up has replaced dating and relationships on college campuses. However, in a recent survey of more than 22,000 students from twenty-two campuses, Kuperberg and Padgett (2015) found that 62 percent reported hooking up, 61 percent reported going on a traditional date, and 51 percent reported being in a long-term relationship since starting college. In this study, White women were more likely to hook up than racial/ethnic minority women, while rates of hooking up were comparable among men of different races/ethnicities with the exception that Asian men reported lower rates than White men. These authors also found that homosexual men were more likely to engage in hookups than heterosexual and bisexual men, while sexual orientation was not related to frequency of hooking up for women.

Alcohol and casual sex frequently co-occur (see Claxton, DeLuca, and van Dulmen 2015 for a meta-analysis). In a random sample of more than seven thousand undergraduates, frequency of attending parties in off-campus apartments, residence halls, and fraternities was positively associated with having casual sex with a stranger while intoxicated (Bersamin et al. 2012). In qualitative narratives of hookup experiences, male and female college students report that they are usually intoxicated and require the liquid courage induced by alcohol to feel comfortable engaging in casual sex (Cowley 2014; Jozkowski and Wiersma 2015). For women, intoxication makes it easier to ignore traditional sexual scripts and seek out sex with someone they do not know well. Being drunk can also protect a woman's sexual reputation by allowing her to attribute hookups to the effects of alcohol rather than to her own sexual desire and agency (Lindgren et al. 2009).

Pathways Linking Alcohol to Sexual Assault: Psychological Effects of Alcohol

How Beliefs about Alcohol Influence Perceptions and Behavior

Perceptions have a powerful impact on behavior; how people perceive a situation and the people in that situation affects how they act and how others respond to them (Snyder and Stukas 1999). Thus, apart from alcohol's pharmacological effects, what people believe about alcohol influences their behavior. A large body of research documents the effects that people expect alcohol to have on themselves and others (Brown et al. 1987; Ham et al. 2013). Because alcohol expectancies reflect societal norms, children aged eight to ten already know and endorse common alcohol expectancies (Miller, Smith, and Goldman 1990). For adults, commonly endorsed alcohol expectancies are that alcohol increases sociability, sexual desire, disinhibited risk taking, and aggression, as well as decreases anxiety and cognitive and motor skills (Fromme, Stroot, and Kaplan 1993; Ham et al. 2013). Overall, male and female college students, as well as White, African American, Asian American, and Hispanic/Latino college students share similar alcohol expectancies (Ham et al. 2013). However, college students expect men to have a stronger sex drive and to feel more aggressive and disinhibited when intoxicated, while women are expected to have stronger sexual feelings and to be more vulnerable to sexual coercion when intoxicated (Abbey et al. 1999; Dermen and Cooper 1994). Other studies have shown that as compared to White students, African American students tend to drink lower quantities of alcohol and have less positive alcohol expectancies (McCarthy et al. 2001).

Alcohol and sex are consistently linked in books, magazines, movies, television shows, music lyrics, social media, and alcohol advertisements (Morgenstern et al. 2015; Nicholls 2012). Not only do these messages pair alcohol and sex, but they also often demonstrate the use of alcohol as a seduction technique. Memorable alcohol ad campaigns include Colt 45: "It works every time"; "Bacardi by Night" (i.e., Inspector by Day depicts a grinning man who has his head cradled between two women's naked thighs as he holds a drink in each hand); and the recent short-lived Budweiser Light campaign: "The perfect beer for removing 'no' from your vocabulary for the night." These "alcohol = uninhibited sex" messages build an automatic nonconscious mental association between these two activities that subtly reinforces the connection between sex and alcohol (Bargh and Ferguson 2000).

These messages also contribute to the standard seduction script, thereby normalizing the use of alcohol, flattery, and persistence to obtain sex from an unwilling companion. By blurring the line between consensual sex and sexual coercion, these stereotypes provide justifications that can be used by perpetrators who view "working a yes out" as normative (Sanday 1990). For example, Bernat, Calhoun, and Stolp (1998) asked male college students to listen to an audiotape of a man and a woman on a date and to stop the tape when they thought the man in the story should stop his attempts to have sex with her. The man initially uses flattery, but then threats and physical force to obtain sexual intercourse, which the woman clearly does not want. Participants were randomly assigned to one of two conditions that varied only in whether or not the man and woman were described as having been drinking alcohol together earlier that evening. Participants who thought they had been drinking alcohol together waited longer to stop the man (thus allowing him to use more extreme force) than participants who did not think they had been drinking together. This finding demonstrates how the mental association between alcohol and consensual sex can bias perceptions of a sexually assaultive situation such that the woman's refusals are not taken seriously (Norris and Cubbins 1992). Other studies have demonstrated that a woman who has just a few drinks of alcohol with a date is perceived as more sexually disinhibited, easier to seduce, and more willing to engage in sex than a woman who does not drink alcohol with her date (Abbey and Harnish 1995; George et al. 1995). Men perceive female targets more sexually than women do (Abbey and Harnish 1995), and both men and women perceive drinking women more sexually than nondrinking women (Abbey and Harnish 1995; George et al. 1995).

Pharmacological Effects of Alcohol on Perpetrators

Controlled laboratory studies have found measurable cognitive deterioration at blood alcohol concentrations (BAC) as low as .04, which typically occurs when two standard drinks of alcohol are consumed within a two-hour period by a man of average weight (Carey and Hustad 2005). These impairments increase with dose and are sizable for most people at blood alcohol levels of .08 and above (Carey and Hustad 2005; Dry et al. 2012). Alcohol impairs executive cognitive functions that are needed to make informed decisions, including working memory, planning, the ability to integrate multiple sources of information, and the capacity to shift one's perspective when new information becomes available (Peterson et al. 1990; Roberts et al. 2014). Relatedly, intoxicated individuals have a difficult time stopping themselves from completing a motor response that has been initiated (in lab studies, decisions are made on computers; Field et al. 2010). In sum, intoxicated individuals focus their attention on the most immediate and salient cues in a situation; they are disinclined to consider distal or subtle cues; and once they have initiated a line of action, they perseverate even when new information suggests they should alter their behavior.

This understanding of the pharmacological effects of alcohol has been used to explain the relationship between perpetrators' alcohol consumption and sexual aggression, as well as links between alcohol and general aggression and risk-taking behavior (Abbey et al. 2014; Heinz et al. 2011). Potential perpetrators' sexual arousal, sense of entitlement, and anger are likely to be much more salient when they are intoxicated than are any concerns about the victim or later negative consequences. For a man predisposed to committing sexual violence, cognitive impairments induced by alcohol may encourage him to act without considering the consequences (Abbey 2002).

Psychological expectancies about alcohol's effects work synergistically with its pharmacological effects (George and Stoner 2000). Thus, an intoxicated man who wants to have sex may interpret almost any response from a woman to whom he is sexually attracted as a sign of sexual interest (e.g., even a direct refusal can be viewed as token resistance). His reduced ability to make complex decisions and inhibit himself further increase the likelihood that he will feel comfortable forcing sex despite the woman's lack of consent. The best evidence for this assertion comes from laboratory studies in which men are randomly assigned to drink alcoholic or nonalcoholic beverages and then respond to a sexual assault scenario (see Abbey et al. 2014 for a review). Using the audiotape paradigm described earlier, male participants who consumed alcohol waited longer to stop the man than those who did not consume alcohol (Marx, Gross, and Adams 1999). Other researchers, using different sexual assault scenarios, have found that drinkers report greater sexual arousal, greater entitlement to have sex in that situation, and greater willingness to use force if they were in that situation (Davis et al. 2012; Noel et al. 2009).

Laboratory studies have also demonstrated that alcohol typically increases aggression only among men already predisposed to be aggressive due to high levels of trait anger and hostility (Heinz et al. 2011). In a sexual assault scenario study, Abbey and colleagues (2009) found that intoxicated participants with high levels of hostility were more likely to report that they would use coercion to obtain sex as compared to intoxicated participants with low levels of hostility and sober participants who were high or low in hostility. In previous reviews, I have labeled this a two-stage process (Abbey 2002). Misperception of a woman's sexual interest does not cause sexual assault, with or without alcohol. However, misperception of a woman's sexual interest can contribute to a sense of entitlement that can trigger aggression among men who are already prone to aggression, especially when they are intoxicated.

A Perfect Storm: Alcohol plus Casual Sex Can Turn into Sexual Assault

As described previously, many college students believe that alcohol makes it easier to talk to someone they do not know well; thus, they strategically drink alcohol in advance of situations in which they might want to engage in some type of sexual hookup (Abbey et al. 1999; Dermen and Cooper 1994). Alcohol provides the initial self-confidence required to act in a sexually disinhibited manner, especially for women who are uncomfortable flaunting the traditional sexual script (Cowley 2014). Many hookups are completely consensual; however, many others begin as consensual but escalate into sexual aggression when the woman refuses some type of sexual activity that the man wants. For example, 78 percent of the sexual assaults reported in a random sample survey of female students at one college occurred during a hookup (Flack et al. 2016). Alcohol consumption is a double-edged sword for women navigating contemporary sexual norms that encourage women to be open to casual sex yet still condemn them for being sexually promiscuous (Conley et al. 2012; Crawford and Popp 2003). Alcohol provides women with an excuse for sexual disinhibition; however, it is often viewed as such a strong sign of sexual availability by men that refusals are ignored (Cowley 2014; Warren, Swan, and Allen 2015).

Numerous studies have documented an association between alcohol and sexual assault with a casual partner. Alcohol is more likely to be consumed by perpetrators and victims during the incident when they know each other casually, as compared to when they are in an established dating relationship (Littleton, Grills-Taquechel, and Axsom 2009; Ullman, Karabatsos, and Koss 1999). In addition, alcohol increases the likelihood that a woman will go to an isolated location with a man she does not know well. In contrast, a perpetrator who is already in a relationship with a woman does not need alcohol to encourage her to spend time alone with him. An intoxicated victim is more likely than a sober victim to miss warning signs and allow a potential perpetrator to isolate her from friends, thereby making it easier to force sex if the woman does not consent or is too intoxicated to consent (Davis et al. 2009; Norris et al. 1999).

Post-Assault Judgments and Justifications

A plethora of vignette studies have demonstrated that alcohol affects college students' perceptions of male perpetrators' and female victims' responsibility for what happened. Many studies have found that victims are held more responsible and perpetrators are held less responsible if the victim had been drinking alcohol (Sims, Noel, and Maisto 2007; Untied et al. 2012). A few studies have contrasted vignettes in which the perpetrator bought or gave the victim drinks with those in which she bought or sought out the drinks herself. Women's voluntary intoxication was associated with increased victim responsibility and decreased perpetrator responsibility as compared to when the perpetrator encouraged or surreptitiously got her intoxicated (Girard and Senn 2008; Lynch et al. 2013). In combination, these studies suggest that intoxicated female victims are held more responsible and their male assailants are held less responsible for what happened, unless the perpetrator appears to have planned the incident and intentionally gotten her intoxicated.

Summary and Implications

Alcohol's role in sexual assault is complicated and multifaceted. Alcohol on its own does not cause sexual assault; however, it increases the likelihood of sexual assault occurring through multiple pathways. Alcohol increases the likelihood of sexual assault perpetration among men who are predisposed to perpetration because of their personalities, attitudes, and past life experiences. Alcohol also increases the likelihood of sexual assault perpetration in contexts that make it easier for perpetrators to justify their behavior as normative. These types of contexts are not unique to college campuses. However, the nexus of heavy drinking, normative expectations for engaging in casual sex, and perceived peer acceptance of verbal coercion and impairment to obtain sex contribute to the high rates of alcohol-involved sexual assault on college campuses.

Alcohol increases the likelihood of victimization to the extent that it makes potential victims less aware of risk cues and less able to resist. As stated in the introductory section, these associations do not legally or morally mitigate perpetrators' responsibility for their actions, nor do they make the victims responsible for what happened. In a civilized society, people should look out for others with permanent or temporary impairments, not take advantage of them. As described earlier, approximately 1,800 college students die each year from alcohol-related unintentional injuries and an additional 599,000 experience nonfatal, alcohol-related injuries (Hingson et al. 2009). Many students express dissatisfaction with the drinking norms on their campus and mistakenly believe that most other students approve of them (Litt, Stock, and Lewis 2012; Merrill, Read, and Colder 2013). Dispelling these misconceptions could encourage healthy levels of alcohol consumption and reduce rates of alcohol-involved sexual assault. However, the elimination of all alcohol-involved sexual assaults would not eliminate sexual assault. Thus, beginning in childhood, comprehensive prevention and treatment programs are needed that address the many risk factors associated with sexual assault perpetration.

REFERENCES

Abbey, A. 1991. Acquaintance rape and alcohol consumption on college campuses: How are they linked? *Journal of American College Health* 39 (4): 165–169.

———. 2002. Alcohol-related sexual assault: A common problem among college students. *Journal of Studies on Alcohol,* Supplement No. 14, 118–128.

———. 2011. Alcohol's role in sexual violence perpetration: Theoretical explanations, existing evidence, and directions for future research. *Drug and Alcohol Review* 30 (5): 481–489.

Abbey, A., and R. J. Harnish. 1995. Perception of sexual intent: The role of gender, alcohol consumption, and rape supportive attitudes. *Sex Roles* 32 (5): 297–313.

Abbey, A., P. McAuslan, L. T. Ross, and T. Zawacki. 1999. Alcohol expectancies regarding sex, aggression, and sexual vulnerability: Reliability and validity assessment. *Psychology of Addictive Behaviors* 13 (3): 174–182.

Abbey, A., M. R. Parkhill, A. J. Jacques-Tiura, and C. Saenz. 2009. Alcohol's role in men's use of coercion to obtain unprotected sex. *Substance Use & Misuse* 44 (0): 1328–1348.

Abbey, A., R. Wegner, J. Woerner, S. E. Pegram, and J. Pierce. 2014. Review of survey and experimental research that examine the relationship between alcohol consumption and men's sexual aggression perpetration. *Trauma, Violence, and Abuse* 15 (4): 265–282.

Bargh, J. A., and M. J. Ferguson. 2000. Beyond behaviorism: The automaticity of higher mental processes. *Psychological Bulletin* 126 (6): 925–945.

Bartoli, A. M., and M. D. Clark. 2006. The dating game: Similarities and differences in dating scripts among college students. *Sexuality and Culture* 10 (4): 54–80.

Bernat, J. A., K. S. Calhoun, and S. Stolp. 1998. Sexually aggressive men's responses to a date rape analogue: Alcohol as a disinhibiting cue. *Journal of Sex Research* 35 (4): 341–348.

Bersamin, M. M., M. J. Paschall, R. F. Saltz, and B. L. Zamboanga. 2012. Young adults and casual sex: The relevance of college drinking settings. *Journal of Sex Research* 49 (2-3): 274–281.

Black, M. C., K. C. Basile, M. J. Breiding, S. G. Smith, M. L. Walters, M. T. Merrick, J. Chen, and M. R. Stevens. 2011. *The national intimate partner and sexual violence survey.* Atlanta, GA: Centers for Disease Control and Prevention.

Brown, S. A., B. A. Christiansen, M. S. Goldman, and L. Anderson. 1987. The alcohol expectancy questionnaire. *Journal of Studies on Alcohol* 48 (5): 483–491.

Carey, K. B., and J. T. P. Hustad. 2005. Methods for determining blood alcohol concentration: Current and retrospective. In *Comprehensive handbook of alcohol related pathology,* vol. 3, ed. V. Preedy and R. Watson, 1429–1444. New York: Elsevier.

Claxton, S. E., H. K. DeLuca, and M. H. van Dulmen. 2015. The association between alcohol use and engagement in casual sexual relationships and experiences: A meta-analytic review on non-experimental studies. *Archives of Sexual Behavior* 44 (4): 837–856.

Conley, T. D., A. Ziegler, and A. C. Moors. 2012. Backlash from the bedroom stigma mediates gender differences in acceptance of casual sex offers. *Psychology of Women Quarterly* 37 (3): 392–407.

Copen, E. E., K. Daniels, J. Vespa, and W. D. Mosher. 2012. *First marriages in the United States: Data from the 2006–2008 National Survey of Family Growth* (National Health Statistics Reports, No. 49). Hyattsville, MD: National Center for Health Statistics.

Cowley, A. D. 2014. "Let's get drunk and have sex": The complex relationship of alcohol, gender, and sexual victimization. *Journal of Interpersonal Violence* 29 (7): 1258–1278.

Crawford, M., and D. Popp. 2003. Sexual double standards: A review and methodological critique of two decades of research. *Journal of Sex Research* 40 (1): 13–26.

Davis, K. C., T. J. Schraufnagel, A. J. Jacques-Tiura, J. Norris, W. H. George, and P. A. Kiekel. 2012. Childhood sexual abuse and acute alcohol effects on men's sexual aggression intentions. *Psychology of Violence* 2 (2): 179–193.

Davis, K. C., S. A. Stoner, J. Norris, W. H. George, and N. T. Masters. 2009. Women's awareness of and discomfort with sexual assault cues. *Violence Against Women* 15 (9): 1106–1125.

DeGue, S., and D. DiLillo. 2004. Understanding perpetrators of nonphysical sexual coercion: Characteristics of those who cross the line. *Violence and Victims* 19 (6): 673–688.

Dermen, K. H., and M. L. C. Cooper. 1994. Sex-related alcohol expectancies among adolescents. *Psychology of Addictive Behaviors* 8 (3): 152–160.

Dry, M. J., N. R. Burns, T. Nettelbeck, A. L. Farquharson, and J. M. White. 2012. Dose-related effects of alcohol on cognitive functioning. *PLOS ONE* 7 (11): 1–8.

Edwards, K. M., K. M. Sylaska, J. E. Barry, M. M. Moyhihan, V. L. Banyard, E. S. Cohn, W. A. Walsh, and S. K. Ward. 2015. Physical dating violence, sexual violence, and unwanted pursuit victimization: A comparison of incidence rates among sexual-minority and heterosexual college students. *Journal of Interpersonal Violence* 30 (4): 580–600.

Field, M., R. W. Wiers, P. Christiansen, M. T. Fillmore, and J. C. Verster. 2010. Acute alcohol effects on inhibitory control and implicit cognition: Implications for loss of control over drinking. *Alcoholism: Clinical and Experimental Research* 34 (8): 1346–1352.

Flack, W. F., B. E. Hansen, A. B. Hopper, L. A. Bryant, K. W. Lang, A. A. Massa, and J. E. Whalen. 2016. Some types of hookups may be riskier than others for campus sexual assault. *Psychological Trauma: Theory, Research, Practice, and Policy* 8 (4): 413–420.

Fromme, K., E. Stroot, and D. Kaplan. 1993. Comprehensive effects of alcohol: Development and psychometric assessment of a new expectancy questionnaire. *Psychological Assessment* 5 (1): 19–26.

Gagnon, J. H., and W. Simon. 1973. *Sexual conduct: The social sources of human sexuality.* Chicago: Aldine.

Garcia, J. R., C. Reiber, S. G. Massey, and A. M. Merriwether. 2012. Sexual hookup culture: A review. *Review of General Psychology* 16 (2): 161–176.

George, W. H., K. L. Cue, P. A. Lopez, L. C. Crowe, and J. Norris. 1995. Self-reported alcohol expectancies and postdrinking sexual inferences about women. *Journal of Applied Social Psychology* 25 (2): 164–186.

George, W. H., and S. A. Stoner. 2000. Understanding acute alcohol effects on sexual behavior. *Annual Review of Sex Research* 11 (1): 92–124.

Girard, A. L., and C. Y. Senn. 2008. The role of the new "date rape drugs" in attributions about date rape. *Journal of Interpersonal Violence* 23 (1): 3–20.

Grello, C. M., D. P. Welsch, and M. S. Harper. 2006. No strings attached: The nature of casual sex in college students. *Journal of Sex Research* 43 (3): 255–267.

Ham, L. S., Y. Wang, S. Y. Kim, and B. L. Zamboanga. 2013. Measurement equivalence of the brief comprehensive effects of alcohol scale in a multiethnic sample of college students. *Journal of Clinical Psychology* 69 (4): 341–363.

Heinz, A. J., A. Beck, A. Meyer-Lindenberg, S. Sterzer, and A. Heinz. 2011. Cognitive and neurobiological mechanisms of alcohol-related aggression. *Nature Reviews* 12 (7): 400–413.

Hingson, R. W., W. Zha, and E. R. Weitzman. 2009. Magnitude of and trends in alcohol-related mortality and morbidity among U.S. college students ages 18–24, 1998–2005. *Journal of Studies on Alcohol and Drugs*, Supplement 16: 12–20.

Johnston, L. D., P. M. O'Malley, J. G. Bachman, J. E. Schulenberg, and R. A. Miech. 2015. *Monitoring the future national survey results on drug use, 1975–2014, volume 2: College students and adults ages 19–55.* Ann Arbor: Institute for Social Research, University of Michigan.

Jozkowski, K. N., and J. D. Wiersma. 2015. Does drinking alcohol prior to sexual activity influence college students' consent? *International Journal of Sexual Health* 27 (2): 156–174.

Kirkpatrick, C., and E. Kanin. 1957. Male sex aggression on a university campus. *American Sociological Review* 22 (1): 52–58.

Koss, M. P. 1988. *Hidden rape.* In *Rape and sexual assault II,* ed. A. W. Burgess, 3–25. New York: Garland.

Koss, M. P., C. A. Gidycz, and N. Wisniewski. 1987. The scope of rape: Incidence and prevalence of sexual aggression and victimization in a national sample of higher education students. *Journal of Consulting and Clinical Psychology* 55 (2): 162–170.

Kuperberg, A., and J. E. Padgett. 2015. The role of culture in explaining college students' selection into hookups, dates, and long-term romantic relationships. *Journal of Social and Personal Relationships,* 33 (8): 1070–1096.

LaFrance, D. E., M. Loe, and S. C. Brown. 2012. "Yes means yes": A new approach to sexual assault prevention and positive sexuality promotion. *American Journal of Sexuality Education* 7 (4): 445–460.

Lindgren, K. P., D. W. Pantalone, M. A. Lewis, and W. H. George. 2009. College students' perceptions about alcohol and consensual sexual behavior: Alcohol leads to sex. *Journal of Drug Education,* 39 (1): 1–21.

Litt, D. M., M. L. Stock, and M. A. Lewis. 2012. Drinking to fit in: Examining the need to belong as a moderator of perceptions of best friends' alcohol use and related risk cognitions among college students. *Basic and Applied Social Psychology* 34 (4): 313–321.

Littleton, H. L., A. Grills-Taquechel, and D. Axsom. 2009. Impaired and incapacitated rape victims: Assault characteristics and post-assault experiences. *Violence and Victims* 24 (4): 439–457.

Liu, G., S. Hariri, H. Bradley, S. L. Gottlieb, J. S. Leichliter, and L. E. Markowitz. 2015. Trends and patterns of sexual behaviors among adolescents and adults aged 14 to 59 years, United States. *Sexually Transmitted Diseases* 42 (1): 20–26.

Lynch, K. R., N. E. Wasarhaley, J. M. Golding, and T. Simic. 2013. Who bought the drinks? Juror perceptions of intoxication in a rape trial. *Journal of Interpersonal Violence* 28 (16): 3205–3222.

Lyons, H., W. Manning, P. Giordano, and M. Longmore. 2013. Predictors of heterosexual casual sex among young adults. *Archives of Sexual Behavior* 42 (4): 585–593.

Malamuth, N. M., R. J. Sockloskie, M. P. Koss, and J. S. Tanaka. 1991. Characteristics of aggressors against women: Testing a model using a national sample of college students. *Journal of Consulting and Clinical Psychology* 59 (5): 670–681.

Marx, B. P., A. M. Gross, and H. E. Adams. 1999. The effect of alcohol on the responses of sexually coercive and noncoercive men to an experimental rape analogue. *Sexual Abuse: A Journal of Research and Treatment* 11 (2): 131–145.

McCarthy, D. M., T. L. Miller, G. T. Smith, and J. A. Smith. 2001. Disinhibition and expectancy in risk for alcohol use: Comparing black and white college samples. *Journal of Studies on Alcohol* 62 (3): 313–321.

Merrill, J. E., J. P. Read, and C. R. Colder. 2013. Normative perceptions and past-year consequences as predictors of subjective evaluations and weekly drinking behavior. *Addictive Behaviors* 38 (11): 2625–2634.

Miller, P. M., G. T. Smith, and M. S. Goldman. 1990. Emergence of alcohol expectancies in childhood: A possible critical period. *Journal of Studies on Alcohol* 51 (4): 343–349.

Morgenstern, M., F. Schoeppe, J. Campbell, W. G. Braam, M. Stoolmiller, and J. D. Sargent. 2015. Content themes of alcohol advertising in U.S. television: Latent class analysis. *Alcoholism: Clinical and Experimental Research* 39 (9): 1766–1774.

Nicholls, J. 2012. Everyday, everywhere—alcohol marketing and social media: Current trends. *Alcohol and Alcoholism* 47 (4): 486–493.

Noel, N. E., S. A. Maisto, J. D. Johnson, and L. A. Jackson Jr. 2009. The effects of alcohol and cue salience on young men's acceptance of sexual aggression. *Addictive Behaviors* 34 (4): 386–394.

Norris, J., and L. A. Cubbins. 1992. Dating, drinking and rape. *Psychology of Women Quarterly* 16 (2): 179–191.

Norris, J., P. S. Nurius, and T. L. Graham. 1999. When a date changes from fun to dangerous: Factors affecting women's ability to distinguish. *Violence Against Women* 5 (3): 230–250.

Owen, J. J., G. K. Rhoades, S. M. Stanley, and F. D. Fincham. 2010. "Hooking up" among college students: Demographic and psychosocial correlates. *Archives of Sexual Behavior* 39 (3): 653–663.

Paschall, M. J., M. Bersamin, and R. L. Flewelling. 2005. Racial/ethnic differences in the association between college attendance and heavy alcohol use: A national study. *Journal of Studies on Alcohol* 66 (2): 266–274.

Peterson, J. B., J. Rothfleisch, P. D. Zelazo, and P. O. Pihl. 1990. Acute alcohol intoxication and cognitive functioning. *Journal of Studies on Alcohol* 51 (2): 114–122.

Powell, A. 2008. *Amor fati?* Gender habitus and young people's negotiation of (hetero) sexual consent. *Journal of Sociology* 44 (2): 167–184.

Reay, B. 2014. Promiscuous intimacies: Rethinking the history of American casual sex. *Journal of Historical Sociology* 27 (1): 1–24.

Roberts, W., M. A. Miller, J. Weafer, and M. T. Fillmore. 2014. Heavy drinking and the role of inhibitory control of attention. *Experimental and Clinical Psychopharmacology* 22 (2): 133–140.

Ryan, K. M. 2011. The relationship between rape myths and sexual scripts: The social construction of rape. *Sex Roles* 65 (11): 774–782.

Sakaluk, J. K., L. M. Todd, R. Milhausen, N. J. Lachowsky, and Undergraduate Research Group in Sexuality. 2014. Dominant heterosexual sexual scripts in emerging adulthood. *Journal of Sex Research* 51 (5): 516–531.

Sanday, P. R. 1990. *Fraternity gang rape: Sex, brotherhood and privilege on campus.* New York: New York University Press.

Sims, C. M., N. E. Noel, and S. A. Maisto. 2007. Rape blame as a function of alcohol presence and resistance type. *Addictive Behaviors* 32 (12): 2766–2775.

Skidmore, J. R., J. G. Murphy, M. Martens, and A. A. Dennhardt. 2012. Alcohol-related consequences in African American and European American college students. *Journal of Ethnicity in Substance Abuse* 11 (2): 174–191.

Snyder, M., and A. A. Stukas Jr. 1999. Interpersonal processes: The interplay of cognitive, motivational, and behavioral activities in social interaction. *Annual Review of Psychology* 50 (1): 273–303.

Sprecher, S., S. Treger, and J. K. Sakaluk. 2013. Premarital sexual standards and socio-sexuality: Gender, ethnicity, and cohort differences. *Archives of Sexual Behavior* 42(8): 1395–1405.

Stinson, R. D. 2010. Hooking up in young adulthood: A review of factors influencing the sexual behavior of college students. *Journal of College Student Psychotherapy* 24 (2): 98–115.

Townsend, J. M., and T. H. Wasserman. 2011. Sexual hookups among college students: Sex differences in emotional reactions. *Archives of Sexual Behavior* 40 (6): 1173–1181.

Ullman, S. E. 2003. A critical review of field studies on the link of alcohol and adult sexual assault in women. *Aggression and Violent Behavior* 8 (5): 471–486.

Ullman, S. E., G. Karabatsos, and M. P. Koss. 1999. Alcohol and sexual aggression in a national sample of college men. *Psychology of Women Quarterly* 23 (4): 673–689.

Untied, A. S., L. M. Orchowski, N. Mastroleo, and C. A. Gidycz. 2012. College students' social reactions to the victim in a hypothetical sexual assault scenario: The role of victim and perpetrator alcohol use. *Violence and Victims* 27 (6): 957–972.

Vannier, S. A., and L. F. O'Sullivan. 2011. Communicating interest in sex: Verbal and nonverbal initiation of sexual activity in young adults' romantic dating relationships. *Archives of Sexual Behavior* 40 (5): 961–969.

Warren, P., S. Swan, and C. T. Allen. 2015. Comprehension of sexual consent as a key factor in the perpetration of sexual aggression among college men. *Journal of Aggression, Maltreatment and Trauma* 24 (8): 897–913.

Wechsler, H., and T. F. Nelson. 2008. What we have learned from the Harvard School of Public Health College Alcohol Study. *Journal of Studies on Alcohol and Drugs* 69 (4): 481–490.

Wheeler, J. G., W. H. George, and B. J. Dahl. 2002. Sexually aggressive college males: Empathy as a moderator in the "Confluence Model" of sexual aggression. *Personality and Individual Differences* 33 (5): 759–775.

White, A., and R. Hingson. 2014. The burden of alcohol use: Excessive alcohol consumption and related consequences among college students. *Alcohol Research: Current Reviews* 35 (2): 201–218.

World Health Organization. 2013. *Global and regional estimates of violence against women: Prevalence and health effects of intimate partner violence and non-partner sexual violence.* Geneva, Switzerland: WHO.

ADDITIONAL RELEVANT READINGS

Abbey, A., A. M. Clinton, P. McAuslan, T. Zawacki, and P. O. Buck. 2002. Alcohol-involved rapes: Are they more violent? *Psychology of Women Quarterly* 26 (2): 99–109.

Abbey, A., A. M. Clinton-Sherrod, P. McAuslan, T. Zawacki, and P. O. Buck. 2003. The relationship between the quantity of alcohol consumed and the severity of sexual assaults committed by college men. *Journal of Interpersonal Violence* 18 (7): 813–833.

Abbey, A., and P. McAuslan. 2004. A longitudinal examination of male college students' perpetration of sexual assault. *Journal of Consulting and Clinical Psychology* 72 (5): 747–756.

Abbey, A., R. Wegner, J. Pierce, and A. J. Jacques-Tiura. 2012. Patterns of sexual aggression in a community sample of young men: Risk factors associated with persistence, desistance, and initiation over a one year interval. *Psychology of Violence* 2 (1): 1–15.

Burkett, M., and K. Hamilton. 2012. Postfeminist sexual agency: Young women's negotiations of sexual consent. *Sexualities* 15 (7): 815–833.

Curtin, J. J., and B. A. Fairchild. 2003. Alcohol and cognitive control: Implications for regulation of behavior during response conflict. *Journal of Abnormal Psychology* 112 (3): 424–436.

Gidycz, C. A., J. B. Warkentin, and L. M. Orchowski. 2007. Predictors of perpetration of verbal, physical, and sexual violence: A prospective analysis of college men. *Psychology of Men and Masculinity* 8 (2): 79–94.

Gross, A. M., T. Bennett, L. Sloan, B. P. Marx, and J. Juergens. 2001. The impact of alcohol and alcohol expectancies on male perception of female sexual arousal in a date rape analog. *Experimental and Clinical Psychopharmacology* 9 (4): 380–388.

Gross, A. M., A. Winslett, M. Roberts, and C. L. Gohm. 2006. An examination of sexual violence against college women. *Violence Against Women* 12 (3): 288–300.

Littleton, H. L., and D. Axson. 2003. Rape and seduction scripts of university students: Implications for rape attributions and unacknowledged rape. *Sex Roles* 49 (9): 465–475.

McCauley, J. L., K. J. Ruggiero, H. S. Resnick, L. M. Conoscenti, and D. G. Kilpatrick. 2009. Forcible, drug-facilitated, and incapacitated rape in relation to substance use problems: Results from a national sample of college women. *Addictive Behaviors* 34 (5): 458–462.

Nicholson, M. E., D. W. Maney, K. Blair, P. M. Wamboldt, B. S. Mahoney, and J. Yuan. 1998. Trends in alcohol-related campus violence: Implications for prevention. *Journal of Alcohol and Drug Education* 43 (3), 34–52.

Paul, E. L., and K. A. Hayes. 2002. The casualties of "casual" sex: A qualitative exploration of the phenomenology of college students' hookups. *Journal of Social and Personal Relationships* 19 (5): 639–661.

Piane, G., and A. Safer. 2008. Drinking behaviors, expectancies and perceived social norms among diverse college women. *Journal of Alcohol and Drug Education* 52 (1): 67–79.

Reese, F. L., and R. Friend. 1994. Alcohol expectancies and drinking practices among black and white undergraduate males. *Journal of College Student Development* 35: 319–323.

Rehm, J., K. D. Shield, N. Joharchi, and P. A. Shuper. 2011. Alcohol consumption and the intention to engage in unprotected sex: Systematic review and meta-analysis of experimental studies. *Addiction* 107 (1): 51–59.

Rhoades, E., and J. H. Jernigan. 2013. Risky messages in alcohol advertising, 2003–2007: Results from content analysis. *Journal of Adolescent Health* 52 (1): 116–121.

Stern, S. R. 2005. Messages from teens on the big screen: Smoking, drinking and drug use in teen-centered films. *Journal of Health Communication* 10 (4): 331–346.

Swartout, K. M., A. G. Swartout, and J. W. White. 2011. A person-centered, longitudinal approach to sexual victimization. *Psychology of Violence* 1 (1): 29–40.

Tharp, A. T., S. DeGue, L. A. Valle, K. A. Brookmeyer, G. M. Massertti, and J. L. Matjasko. 2012. A systematic qualitative review of risk and protective factors for sexual violence perpetration. *Trauma, Violence, and Abuse* 14 (2): 133–167.

Wenger, A. A., and B. H. Bornstein. 2006. The effects of victim's substance use and relationship closeness on mock jurors' judgments in an acquaintance rape case. *Sex Roles* 54 (7): 547–555.

II

Addressing Violence Against Women on College Campuses

Legislation and Federally Mandated Action

7

From Sexual Harassment to Sexual Violence

The Evolution of Title IX's Response to Sexual Victimization

Michelle Hughes Miller

Introduction

With the advent of the Dear Colleague Letter (2011 DCL) from the U.S. Department of Education's (DOE) Office for Civil Rights (OCR) in 2011, institutions of higher education began the process of reconceptualizing their Title IX processes to more directly address sexual violence on college campuses, including peer-on-peer sexual assault (DOE 2011a). In this chapter, I discuss the evolution of the OCR's Title IX demands on universities in relation to sexual violence, but I do so by querying the widely cited claim that the 2011 DCL was a seismic shift in the OCR's expectations for universities. Though there is no doubt that the 2011 DCL ushered in an era of significant and intensive transformation of Title IX prevention and response to sexual violence on college campuses, such changes in implementation do not require a shift in the OCR's understanding or articulation of sexual violence as an element of Title IX. In other words, though the 2011 DCL provided guidance to universities on changing institutional practices, did it in fact reflect a change in the OCR's articulation of Title IX and sexual violence compared to earlier communications?

To answer this question, I analyze the most relevant communications the OCR had with universities prior to the 2011 DCL to detail the evolution of discourse about sexual violence and Title IX in those documents. How did the OCR's guidance for universities on Title IX incorporate sexual violence, and when? By focusing on the discourse in various OCR communications from 1997 to 2011, I am able to both trace the evolution of OCR discourse on sexual violence and understand the context of the 2011 DCL. I use summative content analysis to consider the manifest and latent content of language included within OCR communications, focusing on documents related to or predating the 2011 DCL (see Hsieh and Shannon 2005 for a discussion of summative content analysis). I focus on the use and development of the construct "sexual violence" within these documents. To be clear, I do not discuss the legal or administrative rulings on Title IX (see Smith, Chapter 17 in this volume, for such a review). Instead, I am interested in how the OCR itself, tasked as it is with enforcing and providing information and guidance to schools and universities, talks about issues of sexual violence to its constituents through its published communications. I begin with a brief background on Title IX before I discuss in detail the definitional elements of importance within the 2011 DCL. I then trace the discourse in the 2011 DCL back to its sources in prior OCR communications and documents, noting any shifts and clarifications. Finally, I consider, at the end of this chapter, how the 2011 DCL with its particular focus on sexual violence came to be, focusing on the legal, political, cultural, and advocacy context within which it was written and, ultimately, distributed to universities, thus setting in motion "shockwaves" across the academic community (Jonson-Reid et al. 2016, 235).

I first became interested in sexual harassment policy at my former institution, Southern Illinois University Carbondale, where I chaired a committee tasked with providing recommendations to revise the institution's sexual harassment policy and procedures. At the University of South Florida (USF), I recently served on and chaired the Presidential Advisory Committee on Title IX. Throughout this time actively working on Title IX issues, including two years' dedicated time working on defining and responding to sexual harassment policy in the company of Title IX scholars and practitioners, I can honestly say that the issue of student-on-student sexual assault as an element of Title IX barely came up. That is, until 2011, when the DCL crossed our desks. Since then I have watched USF respond to these new articulations of expected Title IX response, and I have witnessed student activists—many of whom are survivors of sexual violence—hold their universities accountable. In Chapter 10, the story told by Dr. Carmen Suarez, Vice President of Global Diversity and Inclusion at Portland State University, nicely discusses changes to institutional response at her university, and the activist narrative by Ava Blustein in Chapter 16 shares the empowerment that can come from collective action on this topic.

Background

The 2011 DCL was written by the OCR under the guidance of Russlyn Ali, who signed the letter, although she was clear in remarks she made to the press that the guidance was developed by a "team of staffers" charged with reviewing prior OCR communications on sexual violence (Lombardi 2010). Ali was appointed to the position of assistant secretary for civil rights in 2009 by President Barack Obama. The format of the DCL as a letter represents a frequently used format by the OCR, simultaneously invoking a shared obligation to address sexual violence ("Dear Colleague") and a formal description of OCR expectations on how and why to do so. Such a letter is not to be taken lightly: "While this . . . DCL does not in and of itself carry the force of law, the reality is that guidance interpreting a law issued by the very agency that is empowered to enforce that law warrants significant attention and action" (Association of Governing Boards 2015, 9).

As also discussed by Smith in Chapter 17, the letter begins by reminding its intended audience—representatives from school districts, colleges, and universities—of the purpose of Title IX within the broader social and governmental goal of "educational environments free from discrimination" (DOE 2011a, 1). The antidiscrimination clause in Title IX, Education Amendments of 1972, says this:

> No person in the United States shall, on the basis of sex, be excluded from participation in, be denied the benefits of, or be subjected to discrimination under any education program or activity receiving Federal financial assistance. (DOE 1998, para. 2)

The 1972 Education Amendments go on to define "education program or activity" (Department of Labor 1972, section 1687) and to identify institutions that would not be covered by this policy (namely, certain religious institutions, military institutions, and historically single-sex institutions). Within this broader mission to create discrimination-free educational environments carried out by the OCR within the DOE, Title IX prohibits discrimination based on sex and, by doing so, prohibits discrimination arising from sexual harassment.

Discourse in the 2011 DCL

> The sexual harassment of students, including sexual violence, interferes with students' right to receive an education free from discrimination and, in the case of sexual violence, is a crime. (DOE 2011a, 1)

In this one statement, in the first paragraph of the 2011 DCL, readers are reminded of two things: (1) sexual harassment is a form of sex discrimination, which is prohibited by Title IX; and (2) sexual violence is a form of sexual harassment—thus, it too is prohibited by Title IX. The first of these points is nothing new, as universities have been aware of federal expectations

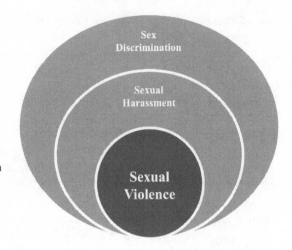

FIGURE 7.1 Visualization of the Discursive Relationship between Sexual Violence and Sex Discrimination in the 2011 DCL

to address sexual harassment under Title IX for decades—thanks to the work of MacKinnon (1979) and others (see Simon 2003)—and have been held accountable for doing so in U.S. Supreme Court rulings such as *Franklin v. Gwinnett Public Schools* (1992) and *Davis v. Monroe County Board of Education* (1999, for student-on-student harassment). But the second point has a more ambiguous history within Title IX guidances from the OCR, as I discuss in this chapter.

In the second paragraph of the 2011 DCL, the OCR repeats itself, saying: "Sexual harassment of students, which includes acts of sexual violence, is a form of sex discrimination prohibited by Title IX" (DOE 2011a, 1). With this argument, the OCR effectively presents an understanding for universities of the interconnections between sex discrimination, sexual harassment, and sexual violence. Figure 7.1 illustrates those interconnections. In the 2011 DCL, the relation between sexual violence and sex discrimination (or coverage of sexual violence under Title IX) is explicit only because of the definitional acceptance of sexual violence as a form of sexual harassment. In other words, the hostile environment arguments that link sexual harassment to sex discrimination create the umbrella under which sexual violence also resides, as a form of sexual harassment.

Having alerted readers twice to the second point that sexual violence is prohibited by Title IX, the purported purpose of the 2011 DCL is disclosed:

> In order to assist recipients, which include school districts, colleges, and universities . . . in meeting these obligations [to address discrimination], this letter explains that the requirements of Title IX pertaining to sexual harassment also cover sexual violence, and lays out the specific Title IX requirements applicable to sexual violence. (DOE 2011a, 1)

The document then defines sexual violence:

> Sexual violence, as that term is used in this letter, refers to physical sexual acts perpetrated against a person's will or where a person is incapable of giving consent due to the victim's use of drugs or alcohol. An individual also may be unable to give consent due to an intellectual or other disability. (DOE 2011a, 1)

The document provides examples of sexual violence, and couples these examples with yet a third statement about the relationship between sexual violence and sexual harassment within Title IX: "A number of different acts fall into the category of sexual violence, including rape, sexual assault, sexual battery, and sexual coercion. All such acts of sexual violence are forms of sexual harassment covered under Title IX" (DOE 2011a, 1–2). Stating three times in short succession the relationship between sexual violence, sexual harassment, and sex discrimination marks this discourse as important. And, indeed, in a footnote, the 2011 DCL calls itself a "significant guidance document" (DOE 2011a, 1). In conjunction with the use of the term "explains" in the prior quote, the letter does appear to express a new (or updated) understanding of sexual violence within Title IX.

But the DCL also is clear that the letter is only providing *more* guidance on these issues to college campuses, grounding itself in its prior communications and also implying that this is not a new issue for the OCR, nor for educational institutions. In explaining this point, the letter points to the OCR's *Revised Sexual Harassment Guidance* (DOE 2001). The 2011 DCL (DOE 2011a, 2) purportedly only "supplements" this 2001 document because sexual harassment and sexual violence "requirements are discussed in detail" in the 2001 guidance. In other words—the 2011 DCL should be read as only providing additional guidance and practical examples to existing OCR regulations. This language suggests that sexual violence has been an element of concern for the OCR and Title IX all along, and the 2011 DCL is only being done to provide additional guidance and recommendations in this area. Indeed, the 2011 DCL specifies that sexual harassment and sexual violence should be addressed by the same set of policies and procedures in an institution: "OCR therefore recommends that a recipient's nondiscrimination policy state that prohibited sex discrimination covers sexual harassment, including sexual violence, and that the policy include examples of the types of conduct that it covers" (DOE 2011a, 7). In saying this, the OCR reinforces its construction of sexual violence within sexual harassment, and "recommends" that universities model this construction explicitly within their Title IX policies, if they have not already done so.

There is a disjunction here in the discourse for the OCR. The repetiveness of the construction of sexual violence under the umbrella of sexual harassment and sex discrimination appears to mark it as not only significant but also transformative. And that is how many institutional actors have responded to the 2011 DCL—as a document that transforms how educational institutions should respond to sexual violence. In the public discussion of the 2011 DCL when it was first distributed, the portrayal by federal actors was absolutely about the presentation of something new. In a press release on April 4, 2011, Vice President Joseph Biden and Secretary of Education Arne Duncan described the 2011 DCL as "the first specifically advising schools, colleges and universities that their responsibilities under Title IX include protecting students from sexual violence" (DOE 2011b, para. 2). However, in making this argument in the 2011 DCL, the OCR is forced to face its own history of communication about Title IX. In doing so, the OCR had to assess the extent to which sexual violence has been an element of concern all along, an analysis I present in the next section.

The 2001 and 1997 Guidances

Directly referenced in the 2011 DCL is the 2001 guidance, which is, in fact, a revision of the 1997 guidance. As the 2001 guidance says in its preamble, "We revised the [1997] guidance in *limited respects* in light of subsequent Supreme Court cases relating to sexual harassment in schools" (DOE 2001, i; emphasis added). Thus, if the 2001 document only involved limited revisions to the 1997 guidance, and the 2011 DCL only supplemented the 2001 document, there should be a clear connection in the language of both sexual harassment and sexual violence in the 1997 and 2001 guidances and the 2011 DCL. Failure to find peer-on-peer sexual violence within these documents cached within sexual harassment policy and procedures, however, would speak to the novelty of the 2011 DCL's discourse.

Both prior guidances indicate that the 2011 DCL is both new and not new, which perhaps explains its disjunctive language. The 1997 guidance, in particular, uses very different language from the 2011 DCL when it comes to both sexual harassment and sexual violence, although the roots of the 2011 DCL are present. For the 1997 guidance, the focus is strictly on sexual harassment, which it divides into two forms: quid pro quo and "hostile environment sexual harassment," the latter of which is the legal mechanism by which both sexual harassment and sexual violence become elements of Title IX. Hostile environment sexual harassment is defined in the 1997 guidance as:

> Sexually harassing conduct (which can include unwelcome sexual advances, requests for sexual favors, and other verbal, nonverbal, or physical conduct of a sexual nature) by an employee, by another student, or by a third party that is sufficiently severe, persistent, or per-

vasive to limit a student's ability to participate in or benefit from an education program or activity, or to create a hostile or abusive educational environment. (DOE 1997, para. 2)

Contained in this definition is the phrase "physical conduct of a sexual nature," a euphemism for sexual violence and as explicit as the document gets definitionally. Also present is the recognition that the harasser (the preferred term in the 2011 DCL) may be another student—an issue of extreme importance in the 2011 DCL. The 1997 guidance further acknowledges that sexual harassment can be from the same sex, and can include "harassing conduct of a sexual nature" against lesbian, gay, bisexual, and transgender (LGBT) individuals, as long as it is severe, persistent, and pervasive (DOE 1997, para. 9). The 1997 guidance also defines gender-based harassment, which it characterizes as "acts of verbal, nonverbal, or physical aggression, intimidation, or hostility based on sex, but not involving conduct of a sexual nature" (para. 10) that is directed at individuals because of their sex. Why gender-based harassment could not include "physical conduct of a sexual nature" is unclear, as research suggests that sexual violence is a type of heteronormative attack, except for the understanding that the OCR's response to sexual harassment has been, from the beginning, heterosexist (Carrigan Wooten 2016).

Two key issues arise for the 1997 guidance. First, it discusses the question of "welcomeness" of the conduct. The authors of the guidance recognize that a person may go along with harassment to avoid a negative outcome. This contextualization of victims' behaviors is important because, as Estrich (1991) explained before the guidance was published, unwelcomeness is a "doctrinal stepchild of the rape standards of consent and resistance" (27) and, as such, puts the burden on victims to explain their conduct. Second, the 1997 guidance considers severe, persistent, and pervasive to be requirements for conduct to be considered sexually harassing, though it concludes— again, in alignment with the 2011 DCL—that a single severe incident such as a rape can signify a sexually hostile environment.

For the 1997 guidance, the concern is predominantly language, especially language as a form of conduct that is harassing. Most of the examples within the document reflect this focus on language. But conduct—or in this case, "conduct of a sexual nature"—is not ignored, with "sexual advances" discussed along with touch and sex. The body of the document does not discuss sexual assault. The word "rape" itself only appears in the footnotes, and then only in reference to the first Supreme Court ruling on Title VII and sexual harassment in which the justices endorsed the legal construct of hostile environment sexual harassment, *Meritor Savings Bank v. Vinson* (1986). In this case, the plaintiff claimed her supervisor subjected her to a hostile environment by, in part, making sexual demands on her and raping her on more than one occasion. Thus, the 1997 guidance includes rape in its description of the coverage of *Meritor*:

> Footnote 6; See e.g. . . . . *Meritor Savings Bank FSB v. Vinson*, 477 U.S. 57, 60–61 (1986) (demands for sexual favors, sexual advances, fondling, indecent exposure, sexual intercourse, rape sufficient to raise hostile environment claim under Title VII). (DOE 1997, 12047)

Note that for the courts, the legality of the conduct and whether it constituted sexual harassment was directly related to its characteristics in terms of hostile environment, namely, whether it met the severity or pervasiveness test (Bartels 1987).

"Sexual assault" as a construct fares a little better in the 1997 guidance. Though it is strikingly absent in the discussion of the definition of sexual harassment or in examples of sexual harassment, it does appear in the procedural section, affecting how schools should respond to claims, handle mediation, or discuss case outcomes. For instance, in a section on responding to claims, the 1997 guidance says:

> It may be appropriate for a school to take interim measures during the investigation of a complaint. For instance, if a student alleges that he or she has been sexually assaulted by another student, the school may decide to immediately place the students in separate classes or in different housing arrangements on a campus, pending the results of the school's investigation. (DOE 1997)

Later, in a discussion of strategies to handle grievances, the document says: "In some cases, such as alleged sexual assaults, mediation will not be appropriate even on a voluntary basis." A third notation, hidden deep within footnote 84, which is about schools' Family Educational Rights and Privacy Act (FERPA) responsibilities for releasing information to complainants about disciplinary action imposed on a student found guilty, does allow for the release of this information if "(2) the harassment involves a crime of violence or a sex offense in a postsecondary institution."

Collectively, the 1997 guidance fails to place peer-on-peer sexual violence under the umbrella of sexual harassment either definitionally or explicitly in the way that the 2011 DCL does, but in discussing responses to sexual harassment, the document clearly gives schools notice that such incidents will require institutional responses. The disconnect between absent policy language and present procedural expectations downplays the importance of sexual violence prevention and response for institutional actors charged with enacting Title IX. Though the procedural discussion and foot-notes mention sexual violence, nowhere in the document is the abject con-nection between the concepts specified.

So how was the 1997 guidance changed in 2001 in relation to the issue of sexual violence? Actually, sexual violence is covered in almost exactly the same muted way in the 2001 guidance, making it a truly "limited" revision of the 1997 guidance on this definitional issue. First, "rape" appears in the 2001 guidance only twice—both of them in footnotes, and both for issues at least marginally covered in 1997 (citing *Meritor* again, and in terms of pro-cedural responses to housing changes for victims of rape as an interim mea-sure). The term "violence" occurs twice also, both in response to concerns about FERPA and Title IX conflicts. Finally, the explicit term "sexual as-sault" appears only in procedural discussions of classroom or living arrange-ment changes and in terms of mediation. In other words, the 2001 guidance does not open up its definition of sexual harassment in ways that would guide a university to understand it needed to directly address sexual assault under Title IX. However, both of these guidances use explicit examples of sexual violence to detail the OCR's recommended responses to such vio-lence. So, without making the discursive connection that is so clear in the 2011 DCL, both of these documents included a procedural connection that gave universities fair warning.

What the 2001 guidance does is create a useful definition of sexual ha-rassment early in the document (DOE 2001, 2), a definition that moves us away from types of sexual harassment (quid pro quo and hostile environ-ment), although it retains the use of euphemisms in its incorporation of sexual violence:

> Sexual harassment is unwelcome conduct of a sexual nature. Sexual harassment can include unwelcome sexual advances, requests for sexual favors, and other verbal, nonverbal, or *physical conduct of a sexual nature*. (DOE 2001, 2; emphasis added)

This euphemism of "physical conduct of a sexual nature" is as close as both of the guidances get to acknowledging that sexual violence is a form of sex-ual harassment. Yet there is some progress in 2001: this definition, unlike the 1997 guidance, is linked via footnote to the *Meritor* cite, which includes rape as conduct that can create a hostile environment. In doing so, the definition of sexual harassment itself creates an opening, albeit a vague one using a Title VII case, for universities to understand expectations that they address sexual assault under their sexual harassment policies.

Other Documents on the Journey to the 2011 DCL

It is important to keep in mind that the issue of sexual assault on campus was well-known before the publication of the 2011 DCL, and was even recognized by the OCR before 2001. For instance, in the 2000 DCL in "Reminder of Responsibilities under Section 504 of the Rehabilitation Act of 1973 and Title II of the Americans with Disabilities Act," the OCR noted that disability harassment included "sexual and physical assault" (DOE 2000, 1). Nowhere in this 2000 DCL, however, did the OCR link Title II to Title IX. In addition, a 2002 National Institute of Justice report (followed in 2005 by a widely publicized summary of this report) by Karjane, Fisher, and Cullen (2002) discussed the prevalence of campus sexual violence and universities' responses. This report, however, failed to turn to Title IX in its recommendation section as it laid out policy and procedure "best practices," hinting at the continuing disconnect between Title IX and campus sexual assault response in 2005. Title IX, as a mechanism to address campus sexual assault, was also not on the radar in the Handbook for Campus Safety and Security Reporting (Westat and Mann 2011), which was published just two months before the 2011 DCL and discussed Clery Act expectations for reporting sexual assault, responding to victims, and adjudicating offenses. It is telling that this document did not identify Title IX as a related and relevant federal law that could or should be used to address campus sexual assault in 2011.

Most of the OCR Title IX-related DCLs published between 2001 and 2011 that I reviewed also did not address the issue of sexual violence. These DCL documents include a 2004 letter regarding Title IX grievance procedures; a 2006 letter that reasserts the importance of sexual harassment response; a 2007 letter celebrating Title IX history and potential, including its "substantial focus to the issue of sexual harassment in schools" (DOE 2007, para. 8); and a 2010 letter on bullying as it relates to Title IX. There is one notable exception, however; in 2008, the OCR released *Sexual Harassment: It's not Academic* (DOE 2008), the fourth version of this document (Henrick 2013). There are two places within this document where the issue of sexual violence is addressed. In a section titled "What if the Sexual Conduct Is Criminal in Nature?" the authors state: "Sexual harassment includes conduct that is criminal in nature, such as rape, sexual assault, dating violence, and sexually motivated stalking" (DOE 2008, 4), and note that if schools report the incidents to the police, they are still obligated to follow Title IX policies. Later, the document illustrates the concept of severity as it relates to hostile environment by using the example of a high school student sexually assaulting a fellow student in a classroom (DOE 2008, 7). However, it should be noted that severity of sexual violence is not a given; the wording in court decisions (including Title VII decisions that often serve as guidance for Title IX decisions; see 2011 DCL, footnote 10; DOE 2011a, 3) remains frustratingly ambiguous regarding the issue of severity in cases of sexual violence, including the use of qualifiers such as "deemed sufficient," "can create," or "may be enough" (see, e.g., *Jennings v. University of North Carolina*; *Berry v. Chicago Transit Authority*; and *Turner v. Saloon Ltd.*, respectively). Nevertheless, the 2008 example makes clear that sexual assault affects the victim's ability to participate in the educational environment, as she is "afraid of attending any classes or coming into contact with the harasser" (DOE 2008, 7).

While these two components of the 2008 document appear to serve as a bridge between the OCR's discussion of sexual violence in the 1997 and 2001 guidances and the 2011 DCL, there are two problems with this perception. First, the 2008 document continues the tradition of the guidances and avoids explicit inclusion of sexual violence within its definition of sexual harassment. Specifically, in the 2008 document, sexual harassment is defined as conduct that is: "(1) sexual in nature; (2) unwelcome; and (3) denies or limits a student's ability to participate in or benefit from a school's education program" (DOE 2008, 3). Though sexual violence has these characteristics, it is notably absent from the examples of sexual conduct provided to illustrate these elements (3). The closest item on the list is the phrase "touching of a sexual nature," which is woefully inappropriate in representing sexual violence. Instead, the document positions sexual violence as a criminal act in a separate section, linking it to behaviors such as dating violence. Though this section explicitly ties sexual harassment to sexual violence, its separation from the definitional elements of the document belies that connection. Second, the rest of the document, with the exception noted earlier, uses the term harassment. As the authors of the guidance take institutional actors through their obligations under Title IX, there is little further recognition that violent victimization may have occurred, with its resultant trauma and physical harm. In contrast, the terminology used in the 2011 DCL is most frequently "sexual harassment and violence," which serves to reinforce the relationship between the two constructs while it constructs sexual violence as a distinctive concern under Title IX.

So, How Did the 2011 DCL Come to Be?

In several of the chapters in *The Crisis of Campus Sexual Violence: Critical Perspectives on Prevention and Response*, edited by Carrigan Wooten and Mitchell (2016), the authors begin from the assumption that the 2011 DCL began campuses' work on sexual violence. I do not disagree. While I have argued in this chapter that earlier OCR Title IX communications implicitly incorporated sexual violence, explicit OCR guidance was lacking until the 2011 DCL, which then set in motion the policy and procedural changes that we discuss in this volume. As stated in the OCR Fact Sheet entitled "Sexual Violence: Background, Summary and Fast Facts" that was released contemporaneously with the 2011 DCL, the "ED is issuing the DCL to *explain* that the requirements of Title IX cover sexual violence and to *remind* schools of their responsibilities to take immediate and effective steps to respond to sexual violence in accordance with the requirements of Title IX" (DOE 2011c, 1; emphasis added). In "explaining" and "reminding" campus authorities, the 2011 DCL both claims its own history recognizing sexual violence within sexual harassment and validates the perception that this is also, in fact, something new. But, that still leaves us with the question, why did the OCR take this vital step in 2011? While my analysis of the OCR documents cannot answer this question, there are other scholars and pundits who have pointed to a confluence of factors.

The earliest of these factors may simply be the growing case law related to campus sexual violence that started in the late 1990s but was "settled law" by the mid-2000s (Lewis, Schuster, and Sokolow 2010). The National Center for Higher Education Risk Management (NCHERM; Lewis, Schuster, and Sokolow 2010) predicted that Title IX would be used to address sexual violence in their report to higher education institutions in 2000—eleven years before the 2011 DCL. In 2010, they repeated this argument and demonstrated that within the courts, at least, Title IX was being used in tort cases to assess institutional liability, as in *Simpson; Gilmore v. University of Colorado Boulder.* Other insiders fully expected that Title IX would or should be used to address sexual violence. Wies (2015), speaking from the perspective of an advocate, reflected on a variety of conversations she had with peers about the use of the "deliberate indifference" expectation of Title IX to hold universities accountable in sexual violence cases well before the 2011 DCL. So, within the campus security domain and the direct service provider domain, there was the understanding even before the 2011 DCL that case law was dictating that universities should respond to sexual violence using Title IX.

In addition, a political shift occurred in 2009, when President Barack Obama took office. Within a year of taking office, President Obama's appointee, Education Secretary Arne Duncan began referencing the DOE's response to school sexual violence in remarks he made before various public entities, such as his speech to the National Urban League in 2010. He claimed that "our Office for Civil Rights has itself undergone a transformation. We have renewed its focus on enforcing civil rights laws and advancing equity" (DOE 2010). Efforts by Ali to guide her staff in the development of the 2011 DCL reflected this new political reality.

At the same time, others were also putting forward legislative and institutional changes, including the OCR itself. In November 2010, Representative Tom Perriello proposed the Campus Sexual Assault Violence Elimination Act (SaVE) to amend the Clery Act. Though the SaVE Act was not passed until 2013, publicity about the 2010 proposal added to the growing political climate urging change (see Chapter 8 by Hughes Miller and Cook for a discussion of the Campus SaVE Act). And the OCR itself pointed to the DOE's 2010 settlements with Notre Dame and Eastern Michigan as models "for how colleges, universities, and the department [will] deal with allegations of campus sexual assault" (Lombardi 2010, para. 6). In these settlements, the DOE fined the two institutions for violations under the Clery Act, and also required them to make changes in their Title IX processes to better address sexual violence. In a December 2010 interview with the Center for Public Integrity, Ali noted that these were "big-picture reform(s)" (Lombardi 2010, para. 14) that would guide the next OCR guidance—what was to become the 2011 DCL.

Finally, within this political realm was also a growing loudness about the prevalence of sexual violence on college campuses. The 2011 DCL itself justifies its focus on sexual violence using statistics on the rates of rape and sexual assault from studies done between 2007 and 2010, saying: "The statistics on sexual violence are both deeply troubling and a call to action for the nation" (DOE 2011a, 2). The phrase "a call to action" implies an immediacy to the concern that ignores the long history of sexual violence on college campuses. But it also acknowledges contemporary research as a justification for the actions required by the 2011 DCL. The Center for Public Integrity's report in 2010, which blatantly called out universities for failing to respond to sexual assault under their Title IX guidelines, has been given significant credit for both sparking and elevating the voices demanding change. Laura Dunn (2014), whose story was one of those profiled in the center's report, argued that such high-profile publicity challenged the status quo. The six-part report, which culminated in a National Public Radio (NPR) piece, was presented in a Senate Judiciary Subcommittee Hearing in September 2010.

Together, these legal, political, and cultural factors created a milieu within which the OCR acted. Though I have argued here that the inclusion of sexual violence under Title IX was not new to the OCR's understanding of sexual harassment, the impetus to articulate this relationship and provide recommendations on implementation for the "unique" topic of sexual violence in the 2011 DCL does illustrate the political and cultural nature of this document.

Conclusion

The framework to address campus sexual violence using Title IX has been present since at least 1997 in OCR communications with universities. The discursive construction of sexual violence as a form of sex discrimination has been present even longer, especially if one considers case law related to Title VII (e.g., *Meritor*) that has direct correlations to Title IX. Educational pundits like NCHERM also have described and predicted this framework relying on case law and OCR communications well before the 2011 DCL. Nevertheless, it is clear that little emphasis or guidance was given to campuses by the OCR on *how* to respond to sexual violence, or even clear instructions *to* respond to sexual violence, until the 2011 DCL.

The articulation of campus responsibilities to address sexual violence under Title IX was made explicit in the 2011 DCL and has been reiterated since in even more detail, such as in the April 2014 Q&A document (DOE 2014). The 2014 Q&A discursively expands the definition of sexual violence to include sexual abuse and coercion and posits a direct relationship between sexual violence and sex discrimination: "All such acts of sexual violence are forms of sex discrimination prohibited by Title IX" (DOE 2014, 1), eliminating the need to retain the phrase "sexual harassment and violence" used in the 2011 DCL. This recent discursive shift may presage a potential bifurcation in the OCR's presentation of sexual harassment and sexual violence, with sexual violence reserved primarily for student-on-student conduct. Note, for instance, the terminology invoked in the 2014 discussion of school employee (as opposed to peer) sexual harassment:

> Although this document and the DCL focus on student-on-student sexual violence, Title IX also protects students from other forms of sexual harassment (including sexual violence and sexual abuse), such as sexual harassment carried out by school employees. . . . Sexual harassment by school employees can include unwelcome sexual advances; requests for sexual favors; and other verbal, nonverbal, or physical conduct of a sexual nature, including but not limited to sexual activity. (DOE 2014, 3)

In talking about Title IX violations by school employees, there may be resistance to referencing sexual violence, as this return to euphemisms illustrates.

Henrick (2013, 60) claims that the 2011 DCL "impose[s] new legal obligations" on institutions. While his concern relates to policy changes that affect student defendants, his point is overstated, according to my analysis. The 2011 DCL "explained" its own prior constructions of sexual violence that, while muted and nondefinitional, explicitly existed prior to 2011. This document has certainly been interpreted as a shift in OCR policy by many institutions, but that also is a problematic claim. Indeed, once sexual harassment was defined as an element of sex discrimination, the stage was set for further articulation of students' experiences. And because Title IX is civil rights legislation, it provides an opportunity to express "the desire of victims and their movements to end these forms of violence, not simply through individualized punishment but by securing collective justice" (Brodsky and Deutsch 2015, 144). Title IX adds a powerful tool to address this widespread and significant problem.

REFERENCES

Association of Governing Boards of Universities and Colleges. 2015. History and context of sexual misconduct. Available at http://agb.org/sites/default/files/agb-statements /statement_2015_sexual_misconduct.pdf.

Bartels, V. T. 1987. *Meritor Savings Bank v. Vinson:* The Supreme Court's recognition of the hostile environment in sexual harassment claims. *Akron Law Review* 23 (3): 575–589.

Berry v. Chicago Transit Authority. 2010. 618 F.3d 688.

Brodsky, A., and E. Deutsch. 2015. The promise of Title IX: Sexual violence and the law. *Dissent* 62 (4): 135–144.

Carrigan Wooten, S. 2016. Heterosexist discourses: How feminist theory shaped campus sexual violence policy. In *The crisis of campus sexual violence: Critical perspectives on prevention and response,* ed. S. Carrigan Wooten and R. W. Mitchell, 33–51. New York: Routledge.

Carrigan Wooten, S., and R. W. Mitchell, eds. 2016. *The crisis of campus sexual violence: Critical perspectives on prevention and response.* New York: Routledge.

Center for Public Integrity. 2010. *Sexual assault on campus.* Available at http://www .publicintegrity.org/accountability/education/sexual-assault-campus.

Davis v. Monroe County Board of Education. 1999. 526 U.S. 629.

Department of Education, Office for Civil Rights (DOE, OCR). 1997. *Sexual harassment guidance 1997.* Available at http://www2.ed.gov/about/offices/list/ocr/docs/sexhar01 .html.

———. 1998. *Title IX and sex discrimination.* Available at http://www2.ed.gov/about /offices/list/ocr/docs/tix_dis.html.

———. 2000. *Prohibited disability harassment.* Available at http://www2.ed.gov/about /offices/list/ocr/docs/disabharassltr.html.

———. 2001. *Revised sexual harassment guidance: Harassment of students by school employees, other students, or third parties.* Available at https://www.atixa.org/wordpress /wp-content/uploads/2012/01/OCR-2001-Revised-Sexual-Harassment-Guidance-Title -IX.pdf.

———. 2007. *Dear Colleague Letter.* Available at http://www2.ed.gov/about/offices/list/ocr /letters/colleague-20070622.html.

———. 2008. *Sexual harassment: It's not academic.* Available at http://www2.ed.gov/about /offices/list/ocr/docs/ocrshpam.html.

———. 2010. *Secretary Arne Duncan's remarks at the National Urban League Centennial Conference.* Available at http://www.ed.gov/news/speeches/secretary-arne-duncans -remarks-national-urban-league-centennial-conference.

———. 2011a. *Dear Colleague.* Available at http://www2.ed.gov/about/offices/list/ocr /letters/colleague-201104.pdf.

———. 2011b. *Vice President Biden announces new administration effort to help nation's schools address sexual violence.* Available at http://www.ed.gov/news/press-releases/vice -president-biden-announces-new-administration-effort-help-nations-schools-address -sexual-violence.

———. 2011c. *Sexual violence: Background, summary and fast facts.* Available at https:// www.whitehouse.gov/sites/default/files/fact_sheet_sexual_violence.pdf.

———. 2014. *Questions and answers on Title IX and sexual violence.* Available at http:// www2.ed.gov/about/offices/list/ocr/docs/qa-201404-title-ix.pdf.

Department of Labor. 1972. *Title IX, Education Amendments of 1972* (Title 20 U.S.C. Sections 1681–1688). Available at http://www.dol.gov/oasam/regs/statutes/titleix.htm.

Dunn, L. L. 2014. Addressing sexual violence in higher education: Ensuring compliance with the Clery Act, Title IX and VAWA. *Georgetown Journal of Gender and the Law* 15: 563–584.

Estrich, S. 1991. Sex at work. *Stanford Law Review* 43: 813.

Franklin v. Gwinnett Public Schools. 1992. 503 U.S. 60.

Henrick, S. 2013. A hostile environment for student defendants: Title IX and sexual assault on college campuses. *Northern Kentucky Law Review* 40 (1): 49–92.

Hsieh, H-F., and S. E. Shannon. 2005. Three approaches to qualitative content analysis. *Qualitative Health Research* 15 (9): 1277–1288.

Jennings v. University of North Carolina. 2007. 444 F.3d 255.

Jonson-Reid, M., J. L. Lauritsen, T. Edmond, and F. D. Schneider. 2016. Public policy and prevention of violence against women. In *Prevention, policy and public health*, ed. A. A. Eyler, J. F. Chriqui, S. Moreland-Russell, and R. C. Brownson, 229–248. New York: Oxford.

Karjane, H. K., B. S. Fisher, and F. T. Cullen. 2002. *Campus sexual assault: How America's institutions of higher education respond* (Final Report, NIJ Grant No. 1999-WA-VX-0008). Newton, MA: Education Development Center.

Lewis, W. S., S. K. Schuster, and B. A. Sokolow. 2010. *Gamechangers: Reshaping campus sexual misconduct through litigation*. The NCHERM 10th Anniversary Whitepaper, 2000–2010. Available at http://students.msstate.edu/clic/pdf/2010_NCHERM _Whitepaper_Gamechangers.pdf.

Lisa Simpson; Anne Gilmore v. University of Colorado Boulder. 2007. No. 06-1184, No. 07-1182; 2007 U.S. App. LEXIS 21478. U.S. Ct. of Appeals, 10th Circuit.

Lombardi, K. 2010. *Education Department touts settlement as "model" for campus sex assault policies: Feds reach agreement with Notre Dame College in Ohio and Eastern Michigan University*. Available at http://www.publicintegrity.org/2010/12/08/2266 /education-department-touts-settlement-model-campus-sex-assault-policies.

MacKinnon, C. A. 1979. *Sexual harassment of working women: A case of sex discrimination*. New Haven, CT: Yale University Press.

Meritor Savings Bank v. Vinson. 1986. 477 U.S. 57.

Simon, A. E. 2003. *Alexander v. Yale University*: An informal history. In *Directions in sexual harassment law*, ed. C. A. MacKinnon and R. B. Siegel, 51–59. New Haven, CT: Yale University Press.

Turner v. Saloon Ltd. 2010. 595 F.3d 679.

Westat, D. W., and J. L. Mann. 2011. *The handbook for campus safety and security reporting*. Washington, DC: U.S. Department of Education, Office of Postsecondary Education.

Wies, J. R. 2015. Title IX and the state of campus sexual violence in the United States: Power, policy, and local bodies. *Human Organization* 74 (3): 276–286. Available at http://dx.doi.org/10.17730/0018-7259-74.3.276.

8

The Reauthorized Violence Against Women Act

The Campus SaVE Act and Its Mandates

MICHELLE HUGHES MILLER
AND SARAH L. COOK

Introduction

On January 22, 2014, President Barack Obama, with longtime advocate Vice President Joseph Biden, launched the White House Task Force to Protect Students from Sexual Assault (White House n.d.). In doing so, he brought the nation's attention to the long-ignored problem of sexual assault on college campuses. But earlier, by signing the Violence Against Women Reauthorization Act of 2013, he brought the problem into sharp focus for the nation's higher education community. Of great interest was section 304 of Title III, the "Campus Sexual Assault, Domestic Violence, Dating Violence, Stalking, Education and Prevention Act," commonly referred to as the Campus SaVE Act (Campus SaVE Act 2016). The intent of Campus SaVE—to make campuses safer through Sexual Assault Violence Elimination—is universally embraced. Sexual violence on campus disrupts the lives of many students and negatively affects an academic community (Murray et al. 2016). It exacts a cascading psychological, social, and economic toll that extends from victims and perpetrators to their peers, families, and communities. This chapter places the Campus SaVE Act in historical and political context, and describes its potential impact on institutions of higher education (IHE) and their students. We conclude by discussing the limits of the legislation and its potential to improve campus environments.

Generally, the Campus SaVE Act utilizes a prevention and awareness framework (Engle 2015) to mandate strategies designed to improve universities' responses to sexual violence. IHE are required to publish annual security reports (ASRs) in which they outline their detailed activities related to specific campus crimes. According to the student activist organization End Rape on Campus (n.d.), the Campus SaVE Act amends the Clery Act in three general ways: (1) by increasing transparency of campus violence through expanded reporting obligations for universities, (2) by clarifying institutional accountability in responding to incidents of violence, and (3) by mandating that institutions provide prevention and awareness programming. More important, the tone of the Campus SaVE Act is different than its predecessors because it "was a legislative attempt to lend clarity to the legal maelstrom confronting college administrators" (Engle 2015, 12) by clarifying and expanding some Clery Act requirements, mandating some Title IX expectations contained in the 2011 Dear Colleague Letter (DCL; Department of Education [DOE] 2011), and emphasizing the interconnectedness among federal agencies in addressing campus violence, particularly sexual violence. In this chapter, we discuss briefly the history of the Violence Against Women Act (VAWA) before detailing the elements of the Campus SaVE Act, including its legislative and activist origins, and focusing specifically on how and why Campus SaVE amends the Clery Act.

The Violence Against Women Act and Its Reauthorizations

The Violence Against Women Act of 1994 essentially codified and addressed what feminists, activists, victim advocates, and legislators had been arguing for decades—that existing laws failed to protect women from violence. For the first time, federal legislation acknowledged women's experiences of sexual assault and interpersonal violence, and in doing so, validated the efforts of various national advocacy groups such as the NOW Legal Defense and Education Fund and the National Task Force to End Sexual and Domestic Violence. The law originally passed during the 103rd Congress (1993–1994). Then senator Joseph Biden and then representative Barbara Boxer tapped widespread national support for the law from a coalition of diverse organizations to generate overwhelming bipartisan support. The result was legislation that established the Office of Violence Against Women within the Department of Justice, revised legal processes in criminal investigations and prosecutions, and made funds available for various activities including victim services, law enforcement training, prevention, and research.

VAWA required continuing legislative reauthorization. In 2000, Congress reauthorized VAWA through the Victims of Trafficking and Violence Prevention Act. This reauthorization filled many holes in the original VAWA, including enhancing protections for marginalized women such as immigrants (who were granted relief in the form of visas for battered women), the elderly, and disabled women. Specific programs were also expanded, including prevention programming and transitional housing. The 2000 reauthorization also created protections for victims of stalking and sex trafficking. Five years later, the Violence Against Women and Department of Justice Reauthorization Act of 2005 was passed. This law continued to broaden the scope of the effort, emphasizing programs for American Indian victims and trafficked nonimmigrants. Its funding opportunities also highlighted explicit collaborations with other public entities such as public health and law enforcement, and across communities and individuals.

In 2011, the 2000 and 2005 VAWA reauthorizations expired, but the programs funded by VAWA fortunately continued to receive funds through 2013. Both chambers of the 112th Congress passed a reauthorization bill, but conservative members of Congress rejected plans to expand VAWA funding to support undocumented immigrant and LGBT (lesbian, gay, bisexual, and transgender) rape victims, and the two chambers could not agree on a suitable compromise. Even efforts to pass VAWA without these protections failed, leaving VAWA—its programs and its funding—in doubt for the first time.

Then, public advocacy, as it did in 1994, reenergized the VAWA debate. Backlash from the prior year's failure led the 113th Congress to move quickly. Not only was VAWA 2013 reauthorized until 2018 but it also incorporated the nondiscrimination provision that had led to nonpassage in the prior Congress. Also on the positive side, the reauthorization prioritized funding for sexual assault prevention and programming, including the rape kit backlog. Unfortunately, the goodwill of Congress to reauthorize VAWA did not extend to its level of funding, which was reduced for most of the grant programs. But most important for our purposes in this chapter, the 2013 reauthorized VAWA also included the Campus SaVE Act in Title III.

The Historical Motivation behind Campus SaVE

Now federal law, the Campus SaVE Act (as Title III, section 304 of VAWA 2013; Campus SAVE Act n.d.) amended the Higher Education Act of 1965 (HEA) and affects institutions operating under Title IV of the HEA, which essentially includes all institutions that receive federal financial assistance for students. Technically, Campus SaVE amends the portion of the HEA, section 485(f), which is called the Jeanne Clery Disclosure of Campus Security Policy and Campus Crime Statistics Act (aka the Clery Act). Problems with institutional compliance with the Clery Act and other limitations of the act—along with significant student activism around reducing sexual violence on college campuses, discussed elsewhere in this volume (see Chapter 16 by Ava Blustein)—motivated Congress and advocates to develop Campus SaVE. Yet it is important to understand what the Clery Act is and why it was developed because its history illuminates why Campus SaVE focuses on *reporting* incidents of crimes on campus and related policies, procedures, and prevention measures.

Jeanne Clery was a nineteen-year-old Lehigh University student who was raped and murdered by another student, Josoph Henry, in 1986. Henry was convicted and sentenced to death by electric chair. Clery's parents sued the university in civil court, claiming that if they had known about the prevalence of violent crimes at Lehigh, they would not have allowed their daughter to enroll. As Mr. Clery stated in 1987, "If you're not warned," he asked, "how can you take precautions as a young adult?" (Kraft 1987, para. 6). They won a $2 million judgment, and in 1987, founded the nonprofit Clery Center for Security on Campus, which has become a highly respected advocacy and training organization (Clery Center 2016). The Clerys were instrumental in the passage of the Crime Awareness and Campus Security Act of 1990, which requires institutions to provide current students and staff (and prospective students and staff, if requested) with a report of basic crime statistics and security policies. As its formal name implies, the original law focuses heavily on increasing awareness and making campuses safer through reporting campus crime information. This perspective continues to drive efforts to improve campus crime reporting, as witnessed in the DOE's 2016 handbook: "Choosing a postsecondary institution is a major decision for students and their families. Along with academic, financial, and geographic considerations, the issue of campus safety is a vital concern" (DOE 2016, 1–1).

Despite the Clerys' victories in civil court and in Congress in the passing of the Clery Act itself, the Henry criminal case continued. In 2002, a U.S. district judge vacated Henry's death sentence due to faulty jury instructions, and Henry is now serving life without parole (Grossman and Coombe 2002). Lehigh University's local newspaper opined at the time that as the criminal case closed, campuses were safer due to the Clerys' efforts. This claim is difficult to assess, however, as the original legislation contained no mechanisms to prevent crime on campus.

Historical Failures in Compliance with the Clery Act

Unfortunately, there is reason to doubt that the Clery Act, through its reporting obligations, has made campuses safer or improved prospective students' knowledge about their future campuses because many institutions historically have not complied. One of the most extreme cases of noncompliance is the 2006 cover-up by administrators of Eastern Michigan University, after they failed to follow Clery reporting and notification requirements after student Orange Taylor III raped and murdered fellow student Laura Dickinson (ABC News 2007). The administration's failure to notify the campus community of the crime left Dickinson's parents and the rest of the Eastern Michigan student body unaware of the murder because campus authorities chose instead to report that Dickinson died of natural causes. This extreme breach of procedure resulted in $350,000 in Clery Act fines, the largest fines to date (Schroeder 2014), and a successful civil suit by Dickinson's parents against Eastern Michigan University (Larcom 2008).

When Jerry Sandusky, assistant football coach at Pennsylvania State University, was indicted with fifty-two counts of child molestation in 2011 (for which he was convicted of forty-five counts of child sex abuse in 2012), the failure of university officials to follow Clery and report known incidents that occurred on their campus became an open question for the general public and the DOE. This resulted in indictments of several university administrators and a review of the university's Clery procedures. At Penn State, the state's flagship institution, the administration was described as treating the football program as a separate entity with respect to compliance with Clery and nearly any other federal law related to higher education (Freeh Sporkin and Sullivan 2012). An investigation by Louis Freeh, former CIA director, severely criticized the university for placing the football program above any code—regulatory, ethical, and even moral. The institution's noncompliance with Clery and state law related to the protection of minors has been argued as allowing the continued sexual abuse of boys and young men by former assistant football coach Sandusky for more than a decade (Lipka 2012). But resolution of the case seems stalled; at the time of this writing, DOE reviewers have yet to release their Clery findings and the indicted administrators continue to argue their ignorance of the abuse in court.

Beyond these egregious examples, underreporting of violent offenses by universities is widespread. VAWA includes amendments to the Clery Act; these changes now require IHE to disclose statistics, policies, and programs related to dating violence, domestic violence, sexual assault, and stalking. Using data from the 2014 Clery Annual Security Report (ASR), which were based on the expectations of the Campus SaVE Act, the American Association of University Women (AAUW 2015) demonstrated that, even with all of the publicity and pressure regarding the need for accurate campus reporting, 91 percent of the almost 11,000 campuses that submitted ASRs in 2014 reported *zero* rapes, and only about 10 percent of campuses reported *any* incidents of dating violence, domestic violence, or stalking. In other words, despite the prevalence of violence (described in Chapters 2–4 and in numerous academic reports), universities themselves are still largely claiming that they have received *no* reports of any of these forms of violence, a clear indication of serious underreporting (Kincade 2016). A total of 8,836 rapes were reported overall (DOE, *Clery Act Reports*, n.d.).

As a result of the AAUW's findings, on July 1, 2016, a group of thirty-one Democrat and Independent senators wrote to Secretary of Education John King and Attorney General Loretta Lynch, expressing concern "that a significant number of schools may be out of compliance" with Clery reporting obligations (Murray et al. 2016, 2). Their concerns are certainly warranted. But while this underreporting appears to be stark, the reason behind it may be particularly problematic. Research suggests that almost twenty years after the Jeanne Clery Act was passed, some university personnel are still ill-informed about Clery Act requirements. In a sample of 1,803 student affairs professionals at four-year institutions, Colaner (2006) found that only 60 percent of respondents earned a C or better on a knowledge-based questionnaire about the Clery Act, and 16 percent reported they had never even heard of the Clery Act. A later study with campus victim advocates shows that this concern remains prevalent, citing administrative confusion or lack of knowledge about the interrelationships between the various federal regulations (Moylan 2016). If campus authorities are not informed or are confused about Clery or Campus SaVE obligations, and campuses are not reporting any offenses, the ability of prospective students to make informed decisions about the relative risk on their campuses is questionable. So, while students and their parents may access the user-friendly database of Clery ASRs through the DOE's Campus Safety and Security (n.d.) website, they should understand the limits of the reports.

Interestingly, the risk of monetary fines with a maximum of $35,000 per incident (Campus SaVE Act 2016), particularly during a period of shrinking university funding, would seem a powerful deterrent to institutions skirting the law. The potential for civil suits—many of which have been successful, such as the case against Eastern Michigan University noted earlier—is another powerful motivator to comply with the Campus SaVE Act. Most of all, the potential threat of losing access to federal student aid would seem to be an even more important consideration for universities that are putting more of their costs on student tuition dollars. Yet the reality is that this final penalty is "almost never imposed" (Novkov 2016, 597), though final program review determination (FPRD) letters from the DOE to universities under review routinely refer to the risk of such loss due to "serious" noncompliance with Clery responsibilities. In addition, the fines imposed by the Administrative Action and Appeals Service Group (for the DOE) for Clery violations are often reduced substantially during negotiations between the office and the university, with eventual payments averaging about 75 percent of the original fine (Stratford 2014). Stratford notes that fine reductions were agreed to in both the Eastern Michigan and Virginia Tech cases, for instance. The largest motivator of compliance may actually be outside the control of the DOE; Moylan's (2016) interviews with victim advocates suggest that institutional efforts to comply with federal regulations were heavily influenced by administrative fears of a "public relations crisis" if breaches to compliance came to the attention of the media (7).

The Obama administration released data in July 2016 on ten Clery investigations completed in 2015 of large and small colleges and universities, both public and private (DOE, *Clery Act Reports* n.d.). FPRD letters show that the DOE relied on guidance and support to bring universities into compliance, primarily since the DOE has no authority to force colleges to change their reporting policies under Clery (Marshall 2014), along with fines and the threat of the removal of federal student aid. For example, in an investigation of the College of William and Mary, federal authorities determined that the institution had: (1) failed to properly classify and disclose crime statistics, (2) failed to distribute an ASR in accordance with federal regulations, and (3) omitted or made inadequate statements of policy and procedures. The FPRD to the College of William and Mary from the DOE contains the boilerplate language on financial risk for the university:

> Due to the serious nature of these findings, this FPRD is being referred to the Administrative Actions and Appeals Service Group (AAASG) for consideration of possible adverse administrative action. Such action may include a fine and/or the limitation, suspension or termination of the eligibility of the College to participate in the Title IV, HEA programs pursuant to *34 C.F.R. Part 668, Subpart G.* Please note that Clery Act violations are normally addressed by the imposition of a fine. (1–2)

The college's failures risked nearly $44 million in federal aid to 59 percent of William and Mary students, though the college is likely to instead receive a fine of up to $35,000 per infraction.

We highlight William and Mary to illustrate how resistant institutional norms are to change: twenty-five years ago, Katie Koestner, a College of William and Mary student, was featured on the cover of *Time* magazine, thrusting the college into the center of national attention for her allegation of date rape and poor treatment by the college when she reported her experience. In 2016, Koestner told Claire Bowes of the *BBC News* magazine that after she began talking about her victimization in 1991, she was told by others: "You're devaluing my degree, people will only know our college for rape" (Koestner and Bowes 2016, para. 52). This sentiment still appears present today, as the historically black college and university (HBCU) activists in the movement #RapedbyMorehouse attest in their protests of poor treatment and protectionism engaged in by Spelman authorities after a Spelman student claimed she was gang-raped by four Morehouse students (theGrio 2016). This sentiment may be at the root of institutional reluctance to report many campus crimes.

Institutional change has also been assessed empirically. A recent examination of university reporting practices before, during, and after Clery audits by the DOE considered the long-term effect of an audit, particularly when fines were levied (Yung 2015). This study used data from ASRs submitted between 2001 and 2012 from 269 four-year universities of 10,000 or more students with on-campus housing to create an overall crime rate per 100,000 reportable crimes. Then, Yung compared ASRs from thirty-one institutions that had been audited by the DOE for Clery violations on their rates of sexual assault reported before, during, and after their DOE audit. On average, the thirty-one institutions had higher rates of sexual assault than those not under investigation. More important, consistent with the study's hypotheses, numbers of incidents reported in the ASRs rose during an investigation, but fell to preaudit levels when the investigation was closed. Specifically, institutions reported a rate of sexual assault 44 percent higher during investigations than before or after investigations. Notably, rates of other Clery reportable crimes (e.g., robbery) did not vary before, during, or after an investigation, which suggests that these increases are the result of reporting practices, not meaningful changes in victimization. These findings held even for institutions that the DOE had fined. Yung's research suggests that institutional practices may be immediately affected by federal oversight, but the impact is time limited.

It is also important to note that the number of institutions investigated is likely to be lower than the actual number of noncomplying institutions because the only way that institutions come to the DOE's attention are through individual complaints, media reports, an independent audit, or a review selection process by the Federal Bureau of Investigation or the DOE itself (DOE, *Clery Act Reports* n.d.). And, as Clery Act investigations open, creating a significant administrative burden for universities in the process, awareness of noncompliance concerns increases in the media, leading to more complaints and a correspondingly greater burden on the DOE. The result is a high number of investigations, with eighty-seven institutions investigated between 1997 and 2015 (DOE, *Clery Act Reports* n.d.) and an unknown number of additional institutions currently under investigation. Some institutions have even been investigated twice (e.g., Georgetown University in 2004 and 2015).

In summary, there is a great deal of evidence to suggest that many institutions have been less than compliant with Clery Act reporting obligations. But this compliance concern is much broader than just the Clery Act. Research conducted in 2014 by the U.S. Senate Subcommittee on Financial and Contracting Oversight—Majority Staff for Senator Claire McCaskill (D-MO) found:

> Federal law requires every institution that knows or reasonably should have known about sexual violence to conduct an investigation to determine what occurred. More than 40% of schools in the national sample have not conducted a single investigation in the past five years. More than 20% of the nation's largest private institutions

conducted fewer investigations than the number of incidents they reported to the Department of Education, with some institutions reporting as many as seven times more incidents of sexual violence than they have investigated. (1)

This failure of institutions to investigate begins with the failure to accurately and consistently record and then report the incidents of sexual violence and other forms of violence on their campuses. While Campus SaVE is designed to strengthen the Clery Act, a widespread lack of compliance could ultimately undermine the law's intent. Ongoing assessment of Campus SaVE is imperative as we consider its potential to reduce violence against women on college campuses.

Campus SaVE Act: Legislative History and Context

The lack of compliance with the Clery Act at the institutional level contrasts with extensive congressional efforts to commemorate and improve the Clery legislation starting in 1992 and culminating in the Campus SaVE Act in 2013 (see Chapter 1, Exhibit 1.1 for a timeline). Such legislative efforts include the Buckley Amendment Clarification (1992); Campus Sexual Assault Victims' Bill of Rights (1992); Campus Courts Disclosure Provision (1998); Jeanne Clery Disclosure of Campus Security Policy and Campus Crime Statistics Act (1998); and Campus Sex Crimes Prevention Act (2000). The 2007 mass shooting at Virginia Polytechnic Institute (where the administrators were found to have delayed notification of risk; Stratford 2014), and the Dickinson murder cover-up at Eastern Michigan were likely to have spurred Congress to further strengthen the Clery Act within the Higher Education Opportunity Act in 2008 (HEOA) and to name September the National Campus Safety Awareness Month that same year. According to the Clery Center (2016), the HEOA in particular added "emergency response and notification provisions to the Clery Act; expand[ed] existing statement of policy on the law enforcement authority of campus security personnel; expand[ed] hate crime statistics . . . to include larceny-theft, simple assault, intimidation and vandalism; establish[ed] safeguards for whistleblowers" (para. 9), and required the DOE to report annually to Congress on compliance and ongoing implementation efforts.

The Campus SaVE Act was one of many bills addressing campus sexual assault that were introduced in the 113th Congress. In this congressional session, the legislation was originally introduced as S. 218 by Senator Robert Casey (D-PA) and H.R. 812 by Representative Carolyn Maloney (D-NY, 12th district), with the intent to reform how colleges and universities respond to sexual assault. When Campus SaVE was eventually incorporated into the Violence Against Women Reauthorization Act of 2013, its passage was nearly guaranteed for two main reasons. First, President Obama insisted that both House and Senate VAWA reauthorization bills include Campus SaVE. Second, VAWA had received nearly full bipartisan support for each reauthorization since its initial passage in 1994, except for Republican opposition in the Senate and the House in 2012 and 2013, respectively.

After the president's signature in March 2013, the secretary of education published in the *Federal Register* a notice of proposed rule making on June 14, 2014 (DOE 2014b), which initiated a public comment period. After the public comment period, final regulations with minimal changes responding to public comment were issued on October 20, 2014, with a July 1, 2015 effective date (DOE 2014a). Institutions of higher education had a little more than eight months to comply with the new regulations. To help, the DOE provides a handbook to assist campus safety authorities comply with the regulations (DOE 2016).

Campus SaVE was not new to the 113rd session. Representative Thomas Perriello (D-VA, 5th District) originally introduced the legislation in 2010 in the 111th Congress to remedy problems with the implementation and effects of the existing Clery Act and Title IX. Neither it nor its companion bill in the Senate succeeded. With great hope from the advocacy community, it was taken up again in 2011, but did not generate momentum. A few matters prevented SaVE from gaining broad support at that time (Marshall 2014), and these are important to note because they are still discussed in proposed legislation and policy discussions and have been subject to a legal ruling. First, the earlier bill required institutions to use the preponderance of evidence standard to determine whether a student committed an assault (as does Title IX), in line with civil proceedings. Critics worried that this evidentiary standard gave the balance of power in an allegation to the victim, whose claim would be held to less scrutiny than if the criminal justice standard of "beyond a reasonable doubt" was implemented. Interestingly, 80 percent of institutions were already using the preponderance of the evidence standard prior to these concerns (New 2016). In the current Campus SaVE Act, a specific evidentiary standard is not required. Instead, institutions are instructed that they must identify their evidentiary standard in their procedures (Coray 2016; Novkov 2016), and they are also referred to the Office of Civil Rights 2011 Title IX guidance on this issue (DOE 2011). Recent court rulings (see Marsh 2015) require the preponderance of the evidence standard in campus sexual assault cases.

Victim advocates had a different concern with the earlier legislation. Campus SaVE required institutions to include in their ASRs only those incidents reported to a "campus security authority." Campus security authorities may not include institutional employees to whom victims may be more likely to report an incident (Marshall 2014), especially as Campus SaVE did not dictate who should be considered mandatory reporters. Advocates worried that continued underreporting would result, which would negate efforts to make incidents of sexual violence (and the other crimes included in Campus SaVE: dating violence, domestic violence, and stalking) transparent to current and prospective students. At the same time, the effects of reporting on the victims had to be considered, something that Clery did not do; fortunately, Campus SaVE requires institutions to inform student survivors about their "campus safety climate" and their rights and the potential outcomes of their reporting choices (Engle 2015, 407). Indeed, Engle (2015) claims that "the SaVE Act brings together victim advocacy language and legal obligations, such as reporting and disciplinary procedures, in a way that neither Title IX nor the Clery Act accomplished" (415).

Efforts are already underway to continue to enhance Campus SaVE through the Campus Accountability and Safety Act (CASA), which had been introduced in the 113th and 114th Congress by Senator Claire McCaskill (D-MO) and Representative Carolyn Maloney (D-NY). This legislation would substantially increase penalties for Clery violations from $35,000 to $150,000 per violation and require institutions to conduct climate surveys to ascertain the scope of victimization on their college campuses, along with a host of other recommendations that would improve responses in sexual assault complaints through the establishment of uniform procedures (Coray 2016). Because of the eventual success of many such legislative proposals in the past, it is possible that the Campus SaVE Act, the first major amendment to the Clery Act since 2008, is just a temporary iteration of the Clery Act and will be replaced and/or amended as we continue to strive for ways to reduce violence against women on college campuses.

A Closer Look at Campus SaVE Provisions

The Campus SaVE Act expands on the Clery Act by mandating that in addition to reporting forcible and nonforcible sex offenses, campuses must report the number of incidents of dating violence, domestic violence, and stalking that occurred during the year, along with an expansion of the hate crimes recorded to individually include gender identity and national origin (American Council on Education 2014). Reporting is the foundation of the Clery Act, as we discussed previously, but it is no longer the sole focus. In addition to these reporting obligations, campuses are also held accountable for having and distributing detailed descriptions of related policies, procedures, and programs for students and staff on issues of campus violence. Institutions must detail procedures for addressing these incidents; describe victims' rights and options for survivors; and outline prompt, fair, and impartial disciplinary hearings. Campus SaVE mandates that institutions develop and implement a policy that outlines the jurisdiction of their security or law enforcement personnel and describes any agreements with other agencies for investigating alleged criminal offenses. The act requires the implementation of primary, universal prevention programs. Tellingly, the act also requires the DOE to partner with the Attorney General's Office and the Department of Health and Human Services to ensure that the best practices for preventing and responding to campus violence are identified and utilized, sharing both the responsibility and the burden of campus security with these other federal offices.

Changes to Reporting Requirements

Institutions must now report incidents of crimes that college students too commonly experience, specifically dating violence, domestic violence, sexual assault, and stalking. These crimes disproportionately affect women, as we discuss in Chapters 2–4 of this volume, but no one is immune. Definitions of each of those crimes is also included in the act, although institutions are expected to also educate their communities about any differences that might exist between the regulations and local crime definitions. Importantly, the Campus SaVE Act aligns its definition of rape with the Federal Bureau of Investigation's 2013 revised definition, which had not been changed since 1927. Where rape used to be defined as "the carnal knowledge of a female forcibly and against her will," it is now defined as "penetration, no matter how slight, of the vagina or anus of any body part or object, or oral penetration of a sex organ of another person without the consent of the victim." The revised definition is gender neutral, and focuses on the core aspects of rape—*penetration* of another's body without that person's *consent* (see American Council on Education 2014).

Campus SaVE also limits and delineates circumstances that allow an institution to remove an incident from a report category, but still requires the institution to report the numbers of unfounded reports (i.e., reports of incidents with insufficient evidence). This provision is presumably meant to reduce the "doctoring" of reports to make crime seem less prevalent than it may be. Confidentiality of victims' names is retained in certain circumstances (Schroeder 2014). The ASR must set out how the institution records and shares data while maintaining survivors' anonymity and keeping information about accommodations or protective measures confidential.

These provisions are relatively noncontroversial. They align the definition of rape, mitigate against misrepresenting data, and clarify definitions of hate crimes. They require little in the way of human or fiscal resources relative to other provisions. But they are much more complicated than they appear, as one guidance from *Campus Legal Advisor* (a newsletter service for university administrators on campus legal issues) attests, because such reporting requires: (1) that individuals know they are campus security authorities, and that they have been trained on what and how to report; (2) that the list of crimes within Clery and Campus SaVE has been informed by local legislation and definitions, and any differences resolved; and (3) that the crimes occurred within appropriate "Clery" geographic areas for counting purposes (McCarthy 2016), which often includes only campus facilities, ignoring the violence that students experience in other off-campus locations (see Fisher, Daigle, and Cullen 2010). All of these issues must be individually handled by campuses, and occur after the complex process victims go through when deciding what they have experienced and whether or how they report it (Cook et al. 2011). A standardized instrument or survey to be used by campuses when completing their ASR may make comparisons between schools more effective (Marshall 2014). Given variability in local crime definitions, this would doubly burden campuses (to report SaVE crimes and also local crimes when definitions differ), but may improve comparability.

Responses to Incidents of Sexual and Relational Violence

Though the reporting changes noted previously appear to broaden the crimes covered by Campus SaVE, the act's true purpose is revealed in its clarification and detailed expectations for campus responses to sexual violence. The 2011 Dear Colleague Letter, which provided guidance to Title IX of the Education Amendments of 1972 (DOE 2011) clarified sexual violence to include all physical sexual acts perpetrated against a person's will or where a person is incapable of giving consent. The guidance noted that this encompasses a number of acts of sexual violence, including rape, sexual assault, sexual battery, and sexual coercion. One of the most important goals of Campus SaVE is "to establish minimum national standards for all college campuses when responding to allegations of sexual assault" (Marshall 2014, 272). Such continuing efforts at the federal (through Campus SaVE) and state levels to improve and clarify higher education disciplinary procedures reflect a continuing dissatisfaction with how universities handle reports of sexual violence, fueled by "public outrage over highly publicized cases of sexual assault victimization that did not result in investigation or disciplinary action against the alleged perpetrator" (Richards and Kafonek 2015, 123). Each provision of Campus SaVE recognizes victim/survivor needs and attends to fairness for the accuser and the accused. The victim-centered nature of the act is exemplified in DOE guidance: "As you compile the section on policy statements, keep the focus of the requirement in mind: disclosure of the procedures, practices and programs your institution uses to *keep students and employees safe and its facilities secure*" (DOE 2016, 9–2; emphasis added).

First, Campus SaVE requires that any institutional officials who conduct investigative or disciplinary proceedings must be trained in a way that "protects the safety of victims" and "promotes accountability." The act requires that victims be informed about their rights and reporting options, including the option of notifying law enforcement, and assured that they will be assisted by campus authorities regardless of their reporting choices. Further, victim information must be kept confidential in record keeping, and institutions are required to describe how they manage these confidentiality expectations in their ASR. Campus policy must also clearly identify the "sanctions or protective measures" that the institution may choose to impose following a determination of sexual assault, dating violence, domestic violence, or stalking. Such measures may include changes to "academic, living, transportation or working situations" (Coray 2016, 72). Victims should also receive information regarding other forms of assistance, such as advocacy, counseling, or legal assistance. Thus, before victims choose to report their victimizations to institutional (or non-institutional) authorities, they should have access to the potential outcomes of their complaints. The Campus SaVE Act makes clear that victim support and services are available to victims regardless of whether their victimization occurred on or off campus, and whether they reported it to campus authorities.

At the same time, Campus SaVE fulfills equity expectations by ensuring that both the accusers and the accused are assured a "prompt, fair, and impartial" process, which includes having access to explicit descriptions of any institutional procedures that may be applicable to the complaint (Smith and Gomez 2013). Both must also have access to information regarding the complaints in a timely manner, including the outcome of the proceedings and any appeals procedures. Similarly, the act recognizes that both accusers and the accused may have any adviser with them during campus hearings. Such obligations can be seen as strategies to assert the validity of campus investigative and disciplinary processes. Konradi (2016) argues:

> The importance of clarity about adjudication procedures extends beyond victim's [sic] immediate concerns. Campus judicial systems must also appear fair and legitimate to members of the campus community, such that students and faculty are willing to play a role in the administration of justice. Procedures that do not provide clear due process protections for accused students increase the likelihood that the outcomes of campus adjudication, both determinations of responsibility and sanctions, will be questioned. . . . In short, the perception of procedural justice is necessary for campus judicial systems to function as remedies for campus sexual assault. (3)

Konradi's own research on Maryland's higher education institutions demonstrated that this focus on fairness is important for both the accused—whose access to due process rights have been widely discussed—and the accusers.

In Konradi's study of public and private universities' policy documents related to sexual assault, the accusers were less likely than those they had accused to have access to procedural measures like the right to call or question witnesses or challenge the procedures for bias. Accusers need to see their rights embodied in the policies purported to support them.

Descriptions of Primary Prevention and Awareness Programming

A substantial contribution of Campus SaVE is its educational mandate, which holds institutions accountable for their efforts to prevent sexual and relational violence. Each campus's ASR must describe the institution's primary prevention and awareness programs for dating violence, domestic violence, sexual assault, and stalking and, because of this, institutions are required to actually have primary prevention and awareness programs to report. Given that only 61 percent of campuses in a recent national study reported any prevention programming in 2015, this is an important yet unrealized mandate (Richards 2016). In addition, Campus SaVE requires particular elements within those programs. For instance, an explicit statement that the institution prohibits these crimes and the definitions of those crimes derived from the final VAWA regulations and the jurisdiction in which the institution is located must both be part of these programs. Key to the prevention efforts is the mandated provision of education about effective, safe, and positive options for bystander intervention (discussed further in Chapter 14 by Sarah McMahon) and information to reduce the risk of sexual violence, emphasizing signs of abusive behavior and strategies to avoid potential attacks. Universities must also define each of the terms they use, from "awareness programs" to "risk reduction" within their ASRs.

Importantly, a definition of consent to sexual activity in the jurisdiction must also be provided. Unfortunately, as Humphrey (2016) notes, in passing the Campus SaVE Act, the DOE has not been successful in its efforts to require all IHE to include a federal definition of consent in their student conduct codes. Under current federal law, colleges and universities must therefore create their own definition of consent. This is incredibly problematic because a recent comprehensive review of all fifty states' statutes to evaluate the extent to which state laws are appropriate and accessible for victims of campus sexual assault concluded that "across statutes, key concepts relating to consent and incapacity were often ill defined or undefined, and many of the statutes appear to be poorly suited to handling campus sexual assaults" (DeMatteo et al. 2015, 227). Nevertheless, recognizing the importance of consent and defining it for the campus community is important because, as Marshall (2014) argues, "by providing a clear definition of what constitutes consent, sexual assault survivors should be able to more clearly recognize an incident that warrants reporting and potential legal action" (285), thus potentially reducing underreporting to campus authorities. Current efforts toward affirmative consent policies in various locales have the potential to contribute even further to this awareness effort.

Expanding on Clery, the Campus SaVE Act requires primary prevention and awareness programming dedicated for both incoming students and employees, and existing students and faculty. Previously, Clery required awareness education regarding sexual violence (Schroeder 2014), and the 2011 DCL (DOE 2011) only recommended prevention programming. With Campus SaVE, universities are expected to go beyond awareness campaigns to provide primary prevention and awareness strategies for all of their current and prospective community members, and describe these strategies in detail in their ASRs. As noted earlier, scholarship suggests that this has not been happening. In *Sexual Violence on Campus*, the authors report that 20 percent of the higher education institutions in their sample provided no sexual assault training at all for their faculty and staff, and more than 30 percent did not provide such training for their students (U.S. Senate Subcommittee 2014).

The goal of primary prevention is to stop an incident from ever happening, a noble goal given the significant trauma that sexual assault, dating violence, domestic violence, and stalking can have on its survivors. Because of this, it is hard to argue against primary prevention and awareness programs, especially since reporting alone, given its challenges, does not appear to make campuses safer. However, as the authors of Chapters 14 and 15 in this volume articulate, evidence for the efficacy of such prevention and awareness programming is still limited, and only a scattering of programs have elicited positive effects in systematic evaluations. Related to this, awareness programs abound, and the Campus SaVE provision has stirred a "cottage industry" of educational programs (New 2014), including those that are online, like the student educational programs Haven and Campus Clarity. Everfi, the company that now owns both of these online programs, notes on its website that it has reached more than 700,000 individuals on more than 650 campuses through Haven, its "premier online program addressing the critical issues of sexual assault, relationship violence, stalking, and sexual harassment—among students, faculty and staff" (Everfi n.d., para. 1). These programs are not without controversy, not only for their claims of effectiveness but also for the intrusiveness of some of their materials (Dockterman 2014). Nevertheless, Everfi (2016) continues to act as if it is the conscience of higher education in terms of prevention programming, especially with its recent publication of *How to Improve Sexual Assault Prevention*.

In terms of risk reduction, while the risk factors for perpetrating SaVE crimes, particularly sexual assault, are well documented (see Tharp et al. 2013), the mechanisms by which these factors work or can be reduced, separately or interactively, are not clearly understood. It is not surprising that scholars found little to encourage perpetration prevention programming in a recent systematic review, with approximately 25 percent of existing programs having no effect or a detrimental effect on the participants (DeGue et al. 2014). DeGue and her colleagues did find, however, that longer-term programming worked better than one-hour educational programs (which tends to be the standard on many college campuses), and they identified two positive middle school programs (Safe Dates and Shifting Boundaries) and one college program that has the potential for positive effects (Bringing in the Bystander). McMahon (Chapter 14 of this volume) also reminds us that while potential victims in risk-reduction programs such as physical defense courses may feel empowered, there is a great deal of controversy about the onus of prevention being placed on prospective victims, who disproportionately are women.

Collectively, Campus SaVE's educational mandate creates the impetus for an expansion of program offerings, along with a renewed focus on social change at the individual and community levels. While the effectiveness of prevention (and risk-reduction) programs is always difficult to ascertain, ongoing evaluation efforts are important to ensure that campuses are instituting programming that fulfills the mission of Campus SaVE. To that end, we encourage higher education administrators to use due diligence when selecting their prevention programming, despite fiscal and resource-driven pressures to choose models such as some online programming that may fundamentally miss the mark and do harm rather than good within their campus communities.

Conclusion

One of the most powerful outcomes of the passage of Campus SaVE was the codification of some elements of the 2011 DCL that sparked Title IX policy and procedural changes by institutions in response to campus sexual violence (see Chapter 7 by Michelle Hughes Miller and Chapter 10 by Carmen Suarez). For example, some of the changes noted previously under disciplinary procedures within Campus SaVE such as the mandate to publish sexual violence complaint procedures were recommended in the 2011 DCL, but their mandate under Campus SaVE creates an affirmative burden on institutions (Marshall 2014). At the same time, the critique that Campus SaVE did not go far enough in codifying 2011 DCL recommendations has also been made, particularly in terms of the failure of Campus SaVE to require the preponderance of the evidence standard in disciplinary hearings.

Nevertheless, Campus SaVE brought together elements of prior reauthorizations of VAWA, elements of the 2011 DCL and Title IX, and Clery to provide an inclusive vision of best practices in response to violence against college women (particularly sexual violence), circa 2013. By weaving accountability across the three areas of enhancement (reporting, education, and disciplinary practices), Campus SaVE put higher education institutions on notice that victims—all of us, really—are entitled to accurate information about campus security; effective and ongoing educational efforts across their campus community; and, if they are victimized, administrative processes that respect their rights as victims and treat them fairly throughout. These are tall orders and, not surprisingly, the number of Clery violations discussed in this chapter suggests that institutions have not yet fulfilled these expectations. Nevertheless, there is progress (Richards 2016). Compared to an earlier study of institutional efforts to respond to campus sexual assault (Karjane, Fisher, and Cullen 2002), Richards (2016) discovered that the majority of institutions in her sample were in compliance with the mandates of the Campus SaVE Act in 2015.

This is key. Campus SaVE ultimately relies on the compliance of higher education institutions to effect the change it desires in levels of sexual, dating, domestic violence, and stalking on college campuses. The compliance culture that such legislation incurs can be valuable if it moves campus authorities to understand their responsibilities toward their communities, including their students, as they clarify and improve policies, programs, and reporting on their campuses. But it can also result in "minimal compliance" (Moylan 2016, 10), which fails to meet the needs of survivors (and the accused) but keeps institutions out of the media. Training courses that allow "checking the boxes," educational programs that are one-shot rather than ongoing, and victim services that are not victim-centric, all meet the demands of the law, but not its spirit. Holding institutions to effective policies and programs is essential, but monitoring and guiding eleven thousand IHE toward effectiveness is a Herculean task.

The victim-centered aspects of the Campus SaVE Act are compelling but not surprising given the cacophony of voices urging greater attention to sexual violence on college campuses, including many survivors and their allies. It is also not surprising that the act is perceived as not going far enough related to concerns about Clery underreporting and dissatisfaction with underevaluated educational programming and highly variable disciplinary practices. Not only has new federal legislation already been proposed to address some of these concerns (CASA, for instance), but Richards and Kafonek (2015) describe state-based legislative efforts that heavily focus on policy, enhancing services for sexual assault victims, and even mandating greater transparency or distribution for the ASRs themselves. The frustration related to addressing campus sexual violence appropriately and adequately may come from "growth of the perception that procedural justice is unattainable [which] has potentially serious consequences for the capacity of colleges and universities to address sexual assault" (Konradi 2016, 2).

Where the Campus SaVE Act gave us hope for progress just a few short years ago, the depth of the need, the complexity of the solutions, and the paucity of resources available to address both reminds us of the continuing need to recognize policy for what it is: an effort to define, within law, our best understandings of what will make a difference. How we implement it, and whether we trust its implementation, depends on the integrity of the higher education community.

REFERENCES

ABC News. 2007. *Eastern Michigan University stays quiet about student's rape and murder for weeks.* Available at http://abcnews.go.com/GMA/story?id=3297153&page=1.

American Association of University Women (AAUW). 2015. *Ninety-one percent of colleges reported zero incidents of rape in 2014.* Available at http://www.aauw.org/article/clery-act-data-analysis/.

American Council on Education. 2014. *New requirements imposed by the Violence Against Women Reauthorization Act.* Available at http://www.acenet.edu/news-room/Documents/VAWA-Summary.pdf.

Campus SaVE Act. 2016. H.R. 2016 (112th): Campus SaVE Act. Available at https://www.govtrack.us/congress/bills/112/hr2016/text.

Clery Center for Security on Campus. 2016. *Policy accomplishments.* Available at http://clerycenter.org/policy-accomplishments.

Colaner, K. T. 2006. "Towards greater campus safety: An explanation of student affairs administrators' knowledge of and compliance with the Clery Act." Ph.D. diss. Available at University of Southern California Digital Library, http://digitallibrary.usc.edu/cdm/ref/collection/p15799coll16/id/621982.

Cook, S. L., C. A. Gidycz, M. Murphy, and M. P. Koss. 2011. Emerging issues in the measurement of rape victimization. *Violence Against Women* 17: 201–218.

Coray, E. 2016. Victim protection or revictimization: Should college disciplinary boards handle sexual assault claims? *Boston College Journal of Law and Social Justice* 36: 59–89.

DeGue, S., L. A. Valle, M. K. Holt, G. M. Massetti, J. L. Matjasko, and A. T. Tharp. 2014. A systematic review of primary prevention strategies for sexual violence prevention. *Aggression and Violent Behavior* 19: 346–362.

DeMatteo, D., M. Galloway, S. Arnold, and U. Patel. 2015. Sexual assault on college campuses: A 50-state survey of criminal sexual assault statutes and their relevance to campus sexual assault. *Psychology, Public Policy, and Law* 21 (3): 227–238.

Department of Education (DOE), Office for Civil Rights. 2011. *Dear Colleague.* Available at http://www2.ed.gov/about/offices/list/ocr/letters/colleague-201104.pdf.

———. 2014a. Violence Against Women Act: Final regulations. *Federal Register* 79 (202): 62751–62790. Available at https://www.federalregister.gov/articles/2014/10/20/2014-24284/violence-against-women-act.

———. 2014b. Violence Against Women Act: Proposed rule. *Federal Register* 79 (119): 35417–35460. Available at https://www.gpo.gov/fdsys/pkg/FR-2014-06-20/pdf/2014-14384.pdf.

———. 2016. *The handbook for campus safety and security reporting, 2016 edition.* Available at https://www2.ed.gov/admins/lead/safety/handbook.pdf.

———. n.d. *Campus safety and security.* Available at http://ope.ed.gov/campussafety/#/.

———. n.d. Federal Student Aid. *Clery Act reports.* Available at https://studentaid.ed.gov /sa/about/data-center/school/clery-act-reports.

Dockterman, E. 2014. Clemson pulls training program that asked students about sex lives. *Time,* September 19. Available at http://time.com/3404430/clemson-sex-training -program/.

End Rape on Campus. n.d. *Campus SaVE Act.* Available at http://endrapeoncampus.org /the-campus-save-act/.

Engle, J. C. 2015. Mandatory reporting of campus sexual assault and domestic violence: Moving to a victim-centric protocol that comports with federal law. *Temple Political and Civil Rights Law Review* 24: 401–421.

Everfi. 2016. *How to improve sexual assault prevention.* Available at http://everfi.com/how -effective-are-your-campus-sexual-assault-prevention-efforts/.

———. n.d. *Online sexual assault prevention programs.* Available at http://everfi.com /higher-education-old/haven/.

Fisher, B., L. Daigle, and F. Cullen. 2010. *Unsafe in the ivory tower: The sexual victimization of college women.* Thousand Oaks, CA: SAGE.

Freeh Sporkin and Sullivan, LLP. 2012. Report of the special investigative counsel regarding the actions of the Pennsylvania State University related to the child sexual abuse committed by Gerald A. Sandusky. *Chicago Tribune,* July 12. Available at http://www .chicagotribune.com/sports/chi-freeh-report-sandusky-penn-state-20120712-pdf -htmlstory.html.

Grossman, E., and T. Coombe. 2002. Death sentence overturned—Judge: jury instructions in Lehigh student's trial were ambiguous. *Morning Call,* May 23. Available at http://articles .mcall.com/2002-05-23/news/3740094_1_death-sentence-life-sentence-federal-judge.

Humphrey, W. A. 2016. "Let's talk about sex": Legislating and educating on the affirmative consent standard. *University of San Francisco Law Review* 50: 35–73.

Karjane, H., B. S. Fisher, and T. Cullen. 2002. *Campus sexual assault: How America's institutions of higher education respond.* Final Report, NIJ Grant #1999-WA-VX-0008. Newton, MA: Education Development Center.

Kincade, T. 2016. *Colleges are likely underreporting sexual assaults, senators warn.* Available at http://www.huffingtonpost.com/entry/colleges-underreporting-sexual-assault -senators_us_577684e8e4b09b4c43c0133e.

Koestner, K., and C. Bowes. 2016. How I convinced the world you can be raped by your date. *BBC News Magazine,* June 2. Available at http://www.bbc.com/news/magazine -36434191.

Konradi, A. 2016. Can justice be served on campus? An examination of due process and victim protection policies in the campus adjudication of sexual assault in Maryland. *Humanity and Society,* 1–32, doi: 10.1177/0160597616651657.

Kraft, J. 1987. Clery's plan litigation, "fight" to save lives. *Morning Call,* April 29, A1–A2. Available at http://articles.mcall.com/1987-04-29/news/2579068_1_lehigh-university -students-trial.

Larcom, G. S. 2008. Eastern Michigan University to pay $350,000 in federal fines over Laura Dickinson case. *Ann Arbor News,* June 6. Available at http://blog.mlive.com /annarbornews/2008/06/eastern_michigan_university_to.html.

Lipka, S. 2012. Ignorance and low priority of Clery Act obligations may extend beyond Penn State. *Chronicle of Higher Education,* July 12. Available at http://chronicle.com /article/IgnoranceLow-Priority-of/132839/.

Marsh, J. R. 2015. Victory! Court rules the Campus SaVE Act has no effect on Title IX. Available at http://title9.us/victory-court-rules-the-campus-save-act-has-no-effect-on -title-ix/#.V5_BCaIqqQl.

Marshall, R. 2014. Will it really SaVE you? Analyzing the Campus Sexual Violence Elimination Act. *Legislation and Policy Brief* 6 (2): 271–293.

McCarthy, C. 2016. Training tools: Avoid common Clery Act compliance pitfalls, challenges. *Campus Legal Advisor,* April 19. Available at Wiley Online Library, http://onlinelibrary.wiley.com/doi/10.1002/cala.30320/full.

Moylan, C. A. 2016. "I fear I'm a checkbox": College and university victim advocates' perspectives of campus rape reforms. *Violence Against Women,* 1–18, doi: 10.1177/1077801216655623.

Murray, P., T. Baldwin, M. F. Bennet, R. Blumenthal, B. Boxer, S. Brown . . . and C. Booker. 2016. VAWA, Clery Anniversary Letter to the Honourable John B. King Jr. and Loretta Lynch. Available at http://www.help.senate.gov/ranking/newsroom/press/on-anniversary-of-violence-against-women-act-reforms-senators-call-on-administration-to-hold-colleges-and-universities-accountable-for-underreporting-sexual-violence-on-campus.

New, J. 2014. Cottage industry on preventing sexual assault. *Inside Higher Education,* August 27. Available at https://www.insidehighered.com/news/2014/08/27/pressure-colleges-deal-sexual-assault-leads-growing-cottage-industry.

———. 2016. Must vs. should: Colleges say the Department of Education's guidance on campus sexual assault is vague and inconsistent. *Inside Higher Education,* February 25. Available at https://www.insidehighered.com/news/2016/02/25/colleges-frustrated-lack-clarification-title-ix-guidance.

Novkov, J. 2016. Equality, process, and campus sexual assault. *Maryland Law Review* 75 (2): 590–619.

Richards, T. N. 2016. An updated review of institutions of higher education's responses to sexual assault: Results from a nationally representative sample. *Journal of Interpersonal Violence,* 1–30, doi: 10.1177/0886260516658757.

Richards, T. N., and K. Kafonek. 2015. Reviewing state legislative agendas regarding sexual assault in higher education: Proliferation of best practices and points of caution. *Feminist Criminology* 11 (1): 91–129.

Schroeder, L. P. 2014. Cracks in the ivory tower: How the Campus Sexual Violence Elimination Act can protect students from sexual assault. *Loyola University-Chicago Law Journal* 45: 1195–1243.

Smith, G. M., and L. M. Gomez. 2013. Effective implementation of the institutional response to sexual misconduct under Title IX and related guidance. *National Association of College and University Attorneys,* 397–400. Available at http://www.higheredcompliance.org/resources/sexual-misconduct.html.

Stratford, M. 2014. Clery fines: Proposed vs. actual. *Inside Higher Education,* July 17. Available at https://www.insidehighered.com/news/2014/07/17/colleges-often-win-reduction-fines-federal-campus-safety-violations.

Tharp, A. T., S. DeGue, L. A. Valle, K. A. Brookmeyer, G. M. Massetti, and J. L. Matjasko. 2013. A systematic qualitative review of risk and protective factors for sexual violence perpetration. *Trauma Violence & Abuse* 14 (2): 133–167.

theGrio. 2016. #RapedbyMorehouse ignites debate about rape allegations on HBCU campus. Available at http://thegrio.com/2016/05/05/rapedbymorehouse-ignites-debate-about-rape-allegations-on-hbcu-campus/.

U.S. Senate Subcommittee on Financial and Contracting Oversight—Majority Staff. 2014. *Sexual violence on campus: How too many institutions of higher education are failing to protect students.* Washington, DC: U.S. Government Printing Office.

Victims of Trafficking and Violence Prevention Act. 2000. P.L. 106-386.

Violence Against Women Act of 1994. 1994. P.L. 103-322.

Violence Against Women and Department of Justice Reauthorization Act. 2005. P.L. 109-162.

Violence Against Women Reauthorization Act of 2013. 2013. P. L. 113-4.

White House. n.d. *Not alone: Together against sexual assault.* Available at https://www .whitehouse.gov/1is2many/notalone.

Yung, C. R. 2015. Concealing campus sexual assault: An empirical examination. *Psychology, Public Policy, and Law* 21 (1): 1–9.

9

The White House Task Force Report on Sexual Violence on College Campuses

CATHERINE KAUKINEN

Sexual violence is more than just a crime against individuals. It threatens our families, it threatens our communities; ultimately, it threatens the entire country. It tears apart the fabric of our communities. And that's why we're here today—because we have the power to do something about it as a government, as a nation. We have the capacity to stop sexual assault, support those who have survived it, and bring perpetrators to justice.—PRESIDENT BARACK OBAMA, *January 22, 2014*

Freedom from sexual assault is a basic human right . . . a nation's decency is in large part measured by how it responds to violence against women . . . our daughters, our sisters, our wives, our mothers, our grandmothers have every single right to expect to be free from violence and sexual abuse.—VICE PRESIDENT JOSEPH BIDEN, *January 22, 2014*

On January 22, 2014, President Obama signed the presidential memorandum establishing the White House Task Force to Protect Students from Sexual Assault (White House Task Force 2014, ii). The president and his administration brought together the task force to strengthen our national response to sexual violence on college and university campuses. For too long, campuses have done far too little to protect students from sexual violence, and they have often failed to hold offenders accountable. The task force's mission was to send a message to victims that they are not alone, and to ensure that colleges and universities are also held accountable for ensuring a safe campus community. Over the months that followed, the task force engaged in a national discussion to answer the president's call to action "to stop sexual assault, support those who have survived it, and bring perpetrators to justice" (White House Task Force 2014, ii). This chapter provides a brief summary of the work of the task force and its recommendations, and highlights the potential of its report for impacting the extent and nature of violence against women on college campuses. Critiques of the task force's work are also discussed, particularly those that relate to a larger backlash to the growing federal response to violence against women on college campuses. This includes critiques by those who have challenged the extent and nature of violence against women on college campuses (in particular, the "1 in 4" statistic on the risk of sexual violence), as well as the perceived impact the White House Task Force's recommendations might have with respect to student due process during investigations and adjudications on campus. An important theme throughout the White House Task Force Report is the need for equipping colleges and universities with the resources to meet the changes required by Title IX, the Campus Sexual Assault Violence Elimination Act (SaVE), and the Clery Act. I highlight how current legislation and statutory requirements have been presented by the report, and the direction for change, improvement, and innovation recommended within the report.

The work of the task force included twenty-seven in-person and online listening sessions with a diverse set of stakeholders from across the country, including campus administrators, faculty, student services staff, and students, community groups, law enforcement, and most important, survivors of sexual violence (survivors; student activists; faculty, staff, and administrators from schools of all types; parents; alumni; national survivors' rights and education associations; local and campus-based service providers and advocates; law enforcement; civil rights activists; school general counsels; men's and women's groups; Greek organizations; athletes; and researchers and academics in the field). At the conclusion of the task force's work, it was noted that there is tremendous variation (and limited success) in what colleges and universities are doing with respect to prevention programming, education, reporting responses, and adjudication. As many of the authors in this volume have noted, and the task force report concluded, the actions taken by campuses to comply with Title IX, Clery, and other federal legislation have not placed protection and response to survivors of violence at the forefront of their campuses' policies and procedures. Checking the Clery box on a list of requirements will not ensure the safety of young men and women on college campuses. As the report notes, what is most often missing are the resources and safe places available to victims. The report's primary goal was to provide colleges and universities with guidance to prevent sexual assault by offering a set of practical and evidence-based tools.

The White House Task Force Report was organized around four objectives: (1) identify the scope of the problem on college campuses; (2) help prevent campus sexual assault by engaging men; (3) help schools respond effectively when a student is assaulted; and (4) improve, and make more transparent, the federal government's enforcement efforts to facilitate universities' protecting and supporting victims during investigations. See Exhibit 9.1 for an executive summary of the White House Task Force (2014) Report on Sexual Violence on College Campuses.

Exhibit 9.1 Not Alone: The First Report of the White House Task Force to Protect Students from Sexual Assault Executive Summary (April 2014)

Why We Need to Act

One in five women is sexually assaulted in college. Most often, it's by someone she knows—and also most often, she does not report what happened. Many survivors are left feeling isolated, ashamed or to blame. Although it happens less often, men, too, are victims of these crimes.

The President created the Task Force to Protect Students From Sexual Assault to turn this tide. As the name of our new website—NotAlone.gov—indicates, we are here to tell sexual assault survivors that they are not alone. And we're also here to help schools live up to their obligation to protect students from sexual violence.

Over the last three months, we have had a national conversation with thousands of people who care about this issue. Today, we offer our first set of action steps and recommendations.

1. **Identifying the Problem: Campus Climate Surveys** The first step in solving a problem is to name it and know the extent of it—and a campus climate survey is the best way to do that. We are providing schools with a toolkit to conduct a survey—and we urge schools to show they're serious about the problem by conducting the survey next year. The Justice Department, too, will partner with Rutgers University's Center on Violence Against Women and Children to pilot, evaluate and further refine the survey—and at the end of this trial period, we will explore legislative or administrative options to require schools to conduct a survey in 2016.

2. **Preventing Sexual Assault—and Engaging Men** Prevention programs can change attitudes, behavior—and the culture. In addition to identifying a number of promising prevention strategies that schools can undertake now, we are also researching new ideas and solutions. But one thing we know for sure: we need to engage men as allies in this cause. Most men are not perpetrators—and when we empower men to step in when someone's in trouble, they become an important part of the solution.

   As the President and Vice President's new Public Service Announcement puts it: if she doesn't consent—or can't consent—it's a crime. And if you see it happening, help her, don't blame her, speak up. We are also providing schools with links and information about how they can implement their own bystander intervention programs on campus.

3. **Effectively Responding When a Student Is Sexually Assaulted** When one of its students is sexually assaulted, a school needs to have all the pieces of a plan in place. And that should include:

Someone a survivor can talk to in confidence

While many victims of sexual assault are ready to file a formal (or even public) complaint against an alleged offender right away—many others want time and privacy to sort through their next steps. For some, having a confidential place to go can mean the difference between getting help and staying silent.

Today, we are providing schools with a model reporting and confidentiality protocol—which, at its heart, aims to give survivors more control over the process. Victims who want their school to fully investigate an incident must be taken seriously—and know where to report. But for those who aren't quite ready, they need to have—and know about—places to go for confidential advice and support.

That means a school should make it clear, up front, who on campus can maintain a victim's confidence and who can't—so a victim can make an informed decision about where best to turn. A school's policy should also explain when it may need to override a confidentiality request (and pursue an alleged perpetrator) in order to help provide a safe campus for everyone. Our sample policy provides recommendations for how a school can strike that often difficult balance, while also being ever mindful of a survivor's well-being.

New guidance from the Department of Education also makes clear that on-campus counselors and advocates—like those who work or volunteer in sexual assault centers, victim advocacy offices, women's and health centers, as well as licensed and pastoral counselors—can talk to a survivor in confidence. In recent years, some schools have indicated that some of these counselors and advocates cannot maintain confidentiality. This new guidance clarifies that they can.

A comprehensive sexual misconduct policy

We are also providing a checklist for schools to use in drafting (or reevaluating) their own sexual misconduct policies. Although every school will need to tailor a policy to its own needs and circumstances, all schools should be sure to bring the key stakeholders—including students—to the table. Among other things, this checklist includes ideas a school could consider in deciding what is—or is not—consent to sexual activity. As we heard from many students, this can often be the essence of the matter—and a school community should work together to come up with a careful and considered understanding.

Trauma-informed training for school officials

Sexual assault is a unique crime: unlike other crimes, victims often blame themselves; the associated trauma can leave their memories fragmented; and insensitive or judgmental questions can compound a victim's distress. Starting this year, the Justice Department, through both its Center for Campus Public Safety and its Office on Violence Against Women, will develop trauma-informed training programs for school officials and campus and local law enforcement. The Department of Education's National Center on Safe and Supportive Learning Environments will do the same for campus health centers. This kind of training has multiple benefits: when survivors are treated with care and wisdom, they start trusting the system, and the strength of their accounts can better hold offenders accountable.

Better school disciplinary systems

Many sexual assault survivors are wary of their school's adjudication process—which can sometimes subject them to harsh and hurtful questioning (like about their prior sexual history) by students or staff unschooled in the dynamics of these crimes. Some schools are experimenting with new models—like having a single, trained investigator do the lion's share of the fact-finding—with very positive results. We need to learn more about these promising new ideas. And so starting this year, the Justice Department will begin assessing different models for investigating and adjudicating campus sexual assault cases with an eye toward identifying best practices.

The Department of Education's new guidance also urges some important improvements to many schools' current disciplinary processes: questions about the survivor's sexual history with anyone other than the alleged perpetrator should not be permitted; adjudicators should know that the mere fact of a previous consensual sexual relationship does not itself imply consent or preclude a finding of sexual violence; and the parties should not be allowed to personally cross-examine each other.

Partnerships with the community

Because students can be sexually assaulted at all hours of the day or night, emergency services should be available 24 hours a day, too. Other types of support can also be crucial—like longer-term therapies and advocates who can accompany survivors to medical and legal appointments. Many schools cannot themselves provide all these services, but in partnership with a local rape crisis center, they can. So, too, when both the college and the local police are simultaneously investigating a case (a criminal investigation does not relieve a school of its duty to itself investigate and respond), coordination can be crucial. So we are providing schools with a sample agreement they can use to partner with their local rape crisis center—and by June, we will provide a similar sample for forging a partnership with local law enforcement.

4. Increasing Transparency and Improving Enforcement

More transparency and information

The government is committed to making our enforcement efforts more transparent—and getting students and schools more resources to help bring an end to this violence. As part of this effort, we will post enforcement data on our new website—NotAlone.gov—and give students a roadmap for filing a complaint if they think their school has not lived up to its obligations.

Among many other things on the website, sexual assault survivors can also locate an array of services by typing in their zip codes, learn about their legal rights, see which colleges have had enforcement actions taken against them, get "plain English" definitions of some complicated legal terms and concepts; and find their states' privacy laws. Schools and advocates can access federal guidance, learn about relevant legislation, and review the best available evidence and research. We invite everyone to take a look.

Improved enforcement

Today, the Department of Education's Office for Civil Rights (OCR) is releasing a 52-point guidance document that answers many frequently asked questions about a student's rights, and a school's obligations, under Title IX. Among many other topics, the new guidance clarifies that Title IX protects all students, regardless of their sexual orientation or gender identity, immigration status, or whether they have a disability. It also makes clear that students who report sexual violence have a right to expect their school to take steps to protect and support them, including while a school investigation is pending. The guidance also clarifies that recent amendments to the Clery Act do not alter a school's responsibility under Title IX to respond to and prevent sexual violence.

OCR is also strengthening its enforcement procedures in a number of ways— by, for example, instituting time limits on negotiating voluntary resolution agreements and making clear that schools should provide survivors with interim relief (like changing housing or class schedules) pending the outcome of an OCR investigation. And OCR will be more visible on campus during its investigations, so students can help give OCR a fuller picture about what's happening and how a school is responding.

The Departments of Education and Justice, which both enforce Title IX, have entered into an agreement to better coordinate their efforts—as have the two offices within the Department of Education charged with enforcing Title IX and the Clery Act.

Next Steps

This report is the first step in the Task Force's work. We will continue to work toward solutions, clarity, and better coordination. We will also review the various laws and regulations that address sexual violence for possible regulatory or statutory improvements, and seek new resources to enhance enforcement. Also, campus law enforcement officials have special expertise to offer—and they should be tapped to play a more central role. We will also consider how our recommendations apply to public elementary and secondary schools—and what more we can do to help there.

The Task Force thanks everyone who has offered their wisdom, stories, expertise, and experiences over the past 90 days. Although the problem is daunting and much of what we heard was heartbreaking, we are more committed than ever to helping bring an end to this violence.

White House Task Force to Protect Students from Sexual Assault. 2014. *Not Alone: The First Report of the White House Task Force to Protect Students from Sexual Assault.* Office of the Vice President and the White House Council on Women and Girls, April. Available at https://www .notalone.gov/assets/report.pdf.

First, the report offered a set of tools and resources to colleges and universities for identifying the problem of sexual violence on their campuses via climate surveys. The Campus Climate Survey Validation Study (CCSVS), funded by the Bureau of Justice Statistics (BJS) and launched by RTI International, was intended to validate a survey instrument and methodology for measuring campus climate and the prevalence of sexual assault (Krebs et al. 2016). These survey instruments are now available for universities to pilot on their own campuses. The full CCSVS report and the associated tool kit provide college and university campuses guidance on the survey methodology, sampling frame, recruitment, and incentives that should be taken into consideration prior to administering a campus climate survey. In Chapter 13, Christine Lindquist and Christopher P. Krebs outline the elements of the CCSVS. The report initially encouraged campus authorities to voluntarily adopt a climate survey on their campuses. The report noted that the task force would explore legislative or administrative options to require colleges and universities to conduct these evidence-based surveys after 2016. If passed, the Campus Accountability and Safety Act of 2015 (CASA) would standardize campus climate surveys and require colleges and universities to collect and maintain these data (see Campus Accountability and Safety Act of 2015, S. 590, 114th Congress, 2015–2016).

Second, the White House Task Force Report notes the importance of preventing sexual violence by utilizing evidence-based practices, including bystander education and engaging men as allies in preventing violence against women. These are fully discussed in Chapter 14 by Sarah McMahon and in Chapter 15 by Ráchael A. Powers and Jennifer Leili. The Campus Grant Program managed by the U.S. Department of Justice's Office on Violence Against Women (OVW) is the ideal site for violence prevention education and evaluation. OVW campus grantees are awarded multiyear funding to implement a four-prong violence prevention initiative that includes efforts to implement mandatory education, build coordinated response team activities, initiate and broaden law enforcement training, and strengthen disciplinary responses. Peterson and colleagues (2016) evaluated the impact of a face-to-face, thirty- to ninety-minute bystander educational program

utilizing a pre- and post-quasi-experimental design with three-month follow-up at an OVW campus grant institution. The results of this evaluation
are similar to other researchers (Banyard et al. 2014; Banyard and Moynihan
2011; Banyard, Moynihan, and Plante 2007) who have shown that bystander
education programs are effective in changing attitudes, beliefs, efficacy,
intentions, and self-reported behaviors as compared to traditional awareness education programs. The findings from the Peterson and colleagues'
study, as well as other evaluations of bystander intervention, need to shape
what we are doing with our students on college campuses with respect to
educational programming. It is important that as educational programming
on college campuses is expanded, such as under the educational mandate
within the Campus SaVE Act (see Chapter 8 by Michelle Hughes Miller and
Sarah L. Cook), researchers collaborate with these institutions to encourage
the use of face-to-face education that utilizes peer role models and mentors.
Presently, as the need for thousands of students to be educated challenges
many campuses to fulfill their educational mandates, university administrators have chosen online commercial modules that have not yet been evaluated with rigorous methodological designs. They are justified in doing so
because these online programs are listed as potential resources for institutions within the task force report. The commitment by the OVW within the
task force report to test and evaluate prevention programs used by its campus grantees, including the online programs, will be an important opportunity to explore the impact of what campuses are doing with respect to
education. These evaluations will need to measure both the quality and impact of these education and prevention efforts, particularly with respect to
those that: (1) combine cognitive-behavioral skills training with norms
clarification and motivational enhancement interventions; (2) have been
shown to be successful with a general population that might be extended to
a college population; (3) take seriously diversity, inclusiveness, and culturally
appropriate language; and (4) make sense intuitively or seem theoretically
sound, but so far lack strong empirical support from well-designed research
evaluations.

Related to educational programming, as the White House Task Force
Report notes, the majority of men on a college campus are not perpetrators
of sexual violence and the prevention efforts adopted need to reflect this fact
to ensure that the men receiving these educational messages are included as
part of the solution to sexual violence. This includes bystander education
and messaging that engages men as allies. There is a growing body of evidence that bystander approaches are effective in both changing attitudes
toward violence and in providing bystanders with the skills and tools to respond to violence. These approaches empower men and women to serve as
active bystanders when they see behavior and actions that threaten those on
their campus. Additionally, it is important to identify role models for men

to emulate and also celebrate the actions of those young men who challenge other men and risk social, personal, and physical costs with their decision to intervene. We are starting to see this happen nationally. While stories of young men recording the sexual violence of their peers is likely as disturbing as the actions of sexual perpetrators, in the summer of 2016, there was national coverage of young men stepping up and intervening to stop sexual violence. This includes the many stories outlining the University of Florida football player's intervention to stop the sexual assault of an unconscious woman behind a garbage dumpster of a bar (Holley 2016). There were stories about the two graduate students on the Stanford campus who happened to come upon an ongoing sexual assault while riding their bicycles. These young men noted that the victim was unconscious while they were with her and that when they assisted her, she did not move the entire time. The victim herself noted the actions of these men in her victim impact statement and keeps a photo of her bystanders above her bed to remind her that there are allies in the world (CBS News 2016).

Third, the report identifies a number of strategies for effectively responding to students who have been sexually assaulted. These include providing confidential assistance to survivors, a comprehensive and well-advertised sexual misconduct policy and disciplinary procedures, trauma-informed training for investigators and other school staff, and collaborations with community partners to offer health and other services to victims. The expansion of training and education on campus would ensure a victim-centered law enforcement approach (e.g., programs on victim-centered investigation skills, dispatch training and protocols, cultural diversity). Particularly important is the provision of resources on campus for victims to seek out prior to deciding to make a report to law enforcement and/or a Title IX officer. The White House Task Force Report notes:

> Sexual assault survivors respond in different ways. Some are ready to make a formal complaint right away, and want their school to move swiftly to hold the perpetrator accountable. Others, however, aren't so sure. Sexual assault can leave victims feeling powerless—and they need support from the beginning to regain a sense of control. If victims don't have a confidential place to go, or think a school will launch a full-scale investigation against their wishes, many will stay silent. (2014, 11)

The report pointed to the need for colleges and universities to identify trained, confidential victim advocates who would be able to offer emergency and ongoing support. The majority of universities now include faculty and student staff as part of their group of responsible employees, which requires them to report all known incidents of dating violence, domestic violence, sexual assault, and stalking. This leaves many students with limited confidential options for their reporting decisions. While, historically, faculty may have served as confidential help sources to students on a host of personal matters, particularly those faculty from disciplines that study or train students for careers within the victim-helping field—such as psychology, women's studies, sociology, and criminology—most universities have placed those faculty within the mandatory reporting group. Instead, because of the confidential nature of their work, the task force report suggests that victim advocates are key to victims' decision making, offering victims options for reporting, access to both on- and off-campus resources, and academic and housing accommodations. Advocates also may serve as mentors to victims in understanding and navigating the campuses' sexual misconduct, grievance, and disciplinary policies and procedures. These advocates would remain with the victims along all of their decisions, including deciding not to participate in a formal investigation, or their decisions to report their complaints and enter a formal set of proceedings, investigations, and adjudications. For a further discussion, see Chapter 11 by Helen Eigenberg and Joanne Belknap.

Fourth, the report notes the government's commitment to making enforcement efforts more transparent while at the same time ensuring that colleges and universities have the resources to be able to address and prevent sexual violence. This includes the provision of a fifty-two-point guidance document that offers information on students' rights and protections, the college and university's obligations under Title IX, and additional clarification of the newest amendments to the Clery Act within the Campus SaVE Act. This fourth objective has at its core to direct universities to a clear understanding of the need to protect and support student victims both during and after investigations.

Who Should Investigate Sexual Assault Complaints?

An important concern of the White House Task Force's recommendations and the federal government's requirement of colleges and universities to fulfill their obligations under Title IX is whether universities are truly capable and equipped to investigate these crimes of sexual violence. Depending on the size of the campus and its historic caseload, they likely lack specialized training, experience, and investigative resources to adequately investigate claims of sexual assault. An important element of the task force report is the recommendation that universities create formally negotiated relationships with local law enforcement agencies. This is particularly crucial when both local law enforcement and campus police are involved in the same case with Title IX investigators. Federal legislation (U.S. Department of Education 2011) has clearly noted that criminal investigations do not mitigate a school's obligation to conduct its own investigation and disciplinary action, or allow universities to wait for the conclusion of a criminal case. Collaboration is therefore key to ensuring the safety of victims and college campuses, along with holding perpetrators accountable. The White House Task Force therefore recommends a memorandum of understanding (MOU) with local law enforcement:

> An MOU can help open lines of communication and increase coordination among campus security, local law enforcement and other community groups that provide victim services. An MOU can also improve security on and around campus, make investigations and prosecutions more efficient, and increase officers' understanding of the unique needs of sexual assault victims. (2014, 15)

To assist universities in building these collaborations, the task force has developed sample MOU documents that campuses may adopt to negotiate the relationships between colleges and local law enforcement. CASA, currently sitting in the Senate (discussed later in this chapter), would require these MOUs with local law enforcement agencies, and they would be reviewed and updated (as needed) every two years. The MOUs would provide a clear delineation of the responsibilities of colleges and universities and police agencies, and facilitate shared information on certain types of crime, including the sexual victimizations of students.

In this vein, the prosecutor for St. Joseph County in Indiana, which covers the jurisdiction of Notre Dame University, has urged victims to report their victimizations to the county's Special Victims Unit, as opposed to campus law enforcement (Emmett 2015). At the same time, the prosecutor invited Notre Dame to take part in the Special Victims Unit when their caseload included Notre Dame students. Emmett (2015) notes that the university responded by stating that as an authorized law enforcement agency in the state of Indiana, the Notre Dame Security Police would be the appropriate reporting agency for crime occurring on its campuses and property. Yet the concern is whether a larger police agency with diverse experience in victim-centered investigations would be better equipped to lead or take over these investigations. At the time this book was published, Notre Dame was under its second Title IX investigation in five years for its mishandling of sexual assault complaints. Notre Dame has company, with 246 additional Title IX investigations of colleges and universities currently under way.

Alternatively, there are reasons to believe that placing the primary investigative element in the hands of universities—in connection with the other recommendations of the report and Title IX guidelines, including prevention messaging and victim services—offers important tools to transform a college campus's cultural norms with respect to sexual violence. An example of this shift is the new set of protocols most recently adopted by the University of Texas system. As of March 2016, all police officers on all fourteen University of Texas campuses will be trained on new investigative protocols that are part of *The Blueprint for Campus Police: Responding to Sexual Assault* (Busch-Armendariz, Sulley, and Hill 2016). These protocols take a victim-centered approach to victim reporting and law enforcement investigations to place supporting victims at the forefront of police interactions. The new investigative techniques are adopted from the work of Rebecca Campbell (2012) and her research on the neurobiology of sexual assault and the implications for police investigations. As New (2016) notes, administrators at the University of Texas offer the manual as guidance for other colleges and universities with the hope that it will lead to an overall cultural shift on campuses and eventually increase victim reporting.

The White House Task Force Report and the LGBT Community

While sexual violence affects all victims in terms of a host of negative consequences, Pérez and Hussey (2014) point out that lesbian, gay, bisexual, and transgender (LGBT) survivors are uniquely affected. LGBT victims encounter obstacles to support, recovery, and justice that are related to their sexual identity and their experiences of sexual violence. This points to the need for specific and culturally competent services that not only address the victimization and its aftermath but also the unique elements of prejudice, stigma, and discrimination encountered by LGBT victims. Pérez and Hussey note that CASA, or S. 2692, will require training of college and university staff that carefully addresses the dynamics and impacts of sexual violence on LGBT victims, as well as information on how this may vary based on cultural background. Similarly, the leadership from Rape, Abuse and Incest National Network (RAINN) has argued for a particular focus on LGBT and other previously ignored communities when considering the adoption of strategies to prevent and respond to sexual violence. In a letter to the White House Task Force, RAINN representatives Scott Berkowitz and Rebecca O'Connor noted:

> There is no shortage of campaigns designed to deliver anti-sexual violence awareness and prevention to college-aged students and other members of the community. While many of these programs seem promising, research to date is insufficient to allow us to know how effective they are or to identify best-in-class programs. There is also insufficient research to know if one-size messages work, or if (and how) they should be tailored for audiences such as male or LGBT survivors or those with disabilities. (2014, 3)

Thus, not only do we need to begin to implement the recommendations of the White House Task Force Report but also do so in ways that allow researchers and policy analysts the opportunity to evaluate their impact on all members of our campus communities.

Critiques of the White House Task Force Report

While many of the task force recommendations suggest how universities might best direct their limited resources to reduce the incidence and impact of sexual violence on their campuses, the White House Task Force Report has also been subject to a number of critiques. Most vocal is the argument that many of the recommendations in the report negatively affect student due process. Some legal scholars, and the Foundation for Individual Rights in Education (FIRE) in particular, have noted concern "about campus civil liberties and the reliability, impartiality, and fundamental fairness of campus judicial proceedings for students accused of sexual harassment and assault" (2014, para. 1). Bader (2014) has a number of critiques of the recommendations in the White House Task Force Report and its position on changes to the obligations of colleges and universities under Title IX. These relate to the burden of proof proposed for campus disciplinary proceedings, attacks on the rights of defendants and their counsel to utilize cross-examinations, and due process. Bader notes that the new guidance will lead to a number of legal problems for colleges and universities since the recommendation ignores the Supreme Court's standing position on cross-examinations. In May 2016, law professors from across the country jointly wrote an "Open Letter Regarding Campus Free Speech and Sexual Assault" (Alexander et al. 2016), which they framed as a protest to a series of directives and enforcement actions by the U.S. Department of Education's Office for Civil Rights (OCR). In particular, they argued that the 2011 Dear Colleague Letter, along with recommendations around its enforcement, "curtailed a number of due process protections for students accused of sexual assault" (2), and that the "lowering" of the standard of proof for on-campus adjudications to preponderance of the evidence was inappropriate.

Other critiques include the recommendation that college and university campuses adopt innovative and different models of investigation and adjudication. The White House Task Force Report notes:

> Schools are experimenting with new ideas. Some are adopting different variations on the "single investigator" model, where a trained investigator or investigators interview the complainant and alleged perpetrator, gather any physical evidence, interview available witnesses—and then either render a finding, present a recommenda-

tion, or even work out an acceptance-of-responsibility agreement with the offender. These models stand in contrast to the more traditional system, where a college hearing or judicial board hears a case (sometimes tracking the adversarial, evidence-gathering criminal justice model), makes a finding, and decides the sanction. Preliminary reports from the field suggest that these innovative models, in which college judicial boards play a much more limited role, encourage reporting and bolster trust in the process, while at the same time safeguarding an alleged perpetrator's right to notice and to be heard. (2014, 14)

A strong criticism of this model lies in the assumption that the single-administrator model "would be empowered to serve as detective, judge and jury, affording the accused no chance to challenge his or her accuser's testimony" (FIRE 2014, para. 5). Given that the task force report is a recommendation document, it is not clear whether the report is suggesting that campuses move to the model. Instead, the recommendation appears to suggest that institutions be empowered to try innovative strategies that still fulfill their legislative mandates. Within the report was also the notation that the single-administrator model might have variations, one being that a set of investigators would present their recommendations to a larger disciplinary board.

Criticism of the single-administrator model has another side to it, one not identified within the legal challenges. For those researchers and advocates who have worked "in the trenches," a fear of this single-administrator model may be that investigations will not have the kind of transparency that will ensure victims' access to a fair and open process that ensures both their safety and offender accountability. One of the greatest ironies of these legal challenges to the 2011 Dear Colleague Letter, the Campus SaVE Act, and the White House Task Force Report is their sharp focus on the rights of the accused. What is lacking is evidence of their concern for the civil liberties of victims, and how these legislative requirements do not yet go far enough to ensure the impartiality and fundamental fairness of campus judicial proceedings for victims.

A critique particularly relevant to one recommendation within the task force report relates to how colleges and universities should adopt a mutually agreed definition of consent to sexual activity, and that this definition should be utilized in both prevention messaging and in disciplinary procedures. Consent is one of the most misunderstood concepts within discussions of interpersonal violence and, in particular, sexual violence. Many educational programs have recently adopted a "yes means yes" affirmative definition of consent—in which consent for sexual activity is understood as clear, knowing, voluntary, freely and actively given in mutually understandable words or actions that indicate a willingness to participate in mutually agreed sexual activity. While consent to sexual activity may be communicated in a variety of ways, it is presumed that consent has not been given in the absence of clear, positive agreement. Many colleges and universities have adopted affirmative consent definitions and policies, and there are also state legislatures that are considering this affirmative definition within their state codes. Recent legislation in California redefined consent to sexual activity to be an affirmative, unambiguous, and conscious decision by each participant to engage in mutually agreed sexual activity. The language with respect to the definition within the White House Task Force Report states:

> We are also providing a checklist for schools to use in drafting (or reevaluating) their own sexual misconduct policies. Although every school will need to tailor a policy to its own needs and circumstances, all schools should be sure to bring the key stakeholders—including students—to the table. Among other things, this checklist includes ideas a school could consider in deciding what is—or is not—consent to sexual activity. As we heard from many students, this can often be the essence of the matter—and a school community should work together to come up with a careful and considered understanding. (2014, 3)

The shift to affirmative consent and the need for higher education institutions to construct campus-specific definitions of consent have important implications for victims, the accused, and campuses responding to sexual violence. Many campus-based definitions included in educational programming emphasize consent with reference to (1) the absence of actual or implied physical force, threats, intimidation, or coercion; and/or (2) the incapacitation or reasonable knowledge of a person's incapacitation or unconscious state due to illness or consumption of alcohol or drugs. These elements are largely consistent with most state laws. Yet many campuses have also adopted the broader definitions of affirmative consent outlined previously. What is less clear is how often colleges and universities within specific states have obviously tied their definition of consent to state statutory language. In contrast to the White House Task Force recommendation, the Campus SaVE Act provision, section 304 of the Violence Against Women Reauthorization Act (VAWA) mandates that the definition of consent should be in reference to sexual offenses in the applicable jurisdiction. Specifically, the Campus SaVE Act requires primary prevention and awareness programs that promote awareness of rape, acquaintance rape, domestic violence, dating violence, sexual assault, and stalking to include the definition of consent, with reference to sexual offenses, in the applicable jurisdiction (American Council on Education 2014). The question is, how should colleges and universities address any differences in the definition of consent to sexual activity that will be used on their campus for prevention education and, potentially, for sexual misconduct investigations that take a preponderance of the evidence as their threshold, when these complaints may ultimately be used by outside prosecution in criminal cases where consent is defined by the state's criminal code? How can university administrators ensure that victims are aware of any differences in the definition of consent and the impact of those differences before victims decide whether to report their victimizations to local police departments?

Assessing University Actions to Respond to Sexual Violence before and after the White House Task Force Report

There is a small literature that has explored the success of college and university efforts to prevent and respond to sexual violence against college students. Research in this area includes work that has examined the response of colleges and universities to sexual violence, as well as an evaluation of campus sexual violence policies and procedures, provision of violence prevention education, confidential reporting, and victim services (Karjane, Fisher, and Cullen 2002; Potter, Krider, and McMahon 2000; Richards 2016). Using a nationally representative sample of 2,438 colleges and universities, Karjane, Fisher, and Cullen (2002) were the first to fully explore campus responses to sexual violence. They concluded that compliance with federal requirements, including Title IX and Clery, was relatively low and that less than 40 percent of campuses reported crime statistics in a manner that was fully consistent with the Clery Act. They also noted that while many colleges and universities, particularly large campuses with residential populations, have moved quickly to develop sexual assault policies and make these easily accessible to their students, smaller, nonresidential campuses have not been as successful in this area. At the same time only 53 percent of campus policy documents explicitly require the inclusion and notification of the complainant during the investigation and adjudication process. Research by Potter, Krider, and McMahon (2000) suggests that less than 30 percent of students who were provided with a URL link to their campuses' sexual assault policies, procedures, and resources actually watched the video. More important, the majority (60 percent) of campuses provided little or no violence prevention education and/or training to their students.

More recent work by Richards (2016) provides both a comparison to the findings reported by Karjane, Fisher, and Cullen, and the opportunity to explore the response of college and university campus authorities to campus sexual assault after the White House Task Force Report was released. In her work, Richards (2016) notes that consistent with the White House Task Force's (2014) recommendations, the majority of universities have clear and accessible Title IX policies and procedures, with 95 percent having a policy on sex discrimination within their Title IX policy, 85 percent of schools having a separate sexual violence policy, and 65 percent providing access to the policies in their student handbook. Campuses have also clarified options for reporting for both victims and bystanders. The majority of campuses (82 percent) outline clear procedures a student should follow if a sexual assault offense occurs, and clearly identify the Title IX Coordinator for their campus (70 percent). With respect to colleges and universities' investigatory and disciplinary policies and procedures, campuses have made progress in ensuring these are accessible to students (79 percent) and that they explicitly distinguish the procedures for sexual misconduct (80 percent). Campuses are not making substantial progress in connecting their students to on- and off-campus victim services and resources. Only 65 percent of campuses offer on-campus counseling for victims of sexual violence, and 55 percent provide victim advocacy. Richards notes that only three-quarters of campuses identify off-campus resources in their online materials. Another area for improvement is in the provision of academic and residential accommodations, with only 70 percent of campuses notifying victims of sexual violence about these measures. Interestingly, Richards found that there has been little upward movement in universities providing violence prevention education related to sexual violence; only 61 percent of campuses provide this education, compared to the 58 percent who did so prior to the 2011 Dear Colleague Letter and the White House Task Force Report (Karjane, Fisher, and Cullen 2002).

While Richards's research was unable to evaluate the types of education provided by campuses, the White House Task Force, along with components of the Campus SaVE Act, have clearly identified a number of key elements of this education, including bystander intervention, defining consent, and how to engage in actions to prevent victimization. Additionally, campuses need to engage in coordinated and cooperative efforts when developing and implementing campus-wide education and violence prevention messaging. This includes identifying existing programming on campus, conducting a needs assessment of the violence and victimization elements to be incorporated in education and messaging, and holding focus groups on campus to identify key stakeholders who will be responsible for implementing the educational programs. Student affairs staff must be actively encouraged to participate, especially from such offices as the counseling center, student health center, housing, athletics, student success, orientation, public safety, and academic and faculty affairs. Students also are key stakeholders, and given the diversity of student experiences and perspectives, their voices in the design and implementation of prevention programming is key to its eventual success.

What should not get lost in this discussion is why we have such federal mandates in the first place: both to prevent victimization and to assist survivors. To be successful at meeting these goals, we must continue to evaluate and assess college and university efforts to respond to and prevent campus sexual violence. Richards's (2016) conclusion echoes what most of the contributors to this volume have argued—that college and university campuses must make a dramatic shift in focus and move beyond a primary emphasis on compliance with federal mandates. Instead, their focus must be on identifying and implementing the best practices for preventing and responding to sexual violence. In particular, Richards (2016) argues that our emphasis for action and evaluation should be on lowering rates of victimization and improving service access and adjudication on our campuses. We need more research to be able to answer these important questions.

It's On Us Initiative

> It's On Us asks everyone—men and women across America—to make a personal commitment to step off the sidelines and be part of the solution to campus sexual assault.
>
> It is on all of us to reject the quiet tolerance of sexual assault and to refuse to accept what's unacceptable.
>
> PRESIDENT BARACK OBAMA, *September 19, 2014*

As an outcome of the work of the White House Task Force, on September 19, 2014, the White House launched the It's On Us initiative (White House 2014). The goal of the It's On Us initiative is to provide a change in how we—as members of a college campus and the communities within which these campuses are located—understand the nature, causes, and solutions to sexual violence. While campuses have historically focused on the actions of victims and perpetrators, the campaign asks campus members to take on the responsibility of preventing sexual violence themselves. In particular, the initiative focuses on engaging men to act in ways that make it clear that sexual violence is unacceptable, and that victims and survivors will be believed and supported. The initiative is a broad public-private partnership with branded name recognition that draws its messaging from college athletics, student leaders, professional athletes and other celebrities, and other stakeholders. Colleges and universities that participate in the It's On Us initiative are asked to have their campus administrators, student leaders, faculty, and entire student body take a pledge that represents a commitment to help keep women and men safe from sexual assault and a promise not to be bystanders to the problem, but to be part of the solution. Specifically, the pledge is "to recognize that non-consensual sex is sexual assault; to identify situations in which sexual assault may occur; to intervene in situations where consent has not or cannot be given; and to create an environment in which sexual assault is unacceptable and survivors are supported" (It's On Us 2016).

Campuses are encouraged to create their own original content and materials while promoting their own campus-specific It's On Us campaign.

The power of the It's On Us campaign is in its endorsement of shared responsibility to prevent and respond to campus sexual violence, an ideology that resonates deeply within many Obama administration proposals. This specific campaign invokes bystander intervention, a well-respected methodology for effecting behavioral change and intervening in situations of danger, while it also asks everyone not to leave the needs of survivors solely in the hands of professionals. In making this argument, the campaign shifts the dialogue from how universities are responding to federal mandates to how we are collectively contributing to the cultures of our campuses. This is an important addition to the arsenal against sexual violence, but it does not negate the importance of codifying the policy recommendations included in the task force report.

Where Do We Go Now?

> When our sons and daughters go to college, they shouldn't have to worry about their safety on campus. The time to address campus sexual assault is now. We have a strong, bipartisan bill that will help combat these crimes and provide survivors with the assistance they need. I will continue working with my colleagues in the Senate to pass the Campus Accountability and Safety Act.
>
> **Senator Dean Heller**

The White House Task Force Report to Protect Students from Sexual Assault outlined important recommendations for colleges and universities, while offering transparency in how campuses will be held accountable for their response to sexual violence. CASA is a bill that was introduced in February 2015, and referred to the Subcommittee on Higher Education and Workforce Training in April 2015 (see Exhibit 9.2). CASA offers the opportunity to formalize the recommendations of the White House Task Force Report. In particular, the bipartisan supporters of the bill have argued that the legislation will help in reforming sexual assault policies, procedures, investigations, and disciplinary practices on college campuses to ensure the safety of victims while holding perpetrators accountable. The bill also pushes forward greater cooperation between college and universities and local law enforcement. It identifies important amendments to the Clery Act, including expanding the types of data that campuses would be required to publish, in particular by adding a requirement to report the outcomes of sexual assault complaints. At the heart of CASA is great accountability and transparency in how colleges and universities address sexual violence.

**Exhibit 9.2 Summary of S.590 Campus Accountability and Safety Act—
114th Congress (2015–2016)**

First Action: Introduced in Senate on 02/26/2015

Latest Action: Referred to the Subcommittee on Higher Education and Workforce
Training on 04/29/2015

Reference:

Campus Accountability and Safety Act of 2015, S.590, 114th Congress (2015–2016).

Hearing before the Committee on Health, Education, Labor, and Pensions
Retrieved from https://www.congress.gov/bill/114th-congress/senate-bill/590

Amends provisions of the Higher Education Act of 1965 (HEA) known as the
Jeanne Clery Disclosure of Campus Security Policy and Campus Crime Statistics
Act to require institutions of higher education (IHE) that participate in title IV
(Student Assistance) programs to include in their annual campus security reports
provided to current and prospective students and employees:

- the memorandum of understanding that this Act requires IHE to enter into
  with local law enforcement agencies (and update, as necessary, every two
  years) to clearly delineate responsibilities and share information about certain serious crimes, including sexual violence, occurring against students or
  other individuals on campus; and
- specified information regarding the number of sex offenses reported to the
  IHE and the IHE's disposition of sex offense cases.

Requires IHE to provide new students and employees with a statement that identifies domestic violence, dating violence, sexual assault, and stalking as crimes
which will be reported and with respect to which, based on the victim's wishes,
the IHE will cooperate with local law enforcement. Requires an IHE's disciplinary
procedures for such offenses to comply with its campus security policy and provide both the accuser and accused written notice of the outcome of such procedures or a change in an outcome within 24 hours after it occurs.

Directs the Secretary to develop and administer through an online portal a standardized, online, and biannual survey of students regarding their experiences with
sexual violence and harassment. Omits survey responses from the annual crime
statistics IHE must report, but requires the Secretary to publish survey information that includes campus-level data for each school on the Department of Education's (ED's) website biannually. Requires IHE to publish the campus-level
results of the survey on their websites and in their annual security reports.

Requires ED to make publicly available guidance regarding the intersection of the
campus security and crime statistics reporting requirements under title IV and
requirements under title IX of the Education Amendments of 1972.

Requires each IHE that receives funding under the HEA to establish a campus security policy that includes:

- the designation of one or more confidential advisors at the IHE to whom non-employee victims of sexual harassment, domestic violence, dating violence, sexual assault, or stalking can report, including anonymously;
- provision on the IHE's website of specified information to assist the victims of such crimes, including contact information for the confidential advisor;
- authorization for the IHE to provide an online reporting system to collect anonymous disclosures of crimes and track patterns of crime on campus;
- an amnesty policy for any student who, in good faith, reports sexual violence to a higher education responsible employee, with respect to a non-violent student conduct violation revealed in the course of such a report;
- a training program, developed by the Secretary, for IHE employees who are involved in implementing the school's student grievance procedures or responsible for interviewing alleged sexual assault victims;
- a uniform process (for each of the IHE's campuses) for student disciplinary proceedings relating to claims of sexual violence against a student attending the IHE;
- the annual provision of information to ED's Office for Civil Rights and the Civil Rights Division of the Department of Justice (DOJ) regarding the IHE's title IX coordinator;
- the provision of written notice to the accuser and accused student within 24 hours of the IHE's decision to proceed with an institutional disciplinary process regarding an allegation of sexual misconduct; and
- the provision of written notice to the accuser and accused student within 24 hours of the determination of responsibility made by the disciplinary board and any sanctions.

Directs the Secretary to establish a title IX website that includes:

- the name and contact information for the title IX coordinator at each IHE, including a brief description of the coordinator's role and the roles of other officials who may be contacted regarding sexual harassment; and
- ED's pending investigations and the actions it has taken regarding all title IX complaints and compliance reviews related to sexual harassment.

Directs the Secretary to develop online training materials for training higher education responsible employees, title IX coordinators, and individuals involved in implementing an IHE's student conduct grievance procedures.

Authorizes the Secretary to impose civil penalties upon IHE that fail to: (1) enter into memorandums of understanding with their local law enforcement agencies, (2) carry out campus security and crime statistics reporting requirements, or (3) establish the requisite campus security policy.

Amends the Violence Against Women and Department of Justice Reauthorization Act of 2005 to: (1) increase the minimum grant that may be provided to IHE to combat domestic violence, dating violence, sexual assault, and stalking on campuses; and (2) authorize the use of such grants to train campus personnel in how to use victim-centered, trauma-informed interview techniques.

Amends the HEA to authorize the Secretary, using amounts collected under this Act's penalty provisions, to award competitive grants to IHE to enhance their ability to address sexual harassment, sexual assault, domestic violence, dating violence, and stalking, on campus.

Amends the Education Amendments of 1972 to authorize the Secretary or DOJ to impose civil penalties on IHE that violate or fail to carry out title IX requirements regarding sexual violence. Gives individuals 180 days after their graduation or disaffiliation with an IHE to file a complaint regarding such a violation with ED's Office for Civil Rights.

The five major components of the proposed legislation are: (1) the establishment of new campus resources and support services for student survivors; (2) ensuring minimum training standards for on-campus personnel; (3) creating historic new transparency requirements; (4) requiring a uniform discipline process and coordination with law enforcement; and (5) establishing enforceable Title IX penalties and stiffer penalties for Clery Act violations. First, given that a key recommendation of the task force report was to expand the confidential reporting options available to student victims, CASA would require colleges and universities to identify confidential advisers who would be trained to assist victims and survivors of all types of interpersonal violence, including sexual harassment, domestic violence, dating violence, sexual assault, and stalking. Most important, the help sought from these confidential advisers would allow victims to weigh their decision-making options and would not automatically initiate a criminal and/or Title IX investigation. Second, CASA would provide a minimum level of training for campus staff and administrators responsible for preventing and responding to sexual violence. The expansion of victim-centered training and culturally appropriate investigative strategies would increase victim reporting and participation in disciplinary proceedings. Third, the requirements under CASA would lead to a transformation in how colleges and universities currently report their crime statistics for Clery. This includes the collection of climate survey data from students on their experiences of victimization, reporting options and decisions, and university processes. The data that universities would be required to collect under the Clery Act would also be expanded. CASA would lead to greater transparency of the actions taken with colleges and universities under Title IX investigations by requiring that the Department of Education disclose the names of all colleges and universities under investigation, as well as the resolution agreements. Fourth, CASA would require a single uniform disciplinary process and set of proceedings that would exclude subgroups on campus from conducting their own investigations. Some elements of this uniformity include the requirement that complainants and accused students would receive notification of a campus's decision to initiate a disciplinary process within twenty-four hours. To facilitate coordination among security officers, campuses would be required to have MOUs with local police agencies responsible for criminal investigations. Finally, CASA would increase college and university accountability for responding to sexual violence. This includes both increasing enforcement of Title IX violations and enhanced penalties for failure to comply with Title IX and the Clery Act.

In examining the potential impact of the White House Task Force Report, the question becomes what more do we need to know to successfully respond to and prevent campus violence against women? We now have decades of data on the extent, nature, and dynamic of violence against college women. Should this not have been enough to identify best practices and direct our prevention and response initiatives? While recent federal interest is a turning point in this effort, the question is whether a change in administration may weaken the efforts we are currently seeing. Additionally, while climate surveys are likely to bring us new information on the types of violence that college women have experienced, at significant institutional expense, how those data can and will be used to inform policies, procedures, and programming on individual campuses has not been fully discussed. More important, will these new standardized data collection efforts bring us any closer to securing a permanent rationale for our ongoing efforts to address, prevent, and respond to violence against women, or must we continue to justify our work, and the expenses of this work, in each new legislative iteration?

This leads to a final important consideration of the recommendations of the task force report: where should we prioritize our efforts, and what policy and political efforts can best help campuses meet these needs? Identifying the problem through climate surveys; preventing sexual assault by fully engaging the campus community, especially men; transforming our processes so we effectively respond when a student is sexually assaulted; and increasing transparency about all of these efforts as we improve our coordinated responses—these are all vital elements of our efforts to end sexual violence on our college campuses. Yet each strategy invokes slightly different stakeholders and committed leaders, and each faces its own backlash, from academic disagreement with prevalence estimates to legalistic claims about biased disciplinary processes. A shared commitment, such as is expressed within the It's On Us campaign, is necessary for our success, but also insufficient. Such resolve must be coupled with political and fiscal accountability measures, frequently embodied within legislative acts like Title IX, Clery, the

Campus SaVE Act, and CASA, which let none of these integrated and interdependent strategies fall to the wayside.

As the report notes, the recommendations by the White House Task Force are merely a starting point in an ongoing set of strategies to ensure that colleges and universities have the resources, tools, and templates to develop a coordinated plan to address and respond to sexual violence. As for next steps, our work, and the work of other researchers, advocates, criminal justice practitioners, and campus administrators continues.

REFERENCES

Alexander, L., S. Bibas, D. Barnhizer, D. A. Candeub, E. Bartholet, and R. J. Cottrol, . . . and A. E. Wilmarth. 2016. Law professors' open letter regarding campus free speech and sexual assault. Available at https://www.lankford.senate.gov/imo/media/doc/Law -Professor-Open-Letter-May-16-2016.pdf.

American Council on Education. 2014. New requirements imposed by the Violence Against Women Reauthorization Act. Available at http://www.acenet.edu/news-room /Documents/VAWA-Summary.pdf.

Bader, H. 2014. White House Task Force attacks cross-examination and due process rights on campus. Foundation for Individual Rights in Education, May 1. Available at https:// www.thefire.org/white-house-task-force-attacks-cross-examination-due-process -rights-on-campus/.

Banyard, V. L., and M. M. Moynihan. 2011. Variation in bystander behavior related to sexual and intimate partner violence prevention: Correlates in a sample of college students. *Psychology of Violence* 1 (4): 287–301.

Banyard, V. L., M. M. Moynihan, A. Cares, and R. Warner. 2014. How do we know if it works? Measuring outcomes in bystander-focused violence prevention on campuses. *Psychology of Violence* 4 (1): 101–115.

Banyard, V. L., M. M. Moynihan, and E. G. Plante. 2007. Sexual violence prevention through bystander education: An experimental evaluation. *Journal of Community Psychology* 35 (4): 463–481.

Berkowitz, S., and R. O'Connor. 2014. Letter to the White House Task Force to Protect Students from Sexual Assault. Available at Rape, Abuse, and Incest National Network, https:// www.rainn.org/images/03-2014/WH-Task-Force-RAINN-Recommendations.pdf.

Busch-Armendariz, N. B., C. Sulley, and K. Hill. 2016. *The blueprint for campus police: Responding to sexual assault.* Austin: University of Texas, Institute on Domestic Violence and Sexual Assault.

Campbell, R. 2012. The neurobiology of sexual assault: Implications for first responders, law enforcement, prosecutors, and victim advocates. Available at the National Institute of Justice, http://nij.gov/multimedia/presenter/presenter-campbell/pages/ presenter -campbell-transcript.aspx.

Campus Accountability and Safety Act. 2015. S.590, 114th Congress (2015–2016). Hearing before the Committee on Health, Education, Labor, and Pensions Available at https:// www.congress.gov/bill/114th-congress/senate-bill/590.

CBS News. 2016. Student who helped stop Stanford sexual assault describes what he saw. Available at http://www.cbsnews.com/news/stanford-university-sexual-assault-former -swimmer-brock-turner-witnesses/.

Emmett, S. 2015. Prosecutor urges victims of sexual assault to report directly to special victims unit; Notre Dame disagrees. Foundation for Individual Rights in Education, May 13. Available at https://www.thefire.org/prosecutor-urges-victims-of-sexual -assault-to-report-directly-to-special-victims-unit-notre-dame-disagrees/.

Foundation for Individual Rights in Education (FIRE). 2014. FIRE responds to White House Task Force's first report on campus sexual assault. Available at https://www .thefire.org/fire-responds-to-white-house-task-forces-first-report-on-campus-sexual -assault/.

Gillibrand, K. 2016. To combat campus sexual assault, republican leaders and sexual assault survivors join Senators Gillibrand and McCaskill to renew push for senate to pass Campus Accountability and Safety Act: Bipartisan legislation would help protect students and create historic transparency requirements at colleges and universities. Press release, April 26. Available at https://www.gillibrand.senate.gov/newsroom/press /release/to-combat-campus-sexual-assault-republican-leaders-and-sexual-assault -survivors-join-senators-gillibrand-and-mccaskill-to-renew-push-for-senate-to-pass -campus-accountability-and-safety-act.

Holley, P. 2016. He thought the couple were having sex outside a bar. Then he realized she was unconscious. *Washington Post,* July 23. Available at https://www.washingtonpost .com/news/morning-mix/wp/2016/07/23/he-saw-a-couple-by-a-dumpster-then-he -realized-what-was-happening-and-took-action/.

It's On Us. 2016. The It's On Us campaign pledge. Available at http://itsonus.org/#pledge.

Karjane, H. K., B. S. Fisher, and F. T. Cullen. 2002. *Campus sexual assault: How America's institutions of higher education respond* (NIJ Grant # 1999-WA-VX-0008). Newton, MA: Education Development Center.

Krebs, C. P., C. Lindquist, M. Berzofsky, B. Shook-Sa, K. Peterson, M. Planty, L. Langton, and J. Stroop. 2016. Campus climate survey validation study final technical report (NCJ 49545). Washington, DC: U.S. Department of Justice, Bureau of Justice Statistics.

New, J. 2016. Replacing "tradition with science." *Inside Higher Education,* March 1. Available at https://www.insidehighered.com/news/2016/03/01/u-texas-announces-new -protocols-investigating-campus-sexual-assault.

Pérez, Z. J., and H. Hussey. 2014. A hidden crisis: Including the LGBT community when addressing sexual violence on college campuses. Center for American Progress, September 19. Available at https://www.americanprogress.org/issues/lgbt/report/2014/09 /19/97504/a-hidden-crisis/.

Peterson, K., P. Sharps, V. Banyard, R. A. Powers, C. Kaukinen, D. Gross, M. R. Decker, C. Baatz, and J. Campbell. 2016. An evaluation of two dating violence prevention programs on a college campus. *Journal of Interpersonal Violence.* doi: 10.1177 /0886260516636069.

Potter, R. H., J. E. Krider, and P. M. McMahon. 2000. Examining elements of campus sexual violence policies is deterrence or health promotion favored? *Violence Against Women* 6 (12): 1345–1362.

Richards, T. N. 2016. An updated review of institutions of higher education's responses to sexual assault results from a nationally representative sample. *Journal of Interpersonal Violence,* doi: 0886260516658757.

U.S. Department of Education, Office for Civil Rights (DOE, OCR). 2011. *Dear Colleague Letter.* Available at http://www2.ed.gov/about/offices/list/ocr/letters/colleague -201104.pdf.

White House. 2014. *Fact Sheet: Launch of the "It's On Us" public awareness campaign to help prevent campus sexual assault.* White House Office of the Press Secretary, September 19.

Available at https://www.whitehouse.gov/the-press-office/2014/09/19/fact-sheet-launch
-it-s-us-public-awareness-campaign-help-prevent-campus-.

White House Task Force to Protect Students from Sexual Assault. 2014. *Not alone: The first
report of the White House Task Force to protect students from sexual assault.* Office of
the Vice President and the White House Council on Women and Girls, April. Available
at https://www.notalone.gov/assets/report.pdf.

10

The (Re)Organization of Campus Responses

Carmen Suarez

Title IX Scope Evolution

Title IX has been part of the lexicon of education, K–12 and higher, for more than forty years. It will be forty-five years old on June 23, 2017. Prior to 2011, Title IX was most widely known as a path for equity in athletics. And, indeed, noticeable progress has been made in the access, inclusion, and success of females pursuing athletics. Resources—while not yet equal or equivalent—are much improved, and women have excelled on the national and global stage. I like to note two things when making presentations with regard to Title IX on my current and former campuses. First, in the 2012 Summer Olympics, U.S. women brought home more gold medals than the U.S. male athletes. I hasten to add that this factoid is not about women versus men à la Billie Jean King and Bobby Riggs. Rather, this is about U.S pride and competitive advantage. This means that by combating systemic and structural discrimination in athletics against women through the use of Title IX, the United States increased its competitive ability and gold medals exponentially (Rapp 2012). The second noteworthy fact to share is that the 2012 Summer Olympics marked the first time every country in the games had at least one female athlete participating (*Los Angeles Times* 2012). Would this be due in part to U.S. global influence? A correlation if not a causation? I like to think so.

Title IX is a law enacted in 1972, and is part of education amendments to the Higher Education Act of 1965. Title IX in part states: "No person in the United States shall, on the basis of sex, be excluded from participation in, be denied the benefits of, or be subjected to discrimination under any education program or activity receiving federal financial assistance" (U.S. Department of Education 2015b, para. 2). The Department of Education (DOE) Office for Civil Rights (OCR) defines the scope of the law to be:

> Title IX applies to institutions that receive federal financial assistance from ED (the U.S. Department of Education), including state and local educational agencies. . . . Educational programs and activities that receive ED funds must operate in a nondiscriminatory manner. Some key issue areas in which recipients have Title IX obligations are: recruitment, admissions, and counseling; financial assistance; athletics; sex-based harassment; treatment of pregnant and parenting students; discipline; single-sex education; and employment. (2015b, para. 3–4)

Title IX has evolved over these four and a half decades. The law stating nondiscrimination in education is relatively short. The regulations published through the years—first by Health, Education, and Welfare, and subsequently by the DOE and the oversight by its OCR—provide us with the evolving definitions and understandings of what constitutes sex discrimination and the expectations of institutional response to the mandate of the law. Two examples of expectations of institutional response include both the affirmative use of Title IX to address systemic and structural discrimination, such as in athletics, and the use of Title IX to address individual and group complaints about sex discrimination and sexual harassment.

During the past years, we have seen a body of regulations and case law build to define sexual discrimination as barriers to full participation in all programs and functions of education, including employment. The purpose of the law was and is understood to be institutional dismantling of such barriers.

Through regulation and court cases, sexual harassment has come to be defined as one barrier, a particularly ugly form, of sex discrimination. Through the language of judicial rulings in court cases about sexual harassment and guidance from the DOE, our understandings moved from the basic quid pro quo definition of sexual harassment to the hostile climate definition and scope.

It is important to note that sexual misconduct as a form of sexual harassment has always been identified as such under Title IX and includes—pre- and post-2011 (more on this watershed year in a moment)—physical acts of a sexual nature, including sexual violence and assault. Such behaviors have long been identified as being barriers that cause a hostile learning and working environment.

In April 2011, colleges and universities nationwide received a Dear Colleague Letter (DCL) from the DOE. In that letter, the DOE "reminded" colleges and universities that sexual harassment included sexual violence and, as other forms of sexual harassment, must be investigated. The letter made it clear that colleges and universities were not meeting their Title IX responsibilities as most did not investigate allegations of sexual violence. In the letter, the DOE defined sexual violence to include:

> physical sexual acts perpetrated against a person's will or where a person is incapable of giving consent due to the victim's use of drugs or alcohol. An individual also may be unable to give consent due to an intellectual or other disability. A number of different acts fall into the category of sexual violence, including rape, sexual assault, sexual battery, and sexual coercion. All such acts of sexual violence are forms of sexual harassment covered under Title IX. (U.S. Department of Education 2011a, 1)

The DOE provided a summary and fact sheet for this April 4, 2011 letter, delineating a school's basic obligations under Title IX:

- Once a school knows or reasonably should know of possible sexual violence, it must take immediate and appropriate action to investigate or otherwise determine what occurred.
- If sexual violence has occurred, a school must take prompt and effective steps to end the sexual violence, prevent its recurrence, and address its effects, whether or not the sexual violence is the subject of a criminal investigation.
- A school must take steps to protect the complainant as necessary, including interim steps taken prior to the final outcome of the investigation.
- A school must provide a grievance procedure for students to file complaints of sex discrimination, including complaints of sexual violence. These procedures must include an equal opportunity for both parties to present witnesses and other evidence and the same appeal rights.
- A school's grievance procedures must use the preponderance of the evidence standard to resolve complaints of sex discrimination.
- A school must notify both parties of the outcome of the complaint. (U.S. Department of Education 2011b, 2)

This April 2011 DCL created a significantly broader Title IX role for colleges and universities and made clear the institutional responsibility for responding to sexual violence perpetrated against its students, faculty, or staff, with the specific focus on students who experience sexual violence.

The pressure to meet this responsibility has intensified over the past five years. Schools have scrambled to revise policies, procedures, management structures, dissemination of educational programming, and information on an arc of topics from prevention to consent; develop substantive training for all involved; redefine safety and protection; and increase standards of care for victims. This is being done while there is emerging and ongoing refinement by the DOE on its expectations and assessments of compliance to both the spirit and regulations of Title IX and the continuing release of DCLs and guidance documents. In tandem, the White House Task Force to Protect Students from Sexual Assault, formed in 2014, also frames the issues and provides guidance, expectations, and recommended resources that colleges and universities must incorporate into their efforts to meet their responsibilities.

Colleges and universities do this rethinking, relearning, and reorganization work amid deep scrutiny from students, activists, media, federal agencies, groups like the Foundation for Individual Rights in Education (FIRE) and the American Association of University Professors (AAUP), legislators, boards of trustees, community members, internal stakeholders, and constituencies, and with the ever-present and ubiquitous instant posting and analysis within social media venues.

The Purpose

As noted, the DOE continues to provide new DCLs and guidance regarding schools' responsibilities to address sexual violence. Two of significance are the April 29, 2014, Questions and Answers on Title IX and Sexual Violence, referred to as the FAQs (U.S. Department of Education 2014), and the April 24, 2015, DCL regarding the role of Title IX coordinators (U.S. Department of Education 2015a).

The document best summarizing the purpose of the renewed call for school attention to, and attendant responsibilities for, combating sexual violence is the White House Task Force to Protect Students from Sexual Assault First Report, entitled *Not Alone* (White House Task Force 2014). The report lays out the troubling statistics of sexual assault of women in college. It discusses issues facing victims, the history of inadequate response by schools, the lack of coordinated prevention work, and the need for better collaboration between government and schools in preventing sexual violence.

Why has the federal government, through the DOE and the White House, stepped up its call for school responsibility and response to sexual violence and Title IX enforcement for this form of sexual harassment? Because of our students. Because of brave women on campuses nationwide who felt abandoned and betrayed by their universities' responses when they filed complaints of sexual violence. Many did not feel they were believed. Many were told that they should not have been wherever they were. They were told they should not have been drinking. They were subjected to victim blaming. They felt revictimized by their campus adjudication processes. They identified rape culture as pervasive and the failure of their schools to change (Newman and Sander 2014). This sense of not being believed, of being shamed and blamed, and of the processes creating revictimization is well documented in scholarly literature about sexual violence in schools (Cantalupo 2010).

Student survivors/activists in such organizations as Know Your IX are turning to Title IX to see if real change can occur. Other student activists are highlighted in *The Hunting Ground*, a documentary film released in 2015 that focuses on accounts of students from various campuses who were sexually assaulted. It details the efforts of two survivor activists to build a national network of college and university sexual assault survivors to create change in what they deemed inadequate and harmful responses by their schools. Utilizing the law of Title IX by filing complaints with the DOE, these students bring the spotlight of a compliance agency to their institutions to prompt change.

Working Hard to Do Better

There are many who work in colleges and universities who care deeply about sexual violence and its prevention, and these individuals have served in their roles since well before the 2011 DCL was written. Post 2011, Title IX coordinators, student affairs professionals, faculty, and students work even more collaboratively, and mightily, to use the renewed Title IX vigilance and guidance of the DOE and the White House to effect the needed systemic and structural changes, and to deconstruct rape culture.

We have observed the outcomes of improvement for women in athletics by the use of Title IX. The use for athletics equity has been steady, ever vigilant, and strategic. The strategies for continuous improvement for gender equity in sports have been well coordinated, multipronged, and with initiatives and actions occurring in concert as well as concurrently. The 2012 Olympics outcomes serve as an example of what systemic and structural change and a focus on institutional response through the use of Title IX can bring about.

However, many would caution that we cannot wait forty or more years for the changes that we need now to reduce sexual violence. Hence, we work as hard and as smart as we can to address the many dimensions we must attend to in order to meet not only our obligations to protect our students from sexual violence but also to meet the spirit of Title IX: everyone should be free of sex discrimination and hostile environment barriers in pursuing all aspects of their education.

Sexual violence is the most pernicious form of hostile environment sexual discrimination. The ways we organizationally address sexual violence prevention and response are many. We have grown in the past five years to be more encompassing of a holistic understanding of, and approach to, prevention and response to sexual violence, as well as turning to theory, scholarship, and practice to ground our work.

The following discussion on several organizational prevention and response dimensions of our colleges and universities is not meant to be exhaustive. As indicated, we are living through the unfolding of this Title IX application to sexual violence, with regularly emerging new perspectives, calls for action, resources, mistakes, failures, successes, and shared best practices.

The discussion is informed by interviews with current Title IX coordinators, as well as student affairs professionals who are deans and assistant deans of students, conduct officers, and investigators tasked with the many institutional Title IX responsibilities. There were six individual interviews that included two males and an additional group interview process of five, of which one was a male participant, held during a Title IX–related conference.

The following subheads were selected after reflection on these interviews and my own professional experience. The headings reflect the areas in which our Title IX work has evolved and changed post-2011.

Victim-Centered Response

Central to the expectations by the DOE regarding school responsibility and accountability for sexual violence prevention and response is a focus on care, interim measures, and remedies for the victim.

By care, we mean the immediate attention to the needs of the victim from multiple dimensions: emotionally, physically, culturally, socially, and psychically. Institutions must enfold the victim with various services (medical, counseling, advocacy, and so on) without overwhelming, and provide partnership for the decision making in which the victim will need to engage, without influencing or suggesting particular decisions. One individual example would be the decision to undergo a rape kit examination.

When an institution becomes aware that sexual violence has occurred, it must gather information about what it knows about the incident thus far. Typically, a review model is activated that includes calling together different staff from counseling, law enforcement, victim advocacy, the Title IX coordinator, and so forth. The purpose is to assess the information as best as possible, such as who the alleged perpetrator might be, what kinds of interactions might subsequently occur between the alleged victim and perpetrator that should be precluded, and whether there is an immediate danger posed to the community.

Of critical and central importance and a key requirement is to assess from the victim's positionality, what interim/intermediate steps and remedies can be taken to allow the victim to continue to attend classes and go about his or her daily activities without further contact with the alleged perpetrator. These interim measures and remedies are put in place while the investigation occurs. Equally, the alleged perpetrator's educational needs must be accommodated.

The DOE's April 2011 DCL was framed by the victim-centered approach and details the various ways that schools must respond.

The concept and practice of victim-centered response to sexual violence is not new, and is considered a best practice (Cantalupo 2010). It calls for a comprehensive focus on the needs, concerns, and individual agency of the victim. For example, the decision to engage with law enforcement and the investigation process must be the decision of the victim. Institutions will provide or refer to victim advocacy services for the law enforcement process, but the ultimate decision resides with the victim. And the decision that is made cannot influence the internal institutional investigation process.

Higher-education institutions were not responding to reports of sexual violence from the victim-centered model, in particular in the student conduct process. With the 2011 DCL, it was clear that a change in approach was needed.

Further guidance on what constitutes a victim-centered approach for colleges and universities can be found in subsequent Title IX documents, including the DOE's April 2015 *Title IX Resource Guide* and the White House report previously mentioned. One example is providing a survivor with someone they can speak with in confidence. This victim-centered approach has given rise to the designation of confidential advisers on campuses. The White House report states:

> While many victims of sexual assault are ready to file a formal (or even public) complaint against an alleged offender right away—many others want time and privacy to sort through their next steps. For some, having a confidential place to go can mean the difference between getting help and staying silent. (White House Task Force 2014, 2)

The case of the University of Montana and the resolution agreement with the Department of Justice (DOJ) addressed the issue of the lack of a victim-centered approach, in particular on the part of the University of Montana Police Department (University of Montana 2015). This and other voluntary consent agreements between schools, the DOE, and the DOJ are used as "blueprints" for meeting expectations and developing best practices by colleges and universities in their sexual violence prevention and response work framed by a victim-centered approach (Evaneski, Baker, and Jayne 2014).

Although victim-centered approaches are considered the best practice to improve the experience of the victim who must go through the process of a sexual assault complaint, there are some who believe that this type of approach creates unfairness for the respondent in an investigation of an allegation, particularly in terms of interim measures that may remove a respondent from school or place other barriers to the respondent's educational participation while the investigation is conducted (Fries 2013). One deputy Title IX coordinator, a dean of students, indicated:

> The Department of Education has put our boat in the right ocean but it hasn't told us the right direction to go in. I asked about balancing the rights between the respondent and complainant early on. They basically refused to answer.

Investigations

Prior to 2011, most schools did not investigate allegations of student-to-student sexual violence, perceiving that, as a crime, it was up to the complainant to report the matter to law enforcement and let them investigate. Founders of Know Your IX and in the *Hunting Ground* movie detail what many of us can acknowledge: survivors were often discouraged from using school conduct processes for pursuing complaints of sexual misconduct. If complainants pursued the matter through the student conduct process, they were often subjected to quasi-courtroom-like hearings with a panel of fellow students, staff, and faculty sitting in judgment, where they would be interrogated about past sexual practices and drinking behaviors, with their character being called into question, and worse.

The 2011 DCL specifically told schools they were not in Title IX compliance and must investigate allegations of sexual misconduct. Furthermore, the investigation should take place whether brought forward by the survivor or a third party. For many colleges and universities, this required a significant change in how student-to-student sexual misconduct investigations were conducted. First, investigations needed to proceed under a civil rights investigation model, typically utilized in investigating allegations of discrimination and sexual harassment, particularly in the workplace (Sexual Assault 2010). Furthermore, school investigation protocols needed review and revision. Over these past five years, gleaned from the DOE letters and guidance plus the consent agreements some schools have entered into, one training business, the Association of Title IX Administrators (ATIXA), has developed a thirty-seven-point checklist for use by schools to improve their investigation protocols. The checklist includes policy requirements; defini-

tions of sexual harassment, including sexual violence; investigation protocols; provisions for training; information about and how to report
complaints and access the Title IX coordinator, grievance procedures; and
more (ATIXA n.d.).

For those investigating sexual misconduct, it rapidly became clear that
additional training and use of a new framework for investigations of this
kind was needed. Typical investigations are conducted by determining timelines; interviewing the complainant, respondent, and witnesses in a linear
fashion; and triangulating information from responses to determine corroboration, verification, credibility, and intersecting statements as well as
outliers. For an investigation into an act or actions of sexual violence, the
complainant has been traumatized and a trauma-framed and influenced investigation process is required, as opposed to the standard linear investigation of question and response, which is ineffective when trauma by violence
has occurred. Those accustomed to doing linear and time frame investigations usually do not believe the victim because he or she does not remember
in the expected way. This has led to decades of retraumatizing victims through
law enforcement investigations, the courts, and our campuses. Trauma investigation training and training about the neurobiology of trauma are at the
heart of a victim-centered investigation model.

Trauma-framed and influenced investigation methods may have been
new to many of us doing discrimination and harassment investigations for
our colleges and universities; however, they were not new to the criminal
justice system. An exemplary leader in the work of trauma-informed investigations as well as throughout all processes of the system is Joanne Archambault, a retired San Diego police department sergeant, executive director of
End Violence Against Women International (EVAWI), and president and
training director of Sexual Assault Training and Investigations (SATI). She
is the developer of the national model "Start by Believing," which looks to
transform how we all respond to victims of sexual violence. Many campuses
use multiple external trainers and models in order to secure for their staff
the most comprehensive knowledge and skills with breadth and depth for
Title IX–related work. EVAWI and Start by Believing comprise a central
training platform (End Violence Against Women International 2016).

College and university investigators are able to take advantage of a rich
and deep field of scholarship, theory, and training on trauma-framed care,
response, and investigations. Additionally, a cottage industry has emerged
with many training programs in Title IX sexual misconduct response and
investigation. These programs are conducted by professional organizations
such as the National Association of College and University Administrators
(NACUA); the American Association for Access, Equity and Diversity
(AAAED); business entities such as ATIXA; and individual trainers such as
Peter Lake, a professor of law at Stetson University College of Law.

Unfortunately, all of this training did not prepare many college and university staff who were charged as investigators for the work ahead. For some, the volume of cases increased exponentially. At the same time that we were retooling our skill sets in investigations, we were also deploying the educational outreach, programming, and training regarding policies, grievance procedures, and prevention programs. For many schools, this led to a large increase in complaints—one Title IX coordinator indicated that during the past five years, complaints of sexual violence went from three to forty-eight to seventy, and today even more. Not only have resources not kept up with need in terms of number of investigators but the impact of listening to the stories of survivors has been overwhelming for many (Flaherty 2014).

We hear stories that range from groping, to sexual assault when incapacitated, to domestic and dating violence of a frightening ferocity, to accounts of gang rapes. Many of us grapple to make sense of what we hear, maintain objectivity, and to rely on the process to lead to an appropriate outcome, but for some of us, as we try to sleep, the voices of our students echo in our heads. One college Title IX investigator reports:

> As time went on, there is an accumulation of seeing hurt people that takes its toll on a person. Self-care didn't include how to take care with a constant barrage of the dark side of humankind. Three or 4 cases a day sometimes. That barrage really got to me mentally. It impacted my outlook on college students and made me look at the world much more negatively.

Another shares:

> The toughest part of this job is having to work with individuals who have experienced a trauma they never expected while pursuing their education. It is as hard to deal with the respondents, many don't yet realize what they did was wrong and it is derailing their education too. . . . What is hard is the heaviness of the work. My husband has questioned if this has affected our sex life.

And a third reveals:

> For me, the sheer numbers of cases that came in and how fast they came in, one on top of the other was beyond challenging. And the things that had happened to these women . . . they were mostly women, I saw maybe 1 male . . . at parties, in their living spaces . . . and drugs and alcohol were almost always involved. I was challenged to be objective and balanced and learned how to detach better. But I took it home with me. I worked 12 hour days, and on weekends

because no additional resources were provided. I was married and now I'm not. The job contributed to the break-up. I had no energy left for my partner. I just wanted to sit and veg in front of the T.V., eat comfort food, have a drink and go to bed. And be left alone.

Prior to the release of the previously mentioned U.S. Department of Education's Questions and Answers (2014), around the country, colleges and universities understood that the DCL required they investigate all allegations of sexual assault that came to their attention, even if the survivor did not wish them to do so. Title IX coordinators and student affairs conduct professionals understood the letter to give very little leeway in making a determination to not investigate. The most difficult investigations were when reported by a third party. A colleague details:

> We would have to email or try and call the student and say a matter has come to our attention and I need to meet with you in person. Then when you saw them, you were basically telling them, "Hey, I hear you were sexually assaulted. I care, the university cares deeply, here's our advocate info, our counseling info, I'd like to walk you over there . . . and also, tell me what happened, I am starting an investigation." And then they crumple, or cry, or freeze, or scream at you.

Another colleague told me:

> As a student affairs professional, trained to be student-centered and help in any and all ways, telling a student we're doing something like this, they didn't want . . . this felt horrible. Give the person all the control you can. Give them the choice, sexual assault makes them lose all that control. That is how we were training. For compliance. For the Department of Education, we now "had to." It was very difficult to see the emotional reaction of students.

The DOE 2014 Questions and Answers specifically address the issue of establishing confidential advisers outside of professionals such as counselors, medical doctors, and clergy. This allows more agency for survivors to determine what steps they wish to take and in what processes they wish to engage. However, the DOE still remains vague on the subject of institutional responsibility; on campuses, we worry about identifying repeat offenders and predators and whether we will be held accountable.

In addition to the retooling of investigation skills, the need to handle personal emotional fallout from sexual violence investigations, and improving investigation protocols to meet DOE expectations, there were other response concerns to address. One was the time frame. It is expected that investigations take place in a timely fashion, with sixty days being the standard. However, with limited investigative staff, the increased caseloads, and the complexities involved, it is a standard that is difficult at times to achieve.

Another part of the response process mandated by the DOE is referred to as interim measures. Steps must be taken while an investigation is ongoing to maintain a safe environment for the complainant to continue his or her education without fear of respondent retaliation; seeing the respondent in classes, in living spaces, and at activities; as well as deploy and follow up with the complainant on accessing and utilizing the resources available to help him or her process and cope with what has happened. And the same care needs to be provided for the respondent. There is also a rise in the number of lawsuits that respondents are bringing against schools that deployed interim measures, as well as found them responsible under the preponderance of the evidence standard (did the behavior in question more likely than not occur) mandated by the DOE and in long use as the standard in organizational civil rights investigations (Grasgreen 2013). These lawsuits do not change our obligations; however, this adds greatly to the pressures and stressors affecting those engaged in this work.

After an investigation is conducted, if a finding emerges that the behavior in question more likely than not did occur, the student conduct code as policy and process becomes the next step.

Conduct Codes: Adjudication and Institutional Response

The 2011 DCL and subsequent 2014 White House report called for review of college and university conduct codes to include all the elements required in appropriate response, from investigation to adjudication and institutional action after the adjudication process. In 2014, the Association for Student Conduct Administration (ASCA) published *Student Conduct Administration and Title IX: Gold Standard Practices for Resolution of Allegations of Sexual Misconduct on College Campuses*. The purpose states:

> There is no one-size-fits-all model for addressing incidents of sexual misconduct. With different missions, resources, staffing models, funding sources, system policies, and especially campus cultures and student populations at postsecondary institutions across the United States, each college or university must develop its own policies and procedures. (1)

The "Not Alone" federal government website also provides a checklist for campus sexual misconduct policies (Not Alone n.d.).

Of particular discussion among Title IX coordinators and student affairs conduct staff is the hearing board model used on many campuses nationwide. For many, a panel of students, faculty, and staff is a critically important part of the adjudication process and a function of the shared-governance culture. However, for adjudication of sexual violence complaints, the involvement of multiple people with limited understandings and training creates complications and barriers to effective adjudication. From panels, workshops, and conversations at national conferences, it is clear that Title IX coordinators and student affairs professionals involved in the conduct process prefer an administrative hearing model whereby the findings of an investigation are presented to well-trained administrative hearing officers to determine institutional response.

However, as the use of hearing panels is widespread, many schools have moved to mandatory in-depth training of hearing board members regarding sexual violence and sexual misconduct charges, the Title IX expectations, the meaning of a victim-centered framing and how to apply it in their deliberations, and an understanding of the neurobiology of trauma. One coordinator shared:

> All panel members get the same training, but they have different filters. Some come with more in-depth knowledge, with a sociological background. They already understand the nature of sexual violence, domestic violence and have frames and lenses that lend itself to the trainings. For others, no, this information is their first learning opportunity. I've had new-to-the-issue members come back for a second year, do the training again and tell me that this second time, the information made much more sense.

Even with such training, individual members of hearing boards bring their own perspectives, experiences, and knowledge. One Title IX coordinator stated:

> Some on a hearing board, they want the process to be courtroom-like. They have a hard time understanding why conduct processes and hearings on campus cannot and should not be like the courts. In one particular instance, the survivor had also filed charges with law enforcement; however, the prosecutor declined to prosecute. A hearing panel member stated that they would not be able to find in favor of the complainant as the prosecutor declined the case.

In some cases, Title IX coordinators have shared that the findings of the investigation detail the conclusion that the behavior in question more likely than not occurred, but the hearing panel dismisses the findings. In other instances, the hearing board may not impose a sanction sufficient to the scale of the offense. One colleague shared that while accepting the findings of the investigation report, the hearing board assigned Green Dot training which is a bystander intervention program that has been implemented on college campuses and in the community (see Chapter 14 by Sarah McMahon for a discussion of bystander programs) rather than expulsion.

As all involved have come to gain more experience and familiarity with victim-centered processes and received training of depth and breadth, concerns such as these with hearing panels are being addressed through hands-on work and relationship building for better communication with others involved in institutional responses to Title IX sexual violence complaints.

Role of Title IX Coordinator

The "Not Alone" federal government website (Not Alone n.d.) provides sample policy language regarding the Title IX coordinator role and responsibilities, from which institutions can use language explaining the need to designate one employee to coordinate compliance with Title IX obligations. The sample policy language section also provides a detailed description of functions and responsibilities specific to sexual assault under the categories of (a) training for students, faculty, and staff; (b) investigations; (c) remedies, including interim measures; and (d) monitoring and advising.

Comprehensive expectations are spelled out in each section for which the Title IX coordinator must provide and/or facilitate. It also outlines the level of accountability held by the Title IX coordinator. The collected list of things to know, do, and be vigilant for is extensive and well beyond expectations pre-2011. A sample of the expectations include:

- Regular training for faculty, staff, and students (with guidance on what should be included).
- Easily accessible and up-to-date websites with policies, procedures, service offices, full listings of Title IX deputy coordinators with contact info, etc.
- Several points about investigations with the overall expectation that the Title IX coordinator will be vigilant for all steps of the process, the prompt and well-trained handling of the investigation, appeals, further grievances, and the attendant comprehensive record keeping.
- Prompt interim measures to ensure the safety of the complainant (and the respondent's attendant rights to full academic access while the investigation is ongoing).
- Coordinate annual climate survey and use data to determine multiple prongs of sexual assault prevention and response.
- Review all complaints and reports; analyze for hot spots and patterns.

- Review all aspects of campus compliance with Title IX.
- Make sure systems are in place to work effectively with police, advocacy groups, rape crisis centers, and other service providers.

The previous list is related specifically to sexual assault. The Title IX coordinator continues to have other substantial and weighty responsibilities under Title IX related to all other forms of sexual discrimination, as well as continuing oversight of athletics compliance to Title IX and relevant National Collegiate Athletic Association (NCAA) requirements and reports. And, for most of us, these responsibilities are in addition to other duties, typically relevant to civil rights compliance, including Affirmative Action/Equal Employment Opportunity and the Americans with Disabilities Act and requirements under Section 504 of the Rehabilitation Act of 1973 that prohibits discrimination based on disability.

What we are seeing increasingly as we scan job notices is the posting of positions whereby the Title IX coordination work is a position in and of itself (Walesby 2013). Institutions of higher education (IHE) receiving federal dollars have always been required to have someone designated as responsible for Title IX. For some longer-term professionals, for whom Title IX is part of a large portfolio of responsibilities, the pre- to post-2011 expectations of investigating sexual assaults and the growth in what to do directly, or facilitate, was more than what they were willing to do. One individual I interviewed noted:

> I went to my president as the case load grew and as the Department of Ed expectations became overwhelming and said we needed to move Title IX out of my area and to another. I want nothing to do with this. This isn't what I signed on for. And I don't want to investigate rapes.

Others successfully worked with their leadership to hire additional staff dedicated for the Title IX work.

On other campuses, decisions were made to move existing Title IX duties. Colleagues share that, in some cases, it was about territory and "politics":

> Now that Title IX is a big thing and it is finally getting resources, the VP [Vice President] came in and said it needs to report to us, we can do it more comprehensively. They get the increased training dollars and staffing I asked for repeatedly and never got. They said I shouldn't take it as a negative, that it wasn't a demotion or anything. How else should I take it? I'm not a VP and so I lost a significant piece of my work and also something I believe in and have stuck with even after (the DCL).

As we can see from the sample of duties and expectations of a Title IX coordinator, it is vital that the coordinator be adept at building relationships. Title IX coordinators must work extensively with student affairs, general counsel, athletics, faculty and faculty governance groups, human resources, communications units, and colleagues institution-wide regarding training, educational programs, investigations, and policies and procedures. They must also build effective working relations with police (both on and off campus), community service groups, boards of trustees, legislators (some states have passed or are considering passing Title IX legislation, and Title IX coordinators report being called to answer questions from legislators; New 2015; Wacks 2014), and students and student groups, including student governing groups, media, parents, and other interested parties.

Beyond relationships, many must lobby for the resources to do the job, in particular for additional investigation personnel as the caseloads have increased. As the following narrative attests, this can be a complicated process:

> At a professional conference recently, several of us sat around and shared our campus situations. For those of us with small staffs, ourselves and maybe one or two others, and with other duties, we can't keep up with the workload and need more investigators. But we are told there is no money in the budget. So what I did, and found out some others did too, was to recruit folks from different departments around campus to become investigators—I first requested permission from their supervisors to ask selected individuals. All asked said yes, which surprised me. It turns out the work is both a professional development opportunity and a task many care about seeing done correctly so that we can improve as a campus. That was very moving to me. . . . We are talking about hours and hours of donated time by staff who routinely give up lunch hours, work well into the evening to do interviews and write reports, for no additional monies or acknowledgement except my and a few others' eternal gratitude. And I set all this up with no help from leadership. I detailed what we were doing, and the attitude I received was basically—ok, so you are doing your job.

And where territorialism and silos overcome relationships, being able to assert authority, even without direct supervision, is an essential though challenging aspect of the job. In big-picture meetings and circumstances, by and large, from vice presidents to directors to coordinators to conduct and front line staff, all sincerely believe in working across units to meet the Title IX expectations and spirit. All truly care. But human nature being what it is, when someone is telling you to ask more questions and disagreeing with your conclusions, it makes for difficulties. A colleague explained:

I was new on the job and trying to do my relationship building, however, we had a tough case and an inexperienced investigator. The investigator did not interview sufficient witnesses nor move at any kind
of quick pace. When I tried to ask that she set up interviews right away
so we could have a chance of meeting the 60 day time period, she replied that she had lots to do, not just this. The complainant came to see
me directly saying she felt she wasn't being taken seriously, that it was
going slow, other students were now coming and asking her questions.
I had to step in and set a meeting with the conduct officer/investigator
and her supervisor and explain what was required and why. Her supervisor, the Dean of Students, also reacted poorly, indicating I was
interfering with the conduct process. . . . I could tell they really hadn't
absorbed the importance of this work, not just for compliance, but for
the complainant and respondent. I had to really control myself and
remain collegial and professional. This affects lives. Both do not talk
to me if they can help it; however, investigations are much improved.

Another critical relationship for Title IX coordinators is with their direct
supervisors and presidents, sometimes one and the same. At the same conference, many colleagues shared that they feel they are respected and that the
complexities and difficulties of the job are well understood. They may not
have the resources they really need, but are grateful they have the leadership
that stands by them, understands the volume, accepts time delays, and refers
e-mails and other communication, media inquiries and the like, that they
receive directly. One said, "I know they have my back." But for others, that
is not the case.
    One colleague shared about a case in which assault by multiple individu-
als occurred while the victim was unconscious from alcohol consumption
and the assault was video recorded:

The right thing to do as the investigator was to watch the video and
analyze and make decisions. I was not trained for how to deal with
the emotions for making those kind of decisions. I worked with the
police and a fellow investigator to get to the alleged rapists as quickly
as possible, before they could share stories and get themselves
aligned. We went over a 48 hour period with no sleep, making sure
we were getting the interviews done, coordinating with the police in
their active investigation, checking repeatedly on the victim and on
impacted third parties, both staff and students. I emailed the president a quick update. At 11 p.m. he replied, "Why did it take so long
for you to get this far?" He had no clue of the pain, no clue of personal toll, no clue of shoulder to the boulder. For him, we do this
work to comply, not because we care, not because we should.

The colleague who shared the story about building a team of volunteer investigators also discussed institutional leadership:

> I had more than 70 cases with a couple dozen fully ongoing, and many others in various beginning and closing stages. As a team, when new allegations came in, we divided up the work of the first contact for the intake. We had one that came in by email to the student affairs general email and one of those staffers said they would follow up. The next week, when we met, she indicated that she hadn't had time yet— she had many investigations already on her plate, she was the sole student affairs investigator as well as the sole investigator and conduct officer for all other types of student conduct code alleged violations. . . . The following week she hadn't yet followed up and so it went on for a few weeks more. Our colleague was assuring us she would get to it . . . and I'm not her boss, we work together extraordinarily well and the pace is killing us all and we just can't get to it—and it wasn't a new case, it was a woman detailing an experience from a year ago and suspecting it was happening again to another. We sometimes prioritize, and got this wrong. The student wrote to the president and indicated no action was happening and how upset she was. Two of us then took over and moved as quickly as we could. . . . When my time came for an evaluation, two months later, he told me he was reducing my evaluation . . . I was the Title IX coordinator and I should have made sure this case was responded to more quickly and it shouldn't get to him. He said he was "gravely concerned." I accepted the determination because objectively, he was correct. However, at no time did he acknowledge the extreme volume, the climate and culture work needed to address the volume, the team—of volunteers!—I put together and cajoled resources from many to have the team properly trained, the relationship building and all the other investigations that have gone well, and my many other duties successfully accomplished. . . . An entire year's evaluation was reduced from above average to average. I have since left and am at another school, doing the same work but in a completely different environment. Being in a new environment has validated my perception of the toxicity of that kind of leadership to the work we do.

Another colleague shared about a sexual harassment case, not assault, of a serial harasser who targeted female graduate students over a period of years. The investigation resulted in a finding that it was more than likely the behavior in question had occurred. The behavior was so pervasive and severe that termination was recommended. The president told the Title IX coordinator: "You will need to select a different recommendation. I will not terminate a tenured faculty member." That Title IX coordinator has also moved to a different institution, after stating: "There is no way to do the work and have legitimacy on campus, in the community, and especially with victims if the leadership will not do the right thing."

Culture Change

This reorganization of the Title IX work in which schools are engaged is leading to significant culture change. As we have progressed in a culture change regarding the "suitability" for athletics of women, we are now engaged in work to change rape culture. We sometimes forget that "compliance" is not an end in and of itself. It is a tool to bring about change. Voters Rights Acts, the Civil Rights Act of 1964, the Americans with Disabilities Act of 1990, subsequent amendments, and many other such legislation are designed to provide the foundation from which to work for equity, access, inclusion, nondiscrimination, and to remove barriers for participation in many societal arenas.

One area for culture change is the call through various avenues for programming regarding bystander intervention. The 2014 Questions and Answers guidance from the DOE addresses the question of "what type of training on sexual violence should a school provide to its students" (U.S. Department of Education 2014, 48)? One section explicitly calls for specific training to "encourage students to report incidents of sexual violence." This is discussed further in Chapters 11 and 14.

This bystander intervention is a significant step in culture change, as it focuses on the idea that "if you see something, say something," deconstructing the long-held cultural value of "don't be a tattletale," along with the "don't get involved" cultural message many of us have received. Further, it is directly aimed at getting men involved as well, helping to disentangle ideas of masculinity, the male role in sex, and the framing of sex. A male colleague shared:

> The message I received was sex as conquest. An athletic situation to be won. That's what we teach our males. The Keith Edwards stuff—a lot of that makes sense to me. The way he talks about the culture men are raised in, really made sense to me because I remember thinking about sex as conquest and those things. Some of the images he would use, for me, helped me lower my defenses, no I am not a bad person, but I see how the world has taught me. We need to get this into the education system at a younger age. I think we need to get that attitude into health teachers, P.E. teachers, coaches of sports at the junior high and high school level.

The front-and-center discussions about consent comprise another significant area of culture change in which we are engaging. The 2011 DCL clarified the concept of consent. It indicated that consent was NOT given in situations where there was impairment by drugs and alcohol, as well as when someone was told no or there were minors involved. And we have gone further down the path of understanding consent and teaching about consent. The Campus Sexual Assault Violence Elimination Act (SaVE) also requires schools to include a definition of consent, and many states have consent statutes.

The concept of consent goes beyond "no means no, to yes means yes" (*Campus Safety* 2015). In a *Campus Safety* magazine article (2015), they cite a DOE consent standard as "the affirmative, unambiguous, and voluntary agreement to engage in a specific sexual activity during a sexual encounter" (2). Under this definition, someone who is asleep, or mentally or physically incapacitated, either through drugs or alcohol or for any reason, or who is under duress, threat, coercion or force, would not be able to consent. "Further, one would not be able to infer consent under circumstances in which consent was not clear, including but not limited to the absence of 'no' or 'stop' or the existence of a prior or current relationship or sexual activity" (3). Silence is *not* affirmative consent.

The critical culture change embodied in consent is the emphasis on what it fundamentally really means to be sexually consenting adults. We are teaching that sexual relations are to be talked about, and that if we do it, we can speak of it. We need to check in with each other about what we are doing, if we want to do it, does this feel good, what we expect, and so forth. We are working on changing the gender role imposition of decades and centuries about how we go about having sex, how a woman should behave, how a man should behave, and how we should feel. .

A related culture change brought about by the use of Title IX to address sexual violence is the concept of mandatory reporters. Almost all faculty, staff, and student workers at an institution are mandatory reporters. Much like bystander intervention, if we know of something, we must say something. This has been difficult for many, who feel they may violate a student's confidentiality. Others feel this should not be part of the job; they do not know what to say or do. Thus, the focus on training—mandatory training— of faculty and staff is critically important. All of us must have the tools and basic skills to help our students who may share with us this crisis situation and traumatic event. Further, mandatory reporting has assisted with the centralization of institutional response and responsibility to the Title IX coordinator. If a problem occurs in athletics, at a particular college, at a fraternity party, or at a house party in town, we have processes in place to quickly deploy care for the victim and begin the investigation process. There is no more "we can take care of this internally" allowed for subunits of an institution. This too is a significant aspect of culture change.

The Intersection of Title IX, VAWA, the Campus SaVE Act, and Clery Act

There has been recent significant legislation important to the work of applying Title IX to sexual violence and that intersects with and generally complements Clery and its amendments through the Violence Against Women Act (VAWA) and the Campus SaVE Act's goal of ending campus sexual violence.

The Clery Act, the Jeanne Clery Disclosure of Campus Security Policy and Campus Crime Statistics, was enacted in 1990 and requires all colleges and universities who receive federal funding to keep track of and share crime statistics occurring on campus (Clery Center 2016). They must also provide information on campus safety efforts and notify the campus and surrounding community of crimes. There is a requirement to provide support to victims of sexual assault, domestic violence, dating violence, and stalking. Additionally, institutions must have specific policies and procedures that are related to safety procedures, timely warnings and emergencies, support for survivors, and information on how to report crimes.

Both SaVE and VAWA are directly related to the Clery Act (see Chapter 8 by Michelle Hughes Miller and Sarah L. Cook for a detailed discussion of the SaVE Act). The SaVE Act of 2013 is a part of the Violence Against Women Reauthorization Act signed by President Obama in 2013. The SaVE Act is a section of VAWA specific to campus sexual assault (see, e.g., American Council on Education 2014). Because VAWA is an amendment to Clery, SaVE is enforced under Clery. All are designed to increase transparency on the reporting of and responding to incidents of sexual violence. In addition, they intersect with Title IX regarding victims' rights and prevention education. Where Title IX DOE guidance provides recommendations, the SaVE Act enacts requirements for education and training, transparency, and reporting and complaint procedures (see, e.g., Dunn 2014). Clery, VAWA, and SaVE intersect with Title IX on these key points:

- Communicate policies and complaint procedures regarding sexual violence (including domestic violence, dating violence, and stalking)
- Intermediate steps to protect the complainant during investigation process
- Written notification to both parties
- Training and prevention education programs for faculty, staff, and students
- Victim-centered response

Having multiple related statutes, requirements, and guidance, while daunting at the outset, has created multiple approaches and vigilance regarding sexual violence on campus. Effective teams have formed to share work on the evaluation of threats; the need for and types of interim measures; continuous review of policies and procedures; sharing and attending, often together, multiple arcs of training to address sexual violence and safety in general; and collectively sending a unified message and modeling a centralized approach to this important intersecting compliance work and the expected outcomes of changing campus climate and culture for the better.

Takeaways

This chapter addresses how we are using federal policy to transform our campus responses to violence against women. A fundamental takeaway is simply that change is possible. The case of campus violence against women requires this real-life and real-time utilization of the law, and of compliance, to drive climate and culture change.

Critical and central is that the work we are engaged in is about people; it affects people. The core of the work is to change the culture of sexual relations and the gendered way our society approaches sexual relations. The purpose of the work is for our students. We must continuously be guided by an ethic of care. That care must be for survivor/complainant and perpetrator/respondent alike. Only with including men can we reach the change we seek. Villainizing and shaming is not effective.

To reach the change we seek, all of us must be continual learners on Title IX, Clery, VAWA, Campus SaVE, and what we do best in higher education: research and scholarship. The pace of how we are evolving ideas, terms, definitions, understandings, gender/gender identity roles, scholarship, and best practices is rapid and multifaceted. We not only need to keep up but we also must be patient with each other throughout our campus communities, seeking and supporting common ground. Change is hard. Fast change is harder still. Taking such concrete action on sexual misconduct we have ignored in the past is shaking some of us to the core as we question our own selves, our own behaviors, our own values.

If you see something, hear something, learn of something—say something. This is a takeaway that needs to be rooted within the ethic of care. It is not about "getting someone in trouble," it is about taking care of one another and taking care of oneself. When we participate in this work, whatever our roles may be—practitioner, coordinator, faculty member, scholar, mandatory reporter—the stories of our survivors impact us deeply.

The linkage of Title IX, Clery, VAWA, and SaVE for transparency, for data collection and reporting, for full information, for easy-to-find information on where to report and the steps of a complaint process, the outcomes and possible sanctions for sexual misconduct, and for a total picture of safety on campuses is a good thing. Leaders rightly worry about the litigation landscape, risk management, the ever-shifting compliance landscape, and institutional reputation. According to Title IX coordinators and related staff with whom I have talked, for the most part, for most institutions, the issues of litigation, compliance, reputation, and so forth do not dominate. The needs of our students dominate. However, it is important to also frame how we respond to these leadership worries. What we have learned is that the decades-old practices of not being transparent caused much harm. We were able to stay in denial about the extent of the problem of campus violence against women, and that rape culture exists and is deeply rooted in our social worlds. Exposure to knowledge forced action, from the original Centers for Disease Control (CDC) data—that one in five women in colleges and universities experience sexual violence—to the information, research, and scholarship of community and campus-based service and advocacy groups. It forced the federal administration to in turn force us to work as hard as we can to stop campus violence against women. Transparency has allowed us to share the work across institutions.

Finally, we have learned that we, and our institutions, are not defined by what happens. We are defined by how we respond. To reach the culture change for which we strive, our response must continuously improve and change.

REFERENCES

American Council on Education. 2014. *New requirements imposed by the Violence Against Women Reauthorization Act.* Available at http://www.acenet.edu/news-room /Documents/VAWA-Summary.pdf.

Association for Student Conduct Administration. 2014. *Student conduct administration and Title IX: Gold standard practices for resolution of allegations of sexual misconduct on college campuses.* Available at http://www.theasca.org/files/Publications/ASCA%20 2014%20Gold%20Standard.pdf.

ATIXA. n.d. *OCR policy checklist.* Available at https://atixa.org/wordpress/wp-content /uploads/2013/05/2016FebruaryOCR37PointPolicyChecklist.pdf.

Campus Safety. 2015. Making sense of affirmative consent, Title IX, VAWA and Clery. Available at http://www.campussafetymagazine.com/article/making_sense_of _affirmative_consent_title_ix_vawa_and_clery#.

Cantalupo, N. C. 2010. How should colleges and universities respond to peer sexual violence on campus? What the current legal environment tells us. *NASPA Journal about Women in Higher Education* 3 (1): 52–87. doi: http://dx.doi.org/10.2202/1940 -7890.1044.

Clery Center for Security on Campus. 2016. *Summary of the Jeanne Clery Act.* Available at http://clerycenter.org/summary-jeanne-clery-act.

Dunn, L. 2014. Addressing sexual violence in higher education: Ensuring compliance with the Clery Act, Title IX and VAWA. *Georgetown Journal of Gender and the Law* 15 (3): 563–584.

End Violence Against Women International (EVAWI). 2016. Available at http://www
.evawintl.org/Default.aspx.

Evaneski, L., N. Baker, and B. Jayne. 2014. *Addressing the day-to-day challenge of Title IX compliance: One size does not fit all.* National Association of College and University Attorneys. Available at http://www.nacua.org/securedocuments/programs/February2014 /03_14-02-3.pdf.

Flaherty, C. 2014. Compassionate but impartial. *Inside Higher Education,* December 19. Available at https://www.insidehighered.com/news/2014/12/19/title-ix-administrators -discuss-emotional-demands-job.

Fries, A. 2013. Student-on-student sexual assault policy: How a victim-centered approach harms men. *Journal of College and University Law* 39 (3): 633–658. Available at http:// www.nacua.org/securedocuments/nonsearched/jcul/39_jcul_633.pdf.

Grasgreen, A. 2013. Going on offense with Title IX. *Inside Higher Education,* August 9. Available at https://www.insidehighered.com/news/2013/08/09/accused-rape-men -allege-discrimination-under-title-ix.

Los Angeles Times. 2012. An Olympic moment for women. Editorial, July 27. Available at http://articles.latimes.com/2012/jul/27/opinion/la-ed-olympics-women-20120727.

New, J. 2015. First, do no harm. *Inside Higher Education,* February 19. Available at https:// www.insidehighered.com/news/2015/02/19/open-letter-calls-legislators-reconsider -campus-sexual-assault-bills.

Newman, J., and L. Sander. 2014. Promise unfulfilled? *Chronicle of Higher Education,* April 30. Available at http://chronicle.com/article/Promise-Unfulfilled-/146299/.

Not Alone. (n.d.). *Developing sexual assault policies and procedures.* Available at https:// www.notalone.gov/schools/#developing-sexual-assault-policies-and-procedures.

Rapp, T. 2012. Olympic medal count 2012: U.S. women stole the show in London. *Bleacher Report,* August 13. Available at http://bleacherreport.com/articles/1294747-olympic -medal-count-2012-us-women-stole-the-show-in-london.

Sexual assault: A matter of civil rights and Title IX. 2010. *Women in Higher Education* 19 (6): 16. Available at http://go.galegroup.com/ps/i.do?id=GALE%7CA229228750&v =2.1&u=s1185784&it=r&p=AONE&sw=w&asid=f2317e5db64bcf23ddae665426d38 af2.

University of Montana Police Department. 2015. Final report of sustained compliance regarding the agreement between the United States Department of Justice and the University of Montana in relation to UMPD's response to sexual assault. Available at http://www.umt.edu/police/docs/DOJ_Reports/Final_Report.pdf.

U.S. Department of Education, Office for Civil Rights (DOE, OCR). 2011a. *Dear Colleague Letter.* Available at http://www2.ed.gov/about/offices/list/ocr/letters/colleague-201104 .pdf.

———. 2011b. Sexual violence: Background, summary and fast facts. Available at https:// www.whitehouse.gov/sites/default/files/fact_sheet_sexual_violence.pdf.

———. 2014. Questions and answers on Title IX and sexual violence. Available at http:// www2.ed.gov/about/offices/list/ocr/docs/qa-201404-title-ix.pdf.

———. 2015a. Dear Colleague. Available at http://www2.ed.gov/policy/rights/guid/ocr /title-ix-coordinators.html.

———. 2015b. Title IX and sex discrimination. Available at http://www2.ed.gov/about /offices/list/ocr/docs/tix_dis.html.

Wacks, J. 2014. Legislators call for transparency in Title IX investigations. *Campus Clarity,* February 5. Available at https://home.campusclarity.com/legislators-call-for -transparency-in-title-ix-investigations/.

Walesby, A. 2013. Title IX coordinators: Five things you MUST know. *Higher Ed Jobs,* January 9. Available at https://www.higheredjobs.com/articles/articleDisplay.cfm?ID =399.

White House Task Force to Protect Students from Sexual Assault. 2014. *Not alone: The first report of the White House Task Force to protect students from sexual assault.* Office of the Vice President and the White House Council on Women and Girls, April. Available at https://www.notalone.gov/assets/report.pdf.

11

Title IX and Mandatory Reporting

A Help or a Hindrance?

HELEN EIGENBERG AND
JOANNE BELKNAP

Educational institutions, especially institutions of higher education (IHE), are facing unprecedented scrutiny with regard to gender-based abuse. While much of this attention appears new, the U.S. Department of Education (DOE) Office for Civil Rights (OCR) has been directing educational systems to deal with a variety of gender-based issues for decades. For example, in 1997 and 2001, the DOE issued detailed guidelines instructing schools of their obligations to address sexual harassment (U.S. Department of Education 1997, 2001). It was the 2011 Dear Colleague Letter (DCL), however, in which the OCR specifically informed schools that sexual violence is a form of sexual harassment and outlined their obligations to address these issues. These documents were followed by several other publications, including: responses to frequently asked questions pertaining to Title IX enforcement, a Dear Colleague Letter to Title IX coordinators, a Title IX Resource Guide, a revised sexual harassment guidance report, and a document notifying students of their rights (U.S. Department of Education 2011, 2014, 2015a, 2015b). The 2013 Violence Against Women Reauthorization Act's (VAWA) Campus Sexual Violence Elimination Act (SaVE) and two White House reports in 2105 also drew additional attention to the issue. The public became more aware of the issue through media reports and documentaries such as *The Hunting Ground* and student activism on campuses. Public attention, student activism, legislative action, and the numerous complaints filed with the DOE's OCR suggest that this issue is not going away any time soon.

Clearly, we are at a unique point and time in history where sexual assault is receiving unprecedented attention, and the roles of lawmakers, campus administrators, law enforcement agencies, service providers, and faculty members are at the center of a national debate on how best to respond to the issue.

Most of the changes in legislation and OCR recommendations address requirements for how universities *and high schools* should address gender-based violence, including sexual assault, intimate partner violence, sexual harassment, and stalking. Most of the recent attention including institutional remedies, legislative action, and prevention efforts have concentrated on sexual assault at the postsecondary level. Intimate partner violence and stalking have largely been ignored at all levels, although the basic requirements outlined for effective Title IX compliance also apply to these crimes. It is beyond the scope of this chapter to discuss the nuances of each of these issues in sufficient depth, so we concentrate on sexual assault at the university level.

There is a growing consensus that universities have a less-than-stellar track record in terms of dealing with sexual assault. The first baseline study on this issue was completed in 2002, and examined sexual assault policies from 2,438 IHE (Karjane, Fisher, and Cullen 2002). This comprehensive study found that many IHE failed to meet Clery requirements. This act (formally the Jeanne Clery Disclosure of Campus Security Policy and Campus Crime Statistics Act) was first passed in 1990, and requires IHE to gather and report data about crimes committed on or near their campuses, and outlines other mandated actions (see Chapter 8 by Michelle Hughes Miller and Sarah L. Cook and Chapter 10 by Carmen Suarez for more details). When the study was conducted, the authors found that sexual assault policies were absent, compliance with Clery requirements was marginal, training was unlikely (especially for students and faculty), victim support services were lacking, and underreporting was a serious problem.

Twelve years later, U.S. senator Claire McCaskill initiated a survey that examined 236 IHE to reexamine these issues (U.S. Senate Subcommittee 2014). Overall, there was some relative improvement in responses; however, there continues to be room for improvement. For example, 21 percent of institutions reported that they offered no sexual assault training for faculty or staff, and 31 percent offered none for students. Campus law enforcement officials in 30 percent of the institutions had no specific training on sexual assault and 73 percent of institutions had no protocols to guide them when working in conjunction with local law enforcement officials. Most surprising, 41 percent of schools had not conducted a single sexual assault investigation in the five years prior to the study. Given the high estimates of victimization repeatedly reported in survey data, it is hard to believe that almost half of the universities either had no reports made to them or had failed to investigate any reports. Moreover, 21 percent of the forty largest private institutions and 6 percent of the largest public schools had conducted fewer investigations than their Clery data indicated. *Thus, underreporting of sexual assault is a significant issue.*

Historically, there have been few incentives for universities to encourage sexual assault reports. There is a general tendency to downplay any crime or violence, as these events obviously do not engender trust in potential students and their parents. While there is no indication to suggest that most universities have any more crime than other similarly situated locations, its very existence shatters the idyllic images that many of us have about universities and the college experience. The notion that it will be the best years of a student's life, full of fun, comradery, discovery, and exploration is challenged. Potential victimization does not work well as a recruitment tool. Universities, then, face a dilemma (Cantalupo 2014). Institutions that work to improve their practices, facilitate reporting, and respond to students' needs risk looking like they have a serious crime problem, especially when compared to those colleges that discourage reporting, fail to respond effectively, and (falsely) appear safer. Thus, there is little incentive to encourage reporting. One of the driving factors in some of the newly evolving and proposed reforms stems from the woefully low numbers of reported sexual assaults on campuses nationwide. This chapter provides an overview of the research on reporting patterns, which suggests that most survivors are unwilling to disclose their victimization to official sources of any kind. It reviews the effects of new Title IX requirements, which have resulted in classifying most university employees as mandatory reporters in the hopes that more victims will come forward and that universities will be more responsive (and therefore can be held more accountable). If victims fail to report, then mandatory reporting options are unlikely to be effective and, in fact, may be harmful. The weaknesses of this approach are discussed and the chapter concludes by discussing other ways that would enhance reporting and accountability.

Mandatory Reporting

There is much debate about the role and advisability of mandatory reporting. The term sometimes is used imprecisely because mandatory reporting can be made either to law enforcement officials (including campus and local police, and prosecutors) or to various campus officials and administrators, most notably Title IX coordinators.

Reporting is a critical issue for several reasons. Most important, survivors who do not report their victimization may fail to be informed about and/or receive essential services such as crisis counseling, victim advocacy, health services, and university accommodations (such as changes in housing, class transfers, and other academic assistance). *In order to receive any of these services, however, students have to recognize and define their experiences as sexual assault, and then also tell someone in an official capacity; that is, they have to disclose.* The problem is that once they do, they may lose control over what happens to "their case."

Defining the Act

For decades, researchers have noted that many rape victims fail to use the word and often do not define their experience as rape. Koss (1985) was one of the first researchers to document this phenomenon and coined the phrase "unacknowledged rape" to represent survivors who had experienced an act that would legally constitute rape without viewing or labeling themselves as someone who had been raped. Several studies have expanded on Koss's work and find consistently high rates of unacknowledged rape; a meta-analysis of this research suggests that this situation occurs on average 60 percent of the time (see Wilson and Miller 2016). This finding also is true in samples of college students where researchers report that between 42 and 73 percent of survivors are unacknowledged victims (Fisher et al. 2003a; Koss 1985; Orchowski, Untied, and Gidycz 2013). College women are less likely to acknowledge a rape when the assault involves offenders who are acquaintances or dates (Cleere and Lynn 2013; Koss 1985), if the incident involves alcohol or drug use (Cleere and Lynn 2013; Kahn et al. 2003), and if little or no aggression or force is used (Bondurant 2001; Cleere and Lynn 2013). Thus, victims are more likely to "see" rape and apply the label to their circumstances when it more closely resembles a stereotypical stranger rape. Victims may be unlikely to recognize acts of rape that fail to meet cultural definitions of "real" rape and/or to identify people they know as offenders who could be subjected to investigations and sanctions by the criminal legal system. (Consistent with some others, we prefer "criminal legal system" to "criminal justice system," as so many cases receive little or no "justice" in the formal system.)

Research on Reporting Patterns

Here again, early work by Koss (1985) provides crucial insight into victim responses. She coined the term "hidden victim" to refer to survivors who met the legal definition of rape, but who failed to report the act to the police or a sexual assault center. Research makes it clear that most victims are unlikely to disclose their victimization to anyone beyond friends and family; therefore, few survivors use campus services (see Sabina and Ho 2014). Studies suggest that while 65 to 88 percent of victims report their experiences to friends, only about 0 to 26 percent of victims report their assaults to any campus officials, including service providers, campus administrative officials, and counselors (with most estimates being at the lower end of this range) (Cantor et al. 2015; Fisher et al. 2003b; Krebs et al. 2007; Lindquist et al. 2013; Orchowski and Gidycz 2012; Tamborra and Narchet 2011). Students are less apt to disclose if the assault involved alcohol use (Fisher et al. 2003b) and if the assailant was an acquaintance (Orchowski and Gidycz 2012). Students report that they do not disclose because it was a private matter and they were ashamed and/or embarrassed about the assault (Walsh et al. 2010). Furthermore, one of the few studies to include male victims finds that males are especially unlikely to disclose (Walsh et al. 2010). Students with prior histories of sexual victimization as adolescents also may be reluctant to disclose (Orchowski and Gidycz 2012), and may have little confidence in sexual assault resources (Burgess-Proctor et al. 2016). At least one study reports that students are more likely to use off-campus than on-campus services (Krebs et al. 2007), and a minority of victims (16 percent) receive assistance from any type of victim services agency (Sinozich and Langton 2014). We were unable to locate research that specifically examined reporting patterns for lesbian, gay, bisexual, and transgender (LGBT) students, students of color, or students with disabilities, all of whom may face significant reporting challenges.

Little research has specifically examined students' use of campus disciplinary procedures or disclosures to campus officials, probably because most students do not reveal their experiences to administrators. It also is common to combine official reports to include campus officials, campus police, and off-campus law enforcement without disaggregating these categories; therefore, it is difficult to understand law enforcement reporting patterns when they are in aggregate categories. In one of the rare studies that specifically looks at this issue, the authors report that less than 1 percent of victims filed a grievance or initiated other disciplinary action with university officials (Krebs et al. 2007).

More research has focused on students' reporting to law enforcement officials. It should not be surprising that most students fail to report their victimizations to the police, as this is a persistent problem with respect to sexual assaults in the community. In fact, the historically poor treatment of rape victims by the criminal legal system has led some to call it the "second victimization" (see Campbell 2008) or the "second assault" (see Orchowski and Gidycz 2012). Recent data from the National Crime Victimization Survey (NCVS) indicates that about 34 percent of rapes and sexual assaults were reported to the police in 2014 (Truman and Langton 2015), which is the lowest reporting rate of any violent crime and lower than all property crimes except theft (29 percent). Furthermore, an eighteen-year summary of rape and sexual assault among college-age females indicates that, on average, only 20 percent of female college victims reported the rape to the police (Sinozich and Langton 2014), and this figure was lower than reporting rates for non-students of the same age (32 percent). This trend is supported by several other studies, which find that between 0 and 13 percent of college women report rapes to the police (Fisher et al. 2003b; Koss et al. 1988; Krebs et al. 2016; Lindquist et al. 2013; Wolitzky-Taylor et al. 2011).

Victims' reasons for not reporting to the police are varied. They commonly state it was not serious enough to report and they were not sure if it was a crime (Fisher et al. 2003b; Krebs et al. 2007). They may feel they lack proof, do not want others to know, fear that the police would not take it seriously, fear reprisal from the perpetrator, are ashamed and embarrassed, and/or have concerns about confidentiality (Fisher et al. 2003b; Krebs et al. 2016). Victims are more apt to report to the police when there is a weapon, physical force, and injuries beyond the rape itself (Fisher et al. 2003b; Wolitzky-Taylor et al. 2011). Lower reporting rates occur when drugs and alcohol are involved (Fisher et al. 2003b; Wolitzky-Taylor et al. 2011), and when the assault was an incapacitated rape (Krebs et al. 2007). One study reports that African American victims are more likely to report (Fisher et al. 2003b), but others suggest that non-Whites are less likely to report to the police (Thompson et al. 2007; Wolitzky-Taylor et al. 2011). Most police reports appear to be made by the victim as opposed to bystanders (Fisher et al. 2003b).

Given that reporting is so rare, there have been both policy and legislative attempts to mandate reporting. Proponents argue several advantages (see Mancini et al. 2016). Universities will no longer be able to minimize the level of victimization. Also, theoretically, if more acts are reported, more victims will receive services, more perpetrators will be held accountable, and campuses ultimately will be safer. Opponents argue that unintended consequences may actually result in reducing reporting because victims lose control over the process, fear that their confidentiality may be violated, and that these policies and laws may result in additional trauma (see Mancini et al. 2016). While there likely is some benefit to having more and better data about the rates of victimization, climate surveys probably offer a better opportunity to amass meaningful data. Climate surveys are institutional surveys that examine the amount of sexual assault occurring on a specific campus and perceptions about the overall campus climate. At this point, they can be different across institutions and they may include diverse measures such as whether or not the institution provides a supportive climate for survivors and whether institutional resources are adequate, and assess overall attitudes toward sexual assault on campus (for more information, refer to Chapter 13 by Christine Lindquist and Christopher P. Krebs). It also is questionable whether or not reporting will ultimately result in an adequate criminal legal system response given its poor track record and high rates of attrition in these cases. It is, however, absolutely clear that victims have already lost control of how information is treated at many (most) universities, in part because of unintended consequences related to Title IX.

Mandatory Reporting to Title IX Coordinators

When most individuals talk about the vast number of Title IX complaints, they are referring to the administrative enforcement of the act, which falls under the auspices of the OCR. This process occurs when a complaint is filed and the OCR investigates whether a university's policies, procedures, and overall practices are in compliance with Title IX. While no monetary damages can be awarded to victims, theoretically, IHE can risk the loss of federal funds (a sanction that has never been used) (Cantalupo 2014). Individuals also may pursue a Title IX action directly with the courts and seek monetary damages. The courts have ruled that IHE can only be held liable if they act with deliberate indifference in the face of actual knowledge of an act of sexual violence (Cantalupo 2016; Richards and Kafonek 2016). Both types of complaints look to determine whether a school has knowledge of an act, to be determined, in part, by ascertaining whether a responsible employee knew or should have known about the act. Thus, to avoid liability and to ensure compliance with Title IX regulations, responsible employees must report any knowledge of sexual assaults to the Title IX coordinator at their university (U.S. Department of Education 2014). Reporting includes information about names of the victim, alleged perpetrator, and all known facts about the incident (e.g., time, dates, etc.).

The OCR does not clearly define who is and is not a responsible employee, with the exception of noting some roles that are exempt (e.g., counselors, health center employees, pastoral counselors, etc.). Given the current legal climate surrounding Title IX and the increasing involvement of university counsel in writing policy in this area, most IHE appear to be defining responsible employees in a very broad manner to include most employees and faculty. While these guidelines intend to increase reporting and accountability, and make victims more aware of services and reporting options, they also compromise confidentiality. For example, in most universities, faculty members are responsible employees and thus are mandated to make reports to their Title IX coordinator. So, when a student confides in a trusted faculty member (or a staff member, for that matter), that faculty or staff member no longer has the ability to assure the student that he or she will keep their confidence, even when a student specifically requests it.

Title IX regulations address confidentiality, but only at the level of the university's Title IX coordinator. This person is charged with evaluating a student's request for confidentiality "in the context of the school's responsibility to provide a safe and nondiscriminatory environment for all students"

(U.S. Department of Education 2014, 11). The guidelines note that "every effort" (17) should be made to respect this request to the "greatest extent possible" (18) and that instances where this is not honored should be limited. They also note that disregarding requests for confidentiality may discourage reporting; however, they do not define specific instances where confidentiality requests can or should be disregarded. Thus, it appears that IHE will be left to balance the needs of the institution to investigate rapes (and avoid claims of deliberate indifference), while also attempting to balance students' requests for confidentiality. This may be a line that is hard to determine, and one that may be implemented inconsistently based on the institution's history of Title IX violations and depending on the training and/or qualifications of the institutional Title IX coordinator (or, more likely, university counsel). It remains to be seen whether this balancing act will be effective.

As discussed previously, confidentiality is a barrier to reporting (Krebs et al. 2016; Sable et al. 2006). Karjane, Fisher, and Cullen note:

> Qualitative data . . . strongly suggest that any policy or procedure that compromises or, worse, eliminates the student victim's ability to make her or his own informed choices throughout the reporting and adjudication process not only reduces reporting rates, but may also be counterproductive to the victim's healing process. (2002, 85)

One problem with the current approach is that while confidentiality may be maintained most of the time, responsible employees cannot guarantee the actions of a Title IX coordinator, which is likely to have a chilling effect on disclosure. Even though, theoretically, students are not likely to be involved in a disciplinary proceeding or criminal process if they have requested confidentiality from the Title IX coordinator, it is not clear how these situations will be defined and under what conditions such requests will be honored (or not). As such, students are likely to fear that they could be involved in these processes against their will. They also may fear that others on campus will find out about their victimization or they may resent having to participate in any process, such as speaking with a Title IX coordinator, simply because they confided in a trusted faculty or staff member. This is especially troubling because some research suggests that faculty members are likely confidants, especially when they teach about victimization (Payne 2008; Richards, Branch, and Hayes 2013). In general, there is too little research to understand how often students report to faculty and how new reporting requirements may affect these disclosures. Anecdotal information suggests that some faculty members are using syllabus statements to warn students about disclosures, which indicates that at least some faculty have sufficient experience to worry about having to violate confidential disclosures.

Mandatory Reporting to Law Enforcement Officials

Given the rapidly changing nature of Title IX enforcement, it should come as no surprise that some states have pursued legislation addressing the issue. Richards and Kafonek (2016) conducted a comprehensive study of proposed state legislation and found that twenty-eight states had considered a total of seventy bills at the end of the study period (November 2015). These bills focused on victim support (including improving information and services), training, policy requirements, due process issues, disciplinary actions, and reporting issues. A total of twenty bills (26 percent) in eleven states were passed. Nine bills (13 percent) were introduced that required sexual assaults be reported to either local law enforcement or the local prosecutor's office, although only one passed. Virginia requires mandatory reporting to a review committee that is tasked with making reporting decisions. For non-felony cases, the committee is required to decide whether or not the case should be referred to law enforcement officials, and all felony assaults must be reported to the prosecutor within twenty-four hours. Similar bills were introduced but defeated in five other states. Thus, Virginia will provide an opportunity to conduct a quasi-experimental design to evaluate the impact of this drastic measure, which, unfortunately, will likely be at the expense of survivors who may be revictimized by this process.

Mandatory reporting laws take away agency from victims and remove their ability to make informed decisions—relegating them, in fact, to the status of children by creating similar laws. Mandatory reporting also takes away control from victims who have experienced an intensely disempowering event. By forcing victims to have their cases referred to the criminal legal system, and thereby to lose control over the process, it is likely that some victims will not disclose and therefore will not have access to many of the fundamental remedies provided under Title IX (such as accommodation provisions).

Legislation requiring mandatory reporting also seeks a simplistic response to a complicated problem (for a full discussion of this issue, see Cantalupo 2012, 2016). Briefly, opponents who wish to move these cases to the criminal legal system argue that colleges are not equipped to investigate sexual assault cases and that these charges are best left to the "experts" in the criminal legal system. Advocates of this perspective argue that accused perpetrators lack sufficient protection in the current campus environment, that the standard of evidence is too low, and that there are too few protections in terms of gathering evidence. Some critics of the existing process have proposed legislation to apply due process rights and other elements of criminal law to the student disciplinary system (Richards and Kafonek 2016). Legislation that would provide students with protections in disciplinary processes that are similar to those found in the criminal court system ignore the fact that many (most) of these provisions would violate Title IX requirements, which proscribe the standard of proof (as preponderance of evidence) and mandate procedural equality (meaning that both accused perpetrators and victims have equal rights in the proceeding). These bills would create rights for students accused of sexual misconduct that would not apply to other types of misconduct. Most important, this approach fails to acknowledge that victims have a right to have their accusers removed from the educational environment so that they can finish their degree, and that the burden of proof in these cases is the same as those required in all civil proceedings. Furthermore, the most extreme sanction for a perpetrator is expulsion. While this is not without consequences, it is a far cry from those sanctions available in the criminal legal system. Critics of the current process fail to acknowledge that universities provide due process rights for accused perpetrators, and that the courts have repeatedly rejected the notion that IHE must use due process standards similar to those in the criminal legal system (Cantalupo 2012). Moreover, IHE already hear cases and provide sanctions for other crimes, ranging from drug offenses to robbery. There is no reason that sexual assault should be viewed as something beyond the scope and capabilities of university disciplinary settings.

Ways to Improve Reporting

As it exists now, there is too little transparency in administrative responses to sexual assault on college campuses. Both students who have been accused of sexual assault and victims report a lack of confidence in the process. As Ridolfi-Starr notes:

> Secrecy stokes mistrust of the process and intensifies suspicions of administrative abuses, which in turn discourages students from coming forward to report and seek the help they need after experiencing rape or abuse on campus. And lastly, whether the ultimate ruling is in favor of the accusing or accused student, this lack of transparency and trust delegitimizes the outcomes of all cases. (2016, 2161)

Clearly, anecdotal reports such as those made in the documentary *The Hunting Ground* and the fact that the OCR has received 295 complaints since 2011 (Title IX 2016), suggest that there are reasons to doubt universities' responses. Advocates for victims claim that unresponsive universities continue to ignore these cases and fail to hold perpetrators accountable. Advocates for perpetrators argue that these cases are unfairly biased against the accused. One of the ways to begin to address this issue is to gather empirical evidence. There is a need for specific information about the number of reports filed, the type of resolutions (e.g., informal resolution or formal investigation), the number of investigations, the types of policy violations, the determinations that are made (and by who), the sanctions that are imposed, the length of investigations, and the results of any appeals (Ridolfi-Starr 2016). Additionally, universities should be required to report the number and types of accommodations provided to victims and the effects of the assault on their academic performance (including withdrawals, academic sanctions, leaves of absence, or leaving the university) (Ridolfi-Starr 2016). If universities were required to report these types of data, one would be better able to ascertain the claims about whether or not IHE are meeting the needs of victims and whether or not the accused are being held accountable.

Transparency also would be enhanced by implementing routine campus climate surveys that use a common methodology. Doing so removes the ability of institutions to manipulate surveys in ways that might affect outcomes and provides a common mode of comparison across universities. It also avoids having universities spend thousands of dollars to deploy commercial surveys that may fail to meet best practices with respect to survey construction and administration. Clearly, much work has been done toward this end (see the comprehensive survey that has been developed by Krebs et al. 2016). Universities could move in this direction on their own, but the bipartisan Campus Accountability and Safety Act that is before Congress would require this action (Ernst 2016; Kingkade 2015).

The routine use of anonymous reporting on campuses also would give victims a way to reveal their victimization without having to relinquish their anonymity. It also offers the added advantage of allowing bystanders, witnesses, and friends to provide information and increase reporting indirectly. This is not a new idea (see Karjane, Fisher, and Cullen 2002); however, it is not often discussed when exploring the myriad of issues surrounding mandatory reporting. It also is rarely employed, according to some research (Englander, McCoy, and Sherman 2015; Krivoshey et al. 2013). Obviously, anonymous reporting does not allow universities to investigate and verify reports, and there might be some instances where more than one person is reporting an act, but it is another way to increase transparency and give some measure of information about the rates of victimization on campus. It also is possible that some victims will report to officials if they gain confidence after filing an anonymous report. If we want to know more about victimization on campuses, we need to make it easier for victims to report, even if they wish to remain anonymous.

Finally, IHE should do a better job educating and training students to be supportive peers. As previously discussed, most victims are reluctant to report to anyone except their friends. Both the OCR and VAWA address student training, especially for new students. While some specific requirements are spelled out (such as defining violations and consent, and focusing on bystander training), there is no particular requirement that education should address ways for friends to assist survivors. In fact, there has been little research in this area to determine whether friends are effective support systems and to establish ways that they could be used to facilitate referrals and reporting. Research suggests that college students often are unaware of services (Burgess-Proctor et al. 2016; Walsh et al. 2010), although it is not clear whether they never received information or whether they simply forgot it. It is possible that they do not retain the information because they think they do not need it; it will never happen to them. Perhaps, if information was provided to demonstrate how a good friend could help a survivor, students might be more likely to retain the information; that is, they might find it useful information to "file away." It also might be possible to use peer education as a way to increase reporting if they understood how it could help their friends secure services. Many IHE are currently implementing bystander education programs that include tertiary intervention. These programs could easily be modified to include more specific information of this nature.

Summary

There are many challenges for IHE as they attempt to respond to sexual assault in an effective manner. Many of the demands that are currently being placed on institutions are relatively new, and to be fair, universities are only beginning to effectively gear up to begin to address this issue in a more comprehensive and meaningful way. It is clear, however, that it is going to be difficult to respond to sexual assault survivors who may not even define their experience as rape. Challenging definitions of rape and views about rapists is part of a massive cultural shift that has been going on for more than forty years. Most victims fail to report their assaults to anyone beyond friends, and they are not likely to report to campus officials or law enforcement (on or off campus). Victims are less apt to define their experiences as rape and to report to campus officials or the police when the circumstances of the assault fail to resemble a stereotypical stranger rape, for example, when the assailant is an acquaintance or intimate partner or when drugs or alcohol are involved (including incapacitated rape). In other words, victims are unlikely to report the types of rape that overwhelmingly occur on college campuses, which suggests that any efforts to enforce mandatory reporting policies and laws are going to be ineffective at best and will likely make matters worse. There also is too little research to understand how males, LGBTQ people, and people of color make decisions about reporting (Richards and Kafonek 2016; Ridolfi-Starr 2016). While the research on reasons for not reporting and underreporting include different methodologies, the reasons victims give for not reporting often suggest that they are unsure about whether or not the act is a crime and they lack confidence in the ability of formal systems (administrative and legal) to protect them and to respond effectively. This fear is not unfounded. Universities and the legal system as a whole have less than a stellar record when it comes to believing victims, providing effective assistance, and holding perpetrators accountable in meaningful ways.

The recent publicity surrounding the former Stanford student Brock Turner illustrates all too well why victims refuse to report. This case is not unusual in many respects. An intoxicated and incapacitated victim was assaulted by a man who claimed he was too intoxicated to be held responsible and who blamed peer pressure, drinking, and promiscuity for his behavior (Stack 2016). Turner was convicted of three felony counts. What is unusual is that there were eyewitnesses, physical evidence, a criminal prosecution, and a conviction by a jury. The judge, a Stanford alumnus, sentenced Turner to a mere six months in jail and probation, in part because he failed to believe Turner would be a danger to others and argued that a prison sentence would have had a severe impact on him. (This outcome is an example of our reluctance to refer to the formal system as the "criminal justice system," instead preferring the more accurate "criminal legal system.")

Unfortunately, this type of treatment of college rape victims is not new, and might not have even warranted national publicity if the case had not involved a Stanford perpetrator and a brave survivor who brilliantly articulated the harm done to her by a privileged perpetrator who was viewed less like a criminal and more like a wayward student who had a promising future destroyed (albeit by his own actions). In other words, the system basically responded by doing business as usual until the profound statement provided by the victim went viral. The fact that it received millions of views, that it was read on air by CNN anchor Ashleigh Banfield, that Vice President Biden issued an open letter in response, and that a recall movement was initiated to sanction the judge suggests that this case and the lack of justice for this rape victim resonated with too many people to be dismissed as an isolated event. We must do better. Should we and can we, in good conscience, ask survivors to report their crimes to a system that is likely to be stacked against them and that historically has been resistant to change? And, if we encourage them to bravely cooperate with our new approaches, we at least need to be fully cognizant of what we are asking and the risks they are taking.

REFERENCES

Bondurant, B. 2001. University women's acknowledgment of rape: Individual, situational, and social factors. *Violence Against Women* 7 (3): 294–314.

Burgess-Proctor, A., S. M. Pickett, M. R. Parkhill, T. S. Hamill, M. Kirwan, and A. T. Kozak. 2016. College women's perceptions of and inclination to use campus sexual assault resources: Comparing the views of students with and without sexual victimization histories. *Criminal Justice Review* 41 (2): 204–218.

Campbell, R. 2008. The psychological impact of rape victims. *American Psychologist* 63 (8): 702–717.

Cantalupo, N. C. 2012. 'Decriminalizing' campus institutional responses to peer sexual violence. *Journal of College and University Law* 38: 483–526.

———. 2014. Institution-specific victimization surveys addressing legal and practical disincentives to gender-based violence reporting on college campuses. *Trauma, Violence, and Abuse* 15 (3): 227–241.

———. 2016. For the Title IX civil rights movement: Congratulations and cautions. *Yale Law Journal Forum*, February 19, 281–303.

Cantor, D., B. S. Fisher, S. Chibnall, R. Townsend, H. Lee, C. Bruce, and G. Thomas. 2015. *Report on the AAU Campus Climate Survey on sexual assault and sexual misconduct.* Rockville, MD: Westat.

Cleere, C., and S. J. Lynn. 2013. Acknowledged versus unacknowledged sexual assault among college women. *Journal of Interpersonal Violence* 28 (12): 2593–2611.

Englander, E., M. McCoy, and S. Sherman. 2015. Sexual assault information on university websites. *Violence and Gender* 3 (1): 64–70.

Ernst, J. 2016. *To combat campus sexual assault, republican leaders and sexual assault survivors join Senators Gillibrand and McCaskill to renew push for Senate to pass Campus Accountability and Safety Act.* Press Release. Available at https://www.gillibrand .senate.gov/newsroom/press/release/to-combat-campus-sexual-assault-republican- leaders-and-sexual-assault-survivors-join-senators-gillibrand-and-mccaskill-to -renew-push-for-senate-to-pass-campus-accountability-and-safety-act.

Fisher, B., L. Daigle, F. Cullen, and M. Turner. 2003a. Acknowledging sexual victimization as rape: Results from a national-level study. *Justice Quarterly* 20 (3): 535–574.

———. 2003b. Reporting sexual victimization to the police and others: Results from a national-level study of college women. *Criminal Justice and Behavior* 30 (1): 6–38.

Kahn, A., A. Jackson, J. Jackson, C. Kully, K. Badger, and J. Halvorsen. 2003. Calling it rape: Differences in experiences of women who do or do not label their sexual assault as rape. *Psychology of Women Quarterly* 27 (3): 233–242.

Kahn, A., V. Mathie, and C. Torgler. 1994. Rape scripts and rape acknowledgment. *Psychology of Women Quarterly* 18 (1): 53–66.

Karjane, H. K., B. S. Fisher, and F. T. Cullen. 2002. *Executive Summary. Campus Sexual Assault: How America's Institutions of Higher Education Respond.* Final Report, NIJ Grant #1999-WA-VX-0008. Newton, MA: Education Development Center.

Kingkade, T. 2015. Bill in Congress would open new route for colleges to get sued over rape cases. *Huffington Post*, June 4. Available at http://www.huffingtonpost.com/2015/06/04 /colleges-sued-rape-cases_n_7511484.html.

Koss, M. P. 1985. The hidden rape victim: Personality, attitudinal, and situational characteristics. *Psychology of Women Quarterly* 9 (2): 193–212.

Koss, M. P., T. E. Dinero, C. A. Seibel, and S. L. Cox. 1988. Stranger and acquaintance rape: Are there differences in the victim's experience? *Psychology of Women Quarterly* 12 (1): 1–24.

Krebs, C. P., C. Lindquist, M. Berzofsky, B. Shook-Sa, K. Peterson, M. Planty, L. Langton, and J. Stroop. 2016. Campus climate survey validation study final technical report (R&DP-2015: 04, NCJ 249545). Washington, DC: Department of Justice.

Krebs, C. P., C. H. Lindquist, T. D. Warner, B. S. Fisher, and S. L. Martin. 2007. *The campus sexual assault (CSA) study.* Washington, DC: U.S. Government Printing Office.

Krivoshey, M. S., R. Adkins, R. Hayes, J. M. Nemeth, and E. G. Klein. 2013. Sexual assault reporting procedures at Ohio colleges. *Journal of American College Health* 61 (3): 142–147.

Lindquist, C. H., K. Barrick, C. P. Krebs, C. M. Crosby, A. J. Lockard, and K. Sanders-Phillips. 2013. The context and consequences of sexual assault among undergraduate women at historically black colleges and universities (HBCUs). *Journal of Interpersonal Violence* 28 (12): 2437–2461.

Mancini, C., J. T. Pickett, C. Call, and S. P. Roche. 2016. Mandatory reporting (MR) in higher education: College students' perceptions of laws designed to reduce campus sexual assault. *Criminal Justice Review* 41 (2): 219–235.

Orchowski, L., and C. Gidycz. 2012. To whom do college women confide following sexual assault? A prospective study of predictors of sexual assault disclosure and social reactions. *Violence Against Women* 18 (3): 264–288.

Orchowski, L., A. Untied, and C. Gidycz. 2013. Factors associated with college women's labeling of sexual victimization. *Violence and Victims* 28 (6): 940–958.

Payne, B. K. 2008. Challenges responding to sexual violence: Differences between college campuses and communities. *Journal of Criminal Justice* 36: 224–230.

Richards, T. N., K. A. Branch, and R. M. Hayes. 2013. An exploratory examination of student to professor disclosures of crime victimization. *Violence Against Women* 19 (11): 1408–1422.

Richards, T. N., and K. Kafonek. 2016. Reviewing state legislative agendas regarding sexual assault in higher education: Proliferation of best practices and points of caution. *Feminist Criminology* 11 (1): 91–129.

Ridolfi-Starr, Z. 2016. Transformation requires transparency: Critical policy reforms to advance campus sexual violence response. *Yale Law Journal* 125 (7): 2156–2181.

Sabina, C., and L. Y. Ho. 2014. Campus and college victim responses to sexual assault and dating violence: Disclosure, service utilization, and service provision. *Trauma, Violence, and Abuse* 15 (3): 201–226.

Sable, M. R., F. Danis, D. L. Mauzy, and S. K. Gallagher. 2006. Barriers to reporting sexual assault for women and men: Perspectives of college students. *Journal of American College Health* 55 (3): 157–162.

Sinozich, S., and L. Langton. 2014. Rape and sexual assault victimization among college-age females, 1995–2013. Report NCJ248471. Washington, DC: U.S. Government Printing Office.

Stack, L. 2016. In Stanford rape case, Brock Turner blamed drinking and promiscuity. *New York Times*, June 8. Available at http://www.nytimes.com/2016/06/09/us/brock-turner -blamed-drinking-and-promiscuity-in-sexual-assault-at-stanford.html?action=click &contentCollection=U.S.&module=RelatedCoverage&region=EndOfArticle&pgtype =article&_r=0.

Tamborra, T. L., and F. M. Narchet. 2011. A university sexual misconduct policy: Prioritizing student victims' voices. *Crime Prevention and Community Safety* 13 (1): 16–33.

Thompson, M., D. Sitterle, G. Clay, and J. Kingree. 2007. Reasons for not reporting victimizations to the police: Do they vary for physical and sexual incidents? *Journal of American College Health* 55 (5): 277–282.

Title IX: Tracking Sexual Assault Investigations. 2016. *Chronicle of Higher Education*. Available at http://projects.chronicle.com/titleix/.

Truman, J. L. and L. Langton. 2015. *Criminal victimization, 2014*. (NCJ 248973). Washington, DC: U.S. Government Printing Office.

U.S. Department of Education, Office for Civil Rights (DOE, OCR). 1997. Sexual harassment guidance: Harassment of students by school employees, other students, or third parties. Available at http://www2.ed.gov/about/offices/list/ocr/docs/sexhar01.html.

———. 2001. Revised sexual harassment guidance: Harassment of students by school employees, other students, or third parties. Available at http://www.ed.gov/offices/OCR/archives/pdf/shguide.pdf.

———. 2011. *Dear Colleague Letter.* Available at http://www2.ed.gov/about/offices/list/ocr/letters/colleague-201104.pdf.

———. 2014. Questions and answers on Title IX and sexual violence. Available at http://www2.ed.gov/about/offices/list/ocr/docs/qa-201404-title-ix.pdf.

———. 2015a. Dear Colleague Letter to Title IX coordinators. Available at http://www.ed.gov/ocr/docs/dcl-title-ix-coordinators-letter-201504.pdf.

———. 2015b. Title IX resource guide. Available at https://www2.ed.gov/about/offices/list/ocr/docs/dcl-title-ix-coordinators-guide-201504.pdf.

U.S. Senate Subcommittee on Financial and Contracting Oversight. 2014. *Sexual violence on campus: How too many institutions of higher education are failing to protect students.* Available at https://www.mccaskill.senate.gov/download/campus-sexual-assault-survey-results.

Walsh, W. A., V. L. Banyard, M. M. Moynihan, S. Ward, and E. S. Cohn. 2010. Disclosure and service use on a college campus after an unwanted sexual experience. *Journal of Trauma and Dissociation* 11 (2): 134–151.

Wilson, L. C., and K. E. Miller. 2016. Meta-analysis of the prevalence of unacknowledged rape. *Trauma, Violence, and Abuse* 17 (2): 149–159.

Wolitzky-Taylor, K. B., H. S. Resnick, J. L. McCauley, A. B. Amstadter, D. G. Kilpatrick, and K. J. Ruggiero. 2011. Is reporting of rape on the rise? A comparison of women with reported versus unreported rape experiences in the National Women's Study-Replication. *Journal of Interpersonal Violence* 26 (4): 807–832.

12

Campus-Based Victim Advocacy Centers

Ráchael A. Powers, Alesha Cameron,
and Christine Mouton

Introduction

The prevalence of sexual assault, intimate partner violence (IPV), and stalking of college students presents a significant concern for students, college administrators, and the community (see Chapters 2–4 of this volume for a more thorough discussion). In 2015, the Association of American Universities (AAU) conducted a survey on sexual assault with more than 150,000 students across twenty-seven university campuses (Cantor et al. 2015). This study found that approximately 23 percent of female undergraduate students had experienced sexual assault, a rate five times higher than their male counterparts (Cantor et al. 2015). Likewise, studies indicate that young women (age nineteen to twenty-nine) are particularly at risk for IPV (Bachman and Saltzman 1995). Besides the disquieting prevalence of these victimizations, violence against college students is unique in several respects. First, because campuses are a microcosm of society, many student survivors know their assailants and it is possible that the offender is in the victim's social group. This can present unique obstacles for safety planning and can compound the adverse consequences of victimization. Second, many students find themselves away from home for the first time. They may not have adequate support systems, especially during the first months of college, which is considered the "Red Zone," a time when students are particularly vulnerable to victimization, particularly sexual violence.

Although victimization on college campuses has long been an issue on the nation's agenda, since 2011, victimization of female college students has risen to the forefront of media and policy attention (Busch-Armendariz, Sulley, and Hill 2016). In 2011, the U.S. Department of Education's Office for Civil Rights issued a Dear Colleague Letter (DCL) to all educational institutions as a sharp reminder of schools' obligations under Title IX to appropriately respond to reports of sexual violence as a form of sex discrimination (White House Council on Women and Girls and the Office of the Vice President 2014). Further, the Campus Sexual Violence Elimination Act (Campus SaVE Act) amended the Clery Act in 2013, as a part of the Violence Against Women Act (VAWA) reauthorization. Campus SaVE details expectations for institutions of higher education (IHE) on how to address, through prevention and intervention strategies, the variety of victimizations noted earlier and also includes mandates for provision of services and remedies.

Such escalated federal attention has renewed media attention on these important issues. Numerous media reports exposing universities' mishandling of allegations of interpersonal violence and documentaries such as *The Hunting Ground* have brought these issues into the spotlight. This has been further amplified by student activism; survivors of campus sexual assault have spoken out about their grievances and the mishandling of their cases by their institutions (Busch-Armendariz, Sulley, and Hill 2016). Student victims and their supporters have coordinated nationally to actively raise awareness with organizations such as Know Your IX (see Chapter 16 for a discussion of student activism). Organized efforts such as Know Your IX and campus-specific protests and outreach efforts have made it clear that students demand a safe learning environment that is free of violence and supportive of survivors (Know Your IX n.d.).

Collectively, legislation, media attention, and student activism have encouraged IHE to handle reports of sexual assault, sexual harassment, stalking, and IPV in a comprehensive, effective, and timely manner (Busch-Armendariz, Sulley, and Hill 2016). In other chapters of this book, authors discuss how IHE are handling these cases with a focus on compliance with Title IX, Clery, and Campus SaVE. Part of these enhanced federal and institutional policies mandate the provision of victim services to student survivors. In this chapter, we situate the purpose of victim services on college and university campuses, and particularly victim advocates, in this larger discussion of compliance and violence prevention. This includes discussing the need, demand, and presence of victim services and victim advocates on campuses, and how their services have changed in recent years due to federal legislation that has placed a heavy burden on campuses to provide interim measures and remedies for victims. We also examine the role(s) campus-based victim advocates play in the prevention, education, and response to female student survivors, including collaborations among victim services and other campus entities, such as campus law enforcement, campus health centers, counseling, Student Affairs, and the Title IX office. We conclude by considering challenges for victim advocates today, which include making their services available and accessible to students and fulfilling their mission despite being inadequately resourced and staffed.

The Role of Victim Advocates

The role of a victim advocate is different from other agencies or offices on campus that handle crime in that there is no requirement of victim advocates to report victimization to IHE administration, investigate offenses, or provide services to respondents. Because their primary responsibility lies in serving the needs of student survivors, victim advocates are sometimes called on to be whistle-blowers against IHE (Hippensteele 1997). However, victim advocacy centers should be viewed, "not only consistent with the intent of Title IX, [but they also] can ultimately help institutions meet important institutional and legal goals" (297). Resources to victims come from three sources: the victims themselves, the advocates, and other agencies/offices. It is the victim advocate's responsibility to empower, inform, and assist the victim in understanding his or her options and help obtain necessary and desired resources (Bozian et al. 2010). The criminal justice system in particular can be difficult to navigate emotionally and procedurally, especially with regard to sexual violence, where the victim is often met with disbelief surrounding the events. As Smith and Fossey (1995) note, "colleges and universities can do little to make the criminal courts more hospitable to rape victims, but they can do a great deal to provide victims with support within the campus community" (197).

It is important to note that student survivors seeking services from a victim advocacy center will not necessarily lead to the victimization being reported to campus/local law enforcement or the Title IX office. A victim advocacy center, like mental health counselors and health care practitioners on campus, is a confidential reporting site under Title IX. Under Title IX, most IHE employees including faculty are required to report incidents of sexual harassment, sexual violence, and sex-based discrimination to the Title IX coordinator (Busch-Armendariz, Sulley, and Hill 2016). As confidential reporting sites, victim advocacy centers are exempt from this reporting requirement. Instead, victim advocates can help victims decide what (if any) resources might best serve their needs and/or help them navigate the reporting process if the student survivors choose.

If survivors choose to report their victimization to law enforcement and/ or to the Title IX office, in addition to services provided by the victim advocacy center, victim advocates can also help them navigate these reporting options by providing tangible and emotional support through the process. Victims have options with regard to disclosing the victimization outside of the victim advocacy office; they can report incidents to police within the criminal justice system, to IHE personnel through the administrative student conduct office, or through a civil suit (Busch-Armendariz, Sulley, and Hill 2016). Students should be informed that each option can produce different outcomes and what those outcomes might entail. To report through the criminal justice process, students can report a sexual assault, IPV, stalking, or other victimization to campus or local police. Although the result of the criminal justice process may end with the offender in jail or prison, victims should be informed that they might not get the desired outcome from the criminal justice system, and victim advocates can ensure that student survivors are informed and prepared for that possibility. Administrative student conduct reporting can take place with student emergency services, student judicial services, or the Title IX office. As these procedures may vary by institution, the explicit administrative sites for reporting should be clearly identified by IHE online and in distributed Title IX materials. An administrative report of victimization can result in the offender receiving IHE-based sanctions, ranging from a verbal warning to being expelled from the institution (Busch-Armendariz, Sulley, and Hill 2016). Further, under Title IX, a report to campus administration will result in immediate interim measures for the victim, including but not limited to changes in housing and academic accommodations if necessary. It is important to note, however, that victim advocates can secure some of these interim measures on behalf of the student survivor without reporting to the Title IX coordinator. Finally, a student can also elect to engage in the civil court system to acquire the recovery of damages (Busch-Armendariz, Sulley, and Hill 2016). These tort actions can involve the perpetrator or third parties, such as school administrators who fail to use reasonable care to protect the student from victimization. This option can be beneficial to victims since they have more control over the process (as opposed to criminal cases where the state is the aggrieved party), there is a lower burden of proof, and survivors may find the process therapeutic. However, advocates should be careful to inform their clients that these procedures can be lengthy (sometimes spanning years), finding legal representation is sometimes difficult, and compensation is not guaranteed, even if a judgment is awarded (Bublick 2009).

Aside from empowering students by informing them of their reporting options, the services offered by victim advocates are varied and include prevention education/trainings, direct client services (e.g., support, interim measures, advocacy, and accompaniment), and referrals/coordination with outside agencies/offices. Thus, campus-based victim advocates interact with clients who are often students, fellow educators, campus administrators, and others on the IHE campus and beyond. As a few examples, victim advocates provide emergency assistance after a crime; crisis intervention; can help coordinate interim measures such as changes in housing; and offer assistance for filing police reports, injunctions, temporary restraining orders, petitions, protective orders, and crime victim compensation requests (Chang et al. 2012). They ease the process of a victim's participation in the criminal justice system or IHE adjudication. Victim advocates provide information and referral to needed resources and help victims navigate the process of obtaining those services. Such referrals and assistance are important because victims may need to interact with several different offices, including campus security, campus police, counseling and psychological services, health services, wellness promotion services, LGBTQ+ services, student legal services, human resources, and student disability services (Bozian et al. 2010). Victim advocates provide referrals and work outside of the office by accompanying student survivors to hospitals, court, and other offices. In doing so, they provide emotional support for victims and are able to advocate on their behalf with other agencies and the criminal justice system.

Victim advocates also play an important role in the prevention of violence. Educational programs, such as those discussed in Chapters 14 and 15, can confront negative aspects of the campus culture, such as binge drinking and bystander apathy. Education, support, and awareness on sexual assault and other forms of victimization can prevent sexual violence, secondary victimization, and the perpetuation of victim-blaming attitudes. Consent is especially important to discuss in educational programs because of the expansion of affirmative consent policies and laws that put clear burdens on all parties to seek and achieve consent for sexual behaviors. A basic definition of consent is an informed, voluntary, mutual agreement for sexual activity that can be withdrawn at any time and is act-specific (consent is not a blanket agreement); silence, absence of resistance, coercion, intimidation, threats and/or duress do not constitute consent (Busch-Armendariz, Sulley, and Hill 2016). Students, in particular, need to be educated on the relationship between voluntary intoxication and sexual consent. Victim advocates can incorporate these ideas of consent within education of campus services and bystander education. In this way, victim advocacy centers can help fulfill the prevention education requirements under the Campus SaVE Act. Furthermore, education and awareness done by victim advocacy centers serves a dual purpose in that they can ensure students are aware of the center and its role in ensuring a safe learning environment and providing services to survivors. This in turn may encourage victims who otherwise would have remained silent to use the victim advocacy center as a confidential reporting site and receive the resources and support they need.

Barriers to Victim Service Utilization

There are barriers that prevent student survivors from seeking victim services. These barriers include a lack of awareness of campus services for victims, logistical barriers pertaining to the center, and cultural barriers.

With regard to awareness, in a large survey done on a southeastern campus, more than 84 percent of both males and females who were surveyed were aware of campus police services, counseling services, health and wellness programs, victim services, emergency alert systems, and blue light safety phones (Pritchard 2016). Around 70 percent of the male and female students were aware of safety escorts, and about 59 percent of the students were aware of sexual consent training (Pritchard 2016). While these numbers indicate that the majority of students are aware of campus resources that may prevent victimization or support survivors, these numbers also indicate that there is a gap in awareness of services available to student survivors.

Therefore, increasing the knowledge of services available and IHE utilization of these services should be a priority. Many schools utilize posters, flyers, stickers, and pamphlets to spread awareness of the resources that are available to students (Centers for Disease Control and Prevention 2014). Posters with information on services that are available to students have been found to have a positive effect on students' knowledge when they are displayed in bathroom stalls, dormitories, and bulletin boards (Garcia et al. 2012). Garcia and colleagues (2012) found that students were receptive to information regarding consent and sexual violence, and messages in public spaces reinforced the IHE commitment to safety. These posters can also send the message that the university or college considers victimization to be a serious issue and will treat victims with respect and compassion. This in turn may encourage victims to seek campus services. Finally, posters with information about resources can also help supporters of survivors to provide information to victims following a disclosure. Aside from passive programming, victim advocates can increase awareness of services by active programming, such as talking at student orientation, speaking in class, using peer educators, tabling in common areas, and engaging student organizations. Given that the majority of victims will disclose an assault informally (to a friend or family member) (Fisher et al. 2003), widely disseminating information about victim services can ensure that the entire campus community is aware of resources to help student survivors.

For the second category of barriers, logistically, research suggests that the location and designation of reporting sites can affect whether students seek services from victim advocacy centers. First, the title that a service center uses is an important feature with regard to student perception and utilization of its services. Student survivors can be discouraged from seeking services available to them simply because of the title of the office. Service centers that include the words "trauma" or "crisis" have been found to be utilized less by students who do not feel that their victimization was on a crisis or traumatic level (Walsh et al. 2010). Some students, such as men and LGBTQ+ students, were less likely to visit victim service centers after they had been victimized if it was titled a "women's" center. College campuses need to be mindful not to alienate or label any students, while also making it clear that services are not gendered or limited to "crisis" situations. Finally, the term "advocacy" may be confusing to some students, so care should be taken to inform the campus community what a victim advocacy center entails.

Second, the location of a victim center is also an important criteria for students' willingness to seek services (Walsh et al. 2010). Students do not want to be stigmatized, shamed, or embarrassed by peers who may see them using victim services (Walsh et al. 2010). Some students may also be concerned that perpetrators might retaliate if they see them use a victim advocacy center. It is fundamental for victim service centers to be secluded in order to provide confidentiality and safety to students entering the office. If centers are not secluded, programs should offer confidential hotlines and alternative private meeting areas, including off-campus locations (DeMatteo et al. 2015). In addition to seclusion, care should be taken not to house the victim advocacy center in another office that may alienate students. For example, students who do not want to report the victimization may not visit a victim advocacy center if it is housed within a police department because they may assume that they are related. Likewise, victim advocacy centers housed in women's health centers may alienate men.

Culturally, rape myth acceptance and gender scripts may prevent victims from seeking services. Common barriers to victim reporting include feelings of shame, guilt, self-blame, and embarrassment (Sable et al. 2006). Female students often report that they did not report their victimization because they feared the perpetrator would retaliate or would not allow them to obtain help, or they were concerned that family members and friends may judge them (Sable et al. 2006). For men and sexual minorities, there may be additional concerns that preclude reporting. For men, these concerns are exacerbated by gender scripts that suggest victimization and seeking help for victimization is emasculating (Sable et al. 2006). Members of the LGBTQ+ community shared with researchers that when they do not report victimization, it is most likely due to fear of being treated unfairly due to their sexual preference, feeling uncomfortable disclosing their sexual preference, and uneasiness about how the police and community would perceive them following the victimization (Potter, Fountain, and Stapleton 2012).

Previous research has shown that prevention programs and sexual assault education help to reduce the cultural barriers preventing students from seeking services. Discussed previously is the role that victim advocacy can play in primary prevention. By addressing rape myth acceptance and increasing awareness of victimization, victim advocates can remove some of these barriers to seeking services. A promising strategy to prevent violence and remove the stigma surrounding victimization is bystander programs. Two common bystander intervention programs that have been implemented on campuses are the Green Dot program and the Bringing in the Bystander campaign (for more information about bystander programs, see Chapter 14). Furthermore, the explicit inclusion of men in anti-violence efforts either through bystander programs or men's anti-violence programs can encourage reporting of victimization for both male and female student victims (for more information about men's anti-violence against women efforts, see Chapter 15). For example, Walk a Mile in Her Shoes events bring awareness to the causes of men's sexualized violence against women, provide men with prevention and remediation strategies, and empower them to implement these skills.

Challenges for Victim Advocacy Centers and the Future of Advocacy

It is important to acknowledge that there is variation among IHE; they vary in terms of size, location, mainly residential compared to commuter, private compared to public, and so on. Some are large urban campuses with easy access to resources both on-campus and in the surrounding community, and some are small colleges in rural areas with less access to on- and off-campus services. Rural communities often face unique challenges when responding to victimization (Littel, Lonsway, and Archambault 2007). First, Littel, Lonsway, and Archambault (2007) suggest that a fear of lack of anonymity and of retaliation are salient factors that prohibit sexual violence victims in rural communities from reporting. This suggests that victim advocacy centers in rural communities should focus a great deal of attention on prevention and education awareness to increase knowledge and amenability of students to seek services. Leveraging technology to allow students to report victimization and seek services may relieve some of their concerns regarding anonymity. Second, colleges in rural areas can sometimes be physically isolated from hospitals, victim services and resources, personnel, and police departments (Littel, Lonsway, and Archambault 2007). When victims do seek services following a victimization and campus resources are not available, they may turn to noncampus support. While worthwhile, noncampus victimization services do not have the same access to campus support for such issues as on-campus residential housing, financial aid, and class accommodations. Although victims may seek help from campus counseling centers as confidential reporting sites that are able to provide interim measures, as discussed earlier, many students may feel hesitant to seek services in a counseling center if they do not feel that their experience requires mental health assistance.

All programs, regardless of their location, can lack funding, sufficient staffing, and institutional support. Victim advocates need adequate resources in order to perform their job correctly and assist victims (Carmody, Ekhomu, and Payne 2009). Beyond the general and ubiquitous need for more resources, however, there are additional gaps in victim services that are rarely discussed. For instance, an important feature that is overlooked in most victim programs and services is access to translation services for international students and accommodations for students with disabilities (Carmody, Ekhomu, and Payne 2009). Furthermore, outside of the victim advocacy center, physical resources such as safety lights, call boxes, emergency buttons, and security patrols are cited by students as important resources before and after a sexual assault or victimization event (Garcia et al. 2012). Again, small campuses might be less likely to have access to a wide array of physical resources like call boxes, or an extensive amount of services available to victims.

Even well-established centers with institutional support may find themselves overwhelmed in light of the changes in the past six years. The media and political attention that violence against women on college campuses has received has been tremendous, particularly with regard to sexual violence. This coupled with innovative primary prevention programs targeting attitudes that condone violence against women (e.g., rape myths) and acts of student activism have represented a cultural shift in how we perceive these issues. Whereas there is still a lot of work to be done, the stigma surrounding victimization is lessening. With that, however, comes an increase in reports of victimization. Many centers report an almost exponential increase in the number of cases they have handled during the past few years. This increase does not represent an increase in perpetration; rather, it reflects a greater willingness of victims to come forward and report and/or seek services that they need. This must be met with increases in funding and staff, but universities are sometimes hard-pressed to meet that demand. Universities and colleges must provide adequate resources to victim advocacy centers and recognize that the increase in reports is likely to continue for some time. Victim advocates, unlike many other offices, operate with an open-ended timeline, so student survivors may be clients for a short time or for years.

It is not just the quantity of agency resources that is important, but also the quality of those resources. One aspect of staffing that is sometimes overlooked is diversity. Diversity in staff is important because victims bring with them identities and potential needs that transcend gender and incorporate race, class, and sexual orientation. For example, victims of same-sex IPV may have unique concerns surrounding being "outed" to friends and family. An international student's experiences with sexual harassment by a professor may stem not only from her gender but also her vulnerabilities being unaccustomed to the United States. As Hippensteele (1997) notes in her discussion of sexual harassment on campuses, "most white, presumably straight, women supporters and advocates lack the experience to fully comprehend the complexity of sexual harassment commingled with race and/or sexual orientation oppression, thus few women of color or lesbians expect influential people within the institution to be sensitive or responsive to their sexual victimization" (301). Acknowledgment of the unique experiences of student survivors and culturally appropriate services are necessary to adequately serve a diverse student body.

One unique challenge facing advocacy centers transcends institutional support and diverse staffing. Advocates are often creative in the remedies that they provide to student survivors. For example, an advocate may help a survivor regain control of her finances after an abusive relationship has ended or find her new routes to school or work that increase her feelings of safety. However, it is more difficult to provide services to victims whose victimization involves technology; there are no interim measures for the Internet. As cyberstalking and cyberharassment are becoming more frequent (Lindsay and Krysik 2012), and the detrimental effects of victims' safety and well-being are being documented in research (Parsons-Pollard and Moriarty 2009), victim advocates must be able to address cybervictimization. Whereas academic accommodations may be similar, housing accommodations are not as simple; removing the victim from the physical space is unlikely to reduce his or her risk or fear. Whereas technology presents unique challenges for victim advocates, it also provides the opportunity to engage students in primary prevention and general awareness. Social media campaigns aimed at sexual and intimate partner violence have shown promising results (Cismaru and Lavack 2011) and advocates should use this platform to continue to change the culture surrounding violence against women.

Conclusion

Victim advocates are essential to the timely and effective response to victimization. They serve to empower survivors and ensure that student victims' voices are heard, respected, and their concerns are remedied. They provide a wide variety of services, including but not limited to safety planning, academic advising, housing accommodations, and personal and systems advocacy. Furthermore, they provide victims the information they need to make informed decisions about reporting and service utilization. This is important, as the process for seeking redress is complicated and victims may be unaware of the resources available to them. Ultimately, victim advocates provide support, both emotional and tangible, to student survivors. Whereas this support is in line with the intentions of Title IX, as discussed in other chapters, it is easy for IHE to get lost in their efforts to comply with regulations and forget the spirit of these policies—to prevent violence against women and support survivors. As these policies evolve, more emphasis will likely be placed on having victim advocates on campuses. Care should be taken to ensure that these centers are and remain victim-centered first and foremost.

ACKNOWLEDGMENT

The authors would like to thank Joni Bernbaum for her assistance and valuable feedback on this chapter.

REFERENCES

Bachman, R., and L. E. Saltzman. 1995. *Violence against women: Estimates from the redesigned National Crime Victimization Survey.* Washington, DC: Department of Justice.
Bozian, R., C. Alexander, M. Burchfield, M. Davis, D. Echesabal, K. Foulke . . . and S. Huntzinger. 2010. *Excellence in advocacy: A victim-centered approach.* National Sexual Violence Resource Center. Available at http://www.nsvrc.org/publications/excellence-advocacy-victim-centered-approach.
Bublick, E. 2009. *Civil tort actions filed by victims of sexual assault: Promise and perils.* National Online Resource Center on Violence Against Women. Available at http://www.vawnet.org/applied-research-papers/print-document.php?doc_id=2150.
Busch-Armendariz, N. B., C. Sulley, and K. Hill. 2016. *The blueprint for campus police: Responding to sexual assault.* Institute on Domestic Violence and Sexual Assault, February. Austin, TX: University of Texas at Austin. Available at the National Center for Campus Public Safety, http://www.nccpsafety.org/resources/library/the-blueprint-for-campus-police-responding-to-sexual-assault/.
Cantor, D., B. Fisher, S. Chibnall, R. Townsend, H. Lee, C. Bruce, and G. Thomas. 2015. *Report on the AAU Campus Climate Survey on sexual assault and sexual misconduct.* Association of American Universities, September. Available at https://www.aau.edu/Climate-Survey.aspx?id=16525.
Carmody, D., J. Ekhomu, and B. K. Payne. 2009. Needs of sexual assault advocates in campus-based sexual assault centers. *College Student Journal* 43 (2): 507–513.
Centers for Disease Control and Prevention. 2014. *Preventing sexual violence on college campuses: Lessons from research and practice. Part one: Evidence-based strategies for the primary prevention of sexual violence perpetration.* The United States Department of Justice, April. Available at https://www.justice.gov/ovw/protecting-student-sexual-assault resources.
Chang, J., T. D. Stucky, R. Thelin, and A. Tynes. 2012. *Review of best practices for ICJI Program areas: Victims of Crime Act (VOCA).* Center for Criminal Justice Research, School of Public and Environmental Affairs, Indiana University, January. Available at https://archives.upui.edu/bitstream/handle/2450/5920/VOCABestPractices_Final_041212.pdf?sequence=1.
Cismaru, M., and A. M. Lavack. 2011. Campaigns targeting perpetrators of intimate partner violence. *Trauma, Violence, and Abuse* 12 (4): 183–197.
DeMatteo, D., M. Galloway, S. Arnold, and U. Patel. 2015. Sexual assault on college campuses: A 50-state survey of criminal sexual assault statutes and their relevance to cam-

pus sexual assault. *Psychology, Public Policy, and Law* 21 (3): 227–238. doi: 10.1037/law0000055.

Fisher, B. S., L. E. Daigle, F. T. Cullen, and M. G. Turner. 2003. Reporting sexual victimization and the police and others: Results from a national-level study of college women. *Criminal Justice and Behavior* 30 (1): 6–38.

Garcia, C. M., K. E. Lechner, E. A. Ferich, K. A. Lust, and M. E. Eisenberg. 2012. Preventing sexual violence instead of just responding to it: Students' perceptions of sexual violence resources on campus. *Journal of Forensic Nursing* 8 (2): 61–71.

Hippensteele, S. 1997. Advocacy and student victims of sexual harassment. In *Sexual harassment on campus: A guide for administrators, faculty, and students,* ed. B. R. Sandler and R. J. Shoop, 293–313. Boston, MA: Allyn and Bacon.

Know Your IX. n.d. *About KYIX.* Available at http://knowyourix.org/about-ky9/.

Lindsay, M., and J. Krysik. 2012. Online harassment among college students. *Information, Communication, and Society* 15 (5): 703–719.

Littel, K., K. A. Lonsway, and J. Archambault. 2007. *Sexual assault response and resource teams (SARRT): A guide for rural and remote communities.* End Violence Against Women International, June. Available at http://www.evawintl.org/PAGEID7/Best-Practices/Resources/SARRTs.

Parsons-Pollard, N., and L. J. Moriarty. 2009. Cyberstalking: Utilizing what we know. *Victims and Offenders* 4 (4): 435–441.

Potter, S., K. Fountain, and J. Stapleton. 2012. Addressing sexual and relationship violence in the LGBT community using a bystander framework. *Harvard Review of Psychiatry* 20 (4): 201–208.

Pritchard, A. 2016. *2016 Campus Safety Survey at the University of Central Florida.* Report to the Title IX Committee. Orlando: University of Central Florida.

Sable, M., F. Danis, D. Mauzy, and S. Gallagher. 2006. Barriers to reporting sexual assault for women and men: Perspectives of college students. *Journal of American College Health* 55 (3): 157–162.

Smith, M. C., and R. Fossey. 1995. *Crime on campus: Legal issues and campus administration.* Phoenix, AZ: American Council on Education; Oryx Press.

Walsh, W. A., V. L. Banyard, M. M. Moynihan, S. Ward, and E. S. Cohn. 2010. Disclosure and service use on a college campus after an unwanted sexual experience. *Journal of Trauma and Dissociation* 11 (2): 134–151.

White House Council on Women and Girls and the Office of the Vice President. 2014. *Rape and sexual assault: A renewed call to action.* White House, January. Available at https://www.whitehouse.gov/the-press-office/2015/09/17/fact-sheet-resource-guide-and-recent-efforts-combat-sexual-violence.

III

Preventing Violence through Knowledge, Education, and Changing Cultural Norms

13

Campus Climate Surveys

Christine Lindquist
and Christopher P. Krebs

Why Campus Climate Surveys?

The prevalence and nature of sexual assaults among college students have been the focus of decades of research. The majority of these studies have focused on documenting the experiences of students at individual colleges or universities, with few coordinated attempts to use standardized data collection instruments and methodologies to facilitate cross-school comparisons or maximize methodological rigor. In addition to research focusing on the extent of sexual assault at individual campuses, two nationally representative studies of undergraduate women were conducted: the National College Women Study (Koss, Gidycz, and Wisniewski 1987) and the National College Women Sexual Victimization (NCWSV) Survey (Fisher, Cullen, and Turner 2000).

Based on the findings from these studies, which generally converged around the estimate that one in five women experiences a sexual assault during her college years (Fisher, Cullen, and Turner 2000; Krebs et al. 2009), campus sexual assault has increasingly been perceived to be a serious problem. Coupled with high-profile media coverage about a student culture that is potentially conducive to sexual assault on some campuses and the egregious handling of reported incidents of sexual assault on the part of university administrators at some schools, the push took shape to measure the "campus climate" associated with sexual misconduct (including sexual assault and other forms of sexual violence or misconduct, such as sexual harassment). This push started with the formation of the White House Task Force to Protect Students from Sexual Assault, which was established in January 2014, with the goals of identifying promising practices for reducing rape and sexual assault among college students and bringing improvements, consistency, and evidence-based practices to campus responses to victimization. A major component of the task force's plan was to encourage schools to administer campus climate surveys to capture self-reported data on students' experiences with sexual assault and perceptions of the climate related to sexual misconduct. The task force recommended that climate assessments measure the incidence and prevalence of sexual assault, as well as "attitudes about the atmosphere of the campus" among students. Among the recommendations was that climate assessments be conducted regularly on campus to allow schools to determine if the implementation of school policies or practices is associated with increases or decreases in the prevalence of sexual assault over time. The White House Task Force released a tool kit for schools interested in conducting campus climate surveys, which included methodological recommendations and a draft survey instrument that was informed by prior research efforts.

After the release of the task force's report, a number of campus climate assessments were initiated, some of which used survey items from the tool kit. (Many other schools already had regular climate survey administration efforts in place; however, such efforts typically focused on the general campus climate, and/or specifically on diversity and inclusion, rather than the climate as it relates to sexual misconduct.) A number of climate surveys with a focus on sexual assault were conducted in 2014 and 2015, including surveys conducted by Rutgers University, University of Michigan, University of Oregon, and the Massachusetts Institute of Technology. Because of methodological differences between these studies (e.g., different definitions of sexual assault, reference periods, measurement strategies, data collection procedures, response rates, etc.), it is not possible to compare results from one survey to another or understand why differences might exist between schools.

In addition to individual climate surveys, several coordinated, cross-school efforts were implemented in 2015. The Association of American Universities (AAU) conducted sexual assault climate surveys using a standardized instrument (and a largely standardized data collection protocol) in twenty-seven institutions of higher education (Cantor et al. 2015). The Administrator Researcher Campus Climate Collaborative (ARC3) consortium of sexual assault researchers and student affairs professionals developed a campus climate survey package (pilot tested in several schools in 2015) and established itself as a coordinating center for schools wishing to use this survey. Finally, the Campus Climate Survey Validation Study

(CCSVS) entailed the use of a standardized instrument and methodology implemented across nine institutions of higher education, with a focus on validating a survey instrument and methodology for collecting precise, school-level data on the prevalence and nature of sexual assault and the campus climate related to sexual misconduct (Krebs et al. 2016). Because of the strong methodological focus of the CCSVS, a number of lessons were learned from this study that can inform future climate survey efforts. This chapter provides an overview of the CCSVS and outlines key methodological considerations for conducting climate surveys to ensure that such assessments are as rigorous as possible and capable of generating data and results that are of maximum utility to schools, students, and parents.

Overview of the CCSVS

The CCSVS was conducted by the Bureau of Justice Statistics (BJS) and RTI International from August 2014 to January 2016 (eighteen months). The purpose of the study was to develop and test a survey instrument and methodology for efficiently collecting valid school-level data on campus climate and sexual victimization. The CCSVS was designed and implemented around three research goals.

1. Develop a survey instrument that uses a collection of techniques to efficiently and confidentially collect valid data from undergraduate students about their sexual victimization experiences and perceptions of campus climate related to sexual harassment and sexual assault.
2. Design and implement a methodology that collects data from a sample of students, achieves response rate and survey completion targets, minimizes nonresponse bias, and ensures that resulting estimates are precise and representative of the undergraduate student populations at participating schools.
3. Collect data from students at multiple schools using a standardized methodology (e.g., within a standardized time period and using a standardized instrument and process) to produce school-specific results that can be compared across schools and are useful to participating schools.

Instrument Development

The CCSVS instrument development process began with an in-depth review of the survey included in the tool kit prepared by the White House Task Force to Protect Students from Sexual Assault. Modifications to the draft tool kit instrument were made to comply with best practices in survey methods research. The new draft survey used behaviorally specific screening questions to identify sexual assault victims and incident-level follow-up questions to capture detailed descriptive information on up to three individual incidents of sexual assault. The survey also covered sexual harassment, coerced sexual contact, intimate partner violence, and perpetration of sexual harassment and sexual assault. Other questions assessed several dimensions of campus climate, including students' school connectedness, perceptions of campus leadership efforts related to sexual misconduct, and student norms related to sexual misconduct. The draft instrument underwent an extensive cognitive testing process with male and female college students, including victims of sexual assault. Cognitive testing entails administering the survey to individuals who are similar to the population that will ultimately be participating in the survey and obtaining in-depth feedback about the cognitive process used by participants to interpret and answer each survey question. Both crowdsourcing and in-person cognitive testing methods were used and, based on the knowledge gained during the cognitive testing process, a number of important revisions were made to the instrument in terms of question ordering, wording, and response options.

Data Collection Methodology

Nine schools were recruited to participate in the CCSVS. The schools together did not constitute a nationally representative sample, but they did offer variation in terms of size, public versus private status, two-year versus four-year status, and region of the country. Memorandums of Understanding and Data Transfer Agreements were established with all participating schools. From rosters provided by each school, stratified random samples of undergraduate, degree-seeking male and female students,[1] who were at least eighteen years of age were drawn, with sample sizes designed to yield school-specific estimates of campus climate and sexual assault victimization during the 2014–2015 academic year (statistical power permitting). All undergraduate students at the participating schools were prenotified about the study via an e-mail from their school leadership. The survey was referred to by the neutral name College Experiences Survey (CES) to broaden its appeal to a cross-section of students. Sampled students were recruited via e-mail to participate in the confidential, web-based survey, which was designed to be fully functional on smartphones, tablets, laptops, and desktop computers. On average, the survey took fifteen minutes for males and sixteen minutes for females to complete. For taking the survey, students received a $25 gift card; however, in four schools, an incentive experiment was conducted to determine whether $25 was more effective than $10, and whether $40 was more effective than $25. The survey was open for approximately fifty-seven days, and up to five reminder e-mails were sent to students who had not responded.

Surveys were completed by more than 23,000 undergraduate students (approximately 15,000 females and 8,000 males). The average response rate across all nine schools was 54 percent for females and 40 percent for males, with response rates varying considerably across schools and exceeding the response rate targets established for the study. Nonresponse bias analyses were conducted at the school level using detailed student roster data provided by the schools. Minimal bias was detected (i.e., differences in characteristics of eligible students who did and did not participate in the survey), but the survey data were nonetheless adjusted or weighted slightly to compensate accordingly. The survey data were thoroughly reviewed for quality and completeness. About 2 percent of respondents started but did not finish the survey. The level of missing data (i.e., the proportion of survey items not answered by survey respondents) was also relatively low for most items. Numerous validity assessments were conducted, with the results indicating that the primary victimization estimates appeared to be valid (i.e., did not appear to be impacted by false positive or false negative bias).

Findings

The CCSVS generated prevalence estimates of sexual assault with the desired level of precision for undergraduate women at eight of nine schools using a representative sample of students. The standardized methodology used in the CCSVS allowed prevalence and incidence rates for key outcomes (such as sexual assault, rape, sexual battery, sexual harassment, and coerced sexual contact) to be compared across schools. Substantial variability in the estimates was evident across schools, and the estimates for several schools could be differentiated from one another statistically. Because only nine schools were included in the pilot test, the study could not identify campus characteristics that were associated with higher or lower victimization rates. The prevalence rate for completed sexual assault experienced by undergraduate females during the 2014–2015 academic year, averaged across the nine schools, was 10 percent, and ranged from 4 percent at one school to 20 percent at another. Incidence rates during this same time period ranged from about 85 to 325 incidents per 1,000 female students. The average prevalence rate for completed sexual assault experienced by undergraduate females since entering college was 21 percent and ranged from 12 to 38 percent across the schools. Sexual assault prevalence rates for undergraduate males were significantly lower than those for females (for men, the cross-school average for completed sexual assault during the 2014–2015 academic year was 3.1 percent, and varied from 1.4 percent at one school to 5.7 percent at another). When examining characteristics of rapes and sexual battery incidents,[2] a large portion of incidents occurred in September or October and were perpetrated by someone the victim knew casually, such as an acquaintance, the friend of a friend, or someone that the victim had just met. Across the nine participating schools, only 4.3 percent of sexual battery incidents and 12.5 percent of rapes were reported by the victim to any official.

In addition to the prevalence and incidence estimates, a number of scales showing campus climate related to sexual misconduct were developed from the CCSVS data, reflecting:

- Students' general perceptions of their school and different types of school staff (e.g., general school connectedness; general perceptions of campus police, faculty, and leadership staff)
- Students' perceptions of their school leadership specific to preventing or responding to sexual assault (e.g., perceptions of school leadership climate for sexual misconduct prevention and response, awareness and perceived fairness of school sexual assault policy and resources, perceptions of school leadership climate for treatment of sexual assault victims)
- Students' perceptions of the student culture related to sexual misconduct on campus (e.g., perceptions of student norms related to sexual misconduct)
- Students' own attitudes toward sexual misconduct and bystander intervention behavior (e.g., personal acceptance of sexual misconduct, likelihood of personal bystander behavior to prevent sexual misconduct)

The scales had high internal consistency and showed some variability across schools, particularly with regard to the percentage of students providing extremely negative ratings. A number of strategies for assessing the relationship between climate and sexual misconduct were explored, and some climate scales were correlated with sexual misconduct such that schools with a high proportion of men and women providing particularly negative ratings (on that particular dimension of climate) also had the highest rates of sexual harassment and sexual assault victimization for women. Specifically, the scales that had the strongest relationship between negative climate ratings and higher sexual harassment and sexual assault victimization were those related to students' perceptions of their school leadership staff (including scales for the "Perceptions of School Leadership Climate for Sexual Misconduct Prevention and Response," "Perceptions of School Leadership Climate for Treatment of Sexual Assault Victims," and "General Perceptions of Leadership Staff").

Methodological Considerations When Conducting Campus Climate Surveys

Based on the experiences and findings of the CCSVS, a number of factors should be considered when designing future climate surveys.

Sampling versus Census

First, researchers must determine, a priori, what estimates are key to meeting study goals (e.g., sexual assault victimization since entering college among the entire student population, sexual assault victimization during a particular academic year among undergraduates) and what subgroup estimates are important (e.g., victimization rates by year of study, sexual orientation, race/ethnicity), and then develop power calculations to guide decisions about the sample size needed to develop such estimates at the desired level of precision.

Many of the campus climate assessments that have been conducted have attempted to collect data from all students at the school. This census approach is appealing from an ideological perspective because it allows every student at the school to provide his or her voice by participating in the study. However, this approach can be logistically challenging and very expensive (particularly if monetary incentives for participation are provided, which is critical for increasing response rates and sample representativeness), and imposes a high level of burden on the student population and on the school. Many schools face constraints related to cost, staff, and the logistical and technical challenges of data collection, data processing, and data analysis. For a large school, conducting a census and collecting and processing thousands of surveys—in some cases, more than thirty thousand—would be a very labor-intensive effort.

A census approach is simply not necessary for most schools to develop precise prevalence estimates for the student population. A census approach does not result in a higher-quality or more precise estimate of the prevalence of sexual victimization than an estimate based on a much smaller, randomly selected sample of students. In fact, if a census approach and nominal or no incentives are used and response rates and/or sample representativeness are rather low as a result, the resulting estimates might lack sufficient statistical precision, have limited utility, or might be inaccurate and misleading. The CCSVS demonstrated that surveying a representative sample of students (rather than the entire student population) can generate school-level sexual assault prevalence and incidence estimates with more than acceptable levels of precision. Sampling smaller but representative groups of students also increases the likelihood that researchers can offer survey incentives in an effort to increase response rates and sample representativeness, and survey-ing only a sample of students minimizes the burden placed on the student population. For small schools, however, it may be necessary to field a census to get enough completed surveys to achieve reasonable levels of precision for key estimates.

Survey Content and Length

Other considerations pertain to the content of the survey instrument and manner of administration. Many survey questions and scales that have been pilot tested and/or validated are publicly available, including the instrument used in the CCSVS. Based on the lessons learned during the CCSVS instru-ment development process regarding the value of cognitive testing, it is critical that new or adapted questions be cognitively tested to ensure that the terminology is clear, understandable, and conveys the intended meaning of questions to a wide variety of college students. Researchers should also pay attention to the potential for certain questions to cause respondent distress, and make support resources available to survey participants. Approximately 15 percent of CCSVS respondents who took the survey viewed the informa-tion made available on school-specific, local, and national resources related to sexual violence.

Another key consideration during survey development is the adminis-tration length. Surveys should be streamlined as much as possible. Previous research has determined that response rates and data quality start to deteriorate after about the twenty-minute mark in web surveys (e.g., Cape 2010; Macer and Wilson 2014). The CCSVS, which took an average of fifteen minutes for men and sixteen minutes for women, had high response rates, very low break-off rates (i.e., surveys that were started, but not finished), and very few individual questions that were skipped. In addition, multiple assessments of data quality and validity returned promising results.

In terms of administration mode, self-administered, web-based surveys offer a number of advantages over other data collection modes (e.g., in-person or telephone interviews, pencil-and-paper surveys administered in a group setting) for collecting data on sensitive topics. Critically, they offer privacy and confidentiality, both of which are particularly important for respondents who may have experienced sexual assault. In addition, this strategy is extremely effective with college populations, who are highly liter-ate, have Internet access, and have active e-mail addresses via which they can be recruited. This mode also offers logistical advantages. Students can take the survey whenever and wherever they want and skip-and-fill patterns can be preprogrammed and seamless for respondents, making for a survey ex-perience that is customized, logical, and as efficient as possible. Based on the experiences of the CCSVS, it is important that climate surveys be accessible on handheld devices, as about 30 percent of respondents took the survey on a smartphone or tablet. In addition, the survey should use question structures and on-screen design features that are clear and readily intuitive to respondents.

Maximizing Response Rates and Sample Representativeness

A critical design consideration for climate assessments is that as many eligible students participate in the survey as possible and that those who participate reflect the general population of students at the schools. If students who take the survey are different in their victimization history, demographics, or attitudes about the school from students who do not take the survey, the data that are collected will have limited or no utility for the school. Typically, sample representativeness and response rates go hand in hand, such that having a high proportion of eligible students participate yields a more representative sample. Several strategies are recommended for maximizing both response rates and sample representativeness.

Most important, incentives should be offered for participation. Incentives are typically the single biggest factor that influence the cost of administering a climate survey, but they are also one of the keys to data quality and the ability to generate estimates with adequate statistical precision. It is thus critical to maximize cost-effectiveness such that the money spent on research and data collection offers a return on investment, so to speak, in the form of high response rates among the students who are invited to participate and low nonresponse bias. Based on the results of the experiment conducted in four of the CCSVS schools, a $25 incentive results in a significantly larger and more representative sample than a $10 incentive. It is less clear, however, whether moving to a $40 incentive offers any advantage. Thus, $20–$30 appears to be an ideal range for maximizing participation. Some recent climate survey efforts that have tried other approaches, such as offering no incentive, a nominal incentive (e.g., $5), or the chance of winning an incentive via a lottery, have obtained relatively low response rates to the point that the collected survey data have had limited utility for the participating schools.

Second, the recruitment strategy should appeal to as many students as possible and convey the legitimacy of the study. For the CCSVS, this was accomplished with a prenotification about the study sent by university leadership and the use of a neutral study name (e.g., "College Experiences Survey") in all recruitment materials. Based on one of the experiments implemented in the CCSVS, recruitment materials should refer to students by their first names as opposed to a generic greeting. Given the lower response rates for men than women in the CCSVS, additional attention should be given to the wording used in recruitment materials such that it is effectively conveyed to men that their participation in climate assessments is needed and important.

The field period and nonresponse follow-up strategy are also important for maximizing response rates and sample representativeness. In most schools, the CCSVS survey was fielded shortly after spring break and was kept open until right before final exam week, which was a fifty-seven-day field period, on average. This timing minimized students' competing demands during spring break and finals. In addition, it allowed time for repeated follow-up reminders with nonrespondents (up to five reminders were sent), which appeared to be effective given that bumps in response rates were observed each time a follow-up was sent. The field period simulations conducted for the CCSVS showed that a shorter field period (e.g., twenty-eight days) can be used to achieve adequate precision for school-level prevalence estimates of sexual assault victimization (provided that the overall study methods, including incentives and recruitment procedures, achieves the targeted sample sizes within this period and that no nonresponse bias results due to the shorter field period). However, keeping the survey open longer (e.g., for fifty-seven days) helps with the precision of subgroup estimates (e.g., victimization by year of study, sexual orientation) because more surveys can be completed.

Finally, it is important that researchers conduct a nonresponse bias analysis to understand if or how students who complete a climate survey differ from those who were invited to participate but did not. The CCSVS used detailed student roster data provided by the schools to compare the characteristics of survey respondents with those who were invited to participate in the survey but declined. As many auxiliary variables as possible (including sex, age, year of study, race/ethnicity, whether the student is living on or off campus, whether the student is attending school part-time or full-time, and grade point average) should be used in the nonresponse bias analysis in an effort to assess the potential for bias. The survey data should also be weighted to adjust for any bias that is detected.

Future Directions for Campus Climate Surveys

Campus climate surveys are an important vehicle for measuring sexual misconduct among college students and collecting information needed to understand which policies and programs are most effective at reducing the prevalence of rape and sexual assault, providing effective and necessary services to victims, investigating sexual victimization incidents, and holding perpetrators accountable. By generating an understanding of the magnitude and nature of the problem, climate surveys can give schools something on which to focus their prevention efforts, modifications to policies, and services for survivors. Given how few sexual assaults are reported to school officials and/or law enforcement agencies, self-reported survey data are, in fact, the only credible source of information on the magnitude and nature of the problem.

At the same time, not all climate survey efforts have captured high-quality data from representative samples of students. For climate surveys to be effective, they must generate valid and reliable estimates of the prevalence of rape and sexual assault victimization; capture sufficient information about the victims, the incidents, the perpetrators, and the campus environment/culture as it relates to sexual misconduct; and help identify school policies or practices that might be associated with increases or decreases in the prevalence of sexual assault. In addition, if comparing the situation at one school to the situation at other schools is of interest, then it is important that the data be collected using a somewhat standardized methodology. Similarly, if a goal is to determine whether schools with certain characteristics (e.g., public versus private, large versus small, geographic region, the presence of a large Greek system, Division I sports teams, or a bystander intervention program) have higher (or lower) rates of sexual assault or poorer campus climates related to sexual misconduct, it will be necessary to collect these data from students across a number of schools, using a rigorous and standardized methodology.

Several federal efforts are under consideration for promoting campus climate surveys. In addition to the recommendations of the White House Task Force to Protect Students from Sexual Assault, there is bipartisan support in Congress for draft legislation designed to address the issue of campus sexual assault, a key goal of which is to accurately and reliably measure the prevalence and nature of sexual assault across colleges and allow for comparisons across schools. The Campus Accountability and Safety Act, if passed, would require that the Department of Education develop, design, and administer a standardized, online, annual survey of students regarding their experiences with sexual violence and harassment every two years.

The outcome of this legislation is unknown, as is the specific framework for such a coordinated federal effort for campus climate surveys, including the funding mechanism, whether school participation would be required, whether it would entail a standardized instrument and methodology across schools or allow for school-level customization, and whether it would be conducted and paid for by the schools themselves or by the federal government. A methodologically rigorous, standardized data collection program would allow for the comparison of results from one school to another. Such an effort would also enable policy makers and school administrators to answer important questions related to which school characteristics and climate factors are associated with the prevalence of sexual assault among college students.

The school-level results generated from the CCSVS could be compared because the same sampling, survey instrument, data collection, and estimation procedures were used at each school. This standardization is what allowed one of the most significant conclusions from the study to be drawn: sexual victimization is a much bigger problem at some schools than others. The ability to compare estimates across schools is critical, but not because schools should be exposed, ranked, or punished because of the rate at which their students are victimized. Rather, schools need valid data to better understand the magnitude and nature of the problem, and to inform their policies and practices. Further, schools that collect these data on a recurrent basis (using the same methods) will learn whether the policies and programs they are implementing are effective at reducing victimization rates over time. Further, valid data that are collected in a standardized manner across schools can help generate an understanding of what factors are associated with high, and low, victimization rates. Only with such data can we begin to understand why some schools have higher rates, and what can be done to prevent sexual assault and make campuses safer for students.

NOTES

1. The rosters provided by the schools reflected students' sex based on school records. Students self-reported their gender identity (with transgender included as a category) in the survey. The number of transgendered students was too small to allow statistically precise estimates for sexual assault victimization to be developed for this population. Therefore, the experiences of transgendered students are reflected in the estimates for males and females, based on their sex as recorded in the school rosters.

2. Sexual battery was defined as any unwanted and nonconsensual sexual contact that involved forced touching of a sexual nature, not involving penetration. This could include forced kissing, touching, grabbing, or fondling of sexual body parts. Rape was defined as any unwanted and nonconsensual sexual contact that involved a penetrative act, including oral sex, anal sex, sexual intercourse, or sexual penetration with a finger or object.

REFERENCES AND RECOMMENDED READING

Cantor, D., B. Fisher, S. Chibnall, C. Bruce, R. Townsend, G. Thomas, and H. Lee. 2015. *Report on the AAU Campus Climate Survey on sexual assault and sexual misconduct.* Rockville, MD: Westat.

Cape, P. 2010. Questionnaire length, fatigue effects and response quality revisited. Available at http://www.surveysampling.com/ssi-media/Corporate/white_papers/SSI _QuestionLength_WP.image.

Couper, M. P. 2008. *Designing effective web surveys.* New York: Cambridge University Press.

Fisher, B. S., F. T. Cullen, and M. G. Turner. 2000. *The sexual victimization of college women* (NCJ 182369). Washington, DC: U.S. Department of Justice, National Institute of Justice and Bureau of Justice Statistics.

Koss, M. P., C. A. Gidycz, and N. Wisniewski. 1987. The scope of rape: Incidence and prevalence of sexual aggression and victimization in a national sample of higher education students. *Journal of Counseling and Clinical Psychology* 55 (2): 162–170.

Krebs, C. P., C. Lindquist, M. Berzofsky, B. Shook-Sa, K. Peterson, M. Planty, . . . and J. Stroop. 2016. *Campus climate survey validation study final technical report* (NCJ 249545). Washington, DC: U.S. Department of Justice, Bureau of Justice Statistics.

Krebs, C. P., C. Lindquist, T. Warner, B. Fisher, and S. L. Martin. 2009. College women's experiences with physically forced, alcohol- or other drug-enabled, and drug-facilitated sexual assault before and since entering college. *Journal of American College Health* 57 (6): 639–647.

Macer, T., and S. Wilson. 2014. *The Confirmit Annual Market Research Software Survey, 2013.* United Kingdom: Meaning.

ADDITIONAL ELECTRONIC RESOURCES

Freyd, J. J. 2016. *The UO Sexual Violence and Institutional Betrayal Surveys: 2014 and 2015.* Available at http://dynamic.uoregon.edu/jjf/campus/index.html.

Georgia State University. 2015. Release: ARC3 Campus Climate Survey. Available at http://campusclimate.gsu.edu/.

Massachusetts Institute of Technology. 2014. *Survey results: 2014 community attitudes on sexual assault.* Available at http://web.mit.edu/surveys/health/MIT-CASA-Survey-Summary.pdf.

University of Michigan. 2015. *Results of 2015 University of Michigan Campus Climate Survey on Sexual Misconduct.* Available at http://Publicaffairs.Vpcomm.Umich.Edu/key-issues/2015-campus-climate-surveys-regarding-sexual-misconduct/aau-campus-climate-survey.

White House. n.d. *Climate surveys: Useful tools to help colleges and universities in their efforts to reduce and prevent sexual assault.* Available at https://www.justice.gov/ovw/protecting-students-sexual-assault.

White House. n.d. *Draft instrument for measuring campus climate related to sexual assault.* Available at https://www.justice.gov/ovw/protecting-students-sexual-assault.

14

Active Bystander Intervention

Sarah McMahon

Introduction

Awareness of the widespread and insidious nature of campus sexual and intimate partner violence (IPV) has increased steadily over the past few decades. As recognition of the problem has grown, universities have responded by providing both services for survivors and prevention programs to educate students about the issues. "Prevention" is interpreted differently on various campuses, however, with no consensus on what the best approach should be. In addition, the field of sexual violence prevention is currently more developed on college campuses than IPV, and thus is the focus of this chapter. In general, three main approaches to sexual violence prevention have emerged on college campuses. One set of programs focuses on risk reduction strategies for women, such as self-defense. While these programs have been found to be empowering for some women, they are controversial for their focus on potential victims rather than focusing on those who perpetrate sexual violence. Another set of programs addresses problematic attitudes related to sexual violence such as reducing rape myths and victim blaming, as well as increasing awareness about sexual assault more generally. Unfortunately, there is limited evidence of the effectiveness of these programs in reducing sexual violence. Additionally, there is growing recognition that a more comprehensive response is needed toward sexual violence; therefore, a focus solely on changing individual-level attitudes and beliefs is insuffi-

cient. In recent years, a third main approach—through bystander intervention education—has rapidly proliferated in an attempt to fill some of these
gaps. Bystander intervention strategies move beyond a focus on individual-
level attitudes and frame sexual violence as a community issue, where all
individuals have the responsibility to interrupt situations that can lead to
sexual assault as well as respond to situations where assaults have occurred.
Evaluation of bystander programs are emerging, and thus far suggest it may
be a potentially powerful strategy.

This chapter reviews traditional approaches to campus sexual violence
prevention (i.e., risk reduction and attitude/knowledge focus) and compares
the bystander intervention approach. Additionally, current trends and future
directions for bystander intervention education programs are discussed.

Risk Reduction

One approach to addressing sexual violence prevention on college campuses,
as well as in broader society, focuses on reducing risk through increasing
awareness of how to prevent victimization. Risk-reduction programs are
typically designed to address women as potential victims and to offer strategies to avoid victimization. Traditional methods have included instructing
women to carry pepper spray or use keys or heels as protective weapons.
Other programs focus on teaching women to defend themselves from rape
through physical and verbal resistance. A body of research has found a number of positive outcomes for participants in rape-resistance programs,
including increased self-esteem and confidence, providing evidence to
support a woman's sexual assault case in the criminal justice system, and
benefits to well-being after an assault occurs (White and Rees 2014). In addition, there is evidence that some physical resistance strategies and some
forms of forceful verbal resistance may be effective strategies to avoid rape
(see Ullman 2007).

Despite some positive outcomes, the risk-reduction approach to sexual
violence has been criticized for focusing on individuals and, in particular,
for holding women responsible for rape. The idea of resistance is rooted in a
long history of blaming women for their assaults. Early rape laws required
some proof of physical resistance, and there is a belief that victims must still
demonstrate some attempt at resistance in order to be believed (Ullman
2007). Some believe that the risk-reduction approach continues to suggest
that women are responsible for their own assaults by sending the message
that sexual violence occurs because the individual did not practice proper
risk-reduction methods (Grove and Zadnik 2012).

In addition to resistance strategies, risk-reduction approaches include
providing "safety tips" to women about how to avoid sexual assault. For a

number of years, many prevention efforts focused on instructing women to regulate their behavior, such as avoiding certain dark areas, not walking alone at night, not wearing certain clothes that may be perceived as promiscuous, and refraining from drinking alcohol (Ullman 2007). Many colleges and universities still provide "safety tips" for students. While universal risk-reduction strategies may be helpful for all students to help lower vulnerability to crime, there is evidence that those tips that are focused on sexual assault tend to place responsibility on women. For example, Bedera and Nordmeyer (2015) analyzed rape-prevention and risk-reduction tips posted on forty college websites in the United States. Their analysis concluded that most tips are directed at women and place the responsibility for prevention of sexual violence primarily on women.

A number of proponents for risk-reduction and resistance strategies recognize the controversial nature and possibility of conveying the message that women are responsible for avoiding sexual assault. However, the argument has been presented that as long as rape occurs, women have the right to be provided with tools to maximize their well-being. Additionally, there are suggestions that risk-reduction education for women be coupled with prevention programs for men, and others indicate that risk reduction can be one piece of a larger prevention approach that includes engaging bystanders to help interrupt situations that could lead to sexual violence (Ullman 2007).

Changing Individual Attitudes, Beliefs, and Knowledge

Many rape-prevention programs on college campuses focus on changing attitudes, beliefs, and knowledge related to sexual assault. In DeGue and colleagues' (2014) review of 140 evaluations of primary prevention strategies to address sexual violence perpetration, the majority were brief, psycho-educational programs designed to affect attitudes or increase knowledge. These programs typically work to change negative attitudes about sexual violence while also providing accurate knowledge about how it occurs.

Most often, these programs focus on changing individuals' beliefs in rape myths, originally defined by Burt (1980) as "prejudicial, stereotyped, or false beliefs about rape, rape victims, and rapists" (217), and later described by Lonsway and Fitzgerald (1994) as "attitudes and beliefs that are generally false yet widely and persistently held and that serve to deny and justify male sexual aggression against women" (134). Common rape myths cited over time include the belief that the way a woman dresses or acts indicates that "she asked for it," or that rape occurs because men cannot control their sexual impulses. A small body of research has demonstrated that the acceptance of rape myths not only indicates problematic attitudes but is also an explanatory predictor in the actual perpetration of sexual violence (Berkowitz 1992; Hinck and Thomas 1999). Because men tend to hold greater rape myths than women, this may be an especially important area for working with male college students.

Other attitude-based programs focus on increasing empathy for survivors, which encourages participants to better understand the post-assault sequelae and the emotions that victims experience (Paul and Gray 2011). Another focus of sexual violence prevention programs is changing attitudes about factors that are theorized to contribute to sexual violence, such as rigid gender roles, sexism, and hostility toward women. These programs tend to address gender socialization and norms related to sexual violence, and oftentimes incorporate IPV as well.

Despite the popularity of sexual violence prevention programs that address attitudes, the evidence that they create meaningful change is limited. Sexual assault program delivery has been criticized for lacking rigorous evaluation as well as theoretical frameworks to explain attitude or behavioral change (e.g., Paul and Gray 2011). In addition, evidence of the effectiveness of sexual violence prevention programs is mixed. In their meta-analysis of rape-prevention programs, DeGue and colleagues (2014) found most programs that focused on changing attitudes and increasing knowledge had no positive effect on perpetration.

Bystander Intervention Education

Bystander Approach

Traditionally, sexual assault prevention efforts have focused on the individual level, such as changing personal attitudes about sexual violence. Increasingly, however, peer and community contexts have been regarded as a salient focus for the prevention of sexual assault as well as IPV (Casey and Lindhorst 2009). Within these peer contexts, social norms and expectations can influence both the occurrence and prevention of sexual assault and IPV. Social norms theories are based on the premise that people behave according to the way they perceive others to behave (Perkins 2003). This is especially relevant for adolescents and young adults, who are developmentally at a stage where the influence of peers is paramount. For example, male peer support theory suggests that sexual assault is more likely to occur in situations where men perceive support for their actions from their peers (Schwartz and DeKeseredy 1997). Research also emphasizes the importance of the peer context for sexual violence prevention. In a study by Fabiano and colleagues (2003), the authors demonstrated that the primary factor impacting men's willingness to intervene to prevent sexual assault was their own perception of other men's willingness to intervene. Similarly, Brown and Messman-Moore (2010) found that perceived peer attitudes about sexual aggression was the most significant factor in predicting men's willingness to intervene in situations involving sexual assault.

Recognizing the potentially prominent role of peer contexts, the bystander approach has been introduced as a way for peers to challenge the social norms in their communities that support sexual violence (Banyard 2015). Introduced by Katz (1995) as part of the Mentors in Violence Prevention program more than twenty years ago, the bystander intervention approach has evolved during the past decade. Its premise is that individuals in a community can intervene before, during, or after a sexual assault occurs (Banyard, Plante, and Moynihan 2004). In addition to interrupting actual behaviors and situations related to sexual violence, peers can intervene by expressing social disapproval for behaviors that are supportive of sexual violence, thereby influencing the larger social norms in the community (Banyard 2015).

Bystanders, or third-party witnesses, are those individuals who are present during an act of negative behavior and have the potential to help the situation, make the situation worse, or do nothing (Banyard 2015; Banyard, Moynihan, and Plante, 2007). Instead of focusing on men as potential perpetrators and women as potential victims, as many attitude-focused prevention programs do, the bystander approach is different by suggesting that everyone, as part of the community, has a responsibility to engage in prevention as active bystanders by intervening before sexual assaults occur (Banyard, Plante, and Moynihan 2004). The bystander intervention approach has received increased recognition as a tool for sexual violence prevention education on college campuses, in high schools, within various communities, and even as a statewide-level prevention strategy in a handful of states (see Banyard 2015 for an in-depth explanation of the evolution of the bystander approach to sexual violence prevention).

The bystander approach holds particular promise for addressing sexual violence and intimate partner violence on college campuses, which may be considered "at-risk" environments. On college campuses, most assaults are committed by someone known to the victim, often involve alcohol intoxication, and occur in social settings with others present, such as in residence halls or fraternities. Burn (2009) suggests that in these settings, bystanders are often present during the "pre-assault phase" where risk markers appear and, if equipped with the correct skills, they can intervene to interrupt these situations. Additionally, bystanders can intervene during or after a sexual assault, and can also take proactive steps to take a public stand against sexual violence and other related forms of oppression and violence.

Bystander Decisional Process

An important facet of the bystander intervention approach is recognition that individuals go through a complex decisional process where they are faced with a number of barriers to taking action. Addressing these barriers as a part of the educational program is therefore critical.

The idea of bystander intervention was borne from the field of social psychology, where researchers studied the motivation for individuals to intervene in emergency situations. The influential work of Latané and Darley (1970) has been instrumental in understanding that the decision to intervene as a bystander is multistaged and occurs through a process of five sequential steps: (1) noticing the event, (2) identifying the situation as intervention-appropriate, (3) taking responsibility, (4) deciding how to help, and (5) acting to intervene.

Burn (2009) applied Latané and Darley's (1970) model to sexual violence and identified common barriers associated with each step that prevent individuals from becoming effective bystanders. For example, during the first step of noticing the event, individuals may fail to even be aware of a high-risk situation due to noise or other sensory distractions, or due to self-focus. For the second step, identifying the situation as intervention-appropriate, individuals may fail to recognize a situation as high-risk due to a number of factors, including: ambiguity regarding consent or danger, pluralistic ignorance (no one else sees it as a problem), or ignorance of sexual assault risk markers. For the third step, take responsibility, individuals may face a number of barriers, including diffusion of responsibility (likelihood to intervene is less if there are many other possible interveners), relationship of bystander to potential victim and potential perpetrator, and attributions of worthiness of the victim (affected by perceived choices of the potential victim that increased her risk, and perception of the potential victim's provocativeness and her intoxication). The fourth step is to decide how to help, which may be inhibited by the individual's lack of knowledge of what to say or do. The fifth step, act to intervene, may be blocked by factors such as audience inhibition and evaluation apprehension, which means that people may be reluctant to intervene because they are concerned that others may judge their actions negatively. There may also be social norms present that run counter to the intervention and therefore create pressure on the individual not to take action.

More recently, Banyard (2015) has put forth a revised decisional model for bystanders that accounts for the fact that the process does not necessarily follow linear steps, but rather involves a number of interactive "bystander action coils," which provide feedback loops that influence one another. These "coils" include Latané and Darley's factors that influence decision making (such as noticing, taking responsibility, etc.), but also incorporates more complex components (timing, peer norms, severity); factors related to the event itself (who is present—whether it is a friend versus a stranger); and outcomes of the action (reactions of the victim, perpetrator, and onlookers; peer response).

Based on these models about decision making, it is important for education programs to address factors that either facilitate or prohibit action at different stages or in different "coils." Effective programs incorporate this research and provide opportunities for participants to discuss barriers, problem solve solutions, and practice intervening in a safe space (National Sexual Violence Resource Center 2013). In this way, bystander programs can incorporate some of the goals of more traditional programs that focus on individual knowledge, attitudes, and beliefs.

Bystander Programs

The bystander approach is increasingly popular on college campuses, and is supported by emerging research that demonstrates a number of encouraging outcomes including decreases in beliefs that support sexual violence and greater willingness to intervene in prosocial ways (see reviews by Katz and Moore 2013; National Sexual Violence Resource Center 2013). The White House Task Force Report highlighted bystander intervention as a "promising practice," and encouraged universities to utilize it as a prevention strategy (White House 2014).

A number of different bystander education programs have emerged over the years. One set of these programs focuses on men by encouraging them to develop the awareness and skills to intervene effectively with other men to prevent sexual violence. For example, one of the first bystander programs was the Mentors in Violence Prevention program, a nationally recognized education program designed to encourage leadership on issues of violence against women (Katz, Heisterkamp, and Fleming 2011). The Men's Project, developed by Berkowitz (1994), was another one of the first bystander intervention education programs that has demonstrated promising results (Gidycz, Orchowski, and Berkowitz 2011). Foubert's The Men's Program works to increase men's empathy toward victims and increase their prosocial behavior, and evaluation of the program finds positive results (Foubert, Newberry, and Tatum 2007; Langhinrichsen-Rohling et al. 2011). For more information on men's anti-violence programs, see Chapter 15 by Ráchael A. Powers and Jennifer Leili.

Another popular bystander intervention program is Green Dot, created by Dorothy Edwards. The program helps participants identify situations that could lead to violence and teaches them how to intervene in safe and effective ways. This is accomplished by first listening to a motivational speech to introduce bystander intervention, and then attending the Students Educating and Empowering to Develop Safety (SEEDS) prevention program that involves small group intensive training sessions. Rigorous evaluations of the Green Dot program have provided evidence of its effectiveness (see Green Dot, etc. n.d.). In one study, Coker and colleagues (2011) surveyed a random sample of 2,504 undergraduates to compare a number of outcomes based on whether participants received the Green Dot speech, SEEDS training, or no intervention. The authors found that those who received Green Dot speeches alone reported more bystander behaviors than those in no intervention program, and those who received both the speech and SEEDS training increased bystander behaviors and lowered rape myth beliefs. This is especially noteworthy because many evaluations only assess whether students' attitudes about intervening improve, and they do not examine whether students' actual positive bystander behaviors change. There is evidence that having the Green Dot program on campus may be beneficial, even for students who are not directly trained. Coker and colleagues' (2014) research found that there were actually lower rates of sexual victimization and perpetration on those campuses as a whole that had the Green Dot program, compared to campuses that did not have any bystander program. Most recently, researchers tested the program in twenty-six high schools across Kentucky and reported a greater than 50 percent reduction in self-reported sexual violence perpetration by students at schools that received Green Dot training, compared to those schools that did not (and reported a slight increase). There were also significant reductions in other types of self-reported perpetration (sexual harassment, stalking, and dating violence) (Hautala 2014).

The most extensively tested bystander intervention model in the literature is Bringing in the Bystander, developed at the University of New Hampshire. The program works to teach safe and effective ways for bystanders to intervene in prosocial, helpful ways in situations related to sexual and intimate partner violence (Moynihan et al. 2011). The model has been developed rigorously over time and found to increase positive bystander attitudes and behaviors with both the general student population (Banyard, Moynihan, and Plante 2007) and groups that the research has indicated may have subcultures that are more supportive of sexual violence, such as athletes and members of sororities and fraternities (Moynihan and Banyard 2008), and both with sexual violence and IPV (Banyard, 2008). Most recently, Moynihan and colleagues (2015) found that the program demonstrated sustained positive behavior changes for a full year.

Bystander programs have utilized other means for education as well. Some programs have utilized peer education theater to educate about bystander intervention, including the InterACT Sexual Assault Prevention Program (Ahrens, Rich, and Ullman 2011) and SCREAM Theater (McMahon et al. 2015), which have both demonstrated success. These programs provide audiences with scenarios that demonstrate situations on campus where sexual violence may occur, and how students can react in positive or negative ways.

The interactive component allows a dialogue between the audience members and characters. Know Your Power is a social marketing campaign that includes poster images and other forms of media that show bystander intervention scenarios across campus. Evaluation of the program found that exposure to the campaign resulted in increased awareness of bystander intervention, increased knowledge about how to safely intervene, and increased active bystander behavior (Potter 2012).

There are a number of online bystander intervention education programs emerging as well. Haven, RealConsent, Not Anymore, and Every Choice are examples of some of the online curricula that include a bystander module. These interactive online programs attempt to prevent sexual assault and interpersonal violence, while adhering to the Campus Sexual Assault Violence Elimination (SaVE) Act's (part of the Violence Against Women Act [VAWA]) mandates that explicitly require prevention education on issues of domestic violence, dating violence, sexual assault, and stalking. Specifically, education programs must address safe and positive options for bystander intervention. In addition, through the 2014 Office for Civil Rights (OCR) guidance on Title IX, bystander intervention education is recommended as a part of training for students. To date, however, these online options have not been empirically evaluated.

Future Directions

While there is increased research available on the effectiveness of bystander intervention programs, there is still a need to continue to employ rigorous evaluation of these curricula through sound research designs such as using random samples to compare students who do and do not receive the curricula. This also requires utilizing tools to measure not only students' willingness to intervene in situations but also their actual behaviors. In addition, it is necessary to determine if the changes are sustained over time, and whether they are more effective for some types of participants (Moynihan et al. 2015). There is increased recognition that the relationship among key outcomes in bystander education—such as efficacy, intentions to intervene, and actual intervention behaviors—are complex and interact with one another over time (McMahon et al. 2015; Moynihan et al. 2015). All of these areas need to be addressed in future evaluations of bystander intervention strategies, including determination of how various subgroups on campus (e.g., cultural groups, LGBTQIA [lesbian, gay, bisexual, transgender, queer, intersex, asexual] students, student leaders, athletes, fraternity members) respond to the programming. There has yet to be rigorous evaluation to determine how the norms of certain subgroups may fit with the premise of bystander intervention, and how current strategies may need to be modified or adapted. For example, the tight bonds experienced by student athletes may serve as a foundation for which bystander intervention can be encouraged as a way to look after one another; yet, at the same time, the norms around loyalty may prevent certain athletes from intervening in ways that would bring negative attention to the team. Developing specific bystander intervention strategies to align with the norms of various subgroups on campus is an important next step.

In addition, as noted by Banyard (2015), a critical question to consider beyond whether students are increasing their bystander intentions and behaviors is the impact of bystander intervention on various situations. It is likely that not all interventions utilized by bystanders are helpful, and some may actually make the situation worse for the survivor. Further work is needed to determine what interventions are successful, and what factors help to make them useful (see McMahon et al. 2015 for a discussion of additional questions to include in the evaluation of bystander behavior).

Additionally, although the bystander approach is often framed as a community-level intervention, much of the programming and research has actually focused largely on the individual level of change, with an emphasis on addressing personal attitudes, beliefs, and behaviors such as an individual's willingness to intervene, his or her efficacy to intervene, or his or her actual behaviors (Banyard 2011; Katz and Moore 2013). Although efforts to address an individual's ability to intervene are important, these provide an incomplete picture by leaving out discussion of the larger environment in which students interact. It is therefore important for colleges and universities to determine what community and environmental-level factors may influence bystander intervention to prevent sexual violence. McMahon (2015) provides some areas of further research for this level of exploration, including factors such as sense of community, community norms, policies, and the physical environment of the campus.

Research is also needed to determine if there is a cumulative effect of prevention programs, and if greater exposure to prevention messages from different levels of the ecology results in better bystander outcomes. As suggested by the recent study by Moynihan and colleagues (2015), a combination of prevention programming (participation in a bystander education program and exposure to social marketing posters) results in a greater willingness by students to engage in bystander actions. Further research like the study by Moynihan and colleagues is needed to determine if ongoing and multiple messages about sexual violence prevention result in stronger outcomes (Banyard 2014).

Lastly, the bulk of bystander intervention research has focused on addressing the topic of sexual violence. There are a few studies that have incorporated IPV as well, but there is a need to have further application and evaluation of the bystander approach that is IPV-specific, as there are a number of critical differences between the occurrence of IPV and sexual violence and the ways in which bystander intervention may be applied (Banyard 2015;

McMahon and Banyard 2012). The bystander intervention approach can potentially be used to educate students on other critical issues such as bullying, harassment, racism, and homophobia.

ACKNOWLEDGMENT

The author would like to thank Khushbu Gandhi for her assistance with this chapter.

REFERENCES

Ahrens, C. E., M. D. Rich, and J. B. Ullman. 2011. Rehearsing for real life: The impact of the InterACT sexual assault prevention program on self-reported likelihood of engaging in bystander interventions. *Violence Against Women* 17 (6): 760–776.
Banyard, V. L. 2008. Measurement and correlates of pro-social bystander behavior: The case of interpersonal violence. *Violence and Victims* 23: 85–99.
———. 2011. Who will help prevent sexual violence: Creating an ecological model of bystander intervention. *Psychology of Violence* 1 (3): 216–229.
———. 2014. Improving college campus–based prevention of violence against women: A strategic plan for research built on multipronged practices and policies. *Trauma, Violence, and Abuse* 15 (4): 339–351.
———. 2015. *Toward the next generation of bystander prevention of sexual and relationship violence: Action coils to engage communities.* New York: Springer.
Banyard, V. L., M. M. Moynihan, and E. G. Plante. 2007. Sexual violence prevention through bystander education: An experimental evaluation. *Journal of Community Psychology* 35 (4): 463–481.
Banyard, V. L., E. G. Plante, and M. M. Moynihan. 2004. Bystander education: Bringing a broader community perspective to sexual violence prevention. *Journal of Community Psychology* 32 (1): 61–79.
Bedera, N., and K. Nordmeyer. 2015. "Never go out alone": An analysis of college rape prevention tips. *Sexuality and Culture* 19 (3): 533–542.
Berkowitz, A. D. 1992. College men as perpetrators of acquaintance rape and sexual assault: A review of recent research. *Journal of American College Health* 40 (4): 175–181.
———. 1994. A model acquaintance rape prevention program for men. In *Men and rape: Theory, research and prevention programs in higher education*, ed. A. D. Berkowitz, 35–42. San Francisco: Jossey-Bass.
Brown, A. L., and T. L. Messman-Moore. 2010. Personal and perceived peer attitudes supporting sexual aggression as predictors of male college students' willingness to intervene against sexual aggression. *Journal of Interpersonal Violence* 25 (3): 503–517.
Burn, S. M. 2009. A situational model of sexual assault prevention through bystander intervention. *Sex Roles* 60: 779–792.
Burt, M. R. 1980. Cultural myths and supports for rape. *Journal of Personality and Social Psychology* 38: 217–230.
Casey, E. A., and T. P. Lindhorst. 2009. Toward a multi-level, ecological approach to the primary prevention of sexual assault. *Trauma, Violence, and Abuse* 10 (2): 91–114.
Coker, A. L., P. G. Cook-Craig, C. M. Williams, B. S. Fisher, E. R. Clear, L. S. Garcia, and L. M. Hegge. 2011. Evaluation of Green Dot: An active bystander intervention to reduce sexual violence on college campuses. *Violence Against Women* 17 (6): 777–796.

Coker, A. L., B. S. Fisher, H. M. Bush, S. C. Swan, C. M. Williams, E. R. Clear, and S. DeGue. 2014. Evaluation of the Green Dot bystander intervention to reduce interpersonal violence among college students across three campuses. *Violence Against Women* 21 (12): 1507–1527.

DeGue, S., L. A. Valle, M. K. Holt, G. M. Massetti, J. L. Matjasko, and A. T. Tharp. 2014. A systematic review of primary prevention strategies for sexual violence perpetration. *Aggression and Violent Behavior* 19 (4): 346–362.

Fabiano, P., H. Perkins, A. Berkowitz, J. Linkenbach, and C. Stark. 2003. Engaging men as social justice allies in ending violence against women: Evidence for a social norms approach. *Journal of American College Health* 52 (3): 105–112.

Foubert, J. D., J. T. Newberry, and J. Tatum. 2007. Behavior differences seven months later: Effects of a rape prevention program. *Journal of Student Affairs Research and Practice* 44 (4): 1125–1146.

Gidycz, C. A., L. M. Orchowski, and A. D. Berkowitz. 2011. Preventing sexual aggression among college men: An evaluation of a social norms and bystander intervention program. *Violence Against Women* 17 (6): 720–742.

Green Dot, etc. n.d. *Evaluation Assessment.* Available at https://www.livethegreendot.com /gd_evalasses.html.

Grove, J., and L. Zadnik. 2012. Prevention versus risk reduction. In *Sexual violence and abuse: An encyclopedia of prevention, impacts and recovery*, ed. J. L. Postmus, 429–431. Santa Barbara, CA: ABC-CLIO.

Hautala, K. 2014. "Green Dot" effective at reducing sexual violence. *University of Kentucky News*, September 10. Available at http://uknow.uky.edu/content/green-dot-effective -reducing-sexual-violence.

Hinck, S., and R. Thomas. 1999. Rape myth acceptance in college students: How far have we come? *Sex Roles* 40 (9–10): 815–832.

Katz, J. 1995. Reconstructing masculinity in the locker room: The Mentors in Violence Prevention Project. *Harvard Educational Review* 65 (2): 163–174.

Katz, J., A. Heisterkamp, and A. M. Fleming. 2011. The social justice roots of the Mentors in Violence Prevention model and its application to a high school setting. *Violence Against Women* 17: 684–702.

Katz, J., and J. Moore. 2013. Bystander education training for campus sexual assault prevention: An initial meta-analysis. *Violence and Victims* 28 (6): 1054–1067.

Langhinrichsen-Rohling, J., J. D. Foubert, H. M. Brasfield, B. Hill, and S. Shelley-Tremblay. 2011. The Men's Program: Does it impact college men's self-reported bystander efficacy and willingness to intervene? *Violence Against Women* 17 (6), 743–759.

Latané, B., and J. M. Darley. 1970. *The unresponsive bystander: Why doesn't he help?* Englewood Cliffs, NJ: Prentice-Hall.

Lonsway, K. A., and L. F. Fitzgerald. 1994. Rape myths in review. *Psychology of Women Quarterly* 18 (2): 133–164.

McMahon, S. 2015. Call for research on bystander intervention to prevent sexual violence: The role of campus environments. *American Journal of Community Psychology* 55 (3): 472–489.

McMahon, S., and V. L. Banyard. 2012. When can I help? A conceptual framework for preventing violence through bystander intervention. *Trauma, Violence and Abuse* 13 (1): 3–14.

McMahon, S., J. E. Palmer, V. Banyard, M. Murphy, and C. A. Gidycz. 2015. Measuring bystander behavior in the context of sexual violence prevention: Lessons learned and new directions. *Journal of Interpersonal Violence*, 1–23. doi: 10.1177/0886260515591979.

Moynihan, M. M., and V. L. Banyard. 2008. Community responsibility for preventing sexual violence: A pilot study with campus Greeks and intercollegiate athletes. *Journal of Prevention and Intervention in the Community* 36 (1/2): 23–38.

Moynihan, M. M., V. L. Banyard, J. S. Arnold, R. P. Eckstein, and J. G. Stapleton. 2011. Sisterhood may be powerful for reducing sexual and intimate partner violence: An evaluation of the Bringing in the Bystander in-person program with sorority members. *Violence Against Women* 17 (6): 703–719.

Moynihan, M. M., V. L. Banyard, A. Cares, S. J. Potter, L. M. Williams, and J. G. Stapleton. 2015. Encouraging responses in sexual and relationship violence prevention: What program effects remain one year later? *Journal of Interpersonal Violence* 30 (1): 110–132.

National Sexual Violence Resource Center. 2013. Engaging bystanders to prevent sexual violence: Annotated bibliography. Available at http://www.nsvrc.org/sites/default/files /publications_nsvrc_bibliographies_engaging-bystanders-prevent-sexual-violence .pdf.

Paul, L. A., and M. J. Gray. 2011. Sexual assault programming on college campuses: Using social psychological belief and behavior change principles to improve outcomes. *Trauma, Violence and Abuse* 12 (2): 99–109.

Perkins, H. W. 2003. *The social norms approach to preventing school and college age substance abuse: A handbook for educators, counselors, and clinicians.* San Francisco: Jossey-Bass.

Potter, S. J. 2012. Using a multi-media social marketing campaign to increase active bystanders on the college campus. *Journal of American College Health* 60: 282–295.

Schwartz, M. D., and W. S. DeKeseredy. 1997. *Sexual assault on the college campus: The role of male peer support.* Thousand Oaks, CA: SAGE.

Ullman, S. 2007. A 10-year update of "Review and critique of empirical studies of rape avoidance." *Criminal Justice and Behavior* 34 (3): 411–429.

White, D., and G. Rees. 2014. Self-defense or undermining the self? Exploring the possibilities and limitations of a novel anti-rape technology. *Violence Against Women* 20 (3): 360–368.

White House. 2014. *The first report of the White House task force to protect students from sexual assault.* Available at https://obamawhitehouse.archives.gov/the-press-office /2014/04/29/fact-sheet-not-alone-protecting-students-sexual-assault.

15

Engaging Men in Anti–Violence Against Women Efforts on College Campuses

RÁCHAEL A. POWERS
AND JENNIFER LEILI

Introduction

Men's anti-violence programs, organized efforts to engage men in combating violence against women, are proliferating on college campuses. These programs are not new, as men have been working alongside women and independently in antisexist campaigns for decades. Building on the work of several notable organizations in the 1970s, such as Men Against Sexist Violence (MASV) in California and Rape and Violence Ends Now (RAVEN) in Boston, men's anti-violence efforts today aim to provide men nonviolent role models and encourage men to hold peers accountable for their sexist attitudes and behavior.

This chapter explores the role of men's anti-violence programs in ending violence against women on college campuses. First, the theoretical framework that guides these efforts is discussed. Second, a brief review of best practices for men's anti-violence programs are presented, followed by examples of several notable national organizations. Subsequently, campus-specific men's anti-violence efforts are discussed. This chapter concludes with an exploration of the future of these programs with a focus on emerging trends in activism.

Why Men's Anti-Violence Programs?

Researchers and practitioners have called for programs that involve men in violence-prevention efforts for a number of reasons. First and foremost, men are the main perpetrators of violence in general and against women specifically (see Kruttschnitt 1994; Tjaden and Thoennes 2000). Although the vast majority of men are not perpetrators, this gendered pattern illustrates that violence against women is not just a "women's issue." Men also have girls/women in their lives who are impacted by violence. Furthermore, men as a whole are viewed as aggressive and violent based on the actions of a few (Berkowitz 2004). The fear of being victimized places strain on relationships between men and women.

Beyond individual risk factors for offending, such as low self-control (Swogger et al. 2012) and alcohol and drug use (Caetano, Schafer, and Cunradi 2001), the form that masculinity has taken in society creates a culture that condones men's use of violence as a means of conflict resolution (Katz 2003). These sexist attitudes and beliefs about gendered violence predict men's use of violence against women (see Stith et al. 2004, for review). Even if men themselves are not violent, these gender norms paired with perceived peer support for violence presents barriers to nonviolent men who are proactively preventing violence (Flood 2006). Men's anti-violence programs address these core beliefs surrounding masculinity and dismantle them as justifiable reasons to use or tolerate violence against women (for a more thorough discussion of the theoretical mechanisms underlying men's perpetration of violence against women, see Chapter 5 by Walter S. DeKeseredy).

Spaces where masculinity scripts can be challenged are important, as gender norms result in the inflated belief that men are supportive of violence against women. For example, in a survey of undergraduate students, Fabiano and colleagues (2003) found that men underestimated the importance their peers placed on sexual consent and the likelihood that their peers would intervene to prevent sexual violence. These beliefs may result in a higher likelihood of sexual violence perpetration and a reduced likelihood of intervening, as men are less likely to intervene when they think their peers are more supportive of violence (Brown and Messman-Moore 2010). As Fabiano and colleagues suggest, prevention programs should correct these misperceptions surrounding social norms and "amplify the voice of the silent majority" (2003, 110). Furthermore, this suggests that male anti-violence programs may be particularly effective because they provide males with prosocial male role models that challenge their notions that men are supportive of violence (Flood 2006; Pease 2008).

Male mentors in anti-violence programs not only act as role models but also possess an "insider's knowledge" about masculinity that better enables them to dispel stereotypes and myths surrounding men and violence (e.g., a man's sex drive can get out of control). Likewise, the use of inclusive pronouns ("us" and "we") when men are facilitating helps break down any defensiveness (Heppner et al. 1999). Furthermore, men's anti-violence programs provide a safe space for men to openly discuss issues related to masculinity (Flood

2006). The explicit inclusivity in involving men is important because research suggests that men may not participate in violence-prevention efforts otherwise. In an interview with men, Garin (2000) found that 21 percent of men do not participate in violence-prevention efforts because no one explicitly sought to involve them. Furthermore, 13 percent reported that they did not know how to help, and a comparable percent reported fears of being vilified. Taken together, this suggests that these programs may be effective in engaging men because they underscore the importance of their involvement and include them as allies in anti-violence against women efforts (Berkowitz 2004).

However, it is important to note that the theoretical bases for men's anti-violence programs are not without their criticisms. Some have expressed apprehension about men's organized involvement because they may compete for limited financial resources to help victims and survivors of violence (Flood 2011). Furthermore, some women activists argue that when men get involved, they are given a disproportionate amount of credit "just for showing up" and that they do not have to "earn their stripes" compared to the women who devote considerable effort to these issues (Messner, Greenberg, and Peretz 2015, 8–9). For example, men's organizations are more likely to make the news as innovative efforts to end violence against women than are the crisis centers, women's shelters, and activist organizations led by women who have been doing this work for decades. Likewise, even when women serve as co-facilitators in presentations with men, it is the men whose message resonates with the audience and who receive accolades. While the appeal of men involved in the movement can be leveraged to widely diffuse anti-violence messages, male anti-violence groups should be careful to define their role as one that is complementary to, but not in competition with, women's anti-violence efforts (Berkowitz 2004).

Best Practices and Examples of Men's Anti-Violence Programs

Prevention research has identified several best practices of men's anti-violence programs on college campuses, including outreach efforts (e.g., social media campaigns) and peer education programs (DeGue et al. 2014; Nation et al. 2003). These include:

- *Male-facilitated programs*—Use men as role models to engage other men in small groups.
- *Variation in teaching methods*—Move beyond lecture-based methods to incorporate skill-based learning and active participation.
- *Sufficient dosage*—Short, one-session programs are less likely to result in lasting change. Programs and outreach efforts should be ongoing.

- *Focus on positive identities and relationships*—Approach men as allies who play a pivotal role in ending violence against women.
- *Comprehensive*—Recognize that violence is caused by a multitude of factors at different levels (individual and societal).
- *Acknowledge the role of masculinity*—Include honest discussions about how masculinity scripts shape the expectations of men and condone violence against women.
- *Be culturally relevant*—Recognize that men bring with them varied experiences and histories that need to be recognized, appreciated, and leveraged.

Many of these best practices are present in local and national men's programs that work to end violence against women. Following are a few examples of national programs that include college student populations.

Mentors in Violence Prevention

The Mentors in Violence Prevention (MVP) program, developed by Jackson Katz in 1993, addresses both men and women as allies in the prevention of violence against women. MVP is also credited with being one of the first bystander programs (see Chapter 14 by Sarah McMahon for more discussion about bystander programs). It originated as a high school and college student-athlete curriculum, but has been adapted to encompass wider audiences (e.g., professional athletes and the military) and accommodates both all-male and mixed-sex audiences. This bystander intervention program employs dynamic learning techniques to skill-building by using scenarios (adapted for the target audience) to prompt discussion of safe interventions before, during, and after a potentially violent situation. The program has been evaluated several times, including a multisite study with universities across the United States including Stanford and Virginia Tech. In this particular evaluation, the program was successful in changing the attitudes of those who would become leaders in their train-the-trainer program (Slaby, Branner, and Martin 2011); after the program, participants were more willing to intervene and felt more confident doing so.

The Men's Program

Developed by John Foubert, The Men's Program is a peer education program traditionally presented by trained male peer educators to all-male groups. The Men's Program is fifty-five minutes long, focuses on preventing violence through bystander intervention and on how sexual assault survivors recover, and challenges men to change the behaviors of themselves and others. There is also a women's version that serves as a complement to The Men's Program.

The Men's Program has at least fifteen chapters at colleges and universities around the country. Research has found the results of The Men's Program to be promising, including lowered acceptance of rape myths seven months after participating in the program (Foubert and Newberry 2006; Foubert 2000). In addition, the program may result in positive behavioral changes; Foubert and colleagues (2007) found that 6 percent of fraternity members who experienced the program reported committing sexual assault during their first year, compared to 10 percent of fraternity members who did not participate in The Men's Program.

The Men's Project

The Men's Project was originally developed by Alan Berkowitz in 1994, and has been revised a number of times since its conception to reflect the latest research and best practices in violence prevention. The Men's Project is based on the integrated model of sexual assault, which focuses on the role of attitudes, peer contexts, and social norms in the perpetration of sexual violence (Gidycz, Orchowski, and Berkowitz 2011). The Men's Project includes programming that lasts as long as eleven weeks (two hours per week) or a shorter, one-and-a-half-hour prevention program and a one-hour booster session. Evaluations have been promising for both formats. For the longer program, Stewart (2014) found that participants reported reductions in rape myth acceptance and sexism, as well as increases in bystander efficacy. Promising results have also been found in the shorter program, including fewer associations with sexually aggressive peers and less reinforcement in sexually aggressive behavior (Gidycz et al. 2011).

Men Can Stop Rape

Founded in 1997 and based out of Washington, D.C., the Men Can Stop Rape (MCSR) campaign focuses on boys and men, age eleven to twenty-two. Men of Strength (MOST) Clubs can be found at more than one hundred middle and high schools around the country, as well as Campus Men of Strength Clubs found at the university level. These clubs aim to commit to the mission of MCSR by engaging men in efforts to prevent violence against women. The MOST club utilizes a twenty-two-week curriculum with the goal of raising awareness of unhealthy masculinity and replacing it with a definition that equates masculine strength with violence prevention. These campus MOST clubs can be found across the United States, including at universities near Washington, D.C., such as American University, George Washington University, and Georgetown University. Evaluations of the MOST club program with high schoolers have found that participants were less likely to endorse beliefs that support violence, and more likely to intervene in situations of sexual and physical violence (Anderson 2011). MCSR also leverages social media to disseminate their anti-violence messaging. The "Where Do You Stand?" campaign is targeted at college-age men and is designed to encourage bystander intervention. There are several different posters that utilize the quote: "I'm the kind of guy who takes a stand. Where do you stand?" The posters offer ways that men can intervene in situations of sexual harassment and violence.

A Call to Men

A Call to Men, cofounded by Ted Bunch and Tony Porter, provides education and training to boys, men, and the community with the goal of shifting social norms to redefine masculinity as embodying respect and equality. There are a number of trainings and initiatives offered by this organization, including keynote speeches, one-day and multiday workshops, community consultations, and outreach efforts. The cofounders have done lectures on campuses or taken part in campus initiatives across the United States, including the University of Connecticut, Duke University, and Ohio University. They work predominately with men in schools and in the community; however, their program also has components for women. While not restricted to athletics, A Call to Men has partnered with the National Football League (NFL) and includes a number of current and former NFL players as spokespersons (e.g., NFL Dads Dedicated to Daughters). They have partnerships with a number of women-led organizations, including the Women of Color Network and V-Day.

Campus-Specific Men's Anti-Violence Efforts

Beyond national organizations, many universities and colleges feature campus-specific men's anti-violence groups aimed at combating violence against women and promoting gender equality. Men's anti-violence programs often join in or compliment the work of women's groups on campuses. For example, Take Back the Night events, which originated in the 1970s as all-women marches and speak-outs, have slowly incorporated men into the rallies and/or marches and sometimes even in the speak-outs. The Vagina Monologues are popular campus events that combine awareness events, such as clothesline projects, with a culmination in Eve Ensler's play that focuses on issues related to women's bodies, identities, and experiences with violence. Some campuses have incorporated men into these events. For example, Connecticut College launched a video (*100 Men Rise for V-Day*) to promote the event, which featured men discussing the importance of vaginas (and the women they are attached to). Some productions on campuses have started to incorporate men as extras or authors of monologues. Some universities such as the University of Colorado, Colorado Springs, have invited male victims to share their stories as well. Men are also often encouraged to participate in SlutWalks alongside female students and community members. So named for a Toronto police officer who remarked to college students that women can prevent sexual assault if they "avoid dressing like sluts," SlutWalks are aimed at confronting victim-blaming beliefs and attitudes. Some campuses and communities actively encourage men to join in these events, as these beliefs negatively impact men as well; they perpetuate stereotypes of men as being animalistic, with sexual drives that cannot be controlled and who therefore are inclined to perpetrate sexual violence.

Men on campuses also host their own events that are designed to empower men to combat violence against women, publicly and privately. For example, Walk a Mile in Her Shoes, which originated in 2001, are popular events that raise awareness of violence against women by featuring marches led by men (many of whom wear women's shoes) and male keynote speakers that rally men in solidarity in support of anti-violence efforts (see Figure 15.1). At these events and many others, men express vocal opposition to violence against women and pledge to engage in prevention efforts. Many men's anti-violence groups have adapted a pledge (see sidebar on next page) originally developed by the California Anti-Sexist Men's Political Caucus, a group formed in the 1970s to support feminist movements. Many men in Messner, Greenberg, and Peretz's (2015) narratives cite a Walk a Mile event as the "pivotal moment" in their pathway to becoming activists.

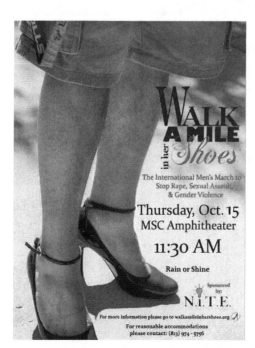

FIGURE 15.1   Walk a Mile Poster. Photo courtesy of Kendyl Muehlenbein, president of NITE at the University of South Florida.

Men's Pledge—Popular with Campus-Based Men's Anti-Violence Groups (originally from the California Anti-Sexist Men's Political Caucus)

Because:

I believe that rape will not end until men become part of the solution;

I take pride in myself as a man;

I care about the women in my life;

I am angry that people I know have been hurt;

I know that more than one woman is raped every minute in this country;

I understand that rape is a crime of violence against a woman's body, a woman's emotional well-being, and a woman's right to do with their bodies what they choose;

I recognize that men and women will not be equal until rape ends;

I know that happiness between men and women is difficult in a world where rape exists;

I accept my responsibility to assist in making this a safer world.

I Pledge To:

Speak about my anger about rape;

Talk with other men about rape;

Look at how men are raised that helps create and perpetuate a culture where rape is possible;

Interrupt sexist and rape jokes;

Support laws that encourage men to take responsibility for ending rape;

Listen to women friends' fears and concerns for their safety;

Pay attention to cries for help;

Challenge images of violence against women in advertising and pornography;

Encourage women to be strong and powerful;

Recognize that cooperation is power;

Examine my behaviors and actions and change whatever I am doing that helps create a climate where rape is possible;

Support women and men working to end rape. (Clothesline Project 1999)

Events like Walk a Mile in Her Shoes are designed to raise awareness, but also do so in a way that is lighthearted or nonthreatening in order to appeal to a wider audience of men who may feel apprehensive about participating in a violence against women prevention/awareness event. There are many examples of campaigns using humor or cleverness to appeal to college students and make anti-violence messages relevant. These campaigns sometimes rely on edginess to get the attention of students, who are bombarded with public service announcement (PSA) messaging daily. For example, Pennsylvania State University launched a campaign where they put urinal splash guards in the men's bathrooms that read, "You have the power to end rape in your hands" (Hartz 2001).

It is important to note that some of these campaigns and events have also brought criticism, as some suggest that these tactics may make light of women's oppression or be "reactionary and anti-feminist" if the message is lost in the means of delivery (Barber and Kretschmer 2013). Care should be taken to underscore the seriousness of violence against women and avoid the possibility of getting lost in the revelry and creativity of some of these campaigns. There is a line between being male-friendly to encourage participation and celebrate men's involvement and undermining the message by distracting from women's experiences or, worse, making light of sexual and domestic violence and thus contributing to the acceptance of violence against women. If done thoughtfully, these events and campaigns can be powerful efforts to combat violence against women because they appeal to students and recognize men's roles as allies in ending violence.

The Future of Men's Anti-Violence Programs

As men continue to define their roles in leading and participating in anti-violence efforts, evaluations of these programs are needed in order to examine their effectiveness and establish best practices in violence prevention. Although the programs mentioned earlier and many others have yielded promising results, more rigorous evaluations are needed of the peer educator training sessions that many of these programs use to educate college students and promote social change. A systematic review of the literature by DeGue and colleagues (2014) suggests that sexual violence prevention programs (including male anti-violence programs) are lacking in methodological rigor (e.g., the use of randomized control trials) and typically focus on changing attitudes instead of changing violent behavior. Although changes in attitudes may be reflective of social change, the ultimate goal of these efforts is to decrease violence perpetration. Furthermore, many of these evaluations focus on the immediate change in attitudes, which may not be indicative of permanent changes in social norms. In order to adequately examine whether cultural shifts in the college climate are occurring, evaluations should incorporate longitudinal assessments.

In addition, the role that social media plays in men's anti-violence programs needs to be more strongly developed. There are two separate avenues that need to be addressed. First, though social media campaigns are being utilized, there is very little empirical evaluation of these efforts. Research does suggest that in order to be effective, social media campaigns need to resonate with the target audience. For example, the Know Your Power poster campaign is a product of the University of New Hampshire's Prevention Innovations Research Center. These posters depict scenarios relevant to college students (e.g., having a friend disclose a sexual assault) and how to intervene to prevent violence or support survivors. The Know Your Power poster campaign found that identifying with the actors of the campaign was critical in increasing responsibility and willingness to get involved in violence prevention (Potter 2012). Having social media efforts that show men actively engaging in violence prevention may confront men's ideas about masculinity and correct misperceptions about men's acceptance of violence against women. Furthermore, just as researchers have suggested that in-person programs are more effective when men serve as facilitators, the best practices with regard to the messengers of anti-violence campaigns on social media need to be explored. In other words, empowering men to use their social media to vocally oppose violence and express solidarity with survivors may be more effective than organizations disseminating comparable sentiments. When men use their personal social media to engage in anti-violence efforts, the message reaches people who would not typically be exposed to these campaigns and may be more influential because it originates from male peers.

Narratives from male activists highlight the importance of culturally relevant programming and the need to make sure that outreach and education is not "ahistorical" (Messner, Greenberg, and Peretz 2015, 105). In particular, programs should aim to be sensitive to diversity beyond gender and recognize that men bring with them experiences that are shaped by their race, socioeconomic class, and sexual orientation (Berkowitz 2004; Flood 2006). Indeed, narratives of men involved in anti-violence efforts suggest that racial minorities may have a different pathway to activism, one where they draw parallels between the marginalization of women and racial oppression (Messner, Greenberg, and Peretz 2015). Programs should aim to address the concerns of minority men, acknowledge their experiences with racial inequality, and draw parallels between violence against women and violence against other men and sexual minorities. Likewise, programs should challenge the stereotypes surrounding different men (e.g., stereotype of the African American male rapist) and recognize that men may be differentially receptive to messages based on their identity, previous education, and interactions with the criminal justice system (Berkowitz 2004). Messner,

Greenberg, and Peretz (2015) suggest that men's programs are doing just this, moving toward a new paradigm that recognizes the larger role of inequality and social justice.

REFERENCES

Anderson, S. 2011. Men of Strength Clubs: 2009–2010 evaluation findings. Washington, DC: Zakiya Consulting.

Barber, K., and K. Kretschmer. 2013. Walking like a man? *Contexts* 12 (2): 40–45.

Berkowitz, A. D. 2004. Working with men to prevent violence against women: An overview (part one). *National Resource Center on Domestic Violence*, 1–7.

Brown, A. L., and T. L. Messman-Moore. 2010. Personal and perceived peer attitudes supporting sexual aggression as predictors of male college students' willingness to intervene against sexual aggression. *Journal of Interpersonal Violence* 25 (3): 503–517.

Caetano, R., J. Schafer, and C. B. Cunradi. 2001. Alcohol-related intimate partner violence among white, black, and Hispanic couples in the United States. *Alcohol Research and Health* 25 (1): 58–65.

Clothesline Project. 1999. Men's pledge to end rape. Available at http://www.clothesline project.org/Men_Pledge.htm.

DeGue, S., L. A. Valle, M. K. Holt, G. M. Massetti, J. L. Matjasko, and A. T. Tharp. 2014. A systematic review of primary prevention strategies for sexual violence perpetration. *Aggression and Violent Behavior* 19 (4): 346–362.

Fabiano, P. M., H. W. Perkins, A. Berkowitz, J. Linkenbach, and C. Stark. 2003. Engaging men as social justice allies in ending violence against women: Evidence for a social norms approach. *Journal of American College Health* 52 (3): 105–112.

Flood, M. 2006. Changing men: Best practice in sexual violence education. *Women Against Violence: An Australian Feminist Journal* 18: 26.

———. 2011. Involving men in efforts to end violence against women. *Men and Masculinities* 14 (3): 358–377.

Foubert, J. D. 2000. The longitudinal effects of a rape-prevention program on fraternity men's attitudes, behavioral intent, and behavior. *Journal of American College Health* 48: 158–163.

Foubert, J., and J. T. Newberry. 2006. Effects of two versions of an empathy-based rape prevention program on fraternity men's survivor empathy, attitudes, and behavioral intent to commit rape or sexual assault. *Journal of College Student Development* 47 (2): 133–148.

Foubert, J. D., J. T. Newberry, and J. L. Tatum. 2007. Behavior differences seven months later: Effects of a rape prevention program. *NASPA Journal* 44 (4): 728–749.

Garin, G. 2000. Report No. #5702c. Washington, DC: Peter D. Hart Research.

Gidycz, C. A., L. M. Orchowski, and A. D. Berkowitz. 2011. Preventing sexual aggression among college men: An evaluation of a social norms and bystander intervention program. *Violence Against Women* 17 (6): 720–742.

Hartz, M. 2001. "Men" distribute splashguards. *Daily Collegian*, July 25. Available at http://www.collegian.psu.edu/archives/article_b5d02a4b-852d-50b3-b8d7-159dc872a1bd .html.

Heppner, M. J., H. A. Neville, K. Smith, D. M. Kivlighan Jr., and B. S. Gershuny. 1999. Examining immediate and long-term efficacy of rape prevention programming with racially diverse college men. *Journal of Counseling Psychology* 46 (1): 16.

Katz, J. 2003. Advertising and the construction of violent white masculinity: From Eminem to Clinique for men. 2nd ed. In *Gender, race, and class in media: A text reader*, ed. G. Dines and J. M. Humez, 349–358. Thousand Oaks: Sage.

Kruttschnitt, C. 1994. Gender and interpersonal violence. In *Understanding and preventing violence: Social influences*, vol. 3, ed. J. A. Roth and A. J. Reiss, 295–378. Washington, DC: National Academy of Sciences Press.

Messner, M. A., M. A. Greenberg, and T. Peretz. 2015. *Some men: Feminist allies and the movement to end violence against women*. New York: Oxford University Press.

Nation, M., C. Crusto, A. Wandersman, K. L. Kumpfer, D. Seybolt, E. Morrissey-Kane, and K. Davino. 2003. What works in prevention: Principles of effective prevention programs. *American Psychologist* 58 (6–7): 449.

Pease, B. 2008. *Engaging men in men's violence prevention: Exploring the tensions, dilemmas and possibilities*. Sydney: Australian Domestic and Family Violence.

Potter, S. J. 2012. Using a multimedia social marketing campaign to increase active bystanders on the college campus. *Journal of American College Health* 60 (4): 282–295.

Slaby, R., A. Branner, and S. Martin. 2011. *Mentors in Violence Prevention: An evaluation of the 2009–2011 campus leadership initiative program*. Washington DC: U.S. Department of Justice, Office on Violence Against Women.

Stewart, A. L. 2014. The Men's Project: A sexual assault prevention program targeting college men. *Psychology of Men and Masculinity* 15 (4): 481.

Stith, S. M., D. B. Smith, C. E. Penn, D. B. Ward, and D. Tritt. 2004. Intimate partner physical abuse perpetration and victimization risk factors: A meta-analytic review. *Aggression and Violent Behavior* 10 (1): 65–98.

Swogger, M. T., Z. Walsh, D. S. Kosson, S. Cashman-Brown, and E. D. Caine. 2012. Self-reported childhood physical abuse and perpetration of intimate partner violence: The moderating role of psychopathic traits. *Criminal Justice and Behavior* 39 (7): 910–922.

Tjaden, P., and N. Thoennes. 2000. *Full report on the prevalence, incidence, and consequences of violence against women: Findings from the National Violence Against Women Survey*. (NCJ 183781). Washington, DC: Office of Justice Programs.

PROGRAM WEBSITES

A Call to Men. http://www.acalltomen.org/
Men Can Stop Rape. http://www.mencanstoprape.org/
The Men's Program. http://www.oneinfourusa.org/themensprogram.php
Mentors in Violence Prevention (MVP). http://www.mvpnational.org/

16

Student Activism

Ava Blustein

Introduction

For most people living in the United States today, rape on college campuses is far from an unfamiliar concept. Stories of violation and trauma inflicted on young university students appear across our social media feeds, in newspapers and magazines, on television and radio, even on the agenda of the White House. Since 2011, the problem of campus sexual violence has risen to public consciousness and held this nation's collective attention in ways that few issues do. This is no accident.

Student activists—the majority of whom are survivors of sexual violence themselves—have built a grassroots movement that not only spotlights sexual assault but also empowers young people to hold powerful institutions accountable and to create meaningful change in their communities. The fact that campus sexual violence continues to garner so much attention across the country is just one of this movement's salient achievements. Student activism represents another side of the campus rape narrative—one of resilience, courage, innovation, and collective power.

This chapter situates the current era of youth and survivor-led organizing in the history of campus anti-rape activism. In doing so, the chapter examines the key elements of the movement, the major tactics activists employ, and the overarching goals of the movement. These goals include raising public consciousness, reclaiming safe spaces, defying silence and institutional denial of sexual violence, dispelling rape myths, and advocating for equitable and fair disciplinary procedures.

Organizing Against Violence and Institutional Betrayal

A 2015 study conducted by the Association of American Universities found that 23.1 percent of female undergraduate respondents had experienced non-consensual sexual contact due to physical force, threats of physical force, or incapacitation since they enrolled at their university. The same study found overall reporting rates to campus officials or law enforcement to range from 5 to 28 percent (Cantor et al. 2015). That means at least one out of every five college women is sexually assaulted while pursuing an education. I once attended a university-sponsored event in which an attendee asked a famous survivor-activist what he could do to help survivors, even though he did not know any survivors personally. The activist bluntly informed him that everyone knows a survivor of sexual assault, whether they are aware of it or not.

The terrifying prevalence of sexual assault, however, is not the only problem. Time and time again, survivors who speak up face social stigmatization, misplaced blame, and the denial of any justice. It is no wonder victims are deterred from identifying themselves publicly, much less trusting that authority figures will believe, support, or help them. Just as no university is immune to sexual assault, students find that institutions of higher education, with few exceptions, choose to protect reputation and money over their students. Common symptoms of this institutional betrayal include administrators denying the realities of sexual assault at their schools, failing to fund adequate confidential support services, giving slap-on-the-wrist sanctions or refusing to find perpetrators responsible for sexual misconduct, creating overly confusing or unfair reporting and adjudication systems, and punishing or silencing survivors of sexual violence. Coast to coast, students have realized that these systemic problems, which continue to harm survivors and leave students at risk, are not isolated to their own campuses.

It is common to hear about students protesting a high-profile sexual assault or their university's mishandling of a particular incident and think those are simply one-off cases. On the contrary, these incidents usually demonstrate the deep-seated and widespread systemic flaws in an institution's response to sexual violence. Survivors who find their own cases mishandled by a school can use their experiences to assess systemic problems. Their resulting campaign demands often fall into three categories: prevention, resources, and response.

Students' specific policy and procedural recommendations vary between campuses due to the unique problems, needs, and characteristics of each school. Still, survivor-activists universally campaign to hold their institutions accountable for complying with federal laws and proactively addressing sexual violence. In response to nonexistent or inadequate prevention efforts, students often demand the implementation of ongoing, comprehensive trainings and awareness campaigns for all students, faculty, and staff. Part of creating effective and evidence-based prevention programming is understanding the unique risk factors that exist on a particular campus. This is commonly accomplished through conducting campus climate surveys and including student input in all programming.

Schools should also make sure to have confidential support resources available on campus. This means the university must hire trained counselors or victims' advocates with expertise in trauma-based therapy to provide survivors with support and information about their options. Many student activists campaign for an on-campus rape crisis center, or recommend that administrators establish a memorandum of understanding with a local rape crisis center. Because sexual assault can inhibit survivors' ability to attend class, participate in extracurricular activities, and even feel safe at school, it is essential for survivors to have safe places to seek refuge, receive culturally competent support, and explore their options for accommodations or reporting.

Prevention and resources are not enough to ensure that student survivors have equal access to their education. An important reason schools must have procedures and policies in place to respond to incidents of sexual violence rather than simply turning reports over to law enforcement is that in most cases, these institutions are best positioned to help student survivors continue their education. The trauma of an assault can be enough to make survivors discontinue their education, let alone the risk of repeatedly encountering the person who harmed them in their dorm, classroom, or club meeting. That is why many survivors seek out protective no-contact orders on campus, extra academic help, a change in their class schedule or dorm assignment, and other accommodations that police cannot typically provide. Beyond enforcing no-contact orders and giving survivors a range of options for accommodations, schools must also understand that with any incident of sexual violence comes the likelihood that the perpetrator will harm other students (Lisak and Miller 2002). Student activists know that college social culture, as well as broken or lenient disciplinary procedures, give sexual predators license to hurt their peers without fear of retribution. That is why many survivor-activists work to ensure that all of their school's policies and procedures are robust and fair.

To understand the student movement against sexual violence and institutional negligence, it is imperative to remember what Dana Bolger, cofounder and executive director of the national youth and survivor-led organization Know Your IX says: survivors and activists are not a monolith (D. Bolger, personal communication, June 21, 2016). Sexual assault happens to individuals of every race, gender identity, sexuality, ability, age, religion, class, and nationality. Those who are most often given a platform to speak

Figure 16.1   Know Your IX (IX on leather jacket). Photo courtesy of Jo Chiang, Found Company.

about sexual assault fit a narrow portrayal of a typical survivor (White, straight, cisgender, able-bodied, petite, Christian, American, class privileged, and Ivy League educated). Yet, this movement is comprised of diverse experiences, backgrounds, and perspectives. Survivors of sexual violence come to this movement from all different places (Figure 16.1). Thus, there are many ways forward toward the goals we share.

This movement also remains intentionally and radically decentralized. In the current landscape, several national organizations and organizers have risen to prominence. These youth-run organizations, however, utilize their power and influence to elevate the campaigns of survivor-activists on the frontlines. They do not dictate the overall direction of the movement or co-opt individual campaigns, working instead to provide students with much-needed resources and opportunities to unite with other activists nationwide. In this decentralized structure, the movement operates on multiple levels, with students advocating for equitable state and federal policies at the same time that others continue to set their own agendas and push boundaries from within their local communities.

Survivor-Led Organizing

Student survivors of sexual assault are the leaders of this movement for many reasons. Perhaps the most important is that survivors know what it is like to pursue an education after trauma and can identify the gaps in their school's response based on their own experiences. Who better to lead the charge against these problems than the young people most directly affected by them? Survivors telling their personal narratives also demands attention in ways that statistics or policy proposals do not, and can have a greater impact on public consciousness.

A movement led by intelligent, daring survivors with organizing savvy flies in the face of the belief that victims of violence are helpless. The very terminology of survivor-led organizing connotes perseverance after trauma. It is not easy to be a public survivor-activist, and many who spearhead campaigns do so at great personal risk. However, survivor-led organizing does not mean that the only or even primary function of survivors in the movement is to tell their stories publicly. This movement is built on the labor and expertise of student survivors. There are those who discount young survivor-activists, not realizing that many of them have dedicated years to learning the law, leading sophisticated campaigns, and advocating for policies everywhere from college administrators' offices to the floor of the U.S. Senate. On top of that, survivors often serve as the most crucial emotional support systems for other survivors. Young activists do all this while working toward earning a degree.

Brief History of Student Activism Against Sexual Violence

In 2014, Columbia University student Emma Sulkowicz began "Mattress Performance (Carry That Weight)," a performance art piece and political protest in which she vowed to carry a standard dorm mattress with her on campus for as long as the person who raped her remained a student at her school (Smith 2014). Her endurance performance, aptly named to reflect survivors' experiences of constantly carrying the burden of their assaults, received widespread media attention. The image of a heavy mattress on the back of a single student (Figure 16.2) became an instant symbol for both the problem of sexual assault and the student movement that rose to end it.

Sulkowicz's performance, occurring two years after she was assaulted during her sophomore year, was a culminating act of defiance and strength after her university failed to hold the perpetrator responsible for sexual misconduct (Smith 2014). For many Americans, "Carry That Weight" was a rude awakening to the pervasive and complex problems of sexual violence and institutional betrayal. In response, some mischaracterized campus sexual violence as a new problem faced only by the millennial generation, not realizing that Sulkowicz's visionary performance and the concurrent resurgence of student activism are part of a long legacy of students working to end a problem that has plagued the college experience for generations.

The term date rape, referring to sexual violence perpetrated by someone the victim knows, was introduced into mainstream vernacular in 1985,

FIGURE 16.2   Mattress Performance (Carry That Weight). Photo courtesy of Jo Chiang, Found Company.

when *Ms. Magazine* published "Date Rape: The Story of an Epidemic and Those Who Deny It" (Sweet 1985). The article featured groundbreaking research conducted by Dr. Mary Koss, which found that approximately one in four college women is the victim of rape or attempted rape (Sweet 2012). This exposed the rampant rate of sexual assault committed by college students against their peers.

Even before 1985, however, college survivors of violence and feminist activists had already connected the dots. In 1972, students at the University of Maryland successfully campaigned to establish one of the first-ever campus rape crisis centers. Student lobbying led to the implementation of campus-wide sexual assault prevention programming for the entire University of California system in 1976 (Heldman and Brown 2014). Before extensive research was conducted and the White House created awareness campaigns, student activists utilized survivors' firsthand experiences to inform solutions.

Anti-rape activists of the 1970s also introduced Take Back the Night, a tradition that occurs annually on university campuses to this day. Part candlelit vigil and part protest, the popular awareness-raising event features chants and readings of survivors' stories (Gibson 2011). During Take Back the Night, participants raise their voices in unison and call out slogans such as "whatever we wear / wherever we go / yes means yes / and no means no."

As its name connotes, Take Back the Night is about the collective reclamation of personal agency and space. When a rape is reported anywhere, from a dorm on campus to a fraternity house or a city street, authority figures like police often advise women to dress differently or adjust their actions to stay safe. Take Back the Night participants defy these dictums and assert their right to move through the world safely.

Another tradition, the Clothesline Project, was born during a 1990 Take Back the Night rally held in Massachusetts (Clothesline Project n.d.). The Clothesline Project is an art installation in which shirts, usually decorated with survivors' experiences of sexual assault, are hung up on clotheslines. The creation of shirts is meant to give survivors a creative outlet to process trauma and heal, while displaying the shirts creates a tangible representation of a problem that is often abstracted or dehumanized by statistics. Rooted in the idea that laundry is a chore traditionally done by women, the project not only confronts viewers with the truth about sexual violence but also invokes a sense of private spaces in which women can exchange knowledge to protect one another and unite in the struggle against violence.

In the face of pervasive violence, women finding ways to communicate with one another for protection and empowerment is a theme that persists throughout the movement. Whether it be creating a Women's Studies department or a feminist club, students have worked to create safe spaces where they could examine violence against women and organize against it. In 1990, anonymous students at Brown University made headlines by writing rapists' names in the stall of a women's restroom on campus. Despite receiving criticism for "vigilantism," students continued to re-create the list in more bathrooms, even after the university repeatedly attempted to paint over the names (Celis 1990). Survivors had previously reported many of the people listed through official university sexual misconduct channels, to no avail. This was a protest against the continued presence of known perpetrators in the Brown community.

As news of the "rape list" gained traction in the media, administrators were forced to publicly recognize a problem students felt had been ignored or denied. The protest exposed sexual assault at Brown and the university's lax response. Moreover, the use of gender-specific restroom stalls enabled activists to share their valuable knowledge when official channels had failed to protect them (Radack 2014). That system served as both a critique of the university's handling of sexual violence and a method by which students could care for one another.

The Movement Today

One challenge that student activists consistently face is institutional memory. Because college activists eventually graduate, turnover is a perpetual impediment to sustaining the movement's cohesion and momentum. So much so, in fact, that a common tactic of university administrators is to stall any substantive improvements so that students will be forced to start over after the current activists graduate. That is why it is important that students build on the philosophical foundations and hard-fought gains of previous activists.

From protests like Take Back the Night to the now repopularized use of zines, the legacy of our predecessors is still integral to the movement. As recently as 2014, Columbia University activists appeared to replicate the Brown bathroom rapist list tactic by writing perpetrators' names on bathroom walls and distributing the list on fliers. Below the printed list, a message said: "To the Columbia Community: Stay safe, protect and support each other, and always always always make sure to have sober, enthusiastic, continuous consent" (Culp-Ressler 2014). Just as the rate of sexual assault on college campuses has changed little since Koss's (1985) study, some of the movement's goals remain much the same. Raising consciousness, dispelling rape myths through survivors' narratives, calling attention to institutional mishandling of violence, as well as eliminating sexual assault and gender-based oppression altogether, are priorities that cannot change until our society changes.

As we struggle toward that future however, we have gained some game-changing tools and explored new goals. In 2014, *Salon* published "Ivy League rape nightmare: My personal reflection of progress—and pain," in which Jesselyn Radack reflected on the 1990 Brown "rape list" and her own disheartening experiences reporting her sexual assault to Brown officials. Writing almost twenty-five years later, Radack said: "In today's activist landscape, students have two additional tools with which they have been able to build the most organized, visible and effective anti-rape movement ever: Title IX and social media" (Radack 2014, para. 18). Radack's insight frames the current state of this movement, which has seen the acceleration of successful student-operated campaigns, heightened visibility in mainstream culture thanks to social media, and the introduction of Title IX to activists' arsenals.

Title IX Activism

Title IX of the Education Amendments of 1972 is a federal civil rights law prohibiting sex discrimination in education. Before student activists began to demand stronger enforcement of Title IX in response to the unmitigated problem of sexual assault, it was best known for gender equity in school athletics programs. In April 2011, the Department of Education's Office for Civil Rights (OCR) published a Dear Colleague Letter, reminding schools that any sexual harassment or violence that creates a hostile environment for students is considered a form of sexual discrimination under Title IX

(Department of Education 2011). Schools that violate students' Title IX rights face investigation by the OCR and risk losing federal funding. (For a more thorough discussion of the evolution of Title IX, see Chapter 7 by Michelle Hughes Miller.) Around the same time, the OCR opened an investigation of Yale University after sixteen students and alumni filed a complaint for Title IX violations (Gasso 2011).

In the years that followed, several survivor-organizers who had campaigned against sexual violence at their own schools began to connect through mutual friends and social media. They realized that colleges across the country had largely ignored their Title IX obligations to address and prevent sexual violence at the expense of survivors' educational opportunities. A few activists—including Dana Bolger and Alexandra Brodsky, founders of Know Your IX, as well as Annie Clark, Andrea Pino, and Sofie Karasek, founders of End Rape on Campus (EROC)—realized that a barrier to students successfully receiving support and protection was that they did not know their rights under Title IX.

Digging deeper, activists learned that even when students filed Title IX complaints, the OCR had "never once sanctioned a college or university for sexual assault–related Title IX violations," instead asking universities to "sign voluntary resolution agreements (VRAs)—essentially signed promises to do better next time" (Know Your IX n.d., para. 1). In July 2013, survivors and organizers traveled from across the United States to protest outside the Department of Education as part of a Know Your IX campaign called ED ACT NOW. Armed with a petition that garnered 100,000 signatures, the students called on the OCR to "conduct timely, transparent, coordinated, and proactive investigations; involve survivor-complainants in the process of arriving at any resolution to an investigation; and issue meaningful sanctions against non-compliant schools" (Know Your IX n.d., para. 2). As a result, organizers were invited to speak with top officials from the White House, the Department of Education, and the Department of Justice. They won a shortened timeline for investigations of schools, as well as a published list of all schools under investigation for Title IX violations. According to the *Chronicle of Higher Education*'s Title IX Tracker, the government conducted 296 such investigations between April 2011 and June 2016, with 247 cases still open (Title IX 2016).

Title IX continues to be an essential tool for survivor-activists at just about every school in America, allowing them to campaign for more comprehensive prevention programming, resources, and fairer and more transparent reporting and disciplinary proceedings. Brodsky and Bolger's organization, Know Your IX, started out as a two-month campaign with a website built using online crowdfunding and a simple mission: to educate students on their rights and schools' Title IX responsibilities. It has now expanded organically into a national clearinghouse for legal information and a vocal leader in the movement against campus violence. Know Your IX, alongside other youth and survivor-led organizations such as SurvJustice and Students Active for Ending Rape (SAFER), empowers more student activists to create change on their campuses, and advocate for equitable policies at the institutional, state, and federal levels. The founders of EROC were recently the focus of a documentary film called *The Hunting Ground*, which brought the fight against sexual violence and institutional negligence to new heights of visibility (Ziering and Dick 2015). Their organization continues to offer advocacy, education, and direct support to survivor-activists.

The use of Title IX in campus activism represents a shift in the way students approach the problem of sexual violence. While the practice of covering up pervasive sexual violence and silencing survivors is unethical, students' appeals for universities to do what is right have not always been successful. Title IX incentivizes administrators to properly address campus sexual violence in order to avoid potential loss of funding and damage to their institution's reputation. The law also reframes sexual violence as a civil rights issue, enabling students to fight for their right to an education free from gender-based violence. The fact that young survivor-organizers are leading influential national campaigns to protect students' civil rights means the very people who have perhaps the most at stake in ending sexual violence now have a seat at the table when it comes to the policies that affect them. This means that survivors no longer need to feel alone when speaking out about their school's mishandling of their cases—they have powerful peers in their corner.

Social Media

Just as Title IX represents an important shift in student organizing around sexual violence, social media has revolutionized the way millennial activists disseminate their messages and create a sustained movement. For young people who have grown up using sites like Facebook to connect with friends, mobilizing support for their activism on social media is a no-brainer.

At my own alma mater, Brandeis University, fellow organizers and I used Tumblr and Facebook to create an awareness campaign in which survivors could anonymously share their stories. The success of that campaign led us to form a coalition of student survivors, peer counselors, and activists called Brandeis Students Against Sexual Violence. Together, we authored a petition detailing eleven proposals to improve our school's prevention efforts, resources, and disciplinary procedures. We delivered the petition to several top administrators and uploaded it to Change.org to be signed and shared by our peers, professors, friends, parents, and Brandeis alumni until we had accumulated enough attention to convince our administration to act. We followed up on the petition by meeting with administrators, disrupting public events, and carrying out protests—all documented on social media. Under pressure to protect the school's image, administrators agreed to work with students and meet our demands, including the establishment of an on-campus rape crisis center. While there is still so much left to be done at Brandeis, using social media to amplify the voices of survivors, spread information, and pressure administrators continues to be one of our most successful tactics.

In today's social media climate, activists not only use the Internet to achieve goals on their own campuses, but to collaborate across state lines and national borders in ways that were unthinkable before. Capitalizing on the attention of Sulkowicz's protest art, student activists in 2014, and again in 2015, rallied to carry mattresses around their own campuses in a nationwide event called the Carry That Weight Day of Action. The Facebook event page read: "Central to the importance of Emma's art is the collaborative and supportive nature of the project" (Carry That Weight National Day of Action 2015), referring to one of the rules of engagement for Sulkowicz's art piece, which stated that she could not seek out assistance carrying the mattress, but was allowed to accept aid when it was offered. The implicit challenge is for everyone, not just survivors, to shoulder the burden of sexual violence. Prior to the day of action, activists could sign up online to host an event on their campuses. Students who did so received advice and encouragement from event organizers, as well as opportunities to be included in press releases and have their photos or demands spotlighted. Using social media, student activists everywhere were able to illuminate systemic problems and mobilize scores of people to demand better.

Moreover, social media has given survivors much-needed access to the masses. The case of a former Stanford swimmer who was caught sexually assaulting an unconscious young woman behind a dumpster outside of a fraternity party sparked national outrage in 2016 (Stack 2016). Many people expressed anger on social media at the details of the case, as well as the perpetrator's six-month jail sentence, which was widely decried as lenient. The outcome of the case may have been unsurprising for many survivor-activists, who are accustomed to college sexual offenders getting off scot-free. For others, however, the case was a shocking revelation that illustrated the perversity of rape culture and just how unattainable justice can be for most survivors.

Stanford student activists' petitions gained traction in the media as more people became enthralled with the injustice of the case. Popular social news and the entertainment media website BuzzFeed published the survivor in the Stanford case's letter to her assailant (Baker 2016). Her powerful account of how the assault impacted her life became one of the most shared articles in BuzzFeed's history. In an era that has seen the propagation of awareness campaigns in response to student activism, it seems no firsthand narrative of a survivor had ever permeated mainstream culture to this degree before.

With any luck, this amplification of survivors' voices on social media indicates meaningful changes to come, not just for campus culture but for our society as well.

Moving Forward

As an organizer in this movement, I see student activism against campus sexual violence reaching a critical juncture. Over several years, generations of student activists have garnered unprecedented visibility and power. The successful utilization of Title IX and social media has given many people reason to hope that with recent successes will come lasting cultural change. Still, there is so much work ahead to end sexual violence and create effective structures for confronting violence in our communities. Activists across the country may also face reactionary backlash, the risk of co-optation, and the problem of media oversaturation. When tackling these future challenges, it seems our movement's greatest strength is that there is no monolithic student campaign against sexual violence.

Campus anti–sexual violence activists organize concurrently with movements against racist police brutality, violent homophobia and transphobia, and gender and class inequity. Every organizer in this movement holds multiple identities. Therefore, we each contribute unique values and experiences to this work, and we are often participating in more than one movement toward a more just future. The diverse experiences, beliefs, and tactics that comprise our movement also make us adaptable and uniquely capable of intersectional organizing. We know that since violence is a part of intricate systems of oppression, we cannot eliminate sexual violence without ending other forms of oppression. It seems essential that in light of our wins, we not become complacent and accept change that benefits only the most privileged. As we share a commitment to ending violence, our entire movement can unite in empowering the most marginalized among us. If we can continue working toward those goals, I believe there is hope that this movement led by young survivors and activists can succeed in realizing long-awaited social change.

REFERENCES

Baker, K. J. 2016. Here is the powerful letter the Stanford victim read aloud to her attacker. *BuzzFeed News*, June 3. Available at https://www.buzzfeed.com/katiejmbaker/heres-the-powerful-letter-the-stanford-victim-read-to-her-ra?utm_term=.tub4QQgl6#.tiGZ99Jrb.

Cantor, D., B. Fisher, S. Chibnall, R. Townsend, H. Lee, C. Bruce, and G. Thomas. 2015. *AAU Campus Survey on sexual assault and sexual misconduct*. Association of American Universities, September 21. Available at https://www.aau.edu/uploadedFiles/AAU_Publications/AAU_Reports/Sexual_Assault_Campus_Survey/AAU_Campus_Climate_Survey_12_14_15.pdf.

Carry That Weight National Day of Action. 2015. Available at https://www.facebook.com /events/1550372131902005/.

Celis, W. 1990. Date rape and a list at Brown. *New York Times*, November 18. Available at http://www.nytimes.com/1990/11/18/us/date-rape-and-a-list-at-brown.html.

Clothesline Project. n.d. *History of the Clothesline Project*. Available at http://www .clotheslineproject.org/History.html.

Culp-Ressler, T. 2014. Columbia students are writing the names of accused rapists on bathroom walls. ThinkProgress, May 14. Available at http://thinkprogress.org/columbia -students-are-writing-the-names-of-accused-rapists-on-bathroom-walls-a948e499c5c#. jwgjgba3c.

Department of Education, Office for Civil Rights. 2011. *Dear Colleague Letter*. Available at https://www2.ed.gov/about/offices/list/ocr/letters/colleague-201104.html.

Gasso, J. 2011. Yale under federal investigation for possible Title IX violations. *Yale Daily News*, April 1. Available at http://yaledailynews.com/blog/2011/04/01/yale-under -federal-investigation-for-possible-title-ix-violations/.

Gibson, M. 2011. A brief history of women's protests. *Time*, August 12. Available at http:// content.time.com/time/specials/packages/article/0,28804,2088114_2087975 _2087967,00.html.

Heldman, C., and B. Brown. 2014. A brief history of sexual violence activism in the U.S. *Ms. Magazine* Blog, August 8. Available at http://msmagazine.com/blog/2014/08/08/a -brief-history-of-sexual-violence-activism-in-the-u-s/.

Know Your IX. n.d. *ED ACT NOW*. Available at http://knowyourix.org/i-want-to/take -national-action/.

Koss, M. P. 1985. The hidden rape victim: Personality, attitudinal, and situational charac- teristics. *Psychology of Women Quarterly* 9 (2): 193–212.

Lisak, D., and P. M. Miller. 2002. Repeat rape and multiple offending among undetected rapists. *Violence and Victims* 17 (1): 73–84. Available at http://www.davidlisak.com/wp -content/uploads/pdf/RepeatRapeinUndetectedRapists.pdf.

Radack, J. 2014. Ivy League rape nightmare: My personal reflection of progress—and pain. *Salon*, October 9. Available at http://www.salon.com/2014/10/09/ivy_leagues_rape _fiasco_a_personal_reflection_of_progress_and_sadness/.

Smith, R. 2014. In a mattress, a lever for art and political protest. *New York Times*, Septem- ber 21, Art and Design. Available at http://www.nytimes.com/2014/09/22/arts/design /in-a-mattress-a-fulcrum-of-art-and-political-protest.html.

Stack, L. 2016. Light sentence for Brock Turner in Stanford rape case draws outrage. *New York Times*, June 6. Available at http://www.nytimes.com/2016/06/07/us/outrage-in -stanford-rape-case-over-dueling-statements-of-victim-and-attackers-father.html.

Sweet, E. 1985. Date rape: The story of an epidemic and those who deny it. *Ms. Magazine*, October, 56.

———. 2012. *Date rape revisited*. Women's Media Center, February 23. Available at http:// www.womensmediacenter.com/feature/entry/date-rape-revisited.

Title IX: Tracking Sexual Assault Investigations. 2016. *Chronicle of Higher Education*. Available at http://projects.chronicle.com/titleix/.

Ziering, A. (Producer), and K. Dick (Director). 2015. *The Hunting Ground*. Motion picture. New York: Weinstein Company.

IV

Preventing Violence Against Women on Campus

Current Challenges and Future Opportunities

17

Title IX Investigations and "Rehabilitated Schools"

MEREDITH M. SMITH

Introduction

In May 2014, the Department of Education's Office for Civil Rights (OCR) released a list of higher education institutions that it was investigating for potential violations of Title IX (U.S. Department of Education 2014). Title IX had been in effect since 1972; this was the first list of its kind. The list had the names of fifty-five institutions, including some of the nation's best colleges such as Harvard, Princeton, Southern California, and the University of North Carolina at Chapel Hill. Dozens of schools—good schools, schools that thousands of students wish for admission to—were alleged to have failed their students by inadequately, indifferently, or even callously responding to reports of sexual violence.

Fifty-five was merely the ground floor. The *Chronicle of Higher Education*'s database of Title IX investigations[1] reveals that in the two years since the release of that list, there was a 200 percent increase in schools under investigation for Title IX noncompliance. As of May 1, 2016, the OCR is investigating 221 sexual violence cases at 175 colleges and universities (Wontorcik 2016). But the dramatic rise in cases becomes truly staggering with a wider perspective. In 2010, there were eleven Title IX complaints filed with the OCR; there were eleven OCR investigations opened in February 2016 *alone*. This investigatory boom is a result of the OCR's 2011 Dear Colleague Letter (DCL) regarding student-on-student sexual assault in school settings, a decision that "clearly determined that Title IX enforcement will play a prominent role on the higher education landscape" (Foerster and Hage 2011, 2).

OCR investigations clearly impact the schools under their review, but the effect on the schools that are not named is as profound. Lewis and colleagues (2013) called the DCL "a sea change on this issue, touching campuses all across the country at the same time in an unprecedented way" (3). To avoid OCR investigation, a school must be letter-perfect in its compliance with the DCL, as well as its progeny, the *2014 Questions and Answers on Title IX and Sexual Violence*, and the 2015 DCL that referenced Title IX coordinators.

As Gersen and Suk (2016) have noted, many institutions of higher education have prematurely revised their policies and procedures in an attempt to be compliant with federal law and to avoid an OCR investigation.

But to what end? The Department of Education's federal regulations state that the purpose of Title IX is "to eliminate . . . discrimination on the basis of sex in any education program or activity" (U.S. Department of Education 1979), yet our driving animus is avoiding OCR investigation. This is not to diminish the incredible good that changes and improvements made in light of OCR guidance have made for sexual violence victims and campus communities. As a Title IX administrator who worked at a school under investigation, I can attest that changes made with an eye to the OCR can better your work. The DCL and subsequent documents from the OCR were a direct and forceful response to chronic systemic failures in higher education's response to sexual violence. Between this guidance and the OCR investigation of schools, higher education is—truly, for the first time—being held responsible to fulfilling its charge under Title IX regarding sexual violence. Yet it is worrisome that the eradication of sexual violence is an aftereffect of the actual goal of avoiding government investigation and public shame. It seems that in our focus on ensuring a perfect response, we have lost sight of what we endeavor to prevent. When compliance is the engine of your work, what can the destination be?

This chapter examines the origins of the DCL and its impact on colleges and the OCR, followed by an examination of how the compliance engine obfuscates the prevention of sexual violence and protection for victims—the real heart of Title IX.

The Roots of the DCL and Its Impact on Colleges and the OCR

The DCL did not materialize out of governmental thin air: its administrative evolution is clear and easy to trace. Sexual violence was not always assumed to be prohibited conduct under Title IX. When Title IX was enacted in 1972, its application did not even extend to sexual harassment. That application was established nearly a decade later when, in 1981, the OCR's director of litigation, enforcement, and policy service sent a memorandum to the office's regional civil rights directors, which prohibited school employees from sexually harassing students (Henrick 2013).

The office went on to issue four pamphlets about sexual harassment in schools (applicable to all educational institutions, K–12 as well as higher education) between 1988 and 2008. More notably, the OCR published two guidance documents on Title IX and sexual harassment in 1997 and 2001, both of which were promulgated following the requirements of the Administrative Procedure Act (APA) with notice-and-comment rule making before issuance, giving their regulations the weight of law (Henrick 2013). The guidances laid out specific mandates for schools with regard to defining, reporting, investigating, and responding to sexual harassment.

The 1997 guidance was the first time the OCR explicitly included sexual assault as a form of sexual harassment (U.S. Department of Education 1997). It mandated that when a school learns about sexual harassment, it has a responsibility to take immediate and effective steps to end sexual harassment, prevent its recurrence, and remedy its effects on the victim and the community. The 2001 revised guidance updated the 1997 publication "in limited respects in light of subsequent Supreme Court cases relating to sexual harassment" (U.S. Department of Education 2001, 2), in particular the ruling of *Davis v. Monroe County Board of Education* (1999). The Supreme Court confirmed what the 1997 guidance had first articulated, that Title IX's application extended to student-on-student sexual harassment as well as to instances where faculty or staff harassed students. The Court noted that "a single instance of sufficiently severe one-on-one peer harassment could be said" to "be serious enough to have the systemic effect of denying the victim equal access to an educational program or activity" (U.S. Department of Education 2001, 22). Student-on-student sexual harassment, said Davis, required schools to respond.

Ten years passed between the 2001 guidance and the 2011 DCL without any major guidance documents from the OCR. As stated previously, the number of schools that were under investigation during this time were few: only eleven schools were under federal inquiry in 2010. Said a student who filed a complaint in 2008: "The message that they are sending to victims is that sexual assault is not something they take seriously" (Jones 2010, para. 89). What, then, was the motivation for the DCL and its "sea change" on enforcement? The answer would make Woodward and Bernstein proud: investigative journalism.

In January 2010, the Center for Public Integrity ("the Center") released the findings of a yearlong investigation into student disciplinary procedures. It found higher education's response to sexual violence inadequate, in particular schools' disciplinary response to students who committed sexual assault against their peers. "Colleges seldom expel men who are found 'responsible' for sexual assault; indeed, these schools permanently kicked out only 10 to 25 percent of such students" (Lombardi 2010, para. 6). The investigation rocked not only higher education but the government as well. When then Department of Education assistant secretary for civil rights Russlyn Ali was informed of the Center's findings, she committed the OCR to a "more aggressive" response to Title IX complaints and the use of strong sanctions not previously exercised by the office, "including referring to (the Department of) Justice [for investigation] or withholding federal funds to ensure that women are free from sexual violence" (Jones 2010, para. 11). Jones (2010), another journalist covering the Center's investigation, pointed out that the Department of Education had already committed to increasing Title IX enforcement in light of the Center's investigation. The ramp-up arrived on April 4, 2011, in the form of the DCL. Even prior to the Center's findings, the OCR had planned to release a new set of guidance documents on the federal law protecting against sex discrimination (including sexual harassment and sexual assault).

Where the 2001 guidance addressed sexual harassment generally, the DCL had a specific focus on student-on-student sexual violence. It proscribes certain measures that schools should follow, "particularly regarding the investigation of complaints and any internal judicial hearings" (Carroll et al. 2013, 46). Among its holdings are: expanded jurisdiction (obligating schools to respond to off-campus incidents), shortened and defined deadlines (an approximate deadline of sixty days to complete the disciplinary investigation and adjudication), and a proscribed standard of evidence to use in a school's adjudication process (the preponderance of evidence standard). It enumerated a school's obligations with regard to sexual violence response and provided the framework for more rigorous and prompt institutional investigation procedures. Cantalupo (2012) credits the DCL with providing a disciplinary system counter to the criminal process, which has "significantly more procedural rights for the accused than the survivor" (507). The college process elevated the victim's rights to put both parties in balance: the DCL mandated victim equity.

The DCL can also be seen as a corrective measure to the issues articulated in the Center's findings. One can draw lines between the Center's findings and the guidance of the DCL, as if the OCR were finding solutions to those frustrations. Frustration: Victims spoke about the deleterious effect of their schools' lengthy investigations (Lombardi 2010). Solution: Schools are required to investigate and resolve complaints within a newly specified sixty-day deadline—and calendar, not business days, to boot. However, the OCR itself was a source of frustration. The Center's investigation presented the office as reacting feebly and infrequently to Title IX complaints, claiming systemic failures in collegiate disciplinary systems through examining nearly five times more schools in their year of reporting than the OCR had investigated in ten years (Lombardi and Jones 2009). The OCR's investigation findings did not identify the same systemic problems that the Center did. Moreover, the OCR is tasked with enforcing Title IX and investigating complaints that schools have violated a student's Title IX rights, and the Center cast the OCR's response to Title IX complaints as lax. Shapiro (2010) notes that between 1998 and 2008, the OCR ruled against only five universities in providing resolutions for twenty-four complaints. None of the five were disciplined for violating Title IX, "even when OCR found that colleges had acted indifferently or even retaliated against students who reported that they had been raped or otherwise sexually assaulted on campus" (Jones 2010, para. 7).

In response, the OCR adopted a "stricter stance in the handling of its investigations" (CLC Staff 2016, para. 1). This was evident in the joint findings issued in 2013 by the OCR and the Department of Justice (DOJ) regarding their investigation into the University of Montana (Bhargava and Jackson 2013). The Montana investigation was a particularly pernicious situation, with both the university and the surrounding town of Missoula under investigation for alleged violations of Title IX. The investigation concluded that from 2010 to 2012, the university and the city failed to fairly and adequately prevent, investigate, discipline, and criminally prosecute sexual assault (Krakauer 2015). Mangan (2016) observed: "In the early days of its shift toward stricter Title IX enforcement, OCR cut colleges some slack, praising them for whatever improvements they were making" (para. 11). In contrast, the Montana findings were critical and unforgiving, noting multiple Title IX violations by the institution; furthermore, the government detailed specific corrective measures that the university must implement in order to be compliant. Given the scope of the systemic failures, the investigation findings were an opportunity to apply almost all of the mandates in the DCL—it was like the government's case study. The offices declared that the Montana findings should serve as a "blueprint" for schools across the country in how to structure their Title IX policies, procedures, and efforts (Bhargava and Jackson 2013, 1). The decision was the DCL made manifest: its guidance turned into the proscriptive measures needed for compliance.

That same year, Title IX complaints against schools picked up in intensity: in 2013, there were 32 complaints. In 2014, it exploded to 102. Talbert (2015) reviewed the 6 complaints that were resolved during 2014 for common themes. He found that the OCR noted problems with all of the institutions' policies on sexual violence, specifically finding recurrent issues with vague and inconsistent procedures. All were also faulted for failing to be sufficiently prompt and equitable in their investigative response to victims' reports; the OCR further concluded that victims at Tufts, Virginia Military

Institute, Ohio State, and Southern Methodist University (SMU) were subjected to hostile environments due to these inadequate responses. Though, not all of the schools were what one could consider flagrantly negligent:

> In its letter to SMU, OCR noted that the university removed and suspended the [accused in one case], issued the accused a no-contact letter within three days, offered counseling and a housing change to the complainant, notified the complainant's professors and requested flexibility on his academic work, and granted the complainant's request for a withdrawal from the university. (Talbert 2015, para. 33)

Still, the OCR found issue with how the university responded to the complainant's later complaints of retaliation, setting a higher standard for the institution's investigative response—an example of the "stricter stance" noted by Campus Law Considered (CLC Staff 2016, para. 1). Mangan (2016) observed that "as the pace of complaints has intensified, the tone [of OCR findings] has become harsher" (para. 11). Even smaller issues or concerns merit the OCR's full force. As Catherine Lhamon, assistant secretary of education for civil rights, said to a 2014 conference of 250 college presidents, Title IX coordinators, and student affairs leaders, if schools did not choose to do what the DCL mandated, "I will do it to you" (Newman and Sander 2014, para. 33).

Each findings report communicates how another school failed its victims; each is a lesson for others to identify their faults and course correct—and quickly. Higher education legal expert Peter Lake observed: "The minute one of these drops, experts are running around saying, 'What's the lesson I'm supposed to take away today?'" (Mangan 2016, para. 7). The findings then become "dear colleague letters" in miniature, reiterating the DCL and how to enact its guidance. Their message is clear: get on board or get on the list.

Under the Microscope: OCR Title IX Investigations

The DCL is a profoundly polarizing document. To some, it is a civil rights landmark, addressing a cultural crisis of sexual violence in college (Cantalupo 2016). Others pilloried it as administrative overreach, legislating how young adults should have sex (Gersen and Suk 2016). A common accusation is that the DCL has irrevocably harmed an accused's right to due process—many go further and claim that it has biased institutional disciplinary processes against men (Henrick 2013). Others argue that the DCL has changed campus culture for the better, markedly improving institutional responses and survivor support (Lewis et al. 2013). The reaction from advocates has been similarly mixed. Some found the letter to be the needed sword to fight sexual assault and shield to protect victims; others have been disappointed that the DCL has not gone far enough to punish schools, with one victim stating: "Title IX enforcement is a horribly broken process that needs to be re-evaluated" (Newman and Sander 2014, para. 57).

To the OCR, it is the measure of a school's commitment to ending sexual violence. The former assistant secretary for civil rights, Catherine Lhamon, articulated this standard when testifying before the Senate:

> I am pleased to see that many colleges and universities are stepping up to the challenge of addressing the problem of sexual assault. For example, within months of the release of the Department of Education's Office for Civil Rights 2011 Dear Colleague Letter on sexual violence, many colleges and universities revised their sexual violence policies and procedures consistent with our guidance. (U.S. Senate Committee 2014)

How compliant a school is with the DCL, then, is the shibboleth, demonstrating how seriously one takes sexual assault.

It must be restated: every school *should* be in compliance with its obligations under Title IX. The substance of the guidance is not at issue, and compliance in and of itself is not the problem. However, compliance with the DCL presents challenges and concerns. As written, the very language of the DCL creates confusion as to what exactly is required. Some passages are written as directives. For example, there are elements of the DCL that clearly note the need for campus policies and procedures to be consistent with Title IX standards, such as the use of the standard of preponderance of the evidence. At the same time, other elements appear to be recommendations. This includes recommendations that campuses should inform complainants that Title IX prohibits retaliation and how they may report such actions. Sometimes they blur, like the discussion about responses to off-campus conduct, where the school *must* process the complaint in accordance with its established procedures—though the sentence immediately preceding it says that "schools *may* have an obligation to respond to student-on-student harassment" that occurs outside of school (U.S. Department of Education 2011, 4). Which *musts* should we follow, and which *shoulds* must be, too? Five years later, there is still no clarity. "Attempts to clarify which parts of the letter should be read as hard regulations and which should be considered recommendations have led only to more confusion and frustration" (New 2016, para. 3).

Yet even if a school were to institute every pronouncement in the DCL, problems would persist because how the DCL *characterized* compliance is an area of concern. The 1997 and 2001 guidance documents both outlined how schools were obliged to investigate all reports of sexual harassment and provide formal complaint procedures to discipline the perpetrator; this did not originate in the DCL. However, Henrick (2013) notes that the DCL has provided very specific procedures that must now be followed by faculty at institutions of higher education during investigations and in resolving complaints. The guidance was responding directly to the Center's findings on the inadequacy of college disciplinary systems by articulating their required elements. Given the energy spent on how to formally resolve complaints, the DCL seemingly indicated that the way to properly address sexual violence was to punish it out of our communities.

This correlation between discipline and effectiveness is reinforced in our cultural conversations around Title IX. Disciplinary outcomes have become the most reliable way to tell if a school is taking sexual violence seriously by examining its expulsion rates, as demonstrated memorably in the 2015 documentary *The Hunting Ground*. When the University of Virginia convened a three-hour meeting of its trustees with administrators and students on how to change the campus culture surrounding sexual assault, New declared that Virginia "does not take a zero-tolerance approach" to the issue because its discipline policy allowed for sanctions other than expulsion (New 2014b, para. 2). Somehow, prevention and education efforts are not our preferred rubric to measure institutional commitment. In the course of my work in Title IX, students, staff, and faculty repeatedly ask about our institution's expulsion rates; if they are perceived to be too low, it is taken as a canary in the coal mine—the proof that the school is failing. And if your community believes you are failing, it stands to reason that the OCR might feel the same way, too.

Colleges double down on disciplinary procedures as the best way of resolving complaints, foreclosing any alternative means of response and resolution. However, as victim advocate and sexual assault survivor Emily Renda observed, "not all victims are comfortable with strictly 'punitive' sanctioning" (New 2014a, para. 15). It can even have a chilling effect on reporting if a victim knows that the only path forward is through the disciplinary process and expulsion, especially when most victims are acquainted with their assailants, and many times they are friends. The DCL, though, promotes a traditional punitive system and as of yet has not permitted restorative justice processes that have been shown to produce resolutions where victims feel treated with respect and fairness, outcomes rarely seen in traditional disciplinary models (Koss, Wilgus, and Williamsen 2014). To be sure, in the aftermath of the Center's findings, schools that do not seriously investigate, adjudicate, and sanction students are not just failing victims—they fail their entire communities; it is understandable that the OCR is promoting more-traditional disciplinary systems when so many schools were struggling with the basics. Still, our current systems do not provide victims with all of the resolutions they are seeking; in showing the OCR our seriousness, we are unable to explore all of the ways that victims can be made whole.

More concerning is how the disciplinary focus of compliance impacts the prevention of sexual violence. In previous guidance, the OCR had equated discipline and prevention since "grievance procedures . . . provide schools with an excellent mechanism to be used in their efforts to prevent sexual harassment before it occurs" (U.S. Department of Education 1997, 1). The DCL moves further, specifying the need for prevention programs, yet the programs still equate prevention and discipline. "OCR recommends that all schools implement preventive education programs. . . . These programs should include a discussion of what constitutes sexual harassment and sexual violence, the school's policies and disciplinary procedures, and the consequences of violating these policies" (U.S. Department of Education 2011, 14–15). Prevention programming did not become a mandate until three years later, in the 2013 Reauthorized Violence Against Women Act (VAWA) under its Campus Sexual Assault Violence Elimination (SaVE) provision. The VAWA requirements were notable in that they required schools to provide new students and employees "primary prevention and awareness programs" that promote awareness of sexual assault, intimate partner violence, and stalking (see Chapter 8 by Michelle Hughes Miller and Sarah L. Cook for a discussion of Campus SaVE). It was a change in degree: the DCL merely recommended that institutions implement preventive education programs; VAWA was more prescriptive in its requirements.

But training on policies and procedures will not change a campus climate; cultural change requires behavioral change, not mere awareness. Researchers from the Centers for Disease Control and Prevention (CDC) studied the kind of brief educational sessions promoted by the DCL and found that "none of these programs have provided consistent evidence of impact on sexual violence outcomes, and most have not shown evidence of lasting impact on the risk factors or related outcomes that were measured" (DeGue et al. 2014, 359). The CDC called for a "paradigm shift in sexual violence prevention" (359) because our current conception of prevention is not effectuating change. Compliance creates a paradox: in fulfilling the DCL's prevention mandates, a school will never actually prevent sexual violence.

Schools need to break free from the compliance chase to actually achieve cultural change—aim higher than what we are required to do. The DeGue report did identify some promising prevention programs, including the VAWA-mandated bystander trainings. More critically, it recognized "'principles of prevention' that were strongly associated with positive effects across multiple literatures" (DeGue et al. 2014, 356). From this, we have a blueprint to create prevention programs that have the ability to truly prevent sexual violence: take one of these promising programs; evaluate it using the rubric of the nine principles, and enhance areas of need; establish behavioral outcomes; and then create rigorous evaluation methods to determine if your program is creating the behavioral change that you are aiming to achieve. Scientific research is rarely in a Title IX coordinator's skill set; however, your faculty is an incredible resource to assist in evaluation and assessment. Find professors who already engage in sexual violence research or encourage junior faculty to take up this area of scholarship. I work closely with faculty in my university's College of Public Health to evaluate our programs, from measuring the impact of the freshman class's reading project on sexual violence to creating an assessment for the football team's training on consent. Not only am I using their expertise, but these collaborations make our school's efforts to address sexual violence something that encompasses the entire school: students, staff, faculty—we are all engaged. We are all change.

This encouragement might seem like a simple call to go above and beyond; as previously stated, the DCL (and VAWA) asks far less of us. Instead, it is quite likely our new normal, as a recent Title IX investigation finding from the DOJ into the University of New Mexico asserted a new standard for prevention programs. The DOJ said it consulted with prevention and training "experts" and also cited the CDC researchers' 2014 study of primary prevention programs in its review of New Mexico's training efforts (Simons and Martinez 2016, 12). While the Montana findings from 2013 articulated the necessary components of training programs for members of the community, the DOJ now expects schools to demonstrate that these trainings comport with the best practices in the prevention field, in which prevention trainings and educational programs "emphasize interaction with participants and use of current case examples" to understand the definitions of sexual violence (Simons and Martinez 2016, 12). With regard to bystander intervention programs, "prevention requires a comprehensive program that teaches knowledge and skills and provides the target audience with opportunities to practice" (Simons and Martinez 2016, 12). Regardless of what type of program one employs, the DOJ stresses that evaluation is essential, as it is the only way to ensure that the programs are effecting change.

In these findings, the DOJ made clear that providing education is not sufficient; schools need to rigorously educate and demonstrate behavioral change in order to be compliant with Title IX. From a prevention standpoint, this is an incredibly welcome message. Of course, our prevention programs should effectively prevent sexual violence; their purpose is in their very definition. But this was not what New Mexico was asked to do; the training programs that the school put in place were in compliance with the directives of the DCL. In applying new criteria to New Mexico's programs—good criteria, yes, but part of a completely different standard—the DOJ changed what it takes to be compliant.

To do Title IX compliance work oftentimes feels like you are trying to hit a moving target—and that sometimes your best aim directs the arrow back at you. Recall the Southern Methodist investigation findings: doing everything that was asked was not enough. What will happen if the OCR begins to evaluate our prevention programs in the same way? There are online programs available from external vendors, like Haven, EverFi, and Third Millennium, among countless others; they are constructed to ensure compliance with every *should* and *must* in the DCL as well as VAWA, easily providing education to hundreds—if not thousands—of students. Yet the CDC's inspection of 140 primary prevention strategies around sexual violence only found that three effectuated behavioral change, two of which were targeted toward precollege students (DeGue et al. 2014). Schools may, in good faith, implement prevention programs only to be found in noncompliance because the change it effects is not profound enough. Are online programs interactive enough? Do they provide enough opportunity for practice? I have yet to meet a university administrator who does not want to do the right thing; the dilemma is that we define what is right as being what is required.

Our frantic chase for compliance reflects the government's disjointed chase for solutions. The DCL was a response to the disciplinary problems raised in the Center's report. The OCR's increasingly critical investigation findings from the DCL forward are a response to the mounting number of complaints. The New Mexico findings are a response to the CDC research on what makes effective prevention programs. It is creating a contradictory patchwork of requirements that seems to bring us no closer to what Title IX asks: to eliminate sexual violence. Wooten and Mitchell (2015) note that this is a function of attempting to find a resolution that will solve a problem we have yet to fully understand—asking what should we do without fully understanding why.

Why does sexual violence persist? Why do students not absorb the information we provide about reporting and resources on campus? Why do certain student groups have higher perpetration rates, and why have we not made any difference in those rates? Why is prevention treated like a lesser institutional effort than discipline? Why do investigations routinely take longer than sixty days? Why would a hearing board not expel someone for rape? Why would a victim refuse to go through the disciplinary process if we mandated expulsion? Why do students take responsibility for violating every behavior prohibited in our Code of Student Conduct—except sexual violence? Why do respondents continually feel like our process is denying them due process? Why do my students, my colleagues, and my campus need Title IX?

These are my questions; they defy compliance. They dig into the very heart of *why Title IX*, and every answer should shape the work that I do. Too often, I catch myself asking, "What does the OCR want? What would the OCR think?" An anonymous administrator wrote an open letter to the OCR in *Inside Higher Education* (Anonymous 2011): "And my fear—yes, it's fear— of seeing my institution's name in *Inside Higher Ed* or the *Chronicle of Higher Education* as the subject of an investigation . . . makes me toe the line in a way I sometimes have trouble justifying to myself" (para. 21). For me, I worry that I am not toeing the *right* line. In focusing on the *what* of compliance in order to satisfy the OCR, I can lose sight of the *why*: doing what is best for victims and our campuses.

Compliance has a strong gravity, and if we are not careful, it can propel us in our work. In response to this, I created a rubric through which I evaluate my decisions on Title IX. My first question cannot be driven by compliance; it must have its roots in the why. I begin with: "Will this do right by my student?" and/or "Will this do right by my community?" I reflect on the *why Title IX?* to eliminate sexual violence, to prevent its recurrence, to remediate its effects. If I can answer yes, then I ask, "Does this comply with the OCR guidance?" If that answer is no, then I start over—but I find that starting with what is right almost always leads me to what is required.

The DCL starts a chase that can corral our thinking to be only about response—responding to reports, investigating reports, adjudicating reports. It does not allow us to contemplate an approach to Title IX that puts equal weight on preventing those incidents, preventing a report from even being filed. Yet I find that my rubric draws me there naturally: anything we do that prevents another act of sexual violence in this community is the right thing. It is the difference between doing trainings and doing trainings that create change. This is where our work from Title IX should—must—start.

NOTE

1. The *Chronicle of Higher Education* has created a database with all Title IX sexual assault complaints that are referred to and referenced in this chapter: Title IX: Tracking Sexual Assault Investigations. 2016. *Chronicle of Higher Education.* Available at http://projects.chronicle.com/titleix/.

REFERENCES

Anonymous. 2011. An open letter to OCR. *Inside Higher Education*, October 28. Available at https://www.insidehighered.com/views/2011/10/28/essay-ocr-guidelines-sexual-assault-hurt-colleges-and-students.

Bhargava, A., and G. Jackson. 2013. *Re: DOJ Case No. DJ 169-44-9, OCR Case No. 10126001.* Civil Rights Division and the Office for Civil Rights, May 9. Washington, DC: Department of Justice and Department of Education. Available at https://www.justice.gov/sites/default/files/opa/legacy/2013/05/09/um-ltr-findings.pdf.

Cantalupo, N. C. 2012. Decriminalizing campus institutional responses to peer sexual violence. *Journal of College and University Law* 38: 481.

———. 2016. For the Title IX civil rights movement: Congratulations and cautions. *Yale Law Journal Forum*, February 19, 281–303.

Carroll, C. M., M. G. Dahlgren, K. L. Grab, M. E. Hasbun, M. A. Hayes, and S. E. Muntis. 2013. Implementing the Dear Colleague Letter: A Title IX case study for university compliance. *Journal of the Student Personnel Association at Indiana University*, 45–63.

CLC Staff. 2016. *Cracking down: What to expect from a tougher OCR.* Available at http://www.campuslawconsidered.com/cracking-down-what-to-expect-from-a-tougher-ocr.

Davis v. Monroe County Board of Education. 1999. 526 U.S. 629.

DeGue, S., L. A. Valle, M. K. Holt, G. M. Massetti, J. L. Matjasko, and A. T. Tharp. 2014. A systematic review of primary prevention strategies for sexual violence perpetration. *Aggression and Violent Behavior* 19 (4): 346–362.

Foerster, A., and G. Hage. 2011. *It's beyond athletics: New efforts to push the frontiers of Title IX liability for sexual misconduct.* NACUA Virtual Seminar, June 26–29. Available at http://www.higheredcompliance.org/resources/publications/x-11-06-3.doc.

Gersen, J. E., and J. Suk. 2016. The sex bureaucracy. *California Law Review* 104: 881–949.

Henrick, S. 2013. A hostile environment for student defendants: Title IX and sexual assault on college campuses. *Northern Kentucky Law Review* 40: 1–44.

Jones, K. 2010. *Lax enforcement of Title IX in campus sexual assault cases.* Available at https://www.publicintegrity.org/2010/02/25/4374/lax-enforcement-title-ix-campus-sexual-assault-cases-0.

Koss, M. P., J. Wilgus, and K. M. Williamsen. 2014. Campus sexual misconduct: Restorative justice approaches to enhance compliance with Title IX guidance. *Trauma, Violence, and Abuse* 15: 242–258.

Krakauer, J. 2015. *Missoula: Rape and the justice system in a college town.* New York: Doubleday.

Lewis, W. S., S. K. Schuster, B. A. Sokolow, and D. C. Swinton. 2013. *The top ten things we need to know about Title IX (that the DCL didn't tell us), the 2013 Whitepaper.* Available at https://www.ncherm.org/wordpress/wp-content/uploads/2012/01/2013-NCHERM-Whitepaper-FINAL-1.18.13.pdf.

Lombardi, K. 2010. *A lack of consequences for sexual assault.* Available at https://www.publicintegrity.org/2010/02/24/4360/lack-consequences-sexual-assault.

Lombardi, K., and K. Jones. 2009. *Campus sexual assault statistics don't add up.* Available at https://www.publicintegrity.org/2009/12/02/9045/campus-sexual-assault-statistics-don-t-add.

Mangan, K. 2016. A closer look at 7 common requirements in resolved federal sex-assault inquiries. *Chronicle of Higher Education*, February 8. Available at http://chronicle.com/article/A-Closer-Look-at-7-Common/235220.

New, J. 2014a. Expulsion presumed. *Inside Higher Education*, June 27. Available at https://www.insidehighered.com/news/2014/06/27/should-expulsion-be-default-discipline-policy-students-accused-sexual-assault.

———. 2014b. Zero tolerance of what? *Inside Higher Education*, November 26. Available at https://www.insidehighered.com/news/2014/11/26/u-virginia-board-adopts-policy-show-it-getting-tough-sexual-assault-policy-lacks.

———. 2016. Must v. should. *Inside Higher Education*, February 25. Available at https://www.insidehighered.com/news/2016/02/25/colleges-frustrated-lack-clarification-title-ix-guidance.

Newman, J., and L. Sander. 2014. Promise unfulfilled? *Chronicle of Higher Education*, April 30. Available at http://chronicle.com/article/Promise-Unfulfilled-/146299/.

Shapiro, J. 2010. *Seeking justice for campus rapes.* Available at http://www.npr.org/series/124073905/seeking-justice-for-campus-rapes.

Simons, S., and D. Martinez. 2016. Title IX and Title IV Investigation of University of New Mexico. Letter to President Robert G. Frank, Office of the President, University of New Mexico, April 22. Available at https://www.justice.gov/crt/file/843926/download.

Talbert, K. 2015. Behind the scenes: A closer look at the Title IX resolution letters and agreements of 2014. *National Association of College and University Attorneys: NACUA Notes* 14 (2). Available at http://counsel.cua.edu/fedlaw/nacuanotebehindthescenestitleix.cfm.

U.S. Department of Education. 1979. *Nondiscrimination on the basis of sex in education programs or activities receiving federal financial assistance.* 34 C.F.R. Sec. 106.1. Available at https://www2.ed.gov/policy/rights/reg/ocr/edlite-34cfr106.html.

——. 2014. *U.S. Department of Education releases list of higher education institutions with open Title IX sexual violence investigations.* Press release, May 1. Available at http://www.ed.gov/news/press-releases/us-department-education-releases-list-higher-education-institutions-open-title-i.

U. S. Department of Education, Office for Civil Rights. 1997. Sexual harassment guidance 1997. Available at http://www2.ed.gov/about/offices/list/ocr/docs/sexhar00.html.

——. 2001. Revised sexual harassment guidance: Harassment of students by school employees, other students, or third parties. Available at https://www.atixa.org/wordpress/wp-content/uploads/2012/01/OCR-2001-Revised-Sexual-Harassment-Guidance-Title-IX.pdf.

——. 2011. *Dear Colleague Letter.* Available at http://www2.ed.gov/about/offices/list/ocr/letters/colleague-201104.pdf.

U.S. Department of Justice. 2012. *Justice Department announces investigations of the handling of sexual assault allegations by the University of Montana, the Missoula, Mont., Police Department and the Missoula County Attorney's Office.* Press release, May 1. Available at https://www.justice.gov/opa/pr/justice-department-announces-investigations-handling-sexual-assault-allegations-university.

U.S. Senate Committee on Health, Education, Labor, and Pensions. 2014. *Sexual assault on campus: Working to ensure student safety.* Full committee hearing, June 26. 113th Congress. (Testimony of Catherine Lhamon). Available at http://www.help.senate.gov/hearings/sexual-assault-on-campus-working-to-ensure-student-safety.

Wontorcik, S. 2016. UNL is still being investigated for potential Title IX violations. What does that mean? *Daily Nebraskan*, April 25. Available at http://www.dailynebraskan.com/news/unl-is-still-being-investigated-for-potential-title-ix-violations/article_89707bde-0a9b-11e6-ad5c-3f8014772cd5.html.

Wooten, S. C., and R. W. Mitchell. 2015. *The crisis of campus sexual violence: Critical perspectives on prevention and response.* New York: Routledge.

18

Managing the Backlash

HELEN EIGENBERG,
STEPHANIE BONNES,
AND JOANNE BELKNAP

A s already noted in this book, there have been significant national and legal challenges associated with the role of the federal government and federally mandated requirements to address campus rape (i.e., through the Clery Act, various Title IX Department of Education [DOE] mandates issued by the Office for Civil Rights [OCR], and provisions outlined in the Campus Sexual Assault Violence Elimination [SaVE] Act). Pressure from federal regulations, the increasing risk of lawsuits (by both victims and accused perpetrators), heightened public attention (such as that which was garnered by *The Hunting Ground* film), and student activism are resulting in new, unprecedented changes in institutions of higher education (IHE) nationwide. Concomitantly, these changes have reinvigorated backlash efforts that were prevalent in the 1980s and 1990s. These early backlash critics misrepresented the research, made inaccurate claims, and often presented findings out of context. Briefly, and as this chapter describes, the backlash critics questioned the validity of the sound scientific research documenting the "one in four" rate of college sexual assault among women, and the Title IX requirements for IHE to address sexual assaults more seriously and formally resulted in both anti-victim and pro-defendant backlash outcomes. These backlash critics rarely addressed the complexity of the issues they purported to know so much about. In addition, they also questioned the feminist motivations of scholars who conducted the research. Instead of having honest debates about social science methodology and the overall veracity of the findings, backlash critics denied the legitimacy of the research (and researchers), even though most of them had little or no training in social science methods and had never collected original data themselves (Kanin and Parcell 1977; Schwartz 1997). Poignantly, these vitriolic responses advanced their careers immeasurably.

Recent backlash critics use many of the tactics employed by their predecessors thirty years ago. They, like those before them, attempt to minimize the extent of the problem, redefine rape in ways that are consistent with rape mythology, challenge procedural and legal responses to rape on campuses, and "blame" feminists for the ways that overzealous officials are responding to this issue. They also argue that IHE are not equipped to address sexual assault, and that they are acting in overzealous ways to unfairly find perpetrators responsible using procedures that offer insufficient due process protections. This chapter provides an overview of both historical and contemporary backlash efforts to demonstrate common themes. It also illustrates how newer backlash efforts continue the tradition of minimizing the extent of rape on campus, while also adding new arguments that challenge the legitimacy of recent reform efforts to hold IHE accountable for responding to the epidemic of rape on campus.

Historical Accounts of Backlash

One of the primary contributions of the second wave of the feminist movement is the recognition that gender-based abuses (i.e., sexual abuse and intimate partner abuse) are widespread, and that these offenses against women and girls are far more likely to be perpetrated by men/boys who are acquaintances or otherwise known to the victims (including family and romantic partners) than by strangers (see Belknap 2015 for a review).[1] As Callie Marie Rennison, Catherine Kaukinen, and Caitlyn Meade ably document in Chapter 2 of this book, a significant body of research consistently has documented that about "1 in 5" college women reports experiencing an attempted or completed sexual assault, and many studies put this figure closer to "1 in 4." This body of literature has been accumulating for almost fifty years (beginning with Kanin 1957; and Kirkpatrick and Kanin 1957) and produces estimates with little substantive variation. In other words, the fundamental findings about the epidemic nature of sexual abuse committed by acquaintances is not, or should not be, viewed as a new revelation. While it is clear that differences in sampling, methods, and operationalization of rape have produced some variation in findings, it is quite remarkable that there is so much consistency in the findings. This remarkable consistency and the "science" behind these findings make it even more perplexing as to why there continues to be a "debate" about the nature and extent of campus rape.

The earliest study to establish a high victimization rate on college campuses was in 1957. Clifford Kirkpatrick and Eugene Kanin (1957) published an article entitled "Male Sex Aggression on a University Campus" in the prestigious journal the *American Sociological Review.* Their study reported that 56 percent of the women reported 1,022 "offensive episodes" of unwanted "erotic intimacy" (including necking, petting above the waist, petting below the waist, attempted intercourse, and attempted intercourse with violence). They found 20.9 percent of the women were offended by attempts at intercourse and 6.2 percent experienced forceful attempts of intercourse where menacing threats or coercive infliction of physical pain were used (or 27.1 percent in total; Kirkpatrick and Kanin 1957, 53). The authors also reported that almost 69.9 percent of these incidents involved perpetrators who had a significant relationship with the victims (e.g., steady dates or engaged, 55)—what we now commonly refer to as "date rape." Kanin (1957) published another similar study in the prestigious *American Journal of Sociology,* this time concentrating on the experiences of seniors in high school. He found a similar rate to his earlier study; 29.5 percent of respondents experienced coerced sexual intercourse or intercourse with violence (198), and 86.2 percent of these acts involved a perpetrator who had a significant relationship with the victim (200).[2] Kanin also reported that 48.1 percent of these incidents of intercourse were not preceded by any voluntary erotic activity on the part of the woman. This study also refuted the idea that date rape generally was miscommunication, where the victim leads the perpetrator on by participating in initial sexual activities. This research experienced backlash challenges to the accuracy of the data and claims of exaggerated risk by those who doubted the veracity of the findings. According to Walter DeKeseredy, a prominent scholar on gender-based abuse, Eugene Kanin faced considerable backlash because critics claimed he fabricated or misrepresented these data, and the editor of the *American Journal of Sociology* also received criticism for publishing Kanin's work (W. DeKeseredy, personal communication, May 21, 2016).

Moving forward three decades, Mary Koss and her colleagues (Koss 1985; Koss, Gidycz, and Wisniewski 1987) published their landmark study, which reported that 27.5 percent of college women stated experiencing attempted or completed rapes. This research also reported that most assaults were perpetrated by acquaintances and/or dates, and coined the term unacknowledged victim to represent rape victims who experienced acts that would legally constitute rape without viewing or labeling themselves as such. Backlash critics especially latched on to this finding and argued that rape estimates were inflated using overly broad definitions of rape that included acts of "bad sex" (Hoff Sommers 1994; Roiphe 1993). This element of the research was useful to backlash critics because some victims did, in fact, label their experiences as "bad sex" or "miscommunication." *That does not mitigate the fact that they also experienced a sexual assault according to the legal definition of rape.* Understanding why survivors fail to label their experiences as rape is a highly complex issue, but backlash critics have not been interested in this subject since it does not fit their definition of reality. Three highly visible backlash critics of the 1990s demonstrate these points: Neil Gilbert, Katie Roiphe, and Christina Hoff Sommers.

Neil Gilbert, a professor of social welfare at the University of California-Berkley, was one of the most prolific critics (1992, 1994, 2005). His initial backlash article, entitled "The Phantom Epidemic of Sexual Assault" (1991), revealed the foundations for his claims. He used three major tactics: first, he refuted the statistics on rape victimization rates by repeatedly comparing prevalence rates (e.g., in Koss's study) to incident rates from official statistics, especially the (then titled) National Crime Survey (NCS). He ignored the fact that one cannot compare lifetime prevalence rates with twelve-month incident rates, and he failed to acknowledge the serious weaknesses inherent in the NCS methodology at the time (Koss 1992; Russell and Bolen 2000). At the time, the NCS did not directly ask respondents if they were raped, which led to gross underestimations of rape (Eigenberg 1990; Koss 1996). Second, he tried to minimize victimization rates by challenging the idea of unacknowledged victims. For example, Gilbert (1998) stated that there was "a notable discrepancy" between Koss's definition of rape and "the way most women she labeled as victims interpreted their experiences. When asked directly, 73% of the students whom Koss categorized as victims of rape did not think that they had been raped" (356). This statement is a serious misrepresentation; Koss (1996) reported that 73 percent of the students who experienced behaviors constituting the *legal* definition of rape did not *label* their experiences as rape. Gilbert's argument is akin to saying that a victim of robbery must know they were robbed and not burglarized in order to count it as such in a survey, even if the victim reported that someone took possessions from them by force. Third, Gilbert accused "radical feminists" of imposing "new norms governing the intimacy between the sexes" (1991, 59), and indoctrinating women to believe that their consensual sex was rape. He equated unacknowledged rape as bad and/or regretted sex. For example, he argued that "advocacy numbers on sexual assault may resonate with their feelings of being, not literally raped, but figuratively 'screwed over' by men. If this is the case, it will require more than objective analysis to dispel the phantom epidemic of sexual assault" (1991, 65). Gilbert's critiques were widely published and cited in the popular press, though he had never collected any data and had no history of substantive research in the field, nor had he published any of his articles in any scholarly, peer-reviewed journal (Russell and Bolen 2000; Schwartz 1997). Currently, Gilbert has an endowed chair as the Chernin professor at the School of Social Welfare at UC-Berkeley and is the codirector of the Center for Child and Youth Policy.

Katie Roiphe, a young, White, woman journalist who had a master's in English at the time, echoed Gilbert's arguments in her 1993 book, *The Morning After: Sex, Fear, and Feminism*. While the book did not offer any substantively new arguments, as a young woman and self-proclaimed feminist who presented these arguments as part of a feminist "debate," she became a media favorite and was featured in periodicals such as the *New York Times* and on numerous television talk shows. More specifically, the feminist debate was Roiphe portraying the "one in four" risk for sexual assault as taking away sexual agency from college women by defining acts as rape that by Roiphe's view were not rape, while the feminist scholars conducting the research (primarily Mary Koss) and their supporters insisted that the self-reported sexual victimizations were consistently and accurately at the "one in four" rate. As Schwartz (1997) noted about Roiphe, "this particular expert was a young graduate student in literature who had never held a job, had never done research, and had made no claim to have interviewed any women except her own personal friends at Harvard and Princeton" (xii). Leveen (1996, 627) describes the irony in how Roiphe "constructs herself as a victim" of the feminists who document IHE rape and how Roiphe's "own trope of victimization succeeded so well that the mainstream press heralded her as one of the leading feminist thinkers of her generation" (626–627). Despite the massive misrepresentations and the unsophisticated understanding of basic research methodology (which is not surprising since she had no training or education in this area), Roiphe's conclusion that rape estimates of college women were "a matter of opinion, not a matter of mathematical fact" (1993, 54) was accepted as "truth." Roiphe went on to earn a doctorate in English literature, has authored other books, and is a contributor to such mainstream media as the *New York Times, Washington Post,* and the *New Yorker.*

Christina Hoff Sommers is another critic who joined the backlash. She has a Ph.D. in philosophy from Brandeis, and thus had academic credentials to legitimize her claims. She argued that there was a feminist conspiracy to inflate rape estimates in her book, *Who Stole Feminism? How Women Have Betrayed Women* (1994). Her work claimed that flawed and biased academic studies were used to overemphasize women's victimization, while they portrayed an overly negative view of men that fundamentally threatened gender relations in society. She contended that "most of the victim statistics are, at best, misleading—at worst, completely inaccurate" (9). She argued that feminist scholars engaged in "victim feminism," using anecdotes and/or folktales to exaggerate rates of gender-based violence. Ironically, she presents herself as a victim of the mainstream feminist establishments for her "heresies" (3), and concludes that it is her "bias toward logic, reason, and fairness that has put [her] at odds with the feminist establishment" (Hoff Sommers 2008, 4). She is a persistent critic of women's studies programs and argues that feminists are using flawed scholarship (and a reckless disregard for the truth) to advance a liberal agenda. Despite her claims of objectivity, her biases are evident in many statements such as this one: "There are a lot of homely women in women's studies. Preaching these anti-male, anti-sex sermons is a way for them to compensate for various heartaches—they're just mad at the beautiful girls" (Friend 1994, 48). Hoff Sommers currently is a resident scholar at the American Enterprise Institute; she has published several books, has appeared on numerous television programs including *Nightline, 60 Minutes,* and the *Oprah Winfrey Show,* and has been featured in articles in the *Wall Street Journal,* the *New York Times,* and the *Washington Post.*

Contemporary Backlash Efforts

Lest one think that these previous examples of backlash represent ancient history, an examination of contemporary backlash efforts demonstrates that many of the same themes continue: (1) that the statistics are wrong because feminists have exaggerated claims using overly broad definitions of rape that include acts of miscommunication often involving intoxicated parties (or "bad sex"); (2) that campus rape cases should be processed by the criminal legal system, which is better suited to deal with "real rape" than are IHE; and (3) federally mandated changes are resulting in unfair treatment of accused perpetrators who are too often presumed to be guilty and who lack adequate protection from charges of rape. The first of these mirrors previous backlash critics and rarely adds new information to claims about false epidemics. Ironically, these backlash critics are ahistorical and fail to note the links between current criticisms of newer data sources, despite using the same arguments. What is new about the current backlash is the extent to which critics are focused on the ways IHE deal with sexual assault cases, in part because of new regulations, but also because there are finally efforts to address the problem. Older backlash arguments had no need to address the ways IHE dealt with sexual assault because there was no response to critique.

The Statistics Are Wrong and Based on Overly
Broad Definitions of Rape

Current backlash critics, like those who came before, generally begin with the data. This "debate" frames critical foundations on both sides of the issue. Those who support a need for substantive change and major regulatory guidance do so in part because of the high rates of victimization as documented by the research. They also point to the low levels of cases reported, processed, and adjudicated as evidence that IHE are not responsive and rape victims do not receive the accommodations or justice they deserve, and that perpetrators are not held accountable so that they are free to revictimize others. Opponents need to undermine the estimates in order to dismantle the argument that there is a need for institutional change based on widespread victimization (the epidemic), and then they can move on to attack the legitimacy of the OCR 2011 Dear Colleague Letter (DCL) and other measures that are used to secure compliance. As in the past, critics use misrepresentation and distortions of the science to make their case that rape, in fact, is not as bad as feminists would have one believe.

Current backlash critics use an ahistorical approach to argue that the OCR uses flawed data to justify its current mandates by citing criticisms of more recent studies (Fisher, Cullen, and Turner 2000; Krebs et al. 2007), while ignoring that the data are part of a body of literature that has been developing for decades. For example, in a commentary for the *Chronicle of Higher Education*, Hoff Sommers (2011) continues her thirty-year-old arguments and applies them to newer empirical studies. She uses the same methodologically flawed argument as she did in prior critiques to compare National Crime Victimization Survey data and incident rates to dispute more recently published prevalence rates. She argues that "the researchers— not the women themselves—decided whether they had been assaulted" (para. 13). This description refers to unacknowledged victims, but Hoff Sommers fails to provide any explanation of this issue. She also casts doubt on the legitimacy of the Krebs et al. (2007) study by stating that there is a disclaimer on "every page of the survey report, advising that it is not a publication of the Justice Department [DOJ] and does not necessarily reflect its positions or policies" (para. 15). She omits that this is a standard disclaimer on publications funded but not written by the DOJ. Her half-truths and misrepresentations are disturbing in that they have not changed over the years despite explanations of her faulty methodological critiques, but one also might hope for a less superficial analysis with some nuance when publishing in a venue that generally is read only by academics.

These arguments are echoed also by Barclay Hendrix (2013), who suggests that reports of the "crisis-level epidemic" have put "pressure on campus officials to clamp down on sexual misconduct as a means of addressing the *perceived crisis*" (595, emphasis added). She also fails to acknowledge the historical consistency in IHE sexual assault estimates, and reports that "ambiguous survey questions have greatly exaggerated the prevalence of sexual assaults" (597). In addition to using arguments that (unacknowledged) victims fail to report they were raped, she challenges the operationalization of sexual assault in the study by Krebs and his colleagues (2007), in part because this study is specifically cited in OCR reports calling for action. Hendrix (2013, 598) states that this "dubious" research exaggerated the amount of rape by including "forced kissing" and "attempted forced kissing"

(596–597).[3] This statement is distorted, lacks context, and omits important details. In fact, the study included sexual battery, which was defined as assaults involving sexual contact only [as opposed to assaults that involved oral, vaginal, or anal penetration], such as *forced kissing or forced fondling* (Krebs et al. 2007, 3–14, emphasis added). These acts amounted to only 1.4 percent of sexual assaults accomplished by physical force and 2.6 percent of incapacitated sexual assaults (5–2). These acts are illegal according to most (if not all) state statutes, and there is no indication that attempted forced kissing was included in their victimization rates.[4] This is a prime example of how backlash critics often fail to provide sufficient detail and context when identifying and discussing methodological "shortcomings." Such inaccurate reporting may be intentional *or* simply represent a lack of training, but either way it distorts the overall reality of rape in IHE. Hendrix has a J.D., practices in a private law firm, and apparently has no postgraduate education in social science methods (Hendrix n.d.).

Other backlash critics focus on incapacitated rape. Hendrix (2013), for example, argues that estimates established in the Krebs et al. (2007) study are flawed because they included "sexual contact with someone when they were unable to give consent because of intoxication or incapacity" (597). She argues that the questions likely had many "gray areas" because they were worded in a way that may have included impaired judgment instead of incapacitation. Or, as Hoff Sommers (2011) puts it, if respondents stated they were "unable to give consent because they were drunk" the study automatically counted it as rape or assault (para. 13). She goes on to state that "if sexual intimacy under the influence of alcohol is by definition assault, then a significant percentage of sexual intercourse throughout the world and down the ages qualifies as crime" (para. 14). In fact, the Krebs et al. (2007) study goes to great lengths to discuss the complexity of constructing this survey item (see, e.g., 1–5). Furthermore, the actual question asks "if someone had sexual contact with you when you were unable to provide consent or stop what was happening because you were passed out, drugged, drunk, incapacitated, or asleep" (A-1). *Incapacitated rape is a crime when victims are incapable of giving consent.* Clearly, being "drunk" does not in and of itself constitute incapacitated sexual assault; however, flippant statements such as those by Hoff Sommers dismiss the complexity of the issue and minimize the frequent nature of these types of sexual assaults.

Backlash critics often present their critiques as neutral, rational, and fair compared to feminists who have an "agenda" and therefore are biased, value-laden researchers who cannot be trusted. For example, French argues that IHE are "in the grip of a feminist-driven hysteria, with university campuses inaccurately portrayed as among America's most dangerous places for young women" (French 2015, para. 6). Young (2015) argues that campus policies, DOE actions, and the White House efforts to address campus rape are "rooted in feminist dogma" (44). Iannone (2015) remarks that "these figures were hotly disputed" because the definition of assault seemingly included "less defined categories of behavior such as abuse, coercion, harassment, misconduct, and victimization," where even an "unwelcome hug at a party" could qualify as rape based on the research definitions (7). Some critics simply dismiss the science altogether. Williamson (2015) notes in his online article for the *National Review*:

> There is no epidemic of rapes on American college campuses. And *Rolling Stone* cannot make that true, nor can 1,000 or 10,000 or 100,000 student activists, bloggers, administrators, compliant law-enforcement agencies, feminist scholars, or *New York Times* columns.

This type of statement clearly is not part of a methodological, empirical debate, but evidence of an ideological war. Ironically, only feminists appear to need to substantiate their claims using science.

Part of the problem when trying to confront this backlash is that claims are often presented by an uncritical media that is ill-prepared to engage in a substantive and methodological debate. Moreover, if these debates are reduced to "cat fights" between warring women representing postfeminists, new feminists, do-me feminists, and antifeminist feminists, all the better (Hammer 2000).[5] Issues such as operationalization of variables, behaviorally grounded screening questions, and differences between incident and prevalence rates are not amenable to sixty-second sound bites or even more-detailed op-eds. As a result, the media often leaves one with the impression that "feminist" studies find drastically higher rates because of overly broad and loose definitions of rape. Rarely, if ever, does media coverage examine the issue in sufficient depth to explain how methodological differences, rather than ideological ones, account for discrepancies in the findings. *Ironically then, feminists are charged with ideological bias even when their positions are, more often than not, grounded in social science and empirical data. In contrast, opponents of recent reforms on college campuses are not required to present data to back up their ideological claims.* This has not prevented them from presenting a whole host of arguments about why Title IX in general, and campus disciplinary procedures specifically, should not be used as a means to address sexual assault.

Title IX Is an Inappropriate Vehicle to Address Sexual Assault

These arguments are lengthy and complex, but they generally assert that Title IX was not written or designed to address sexual assault and that the federal government, especially the OCR, has no business dictating how IHE should respond to campus rape. They contend that the OCR has overreached—reforms have *gone too far* and given undue power to universities who are ill-equipped to deal with these cases. They also contend that IHE are afraid *not* to find perpetrators responsible (guilty) because they fear lawsuits or OCR action. Three notable cases are often presented and used to argue that the risk of lawsuits and the large monetary awards that accompanied them have caused university officials to err on the side of the victim. They rarely discuss that all three of the successful (and expensive) lawsuits involved egregious actions by the universities who failed to take action to protect victims.[6] Despite the rarity of these lawsuits, these three cases are used as evidence of "disastrous consequences" and this "knowledge hangs like a Sword of Damocles over risk-adverse administrators" (Henrick 2013, 75).

Critics also argue that IHE have been pressured to find perpetrators responsible because the 2011 DCL threatened loss of federal funding as a consequence of noncompliance. Ignoring the fact that the OCR has *never* taken away federal funding from an institution of higher education (Anderson 2016), there is little evidence that IHE are unduly afraid of OCR sanctions. The abysmal history of Title IX compliance and the fact that the OCR has received 295 complaints since 2011 (Title IX 2016), suggests *a long pattern of inaction rather than overreaction*. Moreover, evidence demonstrates that IHE historically have failed to comply with various legislative and regulatory requirements. In fact, almost a decade after Clery requirements were mandated, a comprehensive national study found that compliance was marginal, training was unlikely (especially for students and faculty), victim support services were lacking, and underreporting was a serious problem (Karjane, Fisher, and Cullen 2002). And almost twenty-five years after Clery requirements were legislated, another study found that 41 percent of schools had not conducted a single sexual assault investigation in the five years prior to the study, and that 21 percent of the forty largest private institutions and 6 percent of the largest public schools had conducted fewer investigations than their Clery data indicated (U.S. Senate Subcommittee 2014). In other words, these IHE apparently had failed to conduct investigations even though their own records demonstrated official reports of sexual assault. Similarly, recent analyses indicate that between 20 and 30 percent of universities either lack policies on sexual assault or, if they have them, have not posted them to their websites (Englander, McCoy, and Sherman 2015; Krivoshey et al. 2013; Lund and Thomas 2015), despite the fact that IHE have been required to develop and disseminate policies for decades now. Ultimately, whether or not universities are overreacting to OCR mandates is an empirical question that could be answered if universities were more transparent about their disciplinary processes—if they were required to report information about the number of cases filed, adjudicated, and types of sanctions imposed.

Thus, IHE are portrayed as incapable of fair judgment because of their fear of the OCR. At the same time, critics also argue that universities are not equipped to handle sexual assault cases, and that they are best left to the "experts" in the criminal legal system who can provide the "professionalism and impartiality" that is required (Henrick 2013, 3). Carle (2015) asserts that "sexual misconduct tribunals" are "conducted in secret, by amateurs, in emotionally charged settings" (12). Or, as Johnson (2015) notes, "imagine the absurdity of a college president, dean, or prominent law professor implying that students who are victims of attempted murder or felony assault should rely on the college disciplinary process to handle the problem" (28). This sensational argument itself is absurd. If a student is facing these types of serious charges, it would seem critical that university officials immediately respond by removing a dangerous person from campus if there is evidence to support the decision and if the police have failed to act or have not yet acted. In fact, this has happened in a Pennsylvania case, where a student was murdered and the prosecutor failed to file charges for two years (see Anderson 2016). The idea that IHE should ignore felony assaults demonstrates a deep ignorance of interpersonal violence on college campuses. Title IX, in fact, requires universities to deal with intimate partner violence that may involve felony assault charges.

Arguments that the criminal legal processing system should be responsible for all sexual assault cases involving college students are deficient for several reasons. First, it is clear that the criminal legal system has failed to effectively respond to sexual assault cases. Underreporting is rampant because victims realistically worry about negative police responses (Anders and Christopher 2011) and attrition in rape cases is astoundingly high (Alderden and Ullman 2012). Second, even if the case is being addressed by the criminal legal system, this process is incredibly slow and likely offers no immediate assistance to survivors who are likely to graduate before the perpetrator would go to trial. Third, the most common types of campus rape (involving acquaintances, often with alcohol or drugs present, and incapacitated rape) are the same cases that prosecutors are loathe to take to trial (Tracy et al. 2012). Thus, the disciplinary process may be the only option for some victims when the criminal legal system will not address their cases. Fourth, some types of sexual misconduct that are prohibited by university policy (such as failure to secure affirmative consent) may not violate the criminal code, depending on state law. In these cases, university sanctions may be the only available option to survivors. Fifth, the student disciplinary process provides a venue for students who do not wish to use the criminal legal system because it does not meet their needs. Ironically, while backlash critics sometimes present victims as vindictive women seeking retribution, some of them just want university accommodations (such as changes in housing, class transfers, and other academic assistance) or to feel protected from additional victimization or retaliation from their perpetrators. These are actions the criminal legal system cannot provide. Lastly, under current law, victims have a right to pursue their education free from discrimination because of sexual assault. The goal of Title IX is to promote equality in education (Anderson 2016; Cantalupo 2016) and IHE are legally and morally bound to ensure that survivors are able to pursue their education.

Unfair Treatment of Accused Perpetrators

Critics of recent OCR changes also argue that due process rights for accused students have been compromised and that the pendulum has swung too far so that accused students are presumed guilty and the lack of procedural safeguards leaves them vulnerable to mere accusations of misconduct. French (2015), for example, claims that Title IX allows "persecution of anyone who contravenes feminist dogma" and notes that if you are a "dissenting professor or a male student," you might face legal proceedings so "bizarre, so opaque, and so unfair that you won't believe they could happen in the United States of America" (para. 1). In one particularly vitriolic article, the authors argue that accused perpetrators are "guilty until proven innocent" and that "almost all" IHE have been "forced" to "disregard due process in disciplinary proceedings when they involve allegations of sexual assault" (Taylor and Johnson 2015, para. 1). Moreover, they argue that these changes are having a "devastating impact . . . on the lives of dozens—almost certainly soon to be hundreds or thousands—of falsely accused students" (para. 1). Or, as Hoff Sommers (2011) argues, "being a victim of rape is uniquely horrific, but being accused of rape is not far behind. If the person is guilty, then the suffering is deserved. But what if he is innocent? To be found guilty of rape by a campus tribunal can mean both expulsion and a career-destroying black mark on your permanent record. Such occurrences could become routine" (para. 10). The two cases most often used to demonstrate this injustice are the 2006 Duke University lacrosse incident and, more recently, the University of Virginia gang rape falsely reported in *Rolling Stone*. Clearly, both of these cases involved huge misconduct on the part of a prosecutor and a reporter; however, these isolated events are often dwarfed by a more insidious narrative that is used to diminish the responsibility of accusers. Anderson (2016) calls this the "he had such a bright future" argument (1992). She illustrates how opponents of Title IX use this tactic to humanize the offenders in the media, portraying them as "college kids" and "good upstanding citizens"—descriptions that are coded for class and race privilege.[7] *Ultimately, whether or not recent changes in the ways IHE respond to sexual assault have resulted in unfair dispositions is an empirical question. Yet there is no evidence at this time that thousands of students are suffering at the hands of overzealous administrators.*

Other arguments used to supplant the idea that accused students are unfairly treated focus on due process issues. A full discussion of these claims is beyond the scope of this chapter. Critics argue that accused students are denied fundamental fairness because of limits on submitting statements, presenting witnesses, cross-examining witnesses, examining evidence, accessing counsel in hearings, receiving notice of outcomes, and appealing outcomes (Henrick 2013; Taylor and Johnson 2015). Critics especially assert that the change in burden of proof from clear and convincing to preponderance of the evidence is unfair to accused students, even though it is the legal standard used in most civil cases and the standard used by the U.S. military in cases of involuntary discharge (Triplett 2012). Probably the most significant change to current requirements imposed on IHE is that both the 2011 DCL and SaVE specify that if a procedure or process is allowed for one party, it must be granted to the other. In other words, both accused and accusing students must have the same access to whatever procedures are put in place. Critics (Henrick 2013; Ricketts 2015) also have opposed this requirement, although it is unclear why this change is so disturbing. This is not a zero-sum game where victims and accused perpetrators battle for the best advantage in the search for due process and justice. In fact, the best disciplinary systems ensure that students are treated fairly on both sides of the table by having clear policies that are fairly enforced.

Fundamental due process rights are of concern for both victims and accused perpetrators. Students have had basic due process rights guaranteed by the courts for quite some time, including notice of charges, a review of the evidence, a hearing, and the ability to present a defense in cases where they could be expelled or suspended (Dixson v. Alabama State Board of Education 1961; Goss v. Lopez 1975). The courts, however, repeatedly have rejected the notion that IHE must use due process standards similar to those in the criminal legal system (see Cantalupo 2012, 2014). The requirements of the criminal legal system are the wrong metric to use when evaluating due process in student disciplinary hearings. Further, there is currently no evidence that courts are going to drastically alter their approach to student disciplinary hearings. Granting due process rights in disciplinary procedures that parallel those in the criminal legal system is not only inappropriate but it would seem also unlikely. This type of a ruling potentially would affect all types of disciplinary infractions in universities, as well as primary and secondary schools.

Summary

There is no indication that issues surrounding Title IX and enforcement efforts will be going away anytime soon. It is important to place backlash efforts in historical context and attend to the damaging claims critics have made that seek to minimize the prevalance of rape; challenge definitions to minimize rape by acquaintances; portray incapacitated rape as "bad sex"; and identify the IHE changes under Title IX, such as the disciplinary hearings, as unfair and inappropriate. Backlash critics ignore social science because they have to; the nature of the data challenges every domain assumption they have about the nature and prevalence of rape. Backlash efforts are not new, and have often followed feminist efforts to redress inequality, such as the serious challenges to Title IX when significant changes were made with respect to collegiate athletics. Those who opposed change argued that women really did not want to play sports and that Title IX was ruining men's programs (Walton 2010). Indeed, backlash is a historical trend that occurs when women appear to make substantial gains in the pursuit of equal rights (Faludi 2009). The backlash efforts that are currently attacking the transformation of college campuses mirror past efforts to defeat progressive rape law reform, which sought to abolish procedural requirements that required corroboration and resistance (Anderson 2016). Current efforts in rape law reform continue to challenge the way that the legal system defines and addresses consent because "the criminal justice system continues to fail to address the most common form of rape: non-stranger rape without traditional force" (Anderson 2016, 1959). The fight over affirmative consent on campuses also reflects this issue. Such political battles deserve attention by advocates who wish to keep and advance current reforms in the legal system and on college campuses. Vigilance is important; state and federal legislation is pending (Richards and Kafonek 2016), and lawsuits continue to accumulate. Some of them represent efforts to turn back the clock on reform or would institute procedures that are hostile to survivors.

Historically, universities faced more liability for failing to address cases brought forth by survivors than they have for accused perpetrators. Court cases rarely have been successful when filed by accusers and damages have been virtually nonexistent (Cantalupo 2012). This situation may be changing. At the time of this writing, as many as fifty lawsuits have been filed by accused students and some have filed Title IX complaints themselves (Grimmett et al. 2015). *All systems are subject to abuse, and no doubt there are cases where accused students have been treated unfairly in ways that have caused them harm; however, failing to address sexual assault by rarely charging individuals with disciplinary infractions also is harmful.* While backlash critics lament the exceptional harm that even an accusation of sexual assault brings to the accused student, they often fail to examine the effects that assaults have on victims. Survivors experience declines in grades and academic performance, which can lead to losing financial aid and scholarships. They also are likely to take time off, transfer schools, or drop out (Bolger 2016; Jordan, Combs, and Smith 2014).

The problem is that we know too little about how disciplinary systems work, especially when interim or emergency sanctions are put in place pending a full hearing. Until IHE make this process more transparent so that there are data to analyze, arguments will continue to rely on anecdotes and court cases that are not representative of the day-to-day actions of conduct boards. It is possible that case law will ultimately develop that supports enhanced rights for accused students or that strikes down OCR provisions. In the meantime, there are established case law and OCR mandates that outline required actions for IHE. Universities are most at risk when: policies and procedures fail to follow OCR guidelines; they provide substantially fewer procedural rights for victims than accused students; they adopt a higher standard of proof than preponderance of the evidence; they lack clear timelines that result in prompt resolutions; and they have confusing and/or contradictory policies and procedures (Cantalupo 2014). Until there is *empirical evidence* that IHE are treating accused students in ways that are inconsistent with policies and the law, universities would do well to act in accordance with proscribed requirements, in large part *because the science* has demonstrated that there is a tendency to ignore both the extent of sexual assault on campuses and the myriad of ways that IHE have failed to use effective institutional responses. Mary Koss (2011) recently reflected on a personal experience, where a discussant years ago responded to her research presentation by asking: "What is it going to take to convince you people?" (353). Indeed.

NOTES

1. Consistent with Belknap and Sharma (2014), we use the term abuse instead of violence, given that many of the gender-based abuses experienced by college women are not "violent" per se, such as many of the incapacitated and other coerced rapes and attempted rapes, although they are certainly very *violating* and can be equally harmful. The nonviolent aspect of these sexual abuses is what keeps some victims from labeling them rapes or attempted rapes.

2. These findings were replicated two decades later by Kanin as well, when he reported a rate of 26.5 percent (Kanin and Parcell 1977).

3. This argument also is repeated by Hoff Sommers (2011).

4. We were unable to locate any data in the report that specifically described the act of sexual battery, probably because there were so few cases.

5. For an explanation of "do-me" feminists, see Leveen (1996).

6. These cases are *Simpson v. University of Colorado, J. K. v. Arizona Board of Regents*, and *Williams v. Georgia*. Florida State University recently settled a highly publicized lawsuit involving Jameis Winston for $950,000 (Tracy 2016). Most recently, the University of Tennessee also settled a case involving the athletic program for $2.48 million (Rau and Wadhwani 2016). These cases are too new to be included in literature reviews.

7. This occurred most recently when a star athlete (swimmer), Brock Turner, was sentenced to only six months of probation, despite being convicted of three felonies for sexually

assaulting his unconscious victim. The judge stated he was concerned about the "severe impact" that prison would have on the perpetrator, and that he was unlikely to "be a danger to others." Turner's father stated that incarceration would be a "steep price to pay for 20 minutes of action," and noted that Turner could no longer enjoy steak because he barely had an appetite (see Miller 2016).

REFERENCES

Alderden, M. A., and S. E. Ullman. 2012. Creating a more complete and current picture: Examining police and prosecutor decision-making when processing sexual assault cases. *Violence Against Women* 18 (5): 525–551.

Anders, M. C., and F. S. Christopher. 2011. A socioecological model of rape survivors' decisions to aid in case prosecution. *Psychology of Women Quarterly* 35 (1): 92–106.

Anderson, M. J. 2016. Campus sexual assault adjudication and resistance to reform. *Yale Law Journal Forum* 125: 1940–2005.

Belknap, J. 2015. *The invisible woman: Gender, crime, and justice.* 4th ed. Belmont, CA: Cengage Learning.

Belknap, J., and N. Sharma. 2014. The significant frequency and impact of stealth (non-violent) gender-based abuse among college women. *Trauma, Violence, and Abuse* 15 (3): 181–190.

Bolger, D. 2016. Gender violence costs: Schools' financial obligations under Title IX. *Yale Law Journal* 125: 2106.

Cantalupo, N. C. 2012. "Decriminalizing" campus institutional responses to peer sexual violence. *Journal of College and University Law* 38: 483–526.

———. 2014. Institution-specific victimization surveys addressing legal and practical disincentives to gender-based violence reporting on college campuses. *Trauma, Violence, and Abuse* 15 (3): 227–241.

———. 2016. For the Title IX civil rights movement: Congratulations and cautions. *Yale Law Journal Forum*, February 19, 281–303.

Carle, R. 2015. Assault by the DOE. *Academic Questions* 28 (1): 11–21.

Dixson v. Alabama State Board of Education. 1961. 294 F. 2d 150.

Eigenberg, H. 1990. The National Crime Survey and rape: The case of the missing question. *Justice Quarterly* 7 (4): 655–671.

Englander, E., M. McCoy, and S. Sherman. 2015. Sexual assault information on university websites. *Violence and Gender* 3 (1): 64–70.

Faludi, S. 2009. *Backlash: The undeclared war against American women.* New York: Broadway Books.

Fisher, B. S., F. T. Cullen, and M. G. Turner. 2000. *The sexual victimization of college women.* Washington, DC: U.S. Department of Justice, National Institute of Justice and Bureau of Justice Statistics (NCJ 182369). Available at the National Criminal Justice Reference Service: https://www.ncjrs.gov/pdffiles1/nij/182369.pdf.

French, D. 2015. Title IX, the all-purpose leftist excuse. *National Review,* June 4. Available at http://www.nationalreview.com/article/419344/title-ix-all-purpose-leftist-excuse-david-french.

Friend, T. 1994. Yes, feminist women who like sex. *Esquire,* February, 48.

Gilbert, N. 1991. The phantom epidemic of sexual assault. *Public Interest* 103: 54–65.

———. 1992. Realities and mythologies of rape. *Society* 31: 4–10.

———. 1994. Miscounting social ills. *Society* 31: 18–26.

———. 1998. Realities and mythologies of rape. *Society* 35 (2): 356–362.

———. 2005. Examining the facts: Advocacy research overstates the incidence of date rape and acquaintance rape. In *Current controversies on family violence*, ed. D. Loseke, R. Gelles, and M. Cavanaugh, 117–131. Newbury Park, CA: Sage.

Goss v. Lopez. 1975. 95 S. Ct. 729.

Grimmett, J., W. Lewis, S. Schuster, B. Sokolow, D. Swinton, and B. Brunt. 2015. *The challenge of Title IX responses to campus relationship and intimate partner violence*. Available at https://atixa.org/wordpress/wp-content/uploads/2012/01/Challenge-of-TIX-with-Author-Photos.pdf.

Hammer, R. 2000. Anti-feminists as media celebrities. *Review of Education, Pedagogy, and Cultural Studies* 22 (3): 207–222.

Hendrix, B. 2013. A feather on one side, a brick on the other: Tilting the scale against males accused of sexual assault in campus disciplinary proceedings. *Georgia Law Review* 47: 591–621.

———. n.d. Strickland Brockington Lewis LLP. Available at http://www.sbllaw.net/Our-Firm/bhendrix.php.

Henrick, S. 2013. A hostile environment for student defendants: Title IX and sexual assault on college campuses. *Northern Kentucky Law Review* 40 (1): 49–92.

Hoff Sommers, C. 1994. *Who Stole Feminism? How Women Have Betrayed Women*. New York: Simon and Schuster.

———. 2008. *What's wrong and what's right with contemporary feminism*. Washington, DC: American Enterprise Institute. Available at https://www.aei.org/wp-content/uploads/2011/11/20090108_ContemporaryFeminism.pdf.

———. 2011. In making campuses safe for women, a travesty of justice for men. *Chronicle of Higher Education*, June 5. Available at http://chronicle.com/article/In-Making-Campuses-Safe-for/127766.

Iannone, C. 2015. Your sex life, and ours. *Academic Questions* 28 (1): 5–10.

Johnson, K. C. 2015. The war on due process. *Academic Questions* 28 (1): 22–31.

Jordan, C. E., J. L. Combs, and G. T. Smith. 2014. An exploration of sexual victimization and academic performance among college women. *Trauma, Violence, and Abuse* 15 (3): 191–200.

Kanin, E. J. 1957. Male aggression in dating-courtship relations. *American Journal of Sociology* 63 (2): 197–204.

Kanin, E. J., and S. R. Parcell. 1977. Sexual aggression: A second look at the offended female. *Archives of Sexual Behavior* 6 (1): 67–76.

Karjane, H. K., B. S. Fisher, and F. T. Cullen. 2002. *Executive summary—campus sexual assault: How America's institutions of higher education respond*. Final Report, NIJ Grant # 1999-WA-VX-0008. Newton, MA: Education Development Center.

Kirkpatrick, C., and E. J. Kanin. 1957. Male sex aggression on a university campus. *American Sociological Review* 22 (1): 52–58.

Koss, M. P. 1985. The hidden rape victim: Personality, attitudinal, and situational characteristics. *Psychology of Women Quarterly* 9 (2): 193–212.

———. 1992. The under detection of rape: Methodological choices influence incidence estimates. *Journal of Social Issues* 48 (1): 61–75.

———. 1996. The measurement of rape victimization in crime surveys. *Criminal Justice and Behavior* 23 (1): 55–69.

———. 2011. Hidden, unacknowledged, acquaintance, and date rape: Looking back, looking forward. *Psychology of Women Quarterly* 35 (2): 348–354.

Koss, M. P., C. A. Gidycz, and N. Wisniewski. 1987. The scope of rape: Incidence and prevalence of sexual aggression and victimization in a national sample of higher education students. *Journal of Consulting and Clinical Psychology* 55 (2): 162–170.

Krebs, C. P., C. H. Lindquist, T. D. Warner, B. S. Fisher, and S. L. Martin. 2007. *The Campus Sexual Assault (CSA) study*. Washington, DC: U.S. Government Printing Office.

Krivoshey, M. S., R. Adkins, R. Hayes, J. M. Nemeth, and E. G. Klein. 2013. Sexual assault reporting procedures at Ohio colleges. *Journal of American College Health* 61 (3): 142–147.

Leveen, L. 1996. Sex and the scholarly girl: Plugging the feminist generation gap. *Women's Studies: An Interdisciplinary Journal* 25 (6): 619–635.

Lund, E. M., and K. B. Thomas. 2015. Necessary but not sufficient: Sexual assault information on college and university websites. *Psychology of Women Quarterly* 39 (4): 530–538.

Miller, M. B. 2016. "A steep price to pay for 20 minutes of action": Dad defends Stanford sex offender. *Washington Post*, June 6. Available at https://www.washingtonpost.com/news/morning-mix/wp/2016/06/06/a-steep-price-to-pay-for-20-minutes-of-action-dad-defends-stanford-sex-offender/?tid=a_inl.

Rau, N., and A. Wadhwani. 2016. Tennessee settles sexual assault suit for $2.48 million. *Tennessean*, July 6. Available at http://www.tennessean.com/story/news/crime/2016/07/05/tennessee-settles-sexual-assault-suit-248-million/86708442/.

Richards, T. N., and K. Kafonek. 2016. Reviewing state legislative agendas regarding sexual assault in higher education: Proliferation of best practices and points of caution. *Feminist Criminology* 11 (1): 91–129.

Ricketts, G. 2015. The tyranny of allegations. *Academic Questions* 28: 32–39.

Roiphe, K. 1993. *The morning after: Sex, fear, and feminism on campus*. Boston: Little, Brown.

Russell, D. E. H., and R. M. Bolen. 2000. *The epidemic of rape and child sexual abuse in the United States*. Thousand Oaks, CA: Sage.

Schwartz, M. D. 1997. *Researching sexual violence against women: Methodological and personal perspectives*. Thousand Oaks, CA: Sage.

Taylor, S., and K. C. Johnson. 2015. The new standard for campus sexual assault: Guilty until proven innocent. *National Review*, December 7. Available at http://www.nationalreview.com/article/428910/campus-rape-courts-republicans-resisting.

Title IX: Tracking Sexual Assault Investigations. 2016. *Chronicle of Higher Education*. Available at http://projects.chronicle.com/titleix/.

Tracy, C. E., T. L. Fromson, J. Long, and C. Whitman. 2012. *Rape and sexual assault in the legal system*. Paper presented to the National Research Council of the National Academies Panel on Measuring Rape and Sexual Assault in the Bureau of Justice Statistics Household Surveys, Committee on National Statistics. Available at http://sites.nationalacademies.org/cs/groups/dbassesite/documents/webpage/dbasse_080060.pdf.

Tracy, M. 2016. Florida State settles suit over Jameis Winston rape inquiry. *New York Times*, January 25. Available at http://www.nytimes.com/2016/01/26/sports/football/florida-state-to-pay-jameis-winstons-accuser-950000-in-settlement.html?_r=0.

Triplett, M. R. 2012. Sexual assault on college campuses: Seeking the appropriate balance between due process and victim protection. *Duke Law Journal* 62: 487–527.

U.S. Senate Subcommittee on Financial and Contracting Oversight. 2014. *Sexual violence on campus: How too many institutions of higher education are failing to protect students*. Avaiable at https://www.mccaskill.senate.gov/download/campus-sexual-assault-survey-results.

Walton, T. 2010. Reaganism and the dismantling of civil rights: Title IX in the 1980s. *Women in Sport and Physical Activity Journal* 19 (1): 14–25.

Williamson, K. 2015. Campus rape and the "emergency": It's always an excuse for authoritarianism. *National Review*, April 7. Available at http://www.nationalreview.com/article/416551/campus-rape-and-emergency-its-always-excuse-authoritarianism-kevin-d-williamson.

Young, C. 2015. The unsayable. *Academic Questions* 28 (1): 40–47.

Conclusion

Where Do We Go from Here?

MICHELLE HUGHES MILLER,
CATHERINE KAUKINEN,
AND RÁCHAEL A. POWERS

> We have an abundance of rape and violence against women in this country and on this Earth, though it's almost never treated as a civil rights or human rights issue, or a crisis, or even a pattern. Violence doesn't have a race, a class, a religion, or a nationality, but it does have a gender.—REBECCA SOLNIT

A Call to Action

Campus sexual violence has been labeled a crisis; we would be remiss if we did not use the same label in this book, though our focus has been broader because we explored research on sexual violence, dating violence, domestic violence, and stalking. Yet the term crisis implies a newness to the phenomenon of campus violence against women, which we note in our introduction to this volume and throughout Chapters 2–4, written by Callie Marie Rennison, Catherine Kaukinen, Caitlyn Meade, Ráchael A. Powers, Matt R. Nobles, and Kate Fox, that this is a gross misunderstanding of the history and prevalence of these gendered forms of victimization. The reality is, campus violence against women is a crisis because it has been labeled as such by administrative actors, such as the Obama White House and the Office for Civil Rights (OCR) of the Department of Education (DOE), who are (finally) publicly and forcefully acknowledging the violent crimes college women have experienced for decades (see Chapter 9 for Kaukinen's discussion of the 2014 White House Task Force Report, for instance). At the same time, while the violence is not new, we have new ways of identifying, understanding, preventing, and responding to that violence that create the possibility of change. It is this possibility of change (with optimism and perhaps, at times, with a skeptical and challenging lens) that we wanted to highlight in this edited volume—how we got here, what we are doing, and how we might ensure that the change is lasting.

There is reason to continue to be concerned for college women and their safety because of the research discussed in this volume, especially in our foundational Chapters 2–4. Women of college age are most at risk for sexual violence and intimate partner violence (IPV). They experience stalking more than their male counterparts. And some of the newest forms of violence, such as cyberviolence, reflect their significantly heavier involvement in social media, even as we are woefully ill-prepared to address their risks. Women are not the only ones victimized on college campuses, however. Their male peers are also sexually assaulted, abused by their partners, and stalked, but their victimizations are frequently invisible: not reported or not validated. Transgender students are also victimized, and research on transgender victimizations in the general population hints that these experiences might be even more prevalent than cisgender women's, especially among transgender women of color. But rarely do we hear these reports, and rarely are campus personnel adequately trained in transgender issues so as to appropriately respond.

The general public also makes assumptions about which women are survivors of campus violence and who the offenders are. Some of those assumptions are supported by the data presented in our early chapters: sorority women and fraternity men are more likely than those not living in Greek housing to be victims and perpetrators of sexual violence, respectively. According to some research, male athletes, long eschewed as being at higher risk for violence against women, do have higher rates of perpetration than their non-athlete male peers. But focusing solely on heterosexual violence ignores violence within nonheterosexual communities, and such violence and our responses to it can be particularly bound up in societal condemnation of queer relationships, resulting in lesser access to justice and support, particularly for those queer students who are also racial or ethnic minorities. And focusing solely on men as perpetrators or potential perpetrators ignores women's (near) proportionate engagement in IPV and stalking. A men-as-perpetrators/women-as-victims focus also puts limits on the prevention and intervention efforts we develop on college and university campuses. Within these subpopulations of college students, we also cannot forget patterns of victimization by race and ethnicity, discussed more thoroughly in Chapters 2–4. Although research findings are not always consistent, generally, African American female students are more likely to experience forced sexual intercourse and IPV than their White counterparts.

Thus, when we consider the crisis that is campus violence against women, we are actually talking about multiple, diverse experiences of violence, and a wide swath of our campus communities that is intimately connected to it, either as survivors, perpetrators, bystanders, loved ones, friends, or allies. Responding to the crisis, then, must be equally diverse and creative, and involve constituents across and beyond the campus, which has its own set of challenges. To reach today's young college students from diverse backgrounds and perspectives requires meeting these students where they are, utilizing contemporary approaches and relevant language, and taking advantage of their role models and mentors—who are, in many cases, other peers.

Challenges to Addressing Violence Against Women

Violence against college women exists within a culture where violence against women occurs at astonishingly high rates. From IPV to sexual violence to the presumptive nature of street harassment, women in U.S. society confront the reality of their embodied risk throughout their lives. And, clearly, relative risk for victimization is highly related to other forms of marginalization, with women of color, transgender women, nonheterosexual women, and women of varied and differing abilities experiencing differential and frequently higher rates of risk for these crimes than their White, cisgender, heterosexual, and able mind and bodied counterparts. Thus, violence against women on college and university campuses on one level simply illustrates that campuses are a microcosm of our larger society. But at the same time, institutions of higher education are geographically constructed to separate themselves from their surrounding communities, and they are organized so that students are placed in interaction in ways that adults and noncollege students are less likely to experience. Our perceptions about lowered risk and victimization on campuses often reflect that metaphorical distance. Crime reporting by campuses until recent years further perpetuated the sense of campus safety because Clery reporting by institutions frequently downplayed campus-based victimizations and considered off-campus victimizations as noncampus-related and thus irrelevant under Clery. These data (on most campuses) exclude the cases of sexual violence and IPV that come to the attention of the university via health, counseling, and victim service centers that remain confidential but need to be addressed to ensure safety to the broader campus community. Still today, in an era of more accurate Clery reporting (although there are still concerns—see Rennison, Kaukinen, and Meade in Chapter 2; Michelle Hughes Miller and Sarah L. Cook in Chapter 8; and Helen Eigenberg and Joanne Belknap in Chapter 11), universities are hard-pressed to explain to prospective students and their parents how safe their campuses are, while they are simultaneously being honest about the victimizations of students that do occur.

Yet this is not to say that campuses are violent domains. Rather, the research suggests that victimizations occur, at disturbingly high rates, but that risk has much to do with students' lives, parts of which occur off campus. Thus, universities are tasked with ignoring the separation between themselves and their communities to acknowledge and address the risks and victimizations of their students' complex interactions, relationships, living arrangements, and social activities that are related to or affect their student status, often beyond the borders of campus. A false sense of security on campus is not the answer, as Chapters 2 through 4 of this volume attest. Instead, an informed, comprehensive understanding of students' lives and experiences (both on and off campus) is more fruitful in recognizing and addressing the realities of violence against college women.

One important recognition we must make is the challenge of reporting. In Chapter 11, Eigenberg and Belknap detail the demands for mandatory reporting, but the context of reporting for survivors also requires an assessment of victim blaming itself. The structural and cultural factors that facilitate violence against women rest, in part, on the fallacy that victims somehow could have prevented the violence. This is often reinforced by the initial reactions of those to whom victims disclose, and those to whom they ultimately report their victimization. The need to address this belief undergirds theoretical explanations for violence against women (see Walter S. DeKeseredy in Chapter 5 and Antonia Abbey in Chapter 6), justifies the newest prevention efforts including bystander intervention and engaging men as allies (see Sarah McMahon in Chapter 14 and Powers and Jennifer Leili in Chapter 15), and permeates the need for campus-based victim advocacy centers (see Powers, Alesha Cameron, and Christine Mouton in Chapter 12). Several of our authors in this text discussed the damaging nature of victim blaming and its role in silencing women (and others) who face or believe they will face dishonor, disbelief, anger, or rejection if they tell their stories. This is why the work of the student-activists detailed by Ava Blustein in Chapter 16 is so important; to address victimization that has occurred, we must have reports of that victimization. These student-activists tell us that victim silence has felt like an expectation from colleges and universities, or at least victim compliance with stilted procedures that rarely meted out justice for any of the parties. But with the rise of social media activism in this area and widespread public discussion of violence against women on campuses, encouraged by the White House Task Force (see Chapter 9 by Kaukinen), Blustein tells us that survivors are voicing their victimizations and their frustrations with inadequate processes, frequently using the forum of Title IX and collective platforms like knowyourIX.org to do so. The outcome is the increase in reporting (and OCR Title IX investigations) that is challenging institutions tasked with response, detailed by Carmen Suarez and Meredith M. Smith in Chapters 10 and 17, respectfully. Administrators (some of whom are perhaps bemoaning the increased reporting) are struggling to handle the case volume as they work to bring redress to the survivors, accountability to the offenders, and to effect, in Suarez's words, "critical cultural change" on their campuses so as to prevent future victimizations.

Beyond campus communities, systems designed to address violence against women generally have struggled for decades to provide justice and support to women who are raped, harassed, abused, and stalked. Victim services generally are underfunded, understaffed, or worse, virtually nonexistent, especially in rural areas and on small campuses where the perceived caseload does not warrant their existence. The criminal justice system—or as Eigenberg and Belknap call it in Chapter 11, the criminal legal system— struggles (and frequently fails) to adequately and effectively provide justice for survivors at all stages, from arrest to prosecution to punishment. While the systems of response on college campuses vary in appreciable ways from the criminal legal system (as discussed throughout the volume), the parallels between the systems reinforce the backlashers' claim, described in Chapter 18 (by Eigenberg, Stephanie Bonnes, and Belknap), that universities are more often than not ill-prepared to prevent, intervene, and respond to violence against women. The question really is, then, how can universities handle reports of violence against women better than other systems already in place off campus that are struggling to do so? The answer really is at the core of this edited volume.

University Tools for Improving Campus Responses to Violence Against Women

On college and university campuses, we have an opportunity not available within the wider social world. We can merge our existing tripartite mandates of *teaching, research, and service*—held by virtually every institution of higher education—to meet the needs of our students and, in doing so, prevent, intervene in, and respond to violence against women. As educators, we can challenge rape myths, victim-blaming attitudes, stereotypes about survivors and offenders and other cultural beliefs, in a variety of educational and training forums already part of our university mission of teaching. As scholars and researchers, we can gather and analyze data, listening to the voices of all those within our campus communities (and beyond) who can help identify and strategize solutions to the problems and then test these empirically. This includes challenging what we are currently doing and moving past those strategies that are not working to solve the problem of violence against women. And, as service providers, we can provide direct care to our student victims, perpetrators, and bystanders, their loved ones, and allies, as we work together to not just respond to violence against women but to prevent future victimizations. Because we know that it is the synergy when we interconnect our three missions that is most valuable, we can then use the results of our scholarship to inform our education and service practices, and use these activities to guide our research.

The tools we have at our disposal to address violence against women on college campuses are those we already had at our disposal and for which many of us are held accountable as part of our job description: education, scholarship, and praxis. It is not surprising, then, that the tools discussed in this volume overwhelmingly take one of these forms. Even policy, particularly because of its federal nature, is driven in part by scholarship, even as it demands educational and practical behaviors and outcomes.

Ultimately, however, as powerful as it may be to recognize that universities are a priori populated with personnel poised to address violence against college women through our existing mission activities, there is a disconnect in the enactment of this vision. Service providers are housed frequently within student affairs, scholarship is conducted by faculty under the academic affairs mission, and educational programs may be dispersed across various Title IX, Violence Against Women Act (VAWA), and Clery personnel. Where synergy could exist, institutional boundaries that dictate responsibilities and funding streams may preclude the integration and coordination beyond directly mandated actions, along with perceived "turf" and problem ownership. A coordinated system of integrated education, research, and service would be ideal, and it is certainly a goal of many campus administrators (see Chapter 17), but is probably beyond the reality of many institutions struggling to fulfill policy expectations with limited resources. Nevertheless, we are hopeful that increasing collaboration across the missions, and across the domains and personnel of universities, will eventually be the preferred modality for integrating climate surveys and evaluation studies, Title IX and other policy trainings, educational and community programming, student adjudication procedures, and victim advocacy—just as we have done in this volume. Small campuses may lead the way in this endeavor as they manage their mandates using the potentially fewer resources at their disposal, as discussed in Chapter 17. In the meantime, however, our available tools include policies, research, and programming.

As discussed throughout this text, most of the policies of relevance to violence against college women actually encourage integration of research, education, and service. Title IX—discussed deeply in Chapters 7 and 17 by Hughes Miller and Smith, respectively—under the OCR's various guidance documents, expects universities to both respond to sexual assaults in ethical, structured, disciplinary and victim-centered ways, and to work to prevent victimizations through educational means. Institutional compliance to Title IX involves meeting all of these expectations—the disciplinary, the service provision, and the educational (the latter being a detailed mandate specified under the Campus SaVE Act; see Chapter 8). The federally constructed breadth of Title IX currently creates this complex of institutional mandates and expectations. Institutions are then held accountable for the choices they make regarding disciplinary strategies, victim advocacy, and educational programming. Research on campus climate, institutional best practices, and evaluation assessments of programs can provide guidance to administrators seeking to, as Smith says, "do the right thing." This echoes the perspective taken by the authors of this volume: when you listen to and value your students, assist victims, investigate accusations in a timely manner, hold perpetrators accountable, and provide victims with remedies that ensure their safety and recovery, campuses will automatically "do the right thing."

In Chapter 8, Hughes Miller and Cook discuss the Campus SaVE Act. Under this component of the reauthorized VAWA, IPV and stalking gain status as issues of campus concern beyond sexual violence, just as they have in this volume, under enhanced Clery reporting procedures. We also see mandated prevention and bystander intervention educational programming, and explicit expectations for the quality and content of such programming. Campus processes are not ignored either; transparency and clarity are expected, as institutions explain in detail their presumably prompt, fair, and impartial investigative and disciplinary processes. Coupled with the White House Task Force Report that has detailed recommendations for campuses on how to improve their responses to sexual violence (discussed by Kaukinen in Chapter 9), legislative and political statements demonstrate contemporary understandings of violence against women and the strategies that can address it that are still evolving. For instance, we are awaiting word about various proposed legislation (such as the Campus Accountability and Safety Act, which, if passed, would require climate surveys to join our tool kit for violence prevention; see Kaukinen, Chapter 9, and Christine Lindquist and Christopher P. Krebs, Chapter 13) and are following closely new legal requirements (such as affirmative consent laws enacted in California and New York and currently being proposed across the country).

But the real impact of policy arises in the overlap between the various political and administrative calls for action. As Suarez (Chapter 10) and Smith (Chapter 17) discuss, though each of these federal laws and statements creates a particular set of responsibilities for universities, their shared vision of violence-free campuses creates accountability for administrators that can be difficult to achieve. With evolving standards and expanding goals, these policies necessitate integrating educational, scholarly, and service activities within and among campus communities. For instance, both authors consider Title IX a powerful tool, but Title IX Coordinator Smith questions the complexity of the OCR's guidance in implementing prevention programming, noting ongoing questions about the increasingly high bar to fulfill OCR, Department of Justice, the Campus SaVE Act, and even the Center for Disease Control's expectations for appropriate and effective violence prevention. Nevertheless, both authors see compliance with the federal requirements as a prevention strategy, an important way for universities to strive to meet the needs of their students.

Identification and assessment of prevention and intervention programming requires ongoing, dedicated research. Climate surveys (Lindquist and

Krebs, Chapter 13), evaluation studies (highlighted in Chapters 14 and 15), and the academic scholarship discussed throughout this book play an important role in our ability to respond appropriately to violence against women in all its diverse forms and across the range of survivors. As discussed by McMahon in Chapter 14, early efforts to educate women in violence prevention and risk reduction and even general calls for educational programs on rape myths and victim blaming evolved after research identified few long-term changes in behavior or attitudes with these programs, along with significant critiques about putting the onus of violence prevention on women. Today, there is recognition that cultural change and the reduction of violence against women necessitates the active involvement of a broader constituency, which requires including men as a targeted group and directly addressing the important roles that can be played by informed bystanders.

The educational programs that recruit men to work against violence against women, discussed in Powers and Leili's Chapter 15, create an opportunity for men to talk with other men about violence prevention. As a tool, then, this involves establishing a cadre of peer-leaders who can serve as role models within any masculinized community. In programs such as *Men Can Stop Rape*, the organizers encourage educational awareness about unhealthy masculinity, in addition to rape myths. Participants also use social media to claim moral authority in violence prevention, encouraging their peers through campaign posters to take a stand against violence against women. Similarly, bystander intervention programs have themselves evolved over the years, again, through informed research, with emphasis on spreading responsibility of violence prevention among peers, recognizing the cultural basis of violence and its prevention. Identifying the promise of such contemporary programs as Green Dot and Bringing in the Bystander for campus communities, McMahon points out ongoing needs to assess the relevance of such programs within subpopulations of campus communities and to address differences between peers' willingness to intervene after participating in such programming and their actual intervening behaviors. We also need to be sure that we are having our students actively participate in these educational programs. The shift to online bystander education, to ensure compliance with Title IX, VAWA, and SaVE, has created the risk that we are checking the boxes on compliance and not ensuring that our students are engaging with these important educational messages.

These examples of effective prevention programs are time- and often resource-intensive for the participants and for universities. But while they can reach a much larger group of people, their intensiveness pales in comparison to direct victim advocacy services, which are also an essential, integrated requirement of the response to violence against college women. As discussed by Powers, Cameron, and Mouton in Chapter 12, victim advocates create the potential for survivors to feel supported and empowered following their victimization. As bridges between survivors and campus offices or police, campus victim advocates unapologetically ensure that survivors do not get lost in the procedures and the investigations, even as they confidentially help survivors identify their needs. Having worked with victim advocates for a number of years, we are personally humbled by the extent of advocates' compassion and strength as they help guide and encourage survivors through or around systems of justice. Their efforts, though, are hindered frequently by lack of funding, staffing, and integration into the various systems within which they must act, a point that is particularly true when universities rely on external victim advocates in lieu of campus-based centers. As a tool, then, to respond to violence against college women, victim advocacy is both vital and, unfortunately, under-resourced.

Challenges to Improving Our Collegiate Responses to Violence Against Women

Though each of the strategies and tools noted previously has its place in our efforts to respond to and prevent violence against college women, these are, in their own way, also ideal types that must be implemented with thoughtful adaptations within specific college locations. How to select and implement strategies, interventions, and educational programs in ways that reflect the specific demographic, geographic, and cultural uniqueness of an individual college campus may be the most under-researched topic of all. As campus leaders strive to meet the mandates noted earlier, they also find themselves facing choices about implementing those mandates and soliciting educational or cultural programming that is relevant for their constituents. They may have to consider these issues as they negotiate the particular constellation of education, research, and service on their campuses:

1. Who should be the target of their interventions? How should they define and identify survivors? As Smith notes in Chapter 17, campuses must find ways to balance the needs of survivors with a desire to transform their campus communities to create safe, inclusive, supportive environments. This means considering the nature, purpose, and potential downsides of mandatory versus confidential reporting; the role of men and campus authorities in violence prevention; the extent to which campus policies have addressed bias crimes that go beyond the current media focus on sexual violence, along with other forms of violence against women required under the Campus SaVE Act; the location, naming, and inclusiveness of their reporting sites; and the various ways victimization is experienced and therefore must be addressed by members of the diverse populations on their campuses. Of particular relevance is a concern for lesbian, gay, bisexual, transgender, intersex, and queer (LGBTIQ) survivors, whose victimizations can be made invisible by heterosexist or gender-biased interactions. Alleged (and potential) offenders are also part of the campus community, and as such are not only mandated to receive comparable services to victims by universities, but should be considered in educational and prevention programming. In identifying relevant (and not just mandated) strategies, universities should begin from the data about their own institutions, requiring them to also recruit researchers to help answer questions about the nature, prevalence, and experiences of victimization and its aftermath, locally. Research strategies discussed by Lindquist and Krebs in Chapter 13 can help with this.

2. *How and who will manage the cacophony of strategies chosen for each campus?* We previously recommended an integrated approach to system management that not only brings stakeholders together but also shares responsibilities across the missions of the university. However, this model does not answer the question of funding for the mandated actions or the staffing of chosen programming. Our own experiences with systems of response from various campuses parallel the argument made by Suarez in Chapter 10, in that what is key is not just the identification of responsible parties but also the identification of committed parties. Institutional commitment can be focused on liability and compliance concerns, as Smith notes in Chapter 17, but it can also be transformative for campus culture if it includes committed and empowered stakeholders reflective of the entire campus community. This includes funders, educators, scholars, and activists—all of whom must play a role in the work toward violence reduction. Clearly, it is in the implementation of programming and services where the depth of commitment is most visible. At the same time, implementation is only a stage; ongoing assessment (linking research with praxis) is key to ensuring that the campus is adequately addressing its goals and its students' needs.

3. *How can universities design feedback mechanisms so as to generate helpful critique in ways that facilitate their continued improvement?* As Smith (Chapter 17) noted, there are more than 175 universities as of May 2016 being investigated by the OCR under Title IX. What these universities and many others do not yet have in place are mechanisms for feedback that are accessible by the recipients of their services. Assessment research has historically played the role of feedback mechanism, particularly for educational programming. This is valuable because it has allowed us to identify those educational programs that have longer-term positive outcomes for the participants (although longitudinal research is still significantly lacking). But as Eigenberg, Bonnes, and Belknap discuss in Chapter 18, assessment of reporting practices, adjudication procedures, and case outcomes have been stymied by the nature of these activities, meaning that researchers have largely been unable to assess and then identify best practices. And research itself

can be too slow to respond to the ongoing need for review and critique of university implementation that, despite claims to the contrary, can be highly variable. At the same time, victim (or offender) dissatisfaction with processes has driven many of these OCR investigations. Yet rarely do institutions consider the educational benefits of systematic constituent feedback as they internally review their processes.

Part of the issue, of course, is that critique can take the form of backlash, as discussed in Chapter 18. In such situations, the critique is, in fact, a negation of the validity of the university's programming based on a rejection of the need for services in the first place. As the authors note, critics have used various flawed methodological claims to reject the research on prevalence of violence against women. Similarly, current critics have claimed that using Title IX to address sexual assault on college campuses is an inappropriate expansion of the policy's purview, and that the OCR is exerting undue influence over colleges and universities on this issue. Feedback mechanisms that acknowledge the experiences of both survivors and alleged offenders could face the same criticism, especially under the umbrella of the OCR's expectations. Nevertheless, we argue that institutions need to ensure they are systematically listening to all parties—participants and stakeholders alike—about processes, programming, and services if they are committed to fulfilling their responsibilities to their students.

Where Do We Go from Here?

As Suarez states in Chapter 10, our legacy as scholars, activists, and practitioners against campus violence against women will depend not on the crimes our students, colleagues, and peers experience, but on how we collectively respond. Do we stay in a reactive mode, studying and responding to only the last set of guidance documents from the OCR or research funding streams from the National Institute of Justice, or do we challenge ourselves to go beyond these expectations to envision and work toward a future with significantly less violence—dare we hope for none? Each of our scholar writers in this volume has identified what he or she sees as unanswered questions in this area, as have our practitioner writers and activist writers. From Powers and Kaukinen's recommendation that prevention and educational programming address mutually violent relationships (Chapter 3), to Abbey's suggestion that dispelling campus-specific myths about drinking norms could reduce high-risk drinking behaviors and sexual assault (Chapter 6), our authors describe opportunities to learn more, do more, and change more. We ignore these experts' calls at our students' peril.

One issue that arises in almost every chapter is the current predominance of bystander education in our response to campus violence against women (see especially McMahon in Chapter 14). As we previously argued, the demand for bystander intervention is rooted in the most insidious, difficult explanation for campus violence against women—the culture within which it occurs. On college campuses, the culture is particularly conducive to violence against women, despite the policies, programs, and services that attempt to define other ways of social interaction. Our authors variously mention that patterns of alcohol consumption, hookups as relationships, equating sex with conquest, male (and female) bonding rituals, antiquated understandings of women's (and heterosexual) sexuality, and a romanticized coupling of young adults that has more to do with "rom-com" movies than real life, all construct the milieu within which women (and men) seek enjoyment or companionship, and some men (and some women) choose to use coercive or violent means within those interactional opportunities. Afterward, victim-blaming beliefs lead many of us to question the "truth" of the violent incident, and the rest of us bemoan the failures of prevention and response.

In other words, we know from research that culture reinforces and produces violence, but we do not yet have the strategies (or perhaps the will) to change each of the fundamental cultural elements that exist on college campuses that produce the particular criminogenic cultural milieu that contributes to our current crisis in campus violence against women, let alone the synergistic effects of all of these elements combined. Each, alone, is a massive undertaking, as we call into question gendered and heterosexist notions of power and pleasure, alongside normative perceptions of what it means to be a college student. We have to recognize and address the role of alcohol culture, not just the role of alcohol consumption, an issue discussed by Abbey in Chapter 6. We have to hold victimizers accountable, along with those who would ignore or endorse their victimizing behavior (see Chapter 14). We have to shift understandings of masculinity to scale back competition and conquest in favor of empathy and respect—theories and research support this focus (see Chapter 5), while research on engaging men in antiviolence against women work suggests how (see Chapter 15). And we have to somehow find ways to believe survivors, in a culture where social media recordings are the preferred way to recognize "truth" and trust makes us vulnerable.

Policy cannot, by itself, change culture, though the policies we discuss in this volume contain elements that are designed to try (see Chapters 7, 8, and 9 by Hughes Miller, Cook, and Kaukinen). Witness the ongoing racial discord in 2016, as Black Lives Matter protestors speak their realities. This discord harkens back to deeply felt racism from years before the Civil Rights Act was passed. Witness the failures of the Equal Pay Act, the Lily Ledbetter Fair Pay Act, or any of the myriad of federal legislation that denounces gender discrimination in hiring, compensation, or promotion to actually substantially reduce the gap between women's earnings and men's earnings, a gap that most analysts argue is dependent, in part, on ongoing systematic and implicit biases about women's labor. And consider the current national debate over identity and bathrooms that started when a local ordinance attempted to prevent discrimination against transgender individuals, only to be the harbinger of more widespread discriminatory measures passed in the interests of protecting "traditional" values and allegedly at-risk daughters (whose potential later sexual assaults on college campuses will unfortunately be seen as their fault). Policy can take us so far—by delineating explicit expectations for prevention, intervention, and response—and that is a distance we cannot travel without policy. But we also need widespread, endemic cultural change, which Smith argues must additionally involve behavioral change (Chapter 17). We cannot effectively reduce (or even begin to think we could eliminate) the violence against women that we see without larger societal-level changes.

Ultimately, the policies, practices, and proposals discussed in this book are tools we can use to create the change we desire. Each is flawed and incomplete. Each needs continuing research to assess and to improve. And each campus needs the resources, personnel, knowledge, support, and commitment to put into motion its own policies, practices, and proposals to prevent and respond to violence against women on campus. The clarion call has been sounded, but women are still being raped, abused, and stalked. So we must ask ourselves: Do we know enough? And are we doing enough?

Contributors

Editors

CATHERINE KAUKINEN, PH.D., is a professor and chair in the Department of Criminal Justice at the University of Central Florida. Kaukinen's research interests include intimate partner violence, risk and protective factors for *violent* victimization, the history of Title IX and federal initiatives to address violence against college women, and the evaluation of campus-based violence against women prevention and intervention programs. Kaukinen's reputation and distinguished record on violence against women on college campuses includes her invitation to give a keynote address at the annual conference of the Center for Research on Violence Against Women at the University of Kentucky. This presentation has subsequently appeared in *Trauma, Violence, and Abuse: A Review Journal*. Her work on developing programs on campus to address violence against women includes more than $1 million in funding from the Office on Violence Against Women, in which she developed a multicampus victim service intervention and prevention program addressing dating violence, intimate partner violence, sexual assault, and stalking. These grants supported the training of practitioners to address violence against women, policy review and evaluation, violence prevention, outreach, and awareness on five college campuses impacting more than 35,000 students, and the evaluation of campus-wide bystander education programs. The Respect on Campus (ROC) Program she created provided violence prevention education programs for incoming students, as well as

faculty and staff. During her tenure, ROC provided educational programming for more than 17,000 students and 5,500 faculty, administrators, and
staff. Her research has appeared in *Criminology*, the *Journal of Marriage and
Family*, the *Journal of Research in Crime and Delinquency*, the *Journal of
Interpersonal Violence, Trauma, Violence, and Abuse*, and *Violence and Victims*, among other outlets.

MICHELLE HUGHES MILLER, PH.D., is an associate professor in women's
and gender studies at the University of South Florida. She has researched
victim advocacy for more than ten years, focusing on understanding how
advocates mediate the context of their work on behalf of victims. Coupled
with her experience working on Title IX policies, procedures, and assessment at two universities, she brings an important combination of victim-
focused and policy awareness to the book. Her academic interests are in
discursive constructions of motherhood within law and policy and systemic
responses to violence against women. She is particularly interested in trans-
national development discourse related to mothering and gender-based violence and, closer to home, victim advocacy within particular ecological
environments. She is coeditor of the Demeter Press volume *Bad Mothers:
Regulations, Representations and Resistance* (2017). Recent publications have
appeared in *Women and Criminal Justice*, the *Journal of Interpersonal
Violence*, and the *Journal of Community Psychology*.

RÁCHAEL A. POWERS, PH.D., is an assistant professor in the Department
of Criminology at the University of South Florida. She has published numerous studies on the risk for victimization, consequences of victimization, and
how victims interact with the criminal justice system. In addition, she has
served as an adviser, consultant, and/or evaluator of violence prevention programs at two universities. Furthermore, she is actively engaged in violence
prevention in the community. Dr. Powers has previously served in the gov-
ernor of Maryland's Office of Crime Control and Prevention, where she
worked on a variety of issues including the death penalty, racial profiling,
and trends in violent crime. Recent publications have appeared in *Criminal
Justice and Behavior, Deviant Behavior*, the *Journal of Interpersonal Violence*,
and *Violence and Victims*.

Chapter Authors

ANTONIA ABBEY, PH.D., is a professor of psychology at Wayne State University and a Board of Governors Distinguished Faculty Fellow. She received her
doctoral degree in social psychology from Northwestern University and has
a long-standing research interest in women's health, substance use, and reducing violence against women. She has published more than one hundred

empirical articles, review papers, and chapters, with a focus in recent years on alcohol's role in sexual aggression. Her research has been funded by the National Institute on Alcohol Abuse and Alcoholism, the National Institute of Mental Health, the National Institute of Child Health and Human Development, and the Department of Education with total funding of approximately $5.5 million. She has served on a variety of national advisory committees focused on sexual assault prevention and etiology for the Centers for Disease Control and Prevention, the National Institute on Alcohol Abuse and Alcoholism, the National Institute of Justice, and the Pentagon. She also has served on numerous National Institutes of Health grant proposal study sections and has given keynote addresses at international and national conferences. In 2016, Dr. Abbey received the American Psychological Association's Division 35 Strickland-Daniel Mentoring Award.

JOANNE BELKNAP is a professor of ethnic studies at the University of Colorado and adjunct professor, Queensland University of Technology, School of Justice, Faculty of Law (Brisbane, Australia). She received a Ph.D. in criminal justice from Michigan State University in 1986 and was the president of the American Society of Criminology (2013–2014). Her research is primarily on gender-based abuse and the trajectory of trauma to offending among women and youth. Dr. Belknap recently published the fourth edition of her book, *The Invisible Woman: Gender, Crime, and Justice*. She has secured almost $2 million in grant money to conduct research on women, girls, and crime. She has served on state advisory boards for female offenders and women in prison, on U.S. attorney general Janet Reno's Violence Against Women Committee, gave expert testimony to the Warren Christopher Commission investigating the Rodney King police brutality incident in Los Angeles, and served as a pro bono adviser on criminal justice policy for the Obama presidential campaign. Dr. Belknap has won numerous research, teaching, and service awards.

AVA BLUSTEIN is an MSW candidate at the University of California, Berkeley School of Social Welfare, and a student engagement organizer for Know Your IX. She received a BA in creative writing and film, television, and interactive media studies from Brandeis University, where she cofounded Brandeis Students Against Sexual Violence and the Brandeis Rape Crisis Center.

STEPHANIE BONNES, MA, is a doctoral candidate in the Department of Sociology at the University of Colorado, Boulder. Her scholarship explores a variety of areas pertaining to gender and organizations, violence against women, sexual abuse, and identity. Her dissertation takes an intersectional approach to examine sexual abuse in the U.S. military.

ALESHA CAMERON is a Ph.D. student in the Department of Criminal Justice at the University of Central Florida, where she received her MS in criminal justice in 2016. Research interests include violence against women and children, sexual violence and victimization, family structure and adolescent problem behavior, and the impact of childhood exposure to family violence.

SARAH L. COOK, PH.D., is the associate dean of the Honors College at Georgia State University. Her work takes a community psychology approach to understanding the social problem of violence against women. Her primary scholarship goals are to contribute to improving research methods in the field of violence against women (VAW), and to synthesize and apply knowledge about VAW to public policy. Her research balances the creation of new knowledge, synthesis, and application of existing knowledge, and dissemination of knowledge to the general public, policy makers, and an interdisciplinary audience in academia. In addition, she strives to integrate her expertise in two surprisingly disparate fields that coexist but seldom interact: sexual assault (SA) and domestic violence (DV). Her research has been funded by the National Institute of Justice, the Centers for Disease Control and Prevention, and the National Institutes of Health.

WALTER S. DEKESEREDY, PH.D., is Anna Deane Carlson Endowed Chair of Social Sciences, director of the Research Center on Violence, and professor of sociology at West Virginia University. He has published 23 books and more than 160 scientific journal articles and book chapters on violence against women and other social problems. In 2008, the Institute on Violence, Abuse and Trauma gave him the Linda Saltzman Memorial Intimate Partner Violence Researcher Award. He also jointly received the 2004 Distinguished Scholar Award from the American Society of Criminology's (ASC) Division on Women and Crime and the 2007 inaugural UOIT Research Excellence Award. In 1995, he received the Critical Criminologist of the Year Award from the ASC's Division on Critical Criminology (DCC) and, in 2008, the DCC gave him the Lifetime Achievement Award. In 2014, he received the Critical Criminal Justice Scholar Award from the Academy of Criminal Justice Sciences' Section on Critical Criminal Justice and, in 2015, he received the Career Achievement Award from the ASC's Division on Victimology.

HELEN EIGENBERG, PH.D., is a professor in the Social, Cultural and Justice Studies Department at the University of Tennessee (UTC) at Chattanooga. She received her Ph.D. in criminal justice in 1989 from Sam Houston State University. She has been at UTC since 1998. Her research interests include women and crime, victimology, violence against women, institutional corrections, and male rape in prisons. She has published a book on domestic violence: *Woman Battering in the United States* (2001). She also has published more than twenty-five book chapters and articles in a wide variety of journals, including: the *American Journal of Police, Women and Criminal Justice, Criminal Justice Review*, the *Journal of Criminal Justice Education*, the *Journal of Criminal Justice, Justice Quarterly*, and the *Prison Journal*. She was the editor of *Feminist Criminology* for four years, which is an international peer-reviewed journal. She currently sits on their editorial board. She has served on the Tennessee State Coalition Against Domestic and Sexual Violence and the Tennessee Victims of Crime State Coordinating Council (2006–2010). She is the faculty liaison for the Senator Tommy Burks Victim Assistance Academy, which provides training for victim advocates throughout the state of Tennessee and is a joint UTC and Tennessee State Coalition Against Domestic and Sexual Violence project.

KATE FOX, PH.D., is an associate professor in the School of Criminology and Criminal Justice at Arizona State University. Her research focuses primarily on crime victimization, including theoretical tests, the victimization-offending link, and the effects of victimization on fear of crime and protective behavior. Dr. Fox's research primarily focuses on interpersonal victimization, including stalking and intimate partner violence. Her work has recently appeared in *Criminology, Justice Quarterly, Criminal Justice and Behavior*, the *Journal of Interpersonal Violence*, and *Aggression and Violent Behavior*.

CHRISTOPHER P. KREBS, PH.D., is currently a chief scientist in the Center for Justice, Safety, and Resilience at RTI International in Research Triangle Park, North Carolina. He has extensive research experience in the areas of corrections, substance abuse epidemiology and treatment, intimate partner violence and sexual violence, HIV transmission and associated high-risk behaviors among offenders and inmates, criminal justice systems, and program evaluation. He has led and worked on a number of projects for the National Institute of Justice, Bureau of Justice Statistics, National Institute on Drug Abuse, Centers for Disease Control and Prevention, and Substance Abuse and Mental Health Services Administration. He has employed both quantitative and qualitative methods in his research and has extensive experience designing studies, developing survey instruments, analyzing data, and disseminating findings. Dr. Krebs has published and presented numerous research papers on a wide variety of topics.

JENNIFER LEILI is a Ph.D. student in the Department of Criminology at the University of South Florida, where she is the president of the Criminology Graduate Student Organization. She has an MS in criminal justice and a BS in psychology and criminal justice from the University of Central Florida. Her research interests include juvenile justice and program evaluations.

CHRISTINE LINDQUIST, PH.D., is currently a senior research sociologist in the Center for Justice, Safety, and Resilience at RTI International. Her research interests include violence against women, families and incarceration, and prisoner reentry, with a particular focus on evaluating the effectiveness of interventions in these areas. She has played key roles in several major research efforts focused on campus sexual assault, funded by the National Institute of Justice and the Bureau of Justice Statistics. Dr. Lindquist has substantial methodological expertise, including multisite evaluation design, qualitative and quantitative methods, and instrumentation. She has extensively published and presented the results of her research. She has also taught a variety of courses on sociology and health.

SARAH MCMAHON, MSW, PH.D., is an associate professor at Rutgers University School of Social Work and also serves as the associate director for the school's Center on Violence Against Women and Children. Her research focuses on violence against women, with an emphasis on using ecological frameworks to examine prevention and social change. Dr. McMahon has extensive experience in designing and implementing quantitative and qualitative studies with college students to measure their knowledge, attitudes, and behaviors related to sexual violence, with a focus on bystander intervention. She has led a number of research projects related to campus violence, including a randomized control trial funded by the Centers for Disease Control and Prevention (2010–2014) to test a peer education sexual violence prevention program for college students. In 2014, she was invited to collaborate with the White House Task Force to Protect Students from Sexual Assault through the testing of a campus climate survey tool. She currently serves as coinvestigator (principal investigator, Keith Kaufman) for a grant from the Department of Justice's SMART (Sex Offender Sentencing, Monitoring, Apprehending, Registering, and Trafficking) Office to test a situational prevention approach to address campus sexual assault. She has numerous publications on the topic of sexual violence and has presented her work around the country.

CAITLYN MEADE, MA, is a doctoral student in the Department of Criminology at the University of South Florida. She has an MA in legal studies from Texas State University and a BA in criminology from West Virginia University. Her interests include campus victimization, reporting behavior, sexual violence; victim-offender overlap among sex offenders; and law. She has been published on topics concerning juvenile justice, the victim-offender overlap, and group-based trajectory modeling.

CHRISTINE MOUTON is the director of victim services at the University of Central Florida (UCF). She is responsible for maintaining a 24-7 confidential hotline for all UCF community members; providing advocacy services to students, faculty and staff; and providing information regarding the criminal justice/civil justice system, and all UCF administrative processes. Her team provides a wide variety of educational and informative prevention education programs and obtains grants, the most recent of which has funded the UCF mandatory online module for all incoming students regarding issues of consent to sex, dating/domestic violence/stalking and bystander intervention. She recently received a grant to launch Green Dot Bystander Intervention at UCF. Prior to her arrival at UCF, she worked for the Office of the State Attorney for the 18th Judicial Circuit in Sanford, Seminole County. She held several positions, including juvenile advocate and domestic violence advocate; however, the most exciting opportunity was to be one of the first neighborhood advocates in the state of Florida.

MATT R. NOBLES, PH.D., is an associate professor in the Department of Criminal Justice and Doctoral Program in Public Affairs at the University of Central Florida. He earned his Ph.D. in criminology, law, and society from the University of Florida in 2008, and joined UCF's faculty in 2015. Dr. Nobles's research interests include violence and interpersonal crimes, neighborhood social ecology, criminological theory testing, and quantitative methods. His recent work has appeared in outlets including *Justice Quarterly*, the *Journal of Research in Crime and Delinquency*, *Criminal Justice and Behavior*, the *Journal of Quantitative Criminology*, *Crime and Delinquency*, the *Journal of Interpersonal Violence*, *Aggression and Violent Behavior*, and the *American Journal of Public Health*. Additionally, Dr. Nobles has served as principal or coinvestigator on grants awarded by the National Institute of Justice, the U.S. Department of Justice Office for Victims of Crime, and the Environmental Protection Agency.

CALLIE MARIE RENNISON, PH.D., is the associate dean of faculty affairs and professor in the School of Public Affairs at the University of Colorado Denver. She received her Ph.D. in political science from the University of Houston-University Park. Her research interests include the nature, extent, and consequences of violent victimization, with an emphasis on research methodology, quantitative analysis, and measurement. Substantively, her research examines violence against women, violence against minority groups, crime data, and victim interaction with the criminal justice system. Her peer-reviewed work has appeared in outlets including *Trauma, Violence and Abuse*, the *Journal of Quantitative Criminology*, *Justice Quarterly*, *Violence and Victims*, and *Violence Against Women*. Her books are *Introduction to Criminal Justice: Systems, Diversity and Change* (Sage, 2015) with Mary Dodge, and *The Wiley Handbook on the Psychology of Violence* (Wiley-Blackwell, 2016) with Carlos Cuevas.

MEREDITH M. SMITH, JD, MS ED, is the Title IX coordinator at Tulane University. In this role, Ms. Smith oversees the university's Title IX compliance and its prevention and response efforts regarding incidents of sexual violence, sexual harassment, intimate partner violence, and stalking. She is also responsible for the university's training programs around sexual violence education and assists with sexual violence training in New Orleans. Ms. Smith has previously worked as a Title IX investigator and in student conduct. She has been invited to participate in the Office on Violence Against Women roundtable on sexual violence adjudication, has presented at national conferences for Student Affairs Professionals in Higher Education (NASPA) and the Association of Title IX Administrators (ATIXA), and is on the 2017 NASPA Sexual Violence Prevention and Response Conference Planning Committee.

CARMEN SUAREZ, PH.D., is vice president of global diversity and inclusion at Portland State University (PSU). As the chief diversity officer, she reports directly to the president and is a member of the President's Executive Committee. Dr. Suarez heads the Department of Global Diversity and Inclusion, which has the mission of creating a positive campus climate that celebrates diversity, builds partnerships, promotes equity, and supports the entire campus community. This includes making sure that PSU is in compliance with all federal and state laws relating to equity and diversity, such as Title VII, Title IX, Affirmative Action, and the Americans with Disabilities Act.

Index